Hardinge of Penshurst

Hardinge of Penshurst

A Study in the Old Diplomacy

by
Briton Cooper Busch

THE CONFERENCE ON BRITISH STUDIES
BIOGRAPHY SERIES

Volume I, New Series

Published for the Conference on British Studies and Indiana
University at South Bend by Archon Books

1980
Archon Books

Library of Congress Cataloging in Publication Data

Busch, Briton Cooper.
Hardinge of Penshurst.

(Biography series; v. 1)
Bibliography: p.
Includes index.
1. Hardinge, Charles Hardinge, Baron, 1858–1944.
2. Great Britain—Foreign relations—1901–1910.
3. Great Britain—Foreign relations—1910–1936.
4. Diplomats—Great Britain—Biography. 5. Viceroys—India—Biography. I. Title. II. Series: Biography series (New York); v. 1.
DA566.9.H29B87 327.2'092'4 [B] 80-16537
ISBN 0-208-01830-1

First published 1980 as an Archon Book,
an imprint of The Shoe String Press, Inc.,
Hamden, Connecticut 06514

Printed in the United States of America

Contents

List of Illustrations

Series Preface

Biography is one of the most active subdivisions of the historical profession, and there is good reason. While many other forms of writing history have failed to attract readers who are not professional historians, a well written and researched historical biography often stirs a passion for history in a far wider audience. By focusing on the humanistic aspects of good biographical writing, by emphasizing the quality of the writing as well as that of the scholarship, it is the aim of the British Biographies Series to help stimulate this interest.

In attempting to achieve this goal, we are well aware that biography, along with all other forms of historical writing, has its limitations. It is not the best vehicle for analyzing concepts such as nationalism or parliamentary democracy, nor is it the ideal place for an in-depth study of British society or its constituent parts. At its best, biography works in a linear fashion, with relatively little time for sideward or backward glances at the larger world. For continuity it relies on the life of one individual, and herein lies a great deal of biography's virtue: it is as varied and as open as the minds of the people it portrays.

By acknowledging that history includes personality, it is possible to make the past less strange to modern eyes, and thus to give it more reality and greater value. It is also important to remember that it is possible to approach the matter from the opposite vantage point. In selecting subjects for this series, we have made a conscious effort to choose individuals who lived in a mainstream of their age, however far removed the spirit of that period might be from our own. As a rule, these people are not the geniuses who, almost by definition, are alienated from their times, but rather people who reflect the quality and the flavor of their eras. In this manner, by blending the familiar with the unknown, we hope this series will help provide a genuine link with the past and will encourage that passion for history that biography can produce.

Paul Scherer
Roy Schreiber
Indiana University, South Bend

Introduction

Charles Hardinge, first baron Hardinge of Penshurst, was one of the most eminent diplomatists of his age. He would deserve this epitaph had he occupied no other position than that of permanent under secretary in the Foreign Office in the years 1905–10, for at that time he was both principal advisor to Sir Edward Grey in the critical period of the formation of the Triple Entente, and principal diplomatic confidant to Edward VII. Hardinge, however, was also ambassador to Russia (1904–5) and to France (1919–22), permanent under secretary again (1916–20), and viceroy of India (1910–16).

Hardinge was viceroy of India in a period of momentous events for that country—the growth of nationalism, the reunification of Bengal, the declaration of Delhi as all-India capital, the coming of the First World War—and yet for several reasons he is without a biographer. He wrote two volumes of memoirs, which were published posthumously. Although unsatisfactory on a number of points, for Hardinge's professional discretion did not desert him in retirement, these had to serve at least until the official documents for the period of his career were open to researchers.

Another difficulty is that Hardinge had two careers, one in

European diplomacy, another in Indian administration. It is indicative that his memoirs are divided in just this fashion, *Old Diplomacy* and *My Indian Years*. It is not always the easiest of tasks to link two subjects. Indeed, it was just this question which first drew me to Hardinge as a subject for study while pursuing the role of India in British foreign policy formation.

Finally, some of the issues faced by any biographer on the subject's motivation, personal life, and the like, are made more difficult in Hardinge's case by his rather distant and coldly professional public character. "Capability" Hardinge did not suffer fools gladly. The problem is further complicated by Hardinge's longevity, for he had more than two decades after retirement to cull through his papers and destroy documents which he felt were too personal. For example, of the correspondence which his wife which must have existed in their periods of separation, nothing remains but a few notes from the first years of their engagement and from the year of her death. Nor are other sources necessarily more revealing. The Royal Archives at Windsor, to cite one further instance, cannot reveal the complete nature of the relationship between Hardinge and King Edward, given the discretion of both men and of the king's advisors and executors.

And yet, despite these limitations, useful materials do exist and Hardinge can be reexamined to some purpose. These include, above all, the substantial collection of his own papers now in Cambridge University Library, with supplemental volumes in the Kent County Archives, Maidstone. Additional, more personal papers, including the draft volumes of Hardinge's memoirs, have very kindly been put at my disposal by Helen Hardinge (Dowager Lady Hardinge of Penshurst), who not only allowed me the run of her library but gave so generously of her own recollections of Lord Hardinge and the family. In addition to the Royal Archives, much important material is to be found in the official volumes of Foreign Office papers in the Public Record Office, and, for Hardinge's viceroyalty, the India Office Library (London), and the National Archives of India

(New Delhi). These, together with other British private paper collections cited in the bibliography, form the basis of this work.

What Hardinge did not make clear, inevitably, in his own self-study, was the extent of his influence upon policy in Grey's era, and, conversely, the ineffectiveness of that influence during his wartime tenure of the same under secretaryship and at the Paris Peace Conference. To weigh his diplomatic accomplishments, both in his formal diplomatic posts and in the conduct of his responsibilities in India, is a central purpose of this book.

There is another, however. Hardinge was above all a practitioner of the "old diplomacy," a profession in which like-minded men of similar experience and equal social rank quietly and expertly prepared and executed their nation's external policies without recourse to popular demagoguery and all the pressures of public opinion in search of "open covenants openly arrived at." To an extent the isolation of such policymakers was a myth by the end of the nineteenth century, but they yet followed aims of "balance of power" or "security of the empire," not "democracy" or "world socialism." It is not my purpose to argue the merits or otherwise of the "new diplomacy" of the twentieth century, but Hardinge was typical in many ways of the triumphs, and limitations, of the traditional methods of diplomatic practice under assault from the new.

Any errors or omissions in pursuit of these themes are my own. The work would not have been possible, however, without the assistance of others. Helen Hardinge's help was indispensable, but I am also very grateful for the information and hospitality given me by other Hardinge family members, the Honorable Mrs. F. G. Beaumont-Nesbitt, Mrs. J. F. D. Johnson, Mrs. R. Leslie, and Mrs. J. A. J. Murray. The Honorable Mrs. G. G. Marten allowed me to use Alington family records at Crichel, and Viscount Hardinge did the same for other family documents in Montreal. Help in other ways was given to me by Susan Mary Alsop, H. E. Baker, Professor F. R. H. Du Boulay, Sir Philip Magnus-Allcroft, C.B.E., Elizabeth Monroe, C.M.G., Nigel Nicolson, and Rose Novak.

I have worked in a number of libraries and other institutions in preparation of this volume, and I am grateful to the staffs in every case. I owe a particular debt, however, to four individuals for their comments and suggestions: Dr. R. J. Bingle of the India Office Library manuscripts collection; Miss Frances Dimond of the Royal Archives, Windsor, photography collection; Gordon Phillips, archivist of *The Times;* and Mrs. Margaret Richardson, of the drawings collection of the Royal Institute of British Architects.

Finally, to my family and my Colgate University colleagues, my thanks for their patience and support during frequent absences over the last few years. Indeed, the Research Council of Colgate University made those absences possible, and for the Council's support—and that of Deans John Morris and John Rexine—I am very grateful.

Unpublished Crown-copyright material in the India Office Library and India Office Records appears by permission of the Secretary of State for Commonwealth Relations; from the Royal Archives, by the gracious permission of Her Majesty Queen Elizabeth II; and other official material, the bulk of which comes from the Public Record Office, by permission of the controller of Her Majesty's Stationery Office.

Hamilton, New York B.C.B.
June, 1978

I Making of a Diplomat

Charles Hardinge had what used to be known as "good blood," which insured him an upper-class upbringing in Victorian England, with all that meant for opportunity. He was good at games, above all cricket, which probably insured him more success in his school career than superior intelligence would have done. His grandfather, however, gave Hardinge the one thing which set him apart from many of his peers — a driving ambition.

"Spurred by ambition, I know that I worked harder than most young men of my day in the Diplomatic Service," he remarked in the opening pages of his memoirs.[1] Hardinge had not the exceptional gifts of those men who pass without apparent effort into positions of power. Such appearances can be deceptive, for remote heights are seldom scaled without ambition, hidden or otherwise, but Charles Hardinge's was not concealed. That his particular distant peak was the viceroyalty of India was another contribution from his grandfather.

Field Marshal Henry, first viscount Hardinge of Lahore and King's Newton, G.C.B., died two years before his grandson was born, but by Charles Hardinge's later account his grandfather's life overshadowed his own. Henry came from a family which had given dutiful service: Robert Hardinge, for example, was knighted by the hand of Charles II for his loyalty (and his troop of horse raised for Charles I). His descendant Nicholas Hardinge, grandfather of the field marshal, won legal fame defending the Marquis of Hastings and his administration in India.

Henry, however, was the propertyless younger son of a younger son, whose success came from energy, ambition, and the favor of the duke of Wellington. Born in 1785, he entered the army as an ensign and was wounded in Spain. The duke's attention won him promotion, and in 1815 he was appointed British military commissioner under Blücher in the Waterloo campaign, losing his left hand at the wrist to a French cannonball at Quatre Bras. After the war he entered Parliament as a firm supporter of the duke, serving as Wellington's secretary at war and even standing as his second in a well-known duel with the earl of Winchelsea in 1829. Henry remained active in Tory politics after Wellington's retirement, serving as chief secretary for Ireland and as Peel's secretary at war. In 1844, now lieutenant general, G.C.B., he was named governor-general and commander in chief of India.

Lord Hardinge's three and a half years in India are best remembered for the clash with the Sikhs which culminated in the annexation of the Punjab. His leadership was recognized with the rank of viscount, a parliamentary pension of £3,000 a year for three lifetimes, and an East India Company annuity of £5,000 for his own lifetime.[2] Returning in triumph, with the reward for his labors he purchased the estate of South Park, Penshurst, Kent, an attractive house built by a wealthy London merchant in the 1830s, to which he added not only rooms but the atmosphere of India: the obligatory swords and armor were mere ornament for two magnificent Sikh field pieces and limbers from the Sutlej battlefield (now on prominent display respectively at the National Army Museum, Chelsea, and the Kent County Museum, Maidstone). A pair of marvelously handworked copper doors from a major Sikh temple completed the decor, and it was in this atmosphere that Charles Hardinge spent his youth. He never knew his grandfather, however, for after rising to full general, field marshal, and then Wellington's successor as commander in chief (thus dealing with the first repercussions of the Crimean War), Henry Hardinge died in 1856.

Field Marshal Lord Hardinge was an interesting man with a varied career and multiple interests. "If I had been a bachelor and not humanised by a wife and children," he wrote to the wife in question, "I am sure I would have been very ambitious, but my opportunity occurring late in life, I am rather discreet and moderate and somewhat of a philosopher . . . ."[3] This self-portrait conflicts with his extensive double career in politics and the army, and he seems to have been possessed of much the same sort of drive his grandson was to display. It does not appear that his energy passed to his son, Charles Stewart, second viscount Hardinge.

Charles Stewart was the eldest son of Lord Hardinge and Emily Jane, widowed daughter of the first marquess of Londonderry and sister of Lord Castlereagh. Born in 1824, he was educated at Eton and was destined for the army until a disastrous riding accident caused one leg to be amputated below the knee. An artificial leg did not keep him from Oxford (he received a third in classics) or travel to India to serve his father as private secretary through the Sikh Wars. He spent four years in Parliament before coming into his father's title and the £3,000 annuity, and for a year was under secretary of state for war, but he did not advance in politics and soon retired to a quiet life at South Park to pursue a different love, for he was an above average painter whose vivid watercolors and more formal published engravings of India show considerable ability. His friendship with Sir Francis Grant and Sir Edwin Landseer, well-known artists of the day; his exhibitions at the Royal Academy; and his tenure as chairman of the trustees of the National Portrait Gallery (1876–94) testify to the esteem in which he was held by his artistic contemporaries.[4]

There was, of course, a family. Charles Stewart married Lady Lavinia Bingham, daughter of Field Marshal the Earl of Lucan. Lord Lucan commanded the Cavalry Division in the Crimean War, and his name remains associated with the famous, or infamous, charge of the Light Brigade. Hardinge retained a vivid memory of his maternal grandfather (clever and vigorous, but a man "of violent temper and very strong likes and dislikes"), who lived until 1888. Lavinia, however, died in 1864 when Charles was only six. "I can remember her quite well with her tall graceful figure," Hardinge wrote wistfully three-quarters of a century later; "I can see her now lying in bed with her beautiful hair covering the pillow and the evening sun pouring in through the windows as she gave me in her hand a small bunch of grapes . . . ."

This childhood memory offered little solace in a motherless house while Viscount Hardinge wrestled with the difficulties of raising eight small children. "Some people talk and write of the happiness of childhood. On looking back it seems to have been one of dull monotony, of exaggerated childish worries and bothers and of a complete absence of any softening influences . . . . Still, my feelings toward my father have always been those of profound respect and gratitude for his kindness and for the manner in which he brought us up, austere though the system may have been." This is unconvincing, but others speak of Lord Hardinge's kindness, and there is no denying the sense of fun in the few informal sketches of family life at South Park which survive. The death of Lady Hardinge, and an income barely adequate for needs, contributed to the atmosphere Charles Hardinge later recalled; the contrast with the ever-present signs of his grandfather's success must have been one source of his character. Father and son corresponded until the former's death in 1894, but the letters have not survived to permit further insight into their relationship.

At least the children were given an adequate education; at home Lord Hardinge tutored them himself in drawing and painting. This training gave Charles considerable later pleasure, for he too painted at some of his earlier and less demanding diplomatic posts. It also gave him confidence to enter much later into a major controversy over the style and form of India's new capital city, New Delhi. At the customary early age, however, the Hardinge children were packed off to school. In 1868, aged nine, Charles left South Park for Cheam, Harrow, and Cambridge.

Hardinge remembered Cheam, an exclusive school of some one hundred boys, for underfeeding, bullying, and an unpopular headmaster. But a trying regime was not new to him, and he thrived in a school which included not only many future Harrow and Cambridge friends but also his older brother by a year, Henry Charles Hardinge, and his cousin and future fellow diplomatist, Arthur Hardinge. All three played cricket for Cheam on a team captained by Charles. As cricket and football captain and as head of the school for two of his five years there, he could not have found life too unpleasant.

Initially, Hardinge was bound for the navy—his father's idea. In 1870, however, he was rejected by a medical board for a slight hernia (it soon cleared up). Lord Hardinge now decreed that Charles would study for the bar. The principal immediate effect was that Charles took on the study of Greek, not required for sailors, and plans were laid for him to attend Harrow, once more following in brother Henry's footsteps.

Three and a half years at Harrow brought mainly success in cricket and football. Hardinge was little impressed by his "indifferent" teachers except for the headmaster, Rev. Dr. H.M. Butler, and one master, E. Bowen, who managed to excite in him an interest in modern history, French, and German. Perhaps for this reason, at some point in his Harrow career he acquired an ambition for diplomacy rather than law. A small legacy of £400 from Lady Lucan made such a career possible, but only just. At that time a new attaché in the Diplomatic Service required a private income of at least £400 a year, above all in the first two probationary years in which he would receive no pay at all. With the £200-300 a year which was all Lord Hardinge would give him, the legacy was essential for survival. As Hardinge was to discover, the Service would have been more comfortable had the legacy been a permanent annual income.

In October 1876 Hardinge went up to Trinity College, Cambridge. His allowance of £200 a year had to cover all expenses, including college fees, tutorial charges, and books. "It was insufficient and a mistaken policy on the part of my father as it was so harassing." How much this policy was deliberate encouragement of frugality, paternal disfavor, or merely the result of straitened circumstances is a moot point, but it forever colored Hardinge's assessment of his father. Even more galling was the promise his father extracted from him not to play cricket for the university if the chance offered, a condition which rather indicates disapproval. Hardinge did captain the Trinity College eleven, and stretched his promise by playing for Cambridge in the second team.

His academic career was another matter. By his own account, he worked hard and constantly for a degree in Mathematical Honours. Why is not clear, unless it was at his father's urging; he had developed a marked distaste for mathematics at Harrow. It was all the less palatable since he had to spend the early summers in continued study (it was at a Trinity summer that he first met George Curzon). Hardinge assessed his prospects as an acceptable second, but he was frustrated to learn that he had emerged at the top of the third class in the Mathematical Tripos. His third was a permanent disappointment: diligent study and determination had not made up for lack of brilliance.

Passage of the Diplomatic Service entrance examination a few months later was more important to his career. His vacations, even during the height of the cricket season, often found him in France practicing the language. Hardinge took his degree in January 1880 and went abroad immediately to continue his work on French, returning to spend April at the famous crammer's establishment of Scoones' in Garrick Street. Success in the examination ended his formal academic career. On the whole it had been a happy one, more so, if his memoirs are to be believed, than his earlier home life. Each step, Cheam, Harrow, Cambridge, was recalled with more pleasure than the last, and the ten terms in Cambridge "were some of the happiest years of my life." Success came easily to him in those things which at that time and place seemed most valuable, only partially undermined by financial stringency. At twenty-two years of age, well-proportioned if slim (and, unusually for his era, always clean shaven), possessed of the proper family and educational credentials, he had embarked upon a career which in the normal course of affairs could be expected to be secure, gentlemanly, and not overly taxing. Whether he would rise above the herd, however, would depend upon both chance and his own abilities.

As was customary for new diplomats, Hardinge was given a brief assignment in the Foreign Office, beginning work on 31 May 1880. He would be deeply involved in reform of Foreign Office procedures in the years to come, and he learned many of them in this introduction to the workings of "old diplomacy." At that time, both the Foreign Office and the Diplomatic Service, two separate establishments, were small and exclusive, roughly equal in size. In 1914, there were still fewer than 150 career diplomats, and the Foreign Office staff numbered 176, including doorkeepers and cleaners. The Diplomatic Service, which incorporated all those with diplomatic (as opposed to consular) functions abroad, had been formally organized in 1861 into a hierarchy from ambassador to attaché.

The Diplomatic Service examination was similar to (and after 1891 identical with) that of the Foreign Office, but there were fewer candidates for the Diplomatic, mainly because Foreign Office clerks did not need the private income asked of diplomats. Since permission to sit for the examination in either group was dependent upon nomination to and approval by the secretary of state, not surprisingly the candidates were all of aristocratic, gentry, or middle-class professional backgrounds. A majority had university degrees, but few had firsts. The examination included a multiplicity of subjects; just how well the tutors at Scoones' knew the questions Hardinge made clear in his draft memoirs (but deleted from the published version):

> I well recollect a curious incident that occurred during my examination. The French tutor at Scoones' was an Italian, Perrini by name, with a singular gift for teaching French. I

> was somewhat anxious about my "viva voce" examination on French literature. The day before this part of the examination was held I received unexpectedly a telegram from Perrini telling me to read Chateaubriand's *Atilla*. I procured and read it so as to leave no stone unturned to secure success. My surprise may be imagined when the examiner asked if I had read any of Chateaubriand's works and told me to give him the story of *Atilla*. This was very easy for me and whether it was simply a coincidence or not, it made a certainty of my success in that subject.[5]

The examination was meant to provide the right sort of man, not to be a test of stamina. Life in the Foreign Office was not particularly difficult in the 1880s. The work was principally ciphering and deciphering telegrams and copying dispatches by hand, all functions to be done in later years by second-division clerks. The labor required, as Hardinge put it, was "infinitesimal" compared to the later volume of correspondence. Although the experience could be termed valuable, at least for a short time, he came to realize that the lack of opportunity for "political education and initiative" was a serious drawback. This was especially true in the German Department, "regarded as the Social Department of the Foreign Office," to which he was temporarily attached. Much of his time was actually spent in passing the Civil Service examination in public law, which would mean a useful addition of £100 a year (two-thirds of his actual salary) once his probation was over.

In early 1881, at his own request, Hardinge was posted as attaché to the embassy at Constantinople, where he remained for four years. The duties were mainly to prepare dispatches; in other words he was a glorified clerk. It has been rightly remarked that memoirs of prewar diplomats usually concentrated on the social side of life rather than the mundane and rather dull formal work.[6] Hardinge's social life was interesting enough, and not surprisingly included as much sport as possible; he had, however, his ambition and the natural curiosity of youth, coupled with an exceedingly fortuitous association with an influential senior diplomat, to focus his attention upon professional matters.

In June, Lord Dufferin (first marquis of Dufferin and Ava) arrived as ambassador to the Porte. Thirty years Hardinge's senior, Dufferin had vast experience in many appointments, including governor-general of Canada (1872–78) and ambassador to St. Petersburg (1879–81). He was always genuinely interested in and helpful to his juniors, and he expected full participation from his staff in all aspects of the work.[7] Hardinge, for example, was once reprimanded for not staying the full course at a dull Italian embassy ball, but in general, he found that Dufferin's expectations suited him exactly. Dufferin reciprocated in kind, taking time to discuss particular diplomatic issues with Hardinge and eventually making him his private secretary. "By studying his methods of diplomacy and by listening to his views on political questions, I learnt during those three and a half years, more of the science of diplomacy than at any other time . . . ."

Dufferin was occupied in 1882 with the Turkish repercussions of the Egyptian crisis, which culminated in Britain's occupation of that Ottoman dependency. Shortly after the troops landed, the ambassador was sent on a special mission to Cairo to make suggestions for future administration, and two months later he called Hardinge to Egypt for "three of the pleasantest and cheeriest months of my life" (January–March 1883). With little official work to do, much time was spent lounging at the opera, or with convivial friends in the various regimental messes. His reward for a leisurely winter in Cairo, however, was to be stricken with typhoid immediately upon his return to Constantinople. He returned from sick leave at home to serve as Dufferin's private secretary from the fall of 1883 until, a year later, the ambassador returned to England to prepare for his new post as viceroy of India.

Hardinge would normally have been moved when his probationary period was up and he was promoted to third secretary, but Dufferin had pronounced him so valuable that he could not be spared. This hardly hurt Hardinge's career, but the association with Dufferin was more than merely professional apprenticeship. "I could scarcely have been fonder of you if you had been my own son," Dufferin wrote on his departure, and he exerted his influence with both Lord Granville, the foreign secretary, and Thomas Sanderson, Granville's private secretary, who had a key role in appointments, to have Hardinge posted to Berlin.[8] Dufferin remained a useful friend and ally, for he returned from India to be ambassador at Rome (1889–91) and finally at Paris (1891–96).

Hardinge's years at Constantinople had given him both general diplomatic experience and Lord Dufferin's friendship and sponsorship. But he had also learned much about Turkey and — again with effort — received a certificate for knowledge of Turkish (another £100 a year). He had done his best to observe the local scene, including the much publicized trail of Midhat Pasha, a central figure in nineteenth-century Ottoman reforms who had run afoul of Sultan Abdul Hamid II. In the fall of 1881, with only a Turkish servant for company, he rode through the interior of Turkey for six weeks, from Ineboli on the Black Sea to Ankara, then only a village, Eskishehir, and Brusa. Dufferin passed his subsequent report home with praise, and Granville commended the dispatch.[9]

Hardinge took up his post as third secretary in Berlin at the beginning of 1885. Although Bismarck had already initiated a bothersome policy of colonial acquisition, Anglo-German relations were as yet uncomplicated by the intense rivalry of later years. Hardinge resumed tennis with Count Hatzfeldt, first met in Constantinople and now foreign minister, finding in addition that Crown Prince Frederick and his wife Princess Victoria (Queen Victoria's daughter) much enjoyed the sport. Hardinge knew and liked both, and not surprisingly came to know their son William, only a year younger than himself. Hardinge had some vivid recollections of the future ruler:

He was always horrid to his Mother and when playing tennis

> one day at Potsdam, I saw him hit a ball with great violence at the Crown Princess when, in a fit of abstraction and in conversation with Col. Swaine, she crossed a part of the court where he was playing. I shall never forget her expression of shocked dignity when she realised what her son had done in the presence of a considerable number of people.[10]

Another meeting set Hardinge even more on edge:

> On one occasion he stopped me as I was walking to the station to go to Berlin [from Potsdam] & asked me how tall I was. I replied that I was 6 feet in my stockings. He then said that was the right height for the 1st Regt. of the Guard, and he made me quite seriously a proposal that I should join his regiment and that he would see that I had a successful career in the German Army. I am afraid that in my heat at such a proposal I was lacking in courtesy in my reply for I said that I would sooner break stones on the road than join his regiment.[11]

Hardinge's year in Berlin gave him the opportunity to meet and know some important people and to taste the atmosphere of military display which surrounded the German court. In the long run it was unfortunate that Hardinge got on so well with William's parents, as William did not — for such an association adversely colored both men's attitudes, and it was William who would rule Germany as Emperor William II when his father died of cancer in 1888.

Late in 1885 Hardinge was promoted to second secretary; two steps in five years was markedly faster than average. His next post was Washington, D.C. Ordered first to Rio de Janeiro, he learned that the next man below him in seniority had been posted to the more desirable Washington. He protested that he had not been offered his choice of the two vacancies, and tradition supported him. "I succeeded in obtaining my point and was ordered to Washington. . . ." Hardinge was not one to take a personal injustice lightly.

In Washington, he served another short but interesting term (December 1885 to November 1886). In the summer he was for the first time left in command of a legation, but it was a typical hot, muggy, and unhealthy Washington summer, and Hardinge was chargé because everybody else had fled the capital. Nevertheless, he worked hard to prepare several lengthy and detailed reports on subjects such as sugar manufacture and land settlement legislation, two of which were printed as parliamentary papers. His personal friendship with Thomas Bayard, President Cleveland's secretary of state, supplied him with much useful information and a reputation for being really well informed. At the end of 1886, he returned home to temporary assignment in the Eastern Department, and Cecil Spring Rice, who was to enjoy a long association with the United States, was sent to Washington in his place. Hardinge's Foreign Office stay of six months was just long enough for him to form a favorable judgement of his department head, Sir Thomas "Lamps" Sanderson ("though [he was] dreadfully fussy," Hardinge recalled), and to read up on the problems of the Balkans and the East.

In April 1887, Hardinge learned from Eric Barrington, private secretary to Lord Salisbury, now foreign secretary, of an opening in Sofia. Bulgaria was then a center of European diplomatic activity, and British "Agent and Consul General" Sir Nicholas O'Conor's sole secretary would have lengthy opportunities to act as chargé. Hardinge immediately volunteered, departed two days later, and soon arrived at a remote and rather primitive town of twenty thousand, two days' journey by carriage from the nearest important rail terminus at Niš.

The political situation was challenging and complicated. The Berlin Conference of 1878 had by no means settled all Balkan problems, and in September 1885 a revolution in the southern half of Bulgaria, known as "Eastern Rumelia" and still technically under Ottoman rule, opened a further period of tension. The movement was aimed at full union and independence of

Bulgaria. Prince Alexander of Battenberg, elected Prince of Bulgaria in 1879, had little choice but to acknowledge the movement. Fortunately for Bulgaria, the Turks were unwilling to send troops, and European powers were generally sympathetic to Alexander's and Bulgaria's cause. The main immediate problem was neighboring Macedonia, where several national groups competed for supremacy. Serbia in particular, fearing that a powerful united Bulgaria would nullify her Macedonian claims, declared war upon Bulgaria in late 1885, only to be so seriously defeated that Austrian intervention alone prevented a Bulgarian invasion of Serbia.

Bulgarian-Turkish tension abated in early 1886, when an agreement recognized Alexander as governor-general of Eastern Rumelia for five years. Only a few months later, however, he was kidnapped by a group of pro-Russian officers; the Tsar's ill will towards Alexander had been growing for some time. A counterrevolutionary movement in Eastern Rumelia led by Stefan Stambulov managed to overthrow the Russian faction and bring back Alexander, but the prince had had enough of Bulgarian adventures and soon abdicated. The Bulgarian Assembly found it no easy task to locate a willing successor. In July 1887, however, it settled upon Prince Ferdinand of Saxe-Coburg, who fortunately lacked neither fortitude nor ambition, for Russia's determined hostility prevented the powers from recognizing him, and Stambulov and his associates, while giving the prince their formal support, had been effective rulers of the country since Alexander's departure.

Hardinge admired Stambulov's determination and political expertise: dictatorial methods were not entirely out of place in a Bulgaria that in Hardinge's view, was approaching anarchy as the internecine Macedonian struggle welled across the frontier. "Whatever may be the faults of his administration," he reported to Salisbury, "he has shown himself to be gifted with the courage and energy to act up to his opinion of what may be necessary for the welfare of the country without looking too closely into the means employed for the attainment of this object . . . ."[12] Hardinge also got on well with Prince Ferdinand, whom he found witty and amusing, "a typical 'boulevardier'".

It was, all in all, a delicate situation. Russian intrigues were everywhere, and Hardinge noted them in his reports. Austria was not far behind, and Hardinge's greatest personal clash came with Count Stephan von Burian von Rajecz, Austria's diplomatic agent (Austro-Hungarian foreign minister, 1915–16 and 1918), "a very clever, cynical man," who always treated the Bulgarians with contempt. Hardinge had to act in concert with von Burian, for Britain and Austria shared the same policy of informal support for Ferdinand; the task of smoothing relations between von Burian and Stambulov could not have been easy. Hardinge did well in preserving Britain's influence; that such efforts were viewed as "British intrigue" did not bother him, nor did he ever question the propriety of Stambulov's methods.

Aside from politics, life was generally pleasant. There were few of those social functions whose novelty had worn off in Berlin and Washington. Hardinge had ample time for shooting and long rides in the countryside. Finances, however, were as usual a restraint. O'Conor told Salisbury that his own salary was considerably less than that of other diplomatic agents on the spot, and not enough to get by on. It is no surprise, therefore, that Hardinge complained officially when he was denied the normal extra allowance of £1 per day given to chargés at diplomatic posts but not at consulates. To a man whose total income was now in the neighborhood of £400 a year, £1 a day mattered.[13]

At the end of 1888, three attractive offers came Hardinge's way: he was asked to join Lord Dufferin in Rome, Sir Augustus Paget in Vienna, and Sir William White in Constantinople. All offered him a senior second secretaryship as head of chancery, a rank for which, at thirty, he was rather young. "I weighed all these offers very carefully and finally decided to go to Constantinople as being certain to give me work for which I had had both training and local experience, and as more likely to lead to openings for advancement in the service," he said later. He would have preferred Rome, but was discouraged by Barrington. Constantinople, while attractive, was his second choice.[14]

Service with Sir William White was a new experience. "Bluff, very capable and not too scrupulous," tall and leonine, White had come up through the ranks of the Consular Service, in those days the equivalent of a ranker becoming an army officer and sharing the mess with gentlemen: it was done, but rarely. His knowledge of Turkey and the Balkans was extensive, for he had served in Serbia, Rumania, and Bulgaria as well as Constantinople. He was a forceful man, quite the opposite of Dufferin in manner.

> On one occassion when I disagreed with him on a political question he became so angry that he brought his fist down with such violence on a small table that he smashed it to pieces and in his rage told me that he would kick such ideas as I had out of my head. I told him quietly that I would not tolerate such language even from my Ambassador and left the room. When I reached the foot of the stairs I heard him call for me to come up again, and when there he asked me how soon I wanted to take some leave, which I may add he had already refused . . . .

Hardinge went home after only two months in Constantinople.

It was an important leave, for during it he became engaged to his first cousin, Winifred Sturt. Winifred, or "Bena" as she was known to family and close friends, was the daughter of Henry Gerard Sturt, first baron Alington, and Lady Augusta Bingham, Hardinge's aunt. Lord Alington, or "Daddie Darling" (the spelling was his own), was a rich landowner of Dorsetshire and northeastern London, and Conservative M.P. for Dorchester and then Dorset from 1846 until his elevation to the peerage in 1876. The creation was a new one, but the family was long established; the title of Alington came from an old and related Irish peerage of the same name. Lord Alington was famous above all as a sportsman. Long a member of the Jockey Club, he entertained the elite of racing society at Crichel, some twenty miles southwest of Salisbury. His horses did well. He was joint owner of "St. Blaise," Derby winner in 1883, and "Common," triple crown winner in 1891.

The earliest meeting of Charles and Winifred is unrecorded, but is surely was as children (Winifred, born in 1868, was ten years younger than Charles). Brought up with her four sisters in relative simplicity, Winifred was a slim, fair woman of middle height — and her beauty and charm come through even in the worst of old photographs. She had a good sense of fun, which with her other characteristics endeared her to her friends, among whom was Alexandra, Princess of Wales. Edward, Prince of Wales, was a noted member of the sporting set and was entertained more than once at Crichel, while the Sturts visited Sandringham, where Winifred was shocked by illegal gambling at baccarat.[15] She was one of the very few outsiders to be permitted to know the Wales children, particularly Princesses Maud and Victoria, well. A talented violinist, Winifred often played at court and other social gatherings. Her weakness was her health — not Victorian vaporings, but a serious inclination to suffer at the least provocation from colds and coughs.

In 1889, Charles visited Crichel soon after his return to England, and the couple decided upon marriage. Lord Alington's opposition to the union was at first shared by Winifred's brother Humphrey (later second baron Alington). Not only was Hardinge her cousin; he also had no prospects beyond the limited honors and income which could come his way as a diplomat. Hardinge thought briefly of going ahead without Alington's approval, but Winifred refused. "A pure unselfish act of self denial does one good morally and makes one happier in a way that one would not be otherwise & I could not bear that our marriage should have even the semblance of a shadow of selfishness."

Winifred was difficult to deny: she was Lord Alington's favorite daughter, and he had other distractions. Humphrey was in the process of marriage as well, and their sister Hilda was involved in a far more unpopular union (even Hardinge opposed it) to a penniless rector. Lady Augusta had died in 1880, and Lord Alington himself remarried in early 1892. There is a strong likelihood that Princess Alexandra put in a good word for Winifred, who stayed at Sandringham in January 1890. She was ill again, and was nursed by Alexandra, but she sat next to Prince Edward at least once at dinner. Edward had been somewhat critical of her fiancé. "I told him that he was most unkind," she wrote to Hardinge in Constantinople; "he laughed a great deal & said he did not know you & he would not say if he approved of our engagement or not until he knew you — to which I answered that that was all right as he could not help liking you." In any case, the marriage was allowed to go ahead, although Lord Alington was not as cooperative in the matter as a dowry as Hardinge, at least, thought he might be. Winifred had the income from £15,000 settled upon her, but did not inherit the principal until her father's death in 1904.

The wedding took place on 17 April 1890, in the height of the Easter season. Guests at St. Paul's church in Knightsbridge included Princess Alexandra and her daughters, and a splendid reception and ball followed at Alington House on Audley Street. The presents were numerous, with much of an impressive list of jewelry give by Lord Alington. The couple honeymooned at Crichel. "This was the beginning of many years of great happiness and of a very successful period in my career largely due to the help and assistance of my wife." These few words contain the crux of a very satisfactory relationship, but in later years Hardinge obviously found it difficult to write about a wife whom he loved greatly but who died unexpectedly and tragically in 1914.

In mid-May 1890, the couple traveled overland to Constantinople, sending their luggage, including Winifred's trousseau, by Messageries Maritimes from London. Only empty boxes arrived, and the insurance company refused to pay compensation since the loss was not due to "sea risk." The Hardinges reluctantly concluded that their limited financial resources would not permit them to take legal action. In any case, they were soon on the move again, for in November Sir Nicholas O'Conor again required a replacement while he went on leave from Sofia.

Sofia was a further introduction to Winifred of the life of the itinerant diplomat. It was a bad winter and she was often ill, although a number of dispatches in her hand in Hardinge's papers show that she acted as his (unpaid) secretary. Wolves surrounded and occasionally penetrated the streets of the town, attracted by the horses. Nor were politics much solace; the Hardinges heard at dinner the shots — meant for Stambulov — which brought down K.M. Belchev, the popular minister of finance. Lady O'Conor's dachshund, left in Winifred's charge, turned rabid and bit servants and horses alike; altogether, it was not an amusing season.

Hardinge found he got on well with Ferdinand, now ruler for three and a half years despite all predictions (he was to survive until his postwar abdication in 1918). According to Hardinge, Ferdinand was in much better control of the situation, unruffled even by Belchev's murder. Since the powers still had not recognized him, the prince was pleased when Hardinge at least agreed to dine with him in small and intimate meetings.[16] Still, it was with relief, certainly on Winifred's part, that the couple went home via Vienna for four month's leave in April 1891 before returning to Constantinople (although after their son Edward's birth the following May, Winifred returned home for her own and the child's sake).

The situation in the Ottoman capital was not particularly satisfactory. Count Radowitz, the German ambassador, was successfully advancing his country's interests, with considerable support from Berlin. Sir William White, bitterly opposed to Russia by virtue of his experiences in Warsaw and his Polish wife, encouraged German influence if he thought it undercut that of Russia, facilitating such projects as the Baghdad Railway, then in its infancy. This policy did not notably enhance Britain's prestige, however, and when White died suddenly in London, his successor, Sir Clare Ford, previously minister in Madrid, proved wanting "both in capacity and knowledge. The prestige of the Embassy dwindled very rapidly in his hands." Hardinge felt that Ford would neither listen nor learn, and Hardinge—and others—took exception to the fact that he had brought his mistress with him.

Hardinge found his position as head of chancery under Ford impossible, but in July 1892 a telegram from London offered him the chargéship at Bucharest. The appointment included responsibility for concluding a marriage contract between the duke of Edinburgh's daughter and the crown prince of Rumania. Queen Victoria could be expected to take her traditional close interest in such a family matter. After a few weeks' leave at home, the Hardinges went to Bucharest in September 1892.

Bucharest was only a slight improvement over Sofia. The Hardinges found themselves at the only hotel, run by an Englishwomen but forever crowded with Balkan diplomats. Hardinge himself was not impressed by the leading Rumanians, with their "external French veneer which concealed their natural Oriental characteristics." On the other hand, the Carpathians were new ground, and weeks spent at the summer capital at Sinaia provided the opportunity for exploration. King Carol I was hospitable and clever, "but a Hohenzollern through and through." His nephew and heir, Prince Ferdinand, second son of the Prince Leopold of the (Catholic) line of Hohenzollern-Sigmaringen whose candidacy for the Spanish throne was the immediate cause of the Franco-Prussian War of 1870–71, "was a very stupid young man with large protruding ears." A better friend was Take Ionescu, a rising young politician just Hardinge's age with an English wife; Hardinge was to know him in Paris after the war. The diplomatic community included Bernhard von Bülow, in due course German foreign secretary (1897–1900) and chancellor (1900–1909), so it was an important association for Hardinge.

If the political atmosphere was calmer than Sofia's, Hardinge now had sole responsibility. His most worrisome task was negotiation of the marriage contract. Although largely a formality, Princess Marie's renunciation of her claims to the British throne, since she was to marry a Catholic, presented some interest. To Hardinge, the most agonizing part of the job was the regular correspondence with Queen Victoria on the couple's reception in Bucharest after their marriage in Germany, but Dufferin in Paris furnished him with a model of how to address the Queen, and it was pleasing to be the bearer of official treaty seals and to be enshrined on parchment forever as "Onorabilul Carol Hardinge."[17]

Charles and Winifred were nearly too successful in welcoming the rather lonely seventeen-year-old princess. Marie wished to make Winifred her lady-in-waiting, a prospect which might have damned them to Bucharest forever. Queen Victoria wrote to Lord Rosebery on Marie's behalf; Rosebery replied in diplomatic language that Hardinge was to be moved — to Paris as it turned out — as a reward for his conduct in Rumania, and the Hardinges were thus saved.[18] Princess Alexandra had also interceded. So annoyed was she that the prospective loss of a good friend that in July 1893 she made Winifred her own lady-in-waiting.

Hardinge had done more than conclude a marriage contract, as Rosebery knew well. He had also negotiated a separate and unconnected treaty of extradition, a different sort of puzzle, with no legal advisor on the spot to aid him. A recent Rumanian prohibition of English cotton goods was a particular concern to home interests. Hardinge managed to have it removed within a month of his arrival, and for this he received an approving note from Rosebery and the subsequent thanks of commercial interests. Typically, Hardinge was able to get quite close to the center of Rumanian policymaking. In December 1892, a Russo-Rumanian incident flared when a Russian ship attempted to break quarantine. The Rumanians feared that Russia wished a pretext for strained relations precisely at a time when a royal wedding which they opposed was taking place. From confidential sources Hardinge was able to pass to Rosebery the entire Russo-Rumanian correspondence on the affair.[19] Acquiring such "confidential sources" was and is a diplomat's stock-in-trade, but Hardinge was always excellent at the task.

In April 1893, the Hardinges left for Paris and the post of head of chancery. Dufferin was ambassador, which meant a congenial relationship, and in fact he had specifically asked for Hardinge at the same time that Rosebery was suggesting his name. The main problem was finances. The Hardinges at that time had a total income of £1,200 a year — each providing about half — and they had fears that Paris would cost more than they could afford. Winifred's court appointment helped, but they decided to take the gamble before she knew of it. It proved a wise decision, and the family, soon numbering four when Alexander (''Alec'') was born in 1894, spent three and a half happy years in Paris.

After the Balkans, Paris appeared an oasis of civilization. The diary which Hardinge kept at this time mentions a lengthy round of dinners, luncheons, shooting parties and the like, some enjoyable, some not, but many including the elite of French aristocratic, financial, and diplomatic circles, as well as royal English friends. Edward and Alexandra visited, and so did Prince George and Princess Mary, whose wedding the Hardinges attended in 1893. The Prince of Wales's visits to Paris permitted him and Hardinge to become acquainted. Hardinge recorded one luncheon exchange in his diary. Edward had previously condemned Jameson, whose raid in South Africa had touched off an international crisis, but Hardinge now found the Prince of Wales to be Jameson's defender.

> He told Dawson when asked his opinion & having replied that they ought to be shot, to hold his tongue, & when I observed that the leaders certainly deserved punishment he asked if I was a Boer, & said that a diplomat should be more reticent. He is really too absurd.[20]

Hardinge learned to keep his tongue, and he also acquired unswerving, though not always uncritical, loyalty and admiration for Prince Edward. Winifred contributed to social success, not least by her travels to England to do her duty as lady-in-waiting or her occasional violin performances before distinguished audiences at Embassy concerts.

Hardinge's work was challenging. Anglo-French relations could have been happier, and although much internal attention was directed toward the Dreyfus affair, Captain Marchand was already on his mission to the Nile, and the dangerous days of Fashoda were not far off. Dufferin left most of the day-to-day work in Hardinge's hands, "he himself writing only one despatch about every quarter, giving a very full and most able account of the political situation in France." This approach was dangerous if the staff was lethargic, as Hardinge found on his arrival:

> Lord Dufferin naturally knew very little of what went on in the Chancery, but when I explained to him that I found that his own Private Secretary claimed the right to control the work of the Chancery, a situation that I could not and would not tolerate, he promised to support me for all he was worth and within a couple of months the situation was entirely changed.[21]

As usual, Hardinge was industrious, and when political work was slack, he drew up numerous reports on subjects such as canal traffic in France and the French state budget; throughout his early career, whether in the United States, the Balkans, or France, he gave considerably more attention to commercial aspects than was expected from diplomats at the time. In June 1895, as a reward for his work at Bucharest, Hardinge was very pleasantly surprised to be made C.B., an unusual recognition for a second secretary of only thirty-seven. Although he was to be one of the most decorated civilians in the whole of British history, "I need hardly say that though I have more than once refused the offer of a British Order for reasons which I regarded as sufficient, I have never asked for one, and it is difficult to imagine how anybody could have the brass to do so, though I knew such to be frequently the case." The C.B., however, was much appreciated, and he recorded his indebtedness to the foreign minister "for having dragged me out of the ruck of the junior branches of the Diplomatic Service . . . . It gave me the forward impetus that I needed, though he had no further connection in any way with my career."

Equally important was Lord Dufferin, still a sponsor in 1896, the year of his retirement, who commended Hardinge to Salisbury, Rosebery's successor. "Thus ends my official connection with a most distinguished man," Hardinge wrote in his diary when Dufferin left, "which has lasted for more than seven years and during which period I have been treated with unvariable kindness and consideration. I have nothing but the most kindly recollections of both him and Lady Dufferin."[22] As once before when Dufferin had moved on, Hardinge had no desire to serve under a new ambassador. When Sir Eric Barrington mentioned the need of a new first secretary in Teheran, he was somewhat surprised to find that the Hardinges were willing to trade the pleasures of Paris for the more oriental delights of Persia.

In fact, the Hardinges agonized over the decision. It meant not only leaving Paris, but also going to nearly as remote a post as could be conceived, requiring weeks of the most difficult travel to reach. In addition, Winifred had to resign her court appointment and its income — only to be told, happily, that Alexandra would await her return. More difficult was the decision to leave the children behind, for the journey and the conditions at its end were not recommended. To soften the separation, Winifred would have to stay in England until the following spring. Despite all these drawbacks, simple calculation showed that promotion to the coveted post of minister or ambassador was impossible so long as Hardinge remained in the herd of second secretaries. Teheran was the right decision, and letters from Prince Edward and Lords Rosebery and Dufferin showed that they agreed.

Trusting his worldly goods once more to Messageries Maritimes, Hardinge sailed from Marseilles to Constantinople, then on to Batum and by rail to Baku, Caspian steamer to Enzeli, and horseback to Teheran — four days of filthy rest houses and mule tracks in lieu of roads. It could not have been encouraging to remember that Winifred would have to make the same journey. He arrived on 8 December 1896 for a stay of nearly two years' duration. Since the minister, Sir Mortimer Durand, soon went on leave, Hardinge occupied the legation building. With a salary as secretary of legation of £750 a year (and £300 allowance for outfit), finances were not a serious problem. Nor, with shooting, race meetings, and polo, was sport.

The Persia which Hardinge encountered bore little resemblance to its ancient glories. The Qajar monarchy was in serious decline — the more so since Nasiru'd-Din Shah, a ruler with some abilities, had been assassinated the previous May and succeeded by the considerably less impressive Muzaffaru'd-Din, "a weak, well-meaning ruler, but frightfully corrupt." In Hardinge's view the prime minister, Aminu'd-Daulah, "was an agreeable but incompetent man." Hardinge already knew the foreign minister, Mushiru'd-Daulah, who had been Persian ambassador at Constantinople, "where we had always been good friends, and I think he had a weakness for me." In any case, the two men could speak frankly.

The principal feature of Persian affairs, viewed from a diplomatic standpoint, was the long-standing Anglo-Russian rivalry, caused by Russia's creeping approach through Transcaspia towards Persia and the Indian frontier, and Britain's fears for that frontier. By the 1880s, Persia had come to pay considerable attention to her powerful northern neighbor in the matter of concessions and privileges. Not to be outdone, Britain had concentrated its attention on southern and western Persia through concessions for telegraph lines, steamer operations on the Karun River, minerals, and tobacco — although both the latter were canceled by popular pressure. British achievements and rumored plans for extensive railway construction brought successful Russian counter-pressure for a ten-year moratorium on railways from 1890.

There appeared to be little central direction of Persian policy. The rulers were desperate for financial resources, and unable to control large sections of the country where virtually independent provincial governors collected taxes for their own purposes. The shah, if he was to preserve his position and fulfill his own desires — notably expensive trips to Europe — had to turn to other sources, and the result was a further web of outside loans and the security for those loans. Britain and Russia thus had ample scope for pursuing policies that were as often aimed at undercutting the other as at any positive objective.

Hardinge found that British influence had declined under Durand. The minister was an Anglo-Indian official, and he had served as foreign secretary in India. Persians generally disliked such officials, not because their atitude was necessarily condescending, but because their appointment seemed to rank Persia with the native Indian states served by the same cadre. Durand, however, was particularly ill received, because "he was very stiff in his manner toward the Persians . . . they disliked him because of his unbending manner, his unusual reticence and the bad Persian that he spoke and which they termed 'Afghani'." His wife was a perpetual invalid, and he himself was idle; he passed "the whole morning in his bath reading French novels and never appearing till luncheon-time. The afternoon was spent in polo or some other amusement." The only work, Hardinge claimed, was done in the chancery — his own department.

Hardinge's appreciation of Durand was not universally shared. Captain (later Brig. Gen. Sir) Percy Sykes, who served in Persia at this time and won considerable fame as a Persian expert, admired Durand and wrote a laudatory biography of him, pointing out in particular how his knowledge of Persian enabled him to obtain greater familiarity with Persian conditions than any of his predecessors and that his Indian experience insured that he did not view Persia through European eyes only. Hardinge would have responded that Sykes had a biased viewpoint:

> Sir M. [Mortimer] was completely under the domination of a certain Captain Sykes, whom he had picked up somewhere, a terrible bounder, and who was the source of

> much friction at the Legation. Sykes' one good point was that he introduced polo at Tehran and it was thanks to his energy that a beginning was made. I could not bear him, and as he left with Sir M. when the latter went home on leave I took good care that he should not return to Tehran so long as I was in charge of the Legation.[23]

Indeed, he did more than that, and considerably upset Durand by telegraphing to oppose the appointment of Sykes to a consular post for which Durand had recommended him.[24]

Hardinge found more congenial companionship in his two junior secretaries, (Sir) Horace Rumbold and (Sir) Ronald Graham. Both were later ambassadors, and Ronald Graham a close personal friend. Also useful was Lt. Col. M. Picot, the military attaché, who knew Persia and Persian well (Hardinge himself soon added another £100 a year for colloquial Persian).[25]

The official work of the post was much involved in the myriad ramifications of Anglo-Russian rivalry. Little remains but the official record; the diary, begun well enough in Paris, languished and died, although Winifred attempted briefly to keep it up after her arrival. The letters to the Foreign Office, official and private, tell enough of the story. Hardinge's concern for many months was to further the construction of a road by Lynch Brothers, the main British commercial concern operating on the Karun and in the southwest generally. Its route would run through the Bakhtiari country from Ahwaz to the Karun River through the mountains to Isfahan. Hardinge emerged from nearly a year of tedious negotiations with the Bakhtiari chiefs, who lived in Teheran, possessed of the agreements and considerable admiration for the Bakhtiaris, "some of the very few honourable men that I have met in this country . . . ."[26]

In the meantime, Hardinge had to deal with two serious incidents. In June 1897, Mr. E. Graves, English inspector of the telegraph lines in the south, was murdered by Baluchi tribesmen. A punitive expedition resulted, in which men from the British squadron in the Persian Gulf took part. Hardinge found it difficult to restrain the military from rushing in forces while he bargained in Teheran for the £5,000 compensation he had asked for Graves's murder. "The military advice of Col. Meade [Persian Gulf Resident] & the military naval officers on the spot has caused me endless trouble & nothing but the most imperative orders could restrain them from undertaking offensive operations against the Baluchis."[27] In other matters, however, Hardinge got on well with Meade. The two had to work in tandem while Hardinge negotiated an agreement with Persia whereby British ships could search for and seize arms found on ships within Persian territorial waters, thus striking a blow at the alarming trans-Gulf trade in arms to India's northwest frontier.[28]

The second episode was financial. In Teheran, the Russians, aided by rumors of the shah's ill health, organized a run upon the British-owned Imperial Bank of Persia. It nearly worked, for the bank had too few reserves of coin; in fact, Hardinge was most annoyed with "the improvidence & lack of foresight of the local manager Mr. Rabino."[29] The crisis was weathered, and before he left Persia Hardinge concluded an agreement by which Persia obtained a small loan through the bank and as guarantee handed over to the bank control of the customs of the southern ports. "This was an immense advantage to British commerce in the South as it placed a check on corruption, and until the loan was repaid British trade held a very privileged position." The Persians had previously refused just such a guarantee, and it may be argued whether this landmark agreement, which for the first time actually alienated a Persian governmental department, was in Britain's best interest — for the Russians soon made compensatory demands in the north.

Hardinge did his best as champion of Britain's cause wherever he saw Russia enter the lists. Finances, local politics, direct military intervention — all were cards in the "great game." "The object of the Russians was to penetrate as far south as Seistan in order to be able to turn the flank of the frontiers of India," he wrote later, and it was certainly an article of belief held by many at the time. On occasion his advocacy was too energetic: Salisbury, for example, who was hoping for some sort of détente with Russia, made him play down a typical issue regarding Cossack military escorts for Russian doctors establishing frontier quarantine posts.[30] Hardinge overestimated the significance of his own contribution, considering the long history of the Anglo-Russian rivalry, but he conducted Britain's defense with enthusiasm, energy, and considerable ingenuity, seldom able to refer to London for advice. He learned several excellent lessons on the nature of Russia's policy in Persia, and the conflict in his own country's policy between strictly commerical and immediate goals on the one hand and long-range diplomatic aims on the other.

A smaller but nagging problem was the uncertainty of his tenure. Durand left Teheran in February 1897 on leave, scheduled to return in the early fall. He then several times postponed his journey for personal reasons, arriving finally on 31 March 1898.[31] Hardinge thus had been chargé for more than a year, and while he relished the responsibility, the uncertainty meant that he saw little of the country and had to cancel a planned journey to the south.

As soon as Durand reappeared, the Hardinges left for home and children, finding the journey out more difficult than the jouney in, since it was earlier in the season and melting snow still flooded the rivers and roads. Winifred's clothes were largely ruined in one roadside accident. Once safely home, however, Hardinge was praised again from private and official quarters, including an official dispatch from Lord Salisbury.

> When I saw Lord Salisbury at the Foreign Office on my return he asked me whether I had not sometimes been afraid of the responsibilities I had assumed on my own initiative, to which I replied that I had undoubtedly passed through moments of some anxiety. He remarked that it had all turned out very well, but that it might have been awkward if it had not. I agreed.

There can be no question that Salisbury approved of Hardinge's judgment and decisiveness, for within two months he offered him the post of secretary of embassy, or councillor, at St. Petersburg, thus promoting him over seventeen men in a Diplomatic Service as conscious of seniority as any military establishment. Naturally he accepted with alacrity.

> It created considerable stir and questions were asked in Parliament as to why I had passed over the heads of so many senior diplomatists, but Lord Salisbury was always quite firm in his statement that I was, in his opinion, the best suited to succeed Mr. Goschen, who had been appointed Minister in Belgrade from St. Petersburg.

Persia marked a turning point in his career, and Hardinge had been very right to accept the appointment. Although only a first secretary, he had done well in sole command of an important legation. In 1898, with nearly twenty years' experience in a variety of situations behind him, he was thrown by Lord Salisbury's mark of favor into the heart of the important Anglo-Russian great power relationship.

II Royal Road to Success

Charles Hardinge arrived in St. Petersburg in October 1898, barely forty, eager to get on. He was schooled in the traditional manner, however, and had traditional views about the British empire and the function of diplomacy in its defense and protection. Hardinge was never a man of pretence—one of his better attributes—and he never posed as an intellectual. There is little evidence that he yet thought particularly deeply about the long-range trends of world power relationships. Reading Hardinge's memoirs, written after World War I, it is possible to reach a different conclusion about the 1880s and 1890s, for in the memoirs it seems that even then he knew Germany would be the enemy and Russia the ally of Great Britain. It was not at all like that. Hardinge's Berlin experience left him with a marked distaste for the future Emperor William and his military minions, but his stay had been short and generally enjoyable. That the real rival was Russia was borne out by his experiences in Teheran and the Balkans. If he arrived in St. Petersburg with any special sense of "mission," therefore, it was the unquestioning assumption that he must defend British imperial interests against Russian encroachments. There was yet no reason to question either the rightness or the strength of the empire, although a severe test was near at hand in the Boer War.

The first problem was to get settled. Housing was scarce and the cost of living high. Hardinge found a tolerable flat, however, and Winifred and the boys soon arrived. Like many they found the climate very trying, and finances were the usual worry. Hardinge's salary was £900 a year, soon augmented by £100 for mastering Russian, together with £150 house and £166 outfit allowances, but the unfurnished flat alone cost £550 a year. More than ever, social contacts were essential, even for exercise. The short summers made sport difficult save for hunting and fishing; Hardinge was most thankful for the covered Admiralty tennis court which he used frequently through the courtesy of Grand Duke Vladimir.

The Hardinges had little problem winning acceptance in St. Petersburg society, although they hardly fit the spendthrift and frivolous mood. Winifred's court appointment approved an important entrée, and Hardinge had met Nicholas in England when the latter was still tsarevich. He came to know the tsar better in later years, but his attitude did not change: sympathy and friendship, well tempered with awareness of the tsar's several major weaknesses. "The unfortunate Emperor," he calls him in his memoirs, who, "had he been an Englishman, would have been the most perfect type of English gentleman. . . ." Nicholas had little trouble in winning Hardinge by always appearing to be pro-British when all around him were Anglophobes. Hardinge overestimated the tsar's capacity to intervene in state affairs, but he did recognize his lack of determination. The Tsarina Alexandra Fedorovna was another matter, but she was Queen Victoria's granddaughter, "devoted to England and thoroughly English in all her tastes." After a year of observation, Hardinge believed that she was a safeguard to British interest.[1] The tsarina's role in foreign policy is a moot point, but she seems never to have used her influence over the tsar in any anti-British cause.

Of more immediate importance were the Russian foreign ministers, Count M.N. Muraviev, "very Anglophobe and hopelessly untruthful," who was found dead in his study little more than a year after Hardinge's arrival, and his assistant and successor, Count V.N. Lamsdorff (1900–1906). "A strange-looking man, very short, very pale and very bald. He wore very high-heeled shoes to increase his height. Like all Russians, he was slippery in his dealings, but always courteous, and he knew his business, which could not be said of his predecessor." Lamsdorff got on well with Hardinge over the eight years they had to work together. He was an unassuming bureaucrat who had almost no experience abroad. His function was to carry out the tsar's haphazard foreign policy and this he did, although personally he disagreed with expansionist policies in the Far East. The dominant figure was Count S.Y. Witte, minister of finance since 1892. "He was a strong, clever, and unscrupulous man of great ambition. His manners were abrupt and wanting in poise, but his views were clear and decided." Witte advocated peaceful relations with Britain in view of increasing tension with Japan and domestic financial difficulties.

Politics, internal and foreign, were often carried on in an atmosphere of confusion and court intrigue. Hardinge soon had the contacts among official and diplomatic circles he required, but it became clear to him that his superior, Sir Charles Scott, was not really master of the situation or capable of influencing Russian policy. The Scotts were popular in society, but "he had spent most of his career in small German Courts, and in Denmark as Minister, and was inexperienced in dealing with the larger political questions of Europe. Consequently he found himself out of his depth in St. Petersburg and his views carried no weight at the Foreign Office." Hardinge concluded that the Russian authorities were pleased to have Scott precisely because he was malleable: "I know they look upon him here as quite their creature," he wrote in 1901 to his friend Sir Francis Bertie, assistant under secretary in the Foreign Office.[2] So long as Sanderson in London appeared to have considerable faith in Scott, it was not likely that he would be moved. In the meantime, Hardinge set out to learn the intricacies of court politics and to assess the general drift of Russian conditions and policy.

It was obvious that Russia was in an expansionist mood. Her push into Manchuria and Korea had captured official imaginations by the 1890s, and it was a policy steadily pursued throughout Hardinge's first five years in St. Petersburg. On a more detailed level, however, "policy" vacillated unsteadily between support for the integrity of Korea and China against Japan, and desire for a modus vivendi with Japan which would result in the practical partition of the two weaker states. Strong factions in St. Petersburg supported both approaches. The result was a policy which worked for alliance with China in 1896 but absorption of China's Port Arthur in 1897.

Expansion was agreed upon; means for its achievement were not. The rise of the xenophobic Boxer movement in China at the turn of the century, however, gave Russia an excellent pretext for interfering to defend her interests, notably the Chinese Eastern Railway in Manchuria. Manchuria was occupied in mid-1900, and the troops were still there when Hardinge left St. Petersburg more than two years later, despite British, American, and Japanese protests. The efficacy of British protests was offset by severe criticism in the London press of Russian brutalities in Peking, and Hardinge as chargé had to pass home an official complaint by the tsar. Hardinge, for all that, felt that the tsar was sincere in his declarations of nonannexation in China, unlike the ministers and military officials. Nevertheless, he understood that "it is not impossible . . . that Manchuria may eventually prove as difficult to the Russians to abandon as Egypt proved to us. . . ."[3]

In another letter, he reported his conclusion that even the convention with China for Russian withdrawal, on which he had gleaned considerable information from his Foreign Ministry sources, would leave enough railway guards to serve as a permanent reminder to China of Russia's position in Manchuria. Without annexation, in other words, Manchuria "will gradually assume the character of a Chinese Province under a Russian protectorate." Hardinge could take satisfaction that his evaluations were well received at home, and Bertie saw to it that the king and Lord Lansdowne (foreign minister, 1900–1905) read his reports. Since, however, actual negotiation of Britain's interests was left to "Sir Venturesome Scott" (Bertie's phrase), Hardinge had little hope that Russia would alter her policy simply on Britain's account.[4]

Hardinge kept his eye on Far Eastern problems, however, as his reports when chargé show. It was Hardinge, in fact, who was able "through the indiscretion of a high official of the Russian Ministry for Foreign Affairs" to report the mission of Marquis Itō to St. Petersburg in November 1901 to negotiate a division of spheres: Korea for Japan, Manchuria for Russia. Despite Lamsdorff's support, the tsar and his advisors refused to make any concessions in Korea. Itō went on to Berlin where Lansdowne's invitation to London reached him. Itō probably planned a visit to London from the first,[5] but Hardinge remained convinced that it resulted from his own information; "this was, I believe, the most crucial moment in the national history of Russia. . . ." The end result was the Anglo-Japanese alliance of January 1902. To Russia, Britain had now sided openly with the enemy; the acquisition of Japanese support, viewed in this light, was a "coup de maître."

The world at large tended to focus upon these Far Eastern quarrels, but from Britain's standpoint, Tibet, Afghanistan, and Persia were equally sensitive areas. In Tibet, a vacuum resulting from China's weakened hold after the Sino-Japanese War of 1894–95, coupled with the usual frontier incidents and growing evidence of Russian ambitions, demanded action. George Nathaniel Curzon, who became viceroy of India in 1898, was nothing if not forward in the pursuit of such British interests. The danger was not Russian invasion of India through Tibet—even the most nervous observers discounted that possibility—but Russian control over the center of the Buddhist world. Curzon began with negotiations with Tibetan agents on the frontier, advanced to direct correspondence with the Dalai Lama, and eventually administered a dose of force with the Francis Younghusband expedition to Lhasa in 1903–4. Hardinge had an important role in the events leading to this expedition for it was he who first reported, when chargé in October 1900, that the tsar had received a Tibetan agent at Lividia Palace in the Crimea. "I have not been able, so far, to procure any precise information with regard to this person or to the mission on which he is supposed to have come to Russia," he reported; but the existence of the mission, combined with periodic signs of Russian reinforcements in Central Asia, was enough to alarm London. The resulting fears and intrigues did much to explain the march on Lhasa three years later.[6]

In Afghanistan, the problem was twofold. The Amir Habibullah, who succeeded in October 1901, was less cooperative than his predecessor. He was unwilling to accede to the long-standing British India control of Afghan foreign relations. Second, the combined pressures of Russian extension into central Asia and the obvious utility of Afghanistan as a means to apply pressure upon Great Britain led to a direct challenge to that control of foreign relations. Although Scott had doubted Russian intentions of acting there, in 1900 Russia first directly denied Britain's total control and then matched deed to word by using its political agent in Bukhara as a means of suggesting to the Afghanis that Russia wanted more direct relations with Kabul.[7] Many small matters—displaced frontier markers, raided sheep—required settlement. It would not do to let the Russian foot in the door, however, particularly if that foot took the form of an agent in Kabul where Britain had none herself. A good deal of Scott's and Hardinge's time over the next several years was spent futilely in trying to work out an equitable solution.

Hardinge needed no introduction to Persian problems. Even as he arrived in Russia, negotiations for the Persian loan had fallen through, and Russia demonstrated little enthusiasm for new proposals for joint Anglo-Russian financial solutions, preferring to step into the breach herself. With the return to power in 1899 of former Grand Vizier Amin os-Soltān, British fears were confirmed. He had voted against British control of the customs of the south in the shah's council, and he questioned

Britain's ultimate intentions in Persia as least as much as he questioned Russia's. Durand in Teheran thought that the grand vizier merely wished to frighten Britain, but Persia had hard cash in mind. In the fall of 1899, Amin os-Soltān negotiated secretly with Muraviev and Witte, so secretly that only the vaguest rumors leaked out. In January 1900, however, the agreement was signed in St. Petersburg. Persia borrowed 22,500,000 rubles, repayment to be guaranteed by the customs of all of Persia save Fars province and the Persian Gulf coast. If Persia's payments fell below a specified limit, Russia's agent, the Discount and Loan Bank of Teheran, would have the right to exercise effective control of customs receipts. In the meantime, Persia could not borrow abroad without Russian consent until the loan was paid off.

It was a disastrous blow to Britain in Persia, the more so since Britain was foolishly caught completely by surprise. Even Hardinge's usually excellent contacts failed him. Persia's willingness to so entangle itself in Russia's clutches was undoubtedly encouraged by the desire to offset the southern customs concession so proudly won by Hardinge. In less spectacular issues, steady Russian effort resulted in the completion of the Teheran road to Julfa on the Russian Azerbaijan frontier, the growth of subsidized Russian trade and steamer traffic to the Persian Gulf, and other similar signs. The "great game" played out between Russia and Britain required constant watchfulness and produced considerable frustration.

Unfortunately for the peace of mind of Britain's agents in Russia, these Asian events came at an awkward time for Britain in view of the extensive African commitments required of her in the Boer War. It is a commonplace to say that Britain's "splendid isolation" ended in South Africa, and it is quite true that the Anglo-Japanese Alliance should be seen, in more than a Far Eastern context, as an attempt to win an ally and yet not join either of the competing alliance systems, Austro-German or Franco-Russian. Seen from Hardinge's perspective, however, the Boer War badly complicated an already delicate situation, for now, surprisingly, Russian opinion was universally anti-British.

The Russian press, unfriendly at the best of times, "has shown a bitterness and hostility towards our country that it would be almost impossible to exceed," Hardinge reported in October 1899.[8] The Russian government claimed in answer to protests that the press was free, but Hardinge knew that the newspapers reflected the government's attitude. Observers expected ministers and military officials to be anti-British, but it was often thought that the court held a contrary attitude. Two days of shooting with Grand Duke Vladimir and a party of nobility showed Hardinge that this was a "complete delusion,"[9] and his reports when chargé in each of the several following autumns during Scott's leaves have much the same content.

More worrying was Muraviev's direct attempt to end the Boer War by seeking collective mediatory action with France, Germany, and Spain. Hardinge learned of the secret overture to Spain from his good friend Prince Kinsky, Austrian chargé, who had it from Señor Silvela, prime minister of Spain. It was possible that Muraviev attempted this European maneuver on his own, "moved by his vanity to endeavour to obtain off his own bat a diplomatic success, which, if proved to be a failure, could be ignored and so bring him no discredit." Muraviev's plot failed, and his death soon removed him from office, but rumors of Russian volunteers for the Transvaal and the appointment of a military attaché to serve with the Boers kept the issue alive.[10]

It seemed briefly that the Boxer rebellion would quiet Russian hostility toward Britain, if only because Russia found cooperation with Germany in China most difficult. But the Boxers were put down, just in time for Britain's "treacherous" treaty with Japan and aggressive action in Tibet. It is safe to say that Hardinge learned even more than in Teheran about the frustration of disseminating an aura of strength from a position of weakness.

Some solace could be taken from the fact that Russia had many difficulties of her own, and Hardinge, assigned to study and report upon finances and the budget, was well placed to observe them. To Hardinge, careful study of Witte's published figures combined with information from other sources showed that the reported budget surpluses were simple falsification. Witte's peace policy resulted from the fact that Russia had not the money for adventures, nor could additional funds be found in European markets at the right price. The annual report of March 1901 was a typical sample. Even in a manipulated budget, only 11 percent went to such areas as agriculture, education, and justice. Hardinge pulled no punches in his summary.

> Thus with the dawn of the new century, in spite of much material progress made, the dark sides of Russian life are only too apparent, amongst which may be noted the general material insecurity of the population as a whole, the absolute want of and low level of education, the excessive gambling and speculative nature of industrial life, the insufficiency and inferiority of the judicial system, the excessive crippling of individual and corporate initiative or enterprise, and the absence of all freedom of the press, which are factors that cannot but influence the general welfare of the country, and leave it heavily handicapped in the sharp competition with other countries which are all devoting more and more attention to subjects of moral and intellectual improvement, whilst in Russia these are at present altogether neglected.

Witte had talked much in his report of Russia's mission for humanity, but Hardinge's information already indicated the continued growth of expenditure upon railways, army, and navy, with consequent economies in other areas of public expenditure.

> It would be a mistake to place too much confidence in M. Witte's rhapsodies upon Russia as a peace-loving Power in the future, or to think that hymns of peace mean peace in the twentieth century, when in reality Russia wishes to avoid for the moment the discussion of any pending international problems, while she gathers up her strength to solve them later on in accordance with Russian interests and

Russian interests alone.

Scott in his covering dispatch to this report disagreed with Hardinge's interpretation of Witte; the minister's chauvinistic noises were made only to appease court critics. To Hardinge, it was unlikely that Witte would sacrifice his own ambitions for Russian greatness simply to show the military party the cost of their specific Far Eastern plans. It was significant that Count von Aerenthal, the Austrian ambassador (and foreign minister, 1906–12), shared Hardinge's view.[11]

Russia's weaknesses, however, did not disguise the fact that Britain had little leverage with which to bargain. Many years later Hardinge recalled:

> It was a perpetual source of irritation to me to feel the humiliating position of our Embassy during those years in face of the hostility openly displayed towards England by the Russian Government and military and official classes, and our weakness and helplessness to retaliate in any way. I felt the absolute necessity of coming to some sort of agreement with Russia upon the questions in conflict in Asia between the two countries, since we were losing ground all the time, but I realized when I left how helpless it would be to enter upon negotiations with any prospect of success except on terms that would imply complete capitulation with the entire abandonment of our policy in Asia.

Hardinge believed sincerely that the Russians desired peace at that time, "owing to the financial and internal situation of the country which would be plunged by war into a state of inextricable confusion." Britain could be "almost sure" that at least no crisis would be forced on the Afghan frontier pending completion of the Orenburg-Tashkent Railway in 1905, which allowed some time.[12]

Although deeply involved in Russian affairs, Hardinge continued to take a serious interest in the flow of appointments and promotions in the Foreign Office and Diplomatic Service. It was flattering, for example, when in 1900 Spring Rice suggested from Persia that Hardinge might have a shot at the ministership in Teheran. It was less satisfactory when the appointment went to the "professor," his cousin Arthur Hardinge.[13] Charles Hardinge perhaps had no wish to return to Teheran, but a definite disappointment was the fleeting chance of an under secretaryship in mid-1902 when Martin Gosselin went as minister to Lisbon and Bertie, Hardinge's influential Foreign Office partisan, put his name forward.

Bertie, a man of forceful views, thought it a good idea to bring another diplomat from overseas into the Office; he also admired Hardinge's abilities and saw in him a future permanent under secretary.[14] Third, Bertie had been impatient since the Salisbury era at the amount of red tape in Foreign Office methods, due mainly to the attitude of "Sanderson Villiers & Co." (Sanderson had been permanent under secretary since 1894, and Francis Villiers became an assistant under secretary two years later.) Bertie wanted to simplify and speed up the office procedures as well as give more challenging tasks to the junior members. There was also the question of determining the basic task of under secretaries of any rank: would they administer the policy as decided and advise only when asked, or function as regular and permanent advisors to the foreign secretary? Bertie had assumed the advisory role in Salisbury's day, and he could expect Hardinge to do so, too.

Finally, there was the issue of basic policy orientation. Bertie already had a reputation for hostility to Germany and support of the alliance with Japan. Hardinge was no particular friend to Germany, and more than once he had found the influence of German representatives in his various posts pernicious and hostile. He also supported negotiations with Russia, as did Bertie. There is no evidence, however, to indicate that Hardinge yet saw that potential German enmity forced Britain to make a choice of enemies.

In the end, Hardinge was not offered the under secretaryship, which went to Francis Campbell, senior clerk in the China Department. Hardinge had thus to resign himself to staying on in Russia, "tired as I am of the place & its abominable climate." But when he went home on leave at Christmas 1902, he learned that he had a second chance. Bertie himself was going to Rome as ambassador (requiring his exchange from Foreign Office to Diplomatic Service).[15]

Once again Bertie was Hardinge's advocate, this time with the help of Sir Francis Knollys, the king's private secretary, and King Edward himself, who, according to Knollys, pressed Lansdowne to make the appointment. Such intervention was hardly unique; the king took a close interest in diplomatic appointments. He knew the Hardinges from Paris and had read the Russian dispatches; he got on well with Bertie, and he could be expected to listen to his longtime secretary Knollys. On the other hand, the king's relations with Lansdowne were rather strained, above all since an unfortunate quarrel over the Garter for the Shah of Iran.[16] But the heavy artillery was on Hardinge's side. Lansdowne capitulated, apparently with reluctance.

The Hardinges now left St. Petersburg with considerable relief, if only from the climate—particularly since the family now included daughter Diamond, born in June 1900. Hardinge took up his work in February 1903 as the most junior of the three assistant under secretaries (Villiers and Campbell were the others) under Permanent Under Secretary Sanderson. In theory, his responsibilities were Afghanistan, Tibet, Egypt, and Morocco, together with the Treaty and Consular Departments. In actual fact, Sanderson kept Egypt and Morocco together with his own European countries (including Russia) but gave Hardinge Persia, Central Asia, Scandinavia, and the Low Countries.[17]

Hardinge had been in London less than two months when he heard that the king had asked that he accompany the royal visit to Portugal and Italy at the end of March. His selection was unusual, since it was the standard practice for a cabinet minister to attent the sovereign abroad. The king had no wish to ask

Lansdowne, or indeed any cabinet member, to join his small masculine holiday party aboard the royal yacht *Victoria and Albert,* but he did require someone from the diplomatic side to write speeches, deal with protocol problems, and the like, and with Bertie gone to Rome, "Charlie" Hardinge was a known and favored quantity. Strong opposition arose at once. "Lord L.," Hardinge wrote to Sir Frank Lascelles in Berlin, "backed by other high officials at the F.O. [meaning Villiers] objected and twice asked the King to select somebody else but the King insisted and got his way. . . ." Obviously, Lansdowne wished to avoid a second head-on collision with the king. In his memoirs, Hardinge admitted to personal intervention:

> Things drifted till within a week of the date of the King's proposed departure, and as the subject had become one of general knowledge and discussion I called on Lady Lansdowne, whom I knew well, and told her that although I realized of course that I was entirely under Lord Lansdowne's orders, still if there was any likelihood of my having to accompany the King it would only be fair to tell me at once as naturally I would have to make certain preparations for such a journey. She entirely agreed, with the result that she spoke to Lord Lansdowne, who told me very unwillingly that I was to accompany the King and that I was to receive the rank of Minister Plenipotentiary in the Diplomatic Service. I need hardly say that I was greatly pleased and astonished at my exceptional good fortune and was entirely at a loss to understand why I had been selected in this unusual and unexpected manner.

The explanation is disingenuous. Hardinge in fact asked for the rank of minister, and the king supported his request. Hardinge justified the request not only on the grounds of the trip, but because he had been given a verbal promise of the rank (he was still councillor) when he returned to the Foreign Office. Sanderson told the king that Hardinge could have the rank "while in attendance upon the King,'' but Edward, with his notorious eye for detail, spotted the qualification and insisted that the rank be general and permanent. ''You should have seen the commotion in the F.O. when this announcement was made,'' Hardinge told Lascelles; ''I chuckled quietly. . . .''[18]

Since Hardinge was to serve an important role as advisor to King Edward and intermediary between the throne and the Foreign Office for at least the last five years of Edward's reign, the king's small victory was also Hardinge's. ''At first it was said that Hardinge had been selected because he had married one of Queen Alexandra's Ladies-in-Waiting,'' reported Sir Frederick Ponsonby, equerry and acting private secretary to the king, ''but this was quite wrong. King Edward had with unerring judgment discovered Hardinge as the rising man in diplomacy, and thought he would be far more useful than a Cabinet Minister, who would probably be unable to talk French or German.''[19] As those who knew the king well might have added, he was most jealous of his personal comforts, incuding his traveling companions, and he would hardly have included Hardinge solely on account of his admiration for Winifred.

The party left England on 30 March and reached Lisbon on 2 April. Only a half-dozen men accompanied the king, including Hardinge, Ponsonby, and the Marquis de Soveral, Portuguese ambassador and court intimate. Hardinge's duties became onerous as soon as the official receptions and speeches began. He took Knollys's sage advice and pleaded ignorance of bridge, which the king enjoyed, for it would have cut deeply into his time. It was a wise deception, for he often had to attend some state function (standing behind the king's chair at a gala Lisbon opera for the entire performance was only one of the more tiring experiences), rising again at an early hour to write more speeches for the king: ''Gentlemen, it is with great pleasure that I have listened to the loyal and dutiful address which you have presented to me. . . .''

The work was worth the effort. The speeches, which reaffirmed the old Anglo-Portuguese friendship and stressed Britain's lack of ambitions toward Portugal's empire—and implied that others too should keep their hands off—all went well, and the king was properly grateful to their author. After one particularly successful statement, he sent for Hardinge to express his thanks for all that he had done. "I was so pleased that I did not know whether I was standing on my head or my heels," Hardinge wrote to Winifred.[20]

The yacht left Lisbon on 7 April. While at sea the party was told that the king intended to visit Paris once the Mediterranean tour was finished. Hardinge probably did not know the king's intention before leaving England, but he certainly knew at or soon after leaving Lisbon. The argument that King Edward intended a single-handed stroke of royal policymaking is given support by the very fact that he took the junior under secretary Hardinge, who would do as he was told. But much correspondence and ciphering were necessary in making the preparations, and Hardinge usually handled this side of the arrangements. It seemed the best part of discretion to make it appear that the idea developed spontaneously, and Hardinge stuck to this account in *Old Diplomacy*:

> It was during his stay [in Gibraltar] that the King received the news that President Loubet was to pay an official visit to Algiers, and . . . King Edward decided to make an effort to place Anglo-French relations on a better footing. He had the happy idea of sending four battleships of the Channel Squadron, that were lying in the harbour and under the command of Admiral Curzon Howe, to Algiers to salute the French President on his arrival. M. Loubet was delighted with this unexpected act of courtesy and sent a very friendly telegram to the King, thanking him and expressing the hope that his Majesty would visit Paris on his way home. It had been no part of the King's programme to visit Paris, but after receiving this invitation he decided at once to do so and informed the Government of his intention.

The battleships were sent specially from Ireland to pay the

honor to Loubet, however, and as Gordon Brook-Shepherd has shown, Sir Edmund Monson, British ambassador at Paris, wrote to the king on 6 April, when the royal yacht was still in Lisbon, outlining Loubet's ideas on the date and style of King Edward's visit to Paris.[21] Whatever the extent of advance Anglo-French collusion, Hardinge, who handled the correspondence, knew his later account to be untrue, but his strong loyalty to the king explains his perpetuation of the old story. It was never his intention to reveal royal confidences.

In any case, Hardinge had little to do with the decision, and was mainly concerned with the phraseology of the king's efforts to persuade his cabinet. Meanwhile, the progress continued to Gibraltar, where the strain was a bit less. "I think I am getting on all right with my job," Hardinge wrote to Winifred; "the King is always nice to me and as it is a purely military & naval place I keep in the background & do not push myself forward. . . .I *do* think that this trip will be of great advantage to me from a professional point of view."[22]

On the thirteenth the royal yacht and its many escorts sailed for Malta, where Hardinge had an hour to prepare six replies to six addresses; he was writing the last as the king read out the fourth. Such pressure was more than compensated for by the privilege of standing by the king's side at the royal levee, at the king's insistence, as if he were indeed a cabinet minister. Returning at midnight, he worked on to 2:30 A.M., turning out at 7:00 to breakfast with the king. "I cannot think how anybody could have imagined that my present job was one for a Cabinet Minister, as it seems to me that I am at work every spare moment of the day & most of the night cyphering & decyphering, writing letters, interviewing & even composing speeches for the King. No Cabinet Minister could have done this sort of work."[23]

After five days of reviews, receptions, and fêtes, the *Victoria and Albert* sailed for Italy with an escort of eight battleships and four cruisers. If nothing else, the tour was a demonstration of British naval strength. Spending the night at Syracuse, the flotilla arrived at Naples—the king, amazingly, was "incognito''—for a further four days of visits, moving on to Rome on 27 April. The visit was the first by an English Sovereign since, as far as anyone could tell, the Saxon King Ethelwulf spent a year in Rome in 855—hardly a forceful precedent. Hardinge was soon embroiled in Byzantine negotiations to enable the king to visit both the king of Italy and Pope Leo XIII while offending neither Roman rulers nor Protestant (or Catholic) opinion at home. The controversy was of little long-range diplomatic importance, but Hardinge's career unquestionably was advanced by the Roman visit. His collection of honors was enlarged as well, since Portugal had provided the ''Grand Cross of Our Lady of the Conception'' and Italy the ''Grand Cordon of the Crown of Italy.'' ''I shall be like a Xmas tree when I come home,'' he reported to Winifred; ''I am determined not to wear them in England unless the King insists. It will however be very nice someday having these foreign decorations when I am Ambassador & for instance to a function at the Italian Embassy.'' The king's gracious enthusiasm was even more uplifting: ''I like working for the King, he is so appreciative, not like the F.O.''[24]

The trip to Paris was far more important. On 30 April, the king left Rome and was met at Dijon by Monson, who brought with him the address of the British Chamber of Commerce. King Edward asked Hardinge to draft ''a very cordial reply.'' As Hardinge put it, ''with this encouragement and with my own strong conviction that friendship with France should be the keystone of our policy in Europe which would have its reflex in Russia and in Asia, I produced a reply which even the King thought might be going too far,'' and Edward asked Monson to look it over. The ambassador entirely approved the text ''and foretold that it would create a sensation and have an extraordinary effect in Paris when published.''

On arrival on 1 May, Hardinge rode in the second carriage with Delcassé, French minister of foreign affairs, whom Hardinge had known when stationed in Paris years earlier. Delcassé repeated remarks of ''Quel enthousiasme!'' could hardly conceal cries of ''Vive Fashoda!'' ''Vive Marchand!'' or ''Vivent les Boers!'' The immediate publication of the king's Chamber of Commerce speech, however, made a considerably more favorable impression, for it emphasized the king's personal feelings for France and the need ro resolve Anglo-French misunderstanding.[25]

The king's influential stay in Paris has been well recorded by others, and there is no need to review these events in detail once more. For Hardinge, it was another hectic experience. On the busiest day, Saturday, 2 May (declared a public holiday), he witnessed a presidential review at Vincennes at 9:15 A.M., visited the Hôtel de Ville at noon, lunched at the British Embassy at 1:00, watched a special race meeting at Longchamps at 3:00, dined in state at the Elysée Palace at 7:00 (ten courses with legendary wines), attended the king at a gala opera performance at 10:00 (a mélange of song and ballet chosen to match Edward's short cultural attention span), and returned half-dead after midnight.[26]

There were no unusual problems for Hardinge to deal with and he returned to London with the rest of the party, leaving Paris—thanks to Edward's flair for public diplomacy—to cries of "Vive le Roi!" and "Vive l'Angleterre!" Hardinge acquired yet another honor, "Grand Officier" of the Legion d'Honneur, and could now, as he pointed out to Winifred, swagger about with a red rosette in his buttonhole. On crossing to Cherbourg, the king added the C.V.O. and a gold cigarettecase with the royal initials in diamonds.

Hardinge had had more than just an interesting five weeks' journey. He had performed creditably under stress in the most formal of situations and had met the rather demanding test of close association with King Edward. More than the burgeoning collection of ribbons and stars, the king's friendship gave him considerable new leverage in the Foreign Office.

No sooner had Hardinge returned to work than he was embroiled in Foreign Office politics and procedures. Bertie had warned him of the red tape and obstructionism before his arrival, and Hardinge had already found the response lethargic to his ideas on Persia and other subjects under his immediate purview.

> It is hard work endeavouring to infuse a little energy into this Office about Persia. Nobody seems to dare to come to any decision & everybody waits to see which way the cat is going to jump. Sanderson has tried to shove his oar into my provinces but I have resisted and spoke to him very clearly on the subject which I hope will be sufficient for some time to come.[29]

His particular hope in this case was to recognize the Persian consular service as a separate entity along the lines of the Levant Service. Since the cadre was very small, it was just as well that the idea was not accepted.

Hardinge also suffered something of a setback when he unsuccessfully opposed the appointment of George Maycock as head of the Treaty Department (a department under Hardinge's responsibility). It was a typical stand for "Capability" Hardinge (precisely when the nickname was adopted in the Office is unclear), and it naturally brought him enemies. Hardinge, for his part, found that "vested interests and red tape are of more account than efficiency in this Office," as he put it to Bertie. "I hope before long to break down the trade-unionism that reigns here & of which Villiers is the champion. I have told Lord Lansdowne & [Viscount] Cranborne what I think of it all and I shall rub it into Lamps & Villiers when I get a chance."[28]

In fact Villiers had supported a scheme of reform while Hardinge was away, which included points Hardinge also advocated, such as the establishment of a special cipher room, with specific individuals responsible for ciphering and deciphering; a similar establishment for the preparation of parliamentary blue books; a new central system of document registration; and the relief of the clerks from as much nonpolitical work as possible, particularly including making up the diplomatic bags. All of these ideas were in the air at the time: despite recent establishment of second-division, nonpolitical clerks and the introduction of typewriters, younger men fresh from the entrance examination were still working at less than capacity. The plan to correct this situation by allowing the devolution downwards of various types of work was, said Hardinge, "not likely to be put into practice so long as Sanderson & Villiers reign here."[29]

The remark was unfair to Villiers, who supported and suggested the scheme. Sanderson, who claimed to favor devolution and to have worked for it himself, did argue against many of the changes. "The political work of the office is however in a large degree so important and a blunder may produce such serious consequences that much greater supervision by the Secretary and Under-Secretaries of State is required than in most public departments." The first duty of the Office was to see that the work was properly done, "and not that the young men are provided with work which they consider suited to their capacities."[30] It has been argued that Sanderson was not unsympathetic to new ideas and that his hostile comments were indicative of Socratic questioning rather than actual opposition, but it is clear he opposed the cipher and blue book rooms and the central registry.[31]

To Lord Lansdowne, on the other hand, it was clearly time for devolution, in part to give the juniors meaningful work, but also because too much paper arrived at the secretary's desk, and the under secretaries were swamped by a mass of routine matters. He therefore appointed a committee to consider the matter (its favorable recommendation was not made until after Hardinge had again left for Russia). Lansdowne was also attracted by a proposal which was specifically Hardinge's, to facilitate a regular system of exchanges between the Foreign Office and Diplomatic Service.

By the time Hardinge returned in 1906 as permanent under secretary, nearly all the suggested changes had been approved. Sanderson had bowed to the inevitable, for even he could see the mounting pressures of a work load approaching a hundred thousand dispatches a year. The precise authorship of most measures cannot now be traced, but Hardinge was obviously a leading reformer. Directly responsible for the proposal on exchanges, he also successfully recommended a new system of grading in the Diplomatic Service, to obviate the possibility of ten or twelve years spent in the rank of second secretary (he had suffered from this himself). At the time, his frustration led him to give less credit to Sanderson's willingness to move into the twentieth century than he deserved, but he did continue to regard Sanderson as a personal friend, while Villiers, whom he never respected, he disdained professionally ("It generally takes him an hour to do what other people can do in ten minutes."). Perhaps this attitude was due to personal antipathy and resentment of Villiers's influence; in any case, it is clear that the two men differed on the pace of change as well as the promotion of individuals.[32] Both Sanderson and Villiers were traditionalists, and both moved slowly.

The general effect of the reforms was important. Additional staff members were hired, which helped somewhat in handling the volume of work. Separate ciphering and blue book responsibilities made for efficiency as well. As Zara Steiner has pointed out, however, the heart of the reform was the registry system. Previously, department supervisors received and read incoming dispatches, minuted them, adding instructions for further disposal, and passed them to the foreign secretary, who for the most part only initialed and returned them for filing. It was the mass of such trivia of which Lansdowne complained.

The new system registered all dispatches in central and subregistries, then passed the documents to departmental senior clerks. These now "devolved" the matter down to their junior clerks, who tracked down further information if necessary and in some cases suggested the proper course of action to be followed. With devolution, the senior clerk settled roughly half the issues which crossed his desk, passing the rest to the proper assistant under secretary, who did much the same, and so on to the permanent under secretary and the foreign secretary himself. First division clerks were thus transformed: "from being clerks they became advisors engaged in the policy making process."[33] More important than Hardinge's role in initiating these reforms is the use to which he would put them as permanent under secretary after 1906. The new system did more than alter the role of the clerks. As will be seen, it permitted the concentration of authority and policy making to a large extent in the hands of the permanent under secretary.

Hardinge was still the most junior assitant under secretary, for all his royal connections and Lansdowne's support of his reform proposals. It was fortunate, therefore, that Lansdowne proved to be thinking along the same lines as Hardinge regarding the larger issues of foreign policy. Hardinge had now come to see that an understanding with France was the easiest way to arrive at the understanding with Russia he certainly regarded as necessary after his return from Paris in the spring of 1903.

In late 1902, Britain's already noticeable feeling of isolation—only partly offset by the Japanese alliance—was reinforced by a considerable wave of Germanophobia engendered by the irritating Venezuelan blockade problem.[34] In that context Joseph Chamberlain and others in the government advocated an entente with France. Prime Minister Balfour and Foreign Secretary Lansdowne were not yet prepared for such a step, although there had been overtures from France in the past, nor did they see the rivalry with Germany in the same clear light. They did see the danger building in relations with Russia, notably over Central Asia, and it was for that reason that they responded positively to Russian overtures which came through Scott in St. Petersburg. Assurances that Russia had no ambitions in Afghanistan were particularly refreshing, and Lord George Hamilton, secretary of state for India, was a strong advocate of rapprochement on this basis (Curzon in India remained noticeably skeptical). The arrival of Count A. K. Benckendorff as Russian ambassador in early 1903 furthered the movement, for Benckendorff was a supporter of Anglo-Russian agreement.

At the same time, a rebellion in Morocco threatened to bring down the dynasty and precipitate a bitter European scramble for control. France was eager to forestall as much competition as possible, and not unnaturally thought Britain more likely to be responsive than Germany. The result, since the Cabinet was equally eager to avoid an Anglo-French disagreement in Morocco, was the first tentative step towards an Anglo-French entente—not, it should be repeated, because of the effect such an entente would have upon Russian relations, but with a view to settling the specific local Moroccan issue.

Other lines of negotiation tended to lead to the same conclusion, since Russia and France were closely allied. With regard to Central Asia the Cabinet refused Curzon's request to send a mission to Tibet in early 1903, and Benckendorff was similarly conciliatory on Russian interests in that remote country. The perceived desire of Russia to obtain a port in the Persian Gulf was overshadowed by common fears of the German Baghdad Railway project. Negotiations with Germany on the railway were not satisfactorally concluded and led to another round of anti-German feeling in Britain. On 5 May Lansdowne declared in the House of Lords that Britain would regard the establishment of a naval base on the Persian Gulf—as opposed to a commercial outlet—as a grave menace to British interests. The declaration applied to Russia but the immediate target was Germany, and Benckendorff reacted favorably, at the same time indicating that Russia was willing to discuss British proposals on Persia. The way was cleared to the settlement of all outstanding Middle Eastern issues. Hardinge was probably of a mixed mind over Persia and the Gulf, for he had urged a strong line in both areas, but it was hard to reconcile the India Office and Curzon with the Foreign Office.[35]

There remained the Far East. Russia, far from reducing her efforts in that direction, was in the process of reinforcing her garrisons. In August the tsar created a new viceroyalty of the Far East and entrusted it to Admiral E. I. Alekseev, a leader of the expansionists, placing all Manchurian matters under his direction. Later in the same month Witte, spokesman of the less aggressive faction, resigned as minister of finance. The danger of war increased steadily, and with it the danger of British involvement.

British army and naval experts had little faith in Japanese military ability, and in the coming clash Japan might well invoke the alliance and call for British aid against Russia and France. The repercussions of the Anglo-Japanese alliance, designed on Britain's part primarily to ease her own military responsibilities in the Far East, were becoming apparent for the first time.

The best way to restrict the Far Eastern crisis to that part of the world was to reach agreement with France. Such an agreement would require at the minimum British concessions in Morocco—a strategic area in its own right—but by early September Lansdowne had come to the conclusion that the risk was worth it. The further results were spelled out to the Cabinet: "A good understanding with France would not improbably be the precursor of a better understanding with Russia, and I need not insist upon the improvement which would result in our international position, which, in view of our present relations with Germany as well as Russia, I cannot regard with satisfaction."[36] The Cabinet, in the midst of changes (Chamberlain, Hamilton, and others resigned over tariff reform a week after this memorandum was circulated), did not take issue with Lansdowne's analysis. Few saw at the time that closer relations with the Franco-Russian partnership meant worsening relations with Germany, but even if they had, the immediate danger of entanglement in the Far Eastern crisis was too great to do otherwise.

On 1 October, Lansdowne sent the first definite statement of Britain's terms to the French ambassador, Paul Cambon. French negotiations proceeded more swiftly than Russian negotiations, in which there were hopeful signs but few positive results. Lansdowne was not above showing Russia that Britain could also pursue a forward policy while Russia was otherwise occupied. For that reason, he sanctioned both Curzon's tour of the Persian Gulf (but with the stricture that Curzon must not appear to want to alter the status quo there), and, more reluctantly, the mission to Gyangtse in Tibet, halfway to Lhasa. The Tibet policy was confused and in the long run misguided, but it resulted as much from local problems as from the larger issues of policy.

Hardinge's influence in all this is not easy to trace, for he was still the most junior under secretary and he was responsible for neither France nor Russia. "I was pressing my propaganda as to the absolute necessity of an understanding with Russia," he wrote later, "and the easiest way to achieve this was through France." Certainly he supported the conclusions that Lansdowne obviously reached independently. On the other hand, Hardinge did his best to foster Persian and Central Asian interests, and was a particular supporter of the Tibet expedition, advising Curzon that he was confident this would forestall the Russians "who are undoubtedly tampering with the Lamas and trying to get a footing within the country."[37]

Hardinge's chance to make a personal contribution came in late November, when he went to Windsor with the express assignment of carrying on the conversations with Benckendorff, this time on specific issues. In a discussion lasting more than an hour, Benckendorff proposed that each country should suggest, informally, the areas of its special concern. Russia, for example, hoped that Britain would not press for the evacuation of Manchuria. In return Russia would be willing to recognize Tibet and Afghanistan as Britain's sphere, although direct negotiations with the latter on frontier issues would be necessary. Persia was a more difficult nut to crack; Russia opposed partition—but maintained that her aims on the Gulf were purely commercial.

Hardinge always regarded that hour as an important breakthrough. He was convinced that plain speaking had done the trick, as he wrote to Spring Rice, "and I think I managed to get more out of him than has been got before. In fact I have always hitherto been a pessimist as to the possibility of an arrangement with Russia but if Benckendorff reflects in any sense the views of Lamsdorff I think that this is no longer outside the pale of possibility." Lansdowne in the next few days carried the discussions considerably further, including mention of the possibility of partitioning Persia. "I do not wish to be too sanguine as I have witnessd the failure of previous attempts of this nature but I think the question has a more healthy aspect now than heretofore." Benckendorff had been impressed with Britain's earnestness, particularly when the king spoke to him in that sense on Hardinge's request—for Hardinge was convinced that this was the only way to insure that the whole scheme reached the tsar.[38]

Hardinge was already involved in another way with the Russian negotiations. "It was on the 1st December that I learnt for the first time from Lord Knollys that the King intended to put my name forward as a successor to Sir C. Scott," who was retiring in the spring. "To me it was a most unexpected surprise." Hardinge and Bertie had in fact hoped to move Scott for some time. As his retirement approached, Bertie and Knollys pushed Hardinge as his successor, with Bertie to move from Rome to Paris. As Knollys put it, Hardinge knew Russia and was "sound" on the question of Russian relations. "He is also a 'strong' man & combines I think strength of character with tact which is not always the case."[39] King Edward, too, backed Hardinge for St. Petersburg. Hardinge, fearing that Lansdowne would oppose the appointment for he "finds me useful and would like to keep me where I am," claimed to be calm, "as I have done nothing to push my name forward & do not intend to move in the matter."[40] Nevertheless he wanted the appointment. Prestige, the chance to achieve big things without direct oversight, even personal finances—all argued in favor of leaving London after only a year, and he was convinced that he could do the job as well as anyone.

Despite the outbreak of the Russo-Japanese War, Hardinge heard nothing more over the holidays, and his return to the Office was delayed until 10 February by illness. From a personal standpoint, the danger to Hardinge was that Lansdowne might prolong Scott's term in St. Petersburg past his April retirement. As for the war, like most contemporaries, he predicted a Russian victory. "Whatever Japan's initial successes may be, Russia will have to go on until she has crushed any Japanese forces that may be landed even if the struggle is prolonged for years."[41] From a European standpoint, however, Hardinge felt Germany was the power most satisfied with the new conflict, especially since Britain might be drawn in.

On the fifteenth, Hardinge heard with relief that he was to be Ambassador. He was eager to be away to St. Petersburg where he understood the embassy to be socially ostracized and the situation deteriorating, but he did not actually leave until 12 May.[42] The time was spent partly in negotiations by mail with the Scotts on taking over their furniture and equipage, "at famine prices." He had also to shore up the king on Bertie's Paris appointment; "I dinned into him that there is *nobody* else," he wrote to Bertie from Crichel.[43]

As soon as it appeared Hardinge might be leaving London, the problem arose of his own successor in the Foreign Office. The Office was seriously divided on this major appointment, but eventually Eldon Gorst, the choice of King Edward, Lansdowne, and Cromer, was selected. Still another problem was Bertie's Paris ambassadorship. Lansdowne was long cool to this idea, either for personal reasons or because of Bertie's known Germanophobia. Gradually other possibilities—including Lord Esher, advisor on military affairs and friend of the king—were ruled out, greatly enhancing Bertie's chances.[44]

For himself, Hardinge discovered that 1904 was the year of honors. In March he was sworn in as privy councillor and made K.C.M.G., and soon after K.C.V.O., so that he could return to Russia as Sir Charles Hardinge. "I cannot say that I am exhilarated at the prospect & I fail to see the necessity for it. However one cannot say these things without giving offense." Hardinge was not a medal-hunter, but this was surely false modesty directed by an ambitious man at the fruits of that ambition. The salary of £7,800 per annum, with £2,500 outfit allowance, was a startling contrast to the £900 he received at the Foreign Office—reason enough for a poor man to take pride in his success.[45] Hardinge very honestly had never chosen his posts by their pay, although he often worried about finances.

It was altogether a triumph. "I had really never imagined the possibility of becoming an Ambassador when only 45 years old, especially as I had been only a Second Secretary at the age of 38. It surpassed all my wildest dreams.'' Letters of congratulation poured in: the king, Curzon, and Rosebery all wrote. Many mentioned his luck, which to Hardinge was not at all the cause of his success.

> Well, my theory is that one makes one's own luck, and I can honestly say that, during the twenty-four years I had already served, I had worked much harder than most of my contemporaries and had been to much worse posts. My theory in the service was that 'power' was the first aim, regardless of pay or post, and that when the offer of a post was made the consideration to be taken into account was not whether the post was an agreeable one or not, or whether the pay as good or better than the last post held, but whether it would bring more power or opportunities for interesting work and distinction.

This was fair self-evaluation on the whole, though some highly placed friends and a dash of intrigue also had helped. ''Luck,'' however, was still part of the story—for hard work did not necessarily win King Edward's personal friendship and support, nor attract court circles to Winifred's charm.

The king had one last honor to confer before Hardinge went to Russia. In April the king and queen visited the latter's family in Copenhagen for three weeks. The occasion had none of the diplomatic importance of the Paris trip; Alexandra's family was close and she always tried to be present at the birthday of her father, King Christian IX. But once more King Edward selected Hardinge to be in attendance. Aside from the honor, the rather dull trip (for life at Amalienborg Palace was tedious and formal by English standards) allowed Hardinge to spend time with both W. Edward Goschen, the English minister, and Alexander Isvolski, the Russian minister (1903–6). Isvolski, whom Hardinge had known in Washington, was never a personal favorite. The king met Isvolski at a luncheon and, finding the Russian friendly and in favor of an understanding with Britain, took the unusual step of praising Isvolski in a letter to the tsar. This maneuver, Hardinge predicted to Spring Rice, might yet bear fruit, although the moment was not yet opportune; his meaning was clearer when Isvolski became Russian foreign minister in 1906. "The fact is," concluded Hardinge, "that for a King he is a very clever man."[46]

Certainly the king had the cleverness to spot Hardinge's ability, for he did admire properly congenial professional expertise. He had the cleverness, too, to see that it was important to send Hardinge to St. Petersburg, and as a result Hardinge had another chance to display his ability through hard work: the Russo-Japanese War was to threaten seriously any Anglo-Russian rapprochement.

III The Russo-Japanese War

On the 16 May 1904, Ambassador Hardinge arrived in St. Petersburg. Superficially little had changed but Hardinge's own position, for he had been away for only fifteen months. Society was as hospitable—or as hostile—as before, and Hardinge was soon in his old routine, even to shooting with Grand Duke Vladimir. The first several days were spent in a round of formal calls, and the official welcome was warm from all sides. On the twenty-sixth, Hardinge went by train to Tsarskoe Selo with his staff, riding from the station to the palace for the formal reception in a gold carriage with six white horses, postillions, and outriders. Both the tsar and tsarina were friendly in a half-hour's private talk, asking about Winifred and Diamond, who would arrive three weeks later. Hardinge delivered a personal message to Tsar Nicholas from King Edward, and it seemed that the Russian court accepted Hardinge's appointment as an olive branch, a token of Edward's and Britain's desire for good relations.

In fact, things had changed, as the Hardinges were instantly aware if only from the visible decline of official (as opposed to private) social functions. Russia had been at war since early February, with its Port Arthur fleet blockaded, and on 1 May Japanese troops had crossed the Yalu. Russian social and military leaders for the most part remained confident, but all official eyes were turned to the Far East.[1] Hardinge had pointed out to Lansdowne (who needed no such warning) the real danger of strained relations between Russia and Britain as a result of the war, particularly if Russia attempted to take its Black Sea fleet through the Turkish Straits. The Straits were always a potential danger spot, and in the long view Hardinge felt the British control was less necessary than it had been in previous decades so long as Britain controlled Egypt and the Suez Canal. Indeed, conceding passage of the Straits might be a valuable counter in the settlement of Anglo-Russian disagreements. Lansdowne had concurred, but both men knew such a proposal must await the end of the war. Interestingly, King Edward had suggested this bargain to Hardinge, although Hardinge was careful not to say so to Lansdowne; the king obviously found Hardinge as useful in proposing his policy suggestions to the Foreign Office as Hardinge found the king's friendship in furthering his own career.[2]

Hardinge's first discussion with Lamsdorff was friendly but noncommittal. Hardinge gave assurances of Britain's strict neutrality in the war and further explanations about Tibet. Lamsdorff was cooperative; the signature of the Anglo-French Entente in April had obviously made Russia more amenable to friendly discussion of the issues. The difficulty, Hardinge reported privately to Lansdowne, was that the peace party was relatively small. The court and military faction, following the lead of Grand Dukes Alexis and Alexander Mikhailovich, was anti-British and consistently advised the tsar against an Asian settlement with Britain, arguing that a self-limiting agreement on Afghanistan would restrict Russia's ability to exert pressure there to nudge Britain into a cooperative Far Eastern policy. Russia would not be reluctant to reach a settlement on the Balkans and China alone, but this should be avoided: the whole package or nothing.[3]

Few among the general population knew or cared about the details of the war. The first fleeting public enthusiasm had already evaporated, and Hardinge shared none of the military's continued optimism. The commercial classes suffered a serious depression; corruption was rampant; and the minister of the interior, V. K. von Plehve, the "best hated man in Russia," was seriously concerned over the growing revolutionary movement, although Hardinge saw little chance of an explosion unless the bulk of the peasantry became aroused. The difficulty was to know what to do. Some who wished to terminate the war would welcome outside intervention or mediation after the inevitable first big Russian victory, but such a victory would only encourage the tsar and the war party to try to crush the Japanese totally. On the other hand, continued Japanese success would result in an interminable struggle. The role of Germany was also important, for William was attempting to use the war as a means of reaching a rapprochement with Russia.[4]

Up to June the situation deteriorated steadily. Disaffection was spreading rapidly among the lower classes, although there was little cohesion among the critics as a result of the government's control of the post, telegraph, and railway systems. Even among educated Russians, "it is generally felt that some change is necessary in the present system of government by which the whole country has been plunged into a costly and, so far, disastrous war by the pursuit of a policy which had not the concurrence of some of the most prominent members of the Government." Witte in private conversation indicated that reforms might not be possible when the war was over; he also made clear the harsh terms a victorious Russia would demand.[5]

From Hardinge's standpoint, the main task was to demonstrate constantly that Britain was strictly neutral, and to insure that no preventable irritant survived to disturb Anglo-Russian relations. He therefore assured Witte that Britain was unlikely to interfere in peace negotiations, unless of course British interests were jeopardized. Similarly he attempted to alleviate the pressure of a mutual press war. Criticism of Britain, muted at the time of his arrival, soon increased, and he talked to both government officials and journalists in an attempt to alter their attitude.[6] Midsummer, however, brought more than problems with the press.

The most immediate danger came from the so-called "Volunteer Fleet," Russian ships which sailed through the Dardanelles as cargo carriers and then transformed themselves into armed merchantmen for commerce raiding.[7] It was difficult to classify these vessels precisely, but when two of them, the *Smolensk* and *Petersburg*, stopped P. & O. and Indian Steam Navigation Company steamers in the Red Sea, a minor crisis arose. The difficulty was that the Russian navy, notably the department dealing with prizes and the Volunteer Fleet under Grand Duke Alexander Mikhailovitch, cared little for the views of the Foreign Ministry. Alexander Mikhailovitch was himself close to the tsar and paid little attention to his own technical superiors.

The only option available to Britain was to impress Lamsdorff with the dangers, so that he would make a strong case in internal Russian councils. To that end, Hardinge insisted that "if the feelings and susceptibilities of the British people were ignored, as appeared to be the present phase of Russian policy, it would be useless to hope for any amelioration in the relations between the two countries at the conclusion of the war"; in other words, the potential rapprochement was at stake. By mid-July several ships had been seized for carrying contraband to the Far East (one, the P. & O. *Malacca*, had arms on board, but Britain claimed they were meant for the Hong Kong garrison). Lamsdorff deplored the incidents at sea, but was not prepared to admit that Britain was blameless or her flag inviolable.[8]

The sinking of the steamer *Knight Commander* by the Vladivostok squadron without the nicety of a prize court was no help. Lansdowne appreciated Hardinge's problems and cheered him with a private letter to that effect. Fortunately, both agreed that they had to proceed quietly and calmly: "we must blacken their faces as little as possible." Hardinge's persistence began to bear fruit as it was brought home to the Russians how little they controlled even their own authorities. Britain had taken a strong line, although without emotional name-calling, and Hardinge, who had advocated such an approach throughout, believed that this, combined with the display of united public opinion at home, forced new Russian orders to the ships in question (Hardinge had to provide the telegraphic link).[9]

The day that Hardinge wrote this evaluation was one of the most hectic of his stay in St. Petersburg. Plehve, apparently the only minister in the tsar's confidence, was killed by a bomb in the morning, upsetting governmental stability—although few seemed to care about his death. The same day Hardinge's sons arrived from school in England on their first independent journey, only to find Diamond in quarantine with scarlet fever. Hardinge was again keeping a brief diary, mainly of social functions, and he had time for no entries from 16 to 28 July, "a time of great anxiety and very critical."[10]

In August, the atmosphere eased. The birth of the Tsarevich Alexis Nicolaievich on the twelfth was the occasion of royal, if not popular, celebration. Prince Louis of Battenberg, director of Naval Intelligence and King Edward's special envoy for the tsarevich's coronation on the twenty-fourth, was most useful in explaining to the tsar and the Russian Admiralty British views on the seizure of merchant vessels. The arrival of the British Tibetan expedition at Lhasa was an irritation, for the Russians not unnaturally took this as British exploitation of a Russian moment of weakness. Both Hardinge and the Russian government were relieved to find that the troops were withdrawn and no permanent mission left in Lhasa, although the continued occupation of the Chumbi Valley suspiciously resembled Russian procedures in Manchuria.[11]

Hardinge's friendly association with Lamsdorff and his close contact with another, unnamed, official in the same ministry kept him reasonably well informed, but watchfulness was still the order of the day (particularly after Witte told Hardinge privately that Russia deciphered all British telegrams and a spy was uncovered in the embassy itself, a maneuver Hardinge countered by finding his own informant in the Russian secret police).[12] Britain had won most of her points on the Volunteer cruisers; unfortunately, Hardinge was about to face the most difficult Anglo-Russian crisis of the war, alone in an important sense, for Winifred and the children had already left for their winter stay in England.[13]

The war had been going badly as Russia suffered defeat after defeat. It was indicative of the seriousness of the situation that some press references to the possibility of peace were permitted. The Baltic fleet, Russia's main remaining hope, sailed on 14 October for the Far East. Hardinge was worried. Lamsdorff was the target of serious criticism from the Russian admirals as the cause of numerous humiliations to the Russian ensign at Britain's hands, and his position and his willingness to work for a rapprochement with Britain were in danger.[14]

It was in this delicate atmosphere that telegrams arrived on 24 October, informing St. Petersburg that the Baltic fleet had fired upon English fishing trawlers off the Dogger Bank in the North Sea. A number of British trawlermen were killed or injured, and several vessels damaged or sunk (actually one was sunk and two fishermen were killed). The Russians too had injuries—from firing at each other. But the major crisis which Hardinge had feared was at hand.

The immediate reaction from London was in indignant request for apologies, reparations, and assurances against repetition. Hardinge at first had no detailed information, and Lansdowne postponed any specific demands until Russia provided some explanation. Thus without instructions, Hardinge as a friend urged Lamsdorff to declare that if the Russian fleet proved at fault for this "unqualified and brutal outrage," the guilty would be severely punished and reparations made. The crisis was complicated by the fact that Russia had no direct means of communication with the fleet, which was no longer at the site of the incident. In Hardinge's view, it was time for strong words; as he had written earlier on the Volunteer cruisers, "I cannot bear a policy of pin-pricks or of 'rubbing it in' but I am all for coming down on them like a sledge-hammer when they behave illegally.'' Since Lamsdorff was unwilling to make any assurances, ''as I left the room,'' Hardinge recalled in his memoirs, ''I said to him that the incident was so grave that peace might possibly be jeopardized unless he and I made up our minds that war should not under any circumstances result. We gave each other a mutual promise and shook hands over it.''[15]

The Ministries of Foreign Affairs and Marine were giving out no information, but the next day Lamsdorff arrived with a message from the tsar. An exhausted Hardinge wrote to Winifred that

> *at last* the Emperor has expressed his regrets to the King & Govt. through me & has promised to make reparation. This ought to have been done 24 hours earlier. It will I hope have a calming effect. I do not however look forward to quiet as nobody knows where the Baltic fleet is nor where it will be. Not a word has been sent by the fleet from anywhere. Delay will I know exasperate public opinion in England who [sic] very naturally will not be able to undestand such proceedings.[16]

Public opinion was indeed exasperated, particularly by the Russian admiral's apparent callousness in not assisting the damaged fishing boats.

On the same day that Hardinge spoke to Lamsdorff, Lansdowne told Benckendorff, who had no instructions, that if prompt action was not taken, ''we should certainly be obliged to take our own measures for guarding against a repetition of these acts.'' On the twenty-sixth, Benckendorff had instructions to convey regrets, but still no full information on what had happened. Lansdowne was adamant: the fleet had to be intercepted. ''If it were allowed to continue its journey without calling at Vigo, we might find ourselves at war before the week was over. . . .'' As the British fleet gathered at Gibraltar and Portland, Benckendorff and Lansdowne together drafted a telegram to St. Petersburg: it would not be enough to hold an inquiry at Vigo. An absolute British condition for the peaceful termination of the incident was the return of the responsible parties to St. Petersburg."[17]

The admiral's explanation arrived on the twenty-seventh. Lamsdorff sent for Hardinge, who found him in evening clothes and "quite dishevelled. The politest man in the world was very nearly rude to me." Admiral Rozhdestvensky reported that two Japanese torpedo boats had lurked among the trawlers (proving to Russia the obvious British complicity) and had attacked the fleet at night. The admiral regretted the injury to the trawlers, but it was unavoidable in the circumstances. He had not stopped to render aid because of the threat of further attacks. Lamsdorff was more excited than Hardinge had ever seen him. "He was simply spluttering with indignation at the perfidy of the Japanese, whom he termed 'vos chers allies.'"

This was a moment of real danger. Had Hardinge replied in a similar tone and reported Lamsdorff's response to London, war might well have resulted. No historian can be certain on "what might have been," but given the aroused state of British opinion, and the extreme sensitivity of a Russia smitten by interminable and humiliating defeats at the hand of what was regarded as an inferior oriental state, Hardinge's reports and advice might have triggered war—in that regard, this was the most decisive moment in his career. Hardinge remained calm, "for I realized that he was not himself and that he was in an abnormal state, and I did not attempt to argue. I said nothing beyond that I would come and see him the following day." A telegram the same evening advised Lansdowne that demands he had proposed would be too demeaning to Russia, and suggested an immediate proposal of joint inquiries at Vigo, where the fleet now lay, and at Hull.[19]

On the twenty-eighth, the corner was turned. When Hardinge went to see Lamsdorff,

> he literally fell on my neck and with tears in his eyes thanked me for having said nothing to him on the

> preceding day. He told me that he had been up all night at the Council of Ministers struggling against a most bellicose atmosphere, and that it had been decided he should send for me, should read to me the Admiral's telegrams and speak to me with the utmost frankness about them, and that if I or Lord Lansdowne in any message should utter one word of menace he was to say to me, "Well, you want war, and now you shall have it!" He was really in a pitiable state of repentance, and I seized the opportunity to administer a very severe scolding, and to tell him that it was very disgraceful to make the risk of a long and terrible war between two great countries dependent upon what a single Government official like myself might say or do. He agreed, and I felt the danger was over for the moment.

Fortunately, the tsar made a proposal similar to Hardinge's of an international commission of inquiry on the spot. Rodzhdestvensky and the fleet were ordered to wait at Vigo, so no overt British naval threat was necessary. Tempers now calmed, and both parties accepted an appeal to the Hague tribunal. So long as the Baltic fleet remained in existence, however, the danger of a second incident was great. As Lansdowne put it in a letter congratulating Hardinge for the promptitude and wisdom with which he had acted, "nothing that you or I, or Lamsdorff or Benckendorff can do will get them out of a second scrape, and I cannot dismiss from my mind the apprehension that they will through stupidity or preversity or both tumble into another."[20]

On Sunday the thirtieth, Hardinge had a private audience with the tsar at Nicholas's request. The tsar was friendly and personable, much regretting the injuries, and he and the tsarina wanted to give whatever was asked in pecuniary compensation—a suggestion which Hardinge had already discouraged through Lansdowne and which he now tactfully advised should wait until the public had calmed down. The tsar was trying to reconcile his desire for peace with his continued faith in Rodzhdestvensky and in stories of Japanese officials in Hull, military arms shipped to

Japan, and the like: he was "pleased" to hear from Hardinge that his own information was wrong. For more than an hour, the discussion ranged widely over all the issues. From Hardinge's standpoint, however, such conversations were all too rare, and the tsar was generally limited to the views of those around him. "An admirable and most interesting despatch," minuted King Edward rather typically.[21]

Hardinge was still nervous. News agencies reported that the British Admiralty intended British cruisers to follow the Russian fleet once it left Vigo. The Russians were desperate, and as ever convinced that India lay only a few marches away if it came to war against Britain. "In their present frame of mind I do not think it is safe to trifle with them, and for that reason I deprecate the shadowing of the Russian fleet, if it is true, as being provocative and as showing that we place no confidence in the instructions which have been given in connection with neutral shipping."[22]

This was not exactly the "very vigorous protest" Hardinge called it in his memoirs, but the navy's intentions made Hardinge's task no easier. As he pointed out in dispatch after dispatch, the Russians believed that Britain could be and deserved to be beaten, for without British aid Japan would not have gone to war. Many were convinced that British officers fought next to Japanese troops. Only Russian naval personnel opposed war with Great Britain by this point, since war would mean the end of the Baltic fleet and therefore of any chance of victory and recovery of naval honor in the Far East. If war did come, Hardinge advised, Russia would jump at the chance to make peace with Japan and concentrate upon India. In short, Russian opinion was as sensitive to humiliation or menace as ever.[23]

Lansdowne clearly appreciated the situation. So did the king, according to Knollys. The pressure of public opinion in England was very strong, however, and Earl Selborne, First Lord, led a warlike group in the Cabinet which had approved the shadowing (the navy called it "keeping in touch") of the Baltic fleet from Vigo to Tangier.[24] Ultimately, calm and wisdom prevailed, and after lengthy negotiations on details Hardinge finally signed the convention for an inquiry on 25 November.

Hardinge had brought the affair to a successful conclusion, but of course he had not worked alone. In particular he acknowledged the assistance of Maurice Bompard, the French ambassador, and his staff. French cooperation contrasted notably with German attempts to use the incident to move closer to Russia—a situation which made it all the more difficult for France, which could not appear to give her ally Russia less support in this matter or the Japanese war in general than Germany gave. The G.C.M.G. and nice words from the king and others demonstrated that Hardinge's personal contribution was realized and appreciated. "It is quite possible that if Lansdowne had not been Foreign Secretary in 1904 Britain and Russia would have been at war over the Dogger Bank attack," one historian has remarked; the same might well be said of Hardinge at St. Petersburg.[25].

As the New Year approached, Anglo-Russian relations were at least peaceful. The "mad dog fleet," as the British press termed it, was rounding Africa, and Port Arthur was close to surrender. It was hardly conceivable that the Russians would attempt to send the Black Sea fleet as well, for passage through the Straits would be a risky violation of the Treaty of Paris of 1856 and might itself provoke war with Britain. Lansdowne nevertheless told Hardinge to give Lamsdorff a frank warning. Since Hardinge knew that Lamsdorff already opposed forcing the Straits, he preferred to make the point a different way:

> I sent an official despatch by post to the Consul-General at Odessa, instructing him to report to me by telegraph any preparations indicating naval movements and explaining that in the event of the Black Sea Fleet issuing into the Aegean Sea from the Black Sea it would be immediately met and driven back by the Mediterranean Fleet. I have no doubt that this letter was opened in the post as all my others were opened and its contents given to the Government, for

nothing more was heard of the question. I was glad that I had said nothing to Lamsdorff.[26]

There was little else Hardinge could do except to keep a close eye upon the internal situation, an easier task once the Dogger Bank incident had passed. In November the presidents of the zemstvos met in St. Petersburg and proposed to the tsar a comprehensive program of reforms. Plehve's successor, Prince P. D. Sviatopolk-Mirsky, took a more liberal attitude than Plehve to such requests, but Hardinge's sources reported that the conservatives, notably K. P. Pobedonostsev, who had been important in setting the tone of Alexander III's reign, had the tsar's ear. It was a test case for the reform movement; the conservatives were aware of the effect upon public opinion should no reforms at all result, and the tsar did issue an imperial ukase with some positive but hardly satisfactory promises, reasserting autocratic principles when the zemstvo resolution had called for equality before the law, democratization of local self-government, and a legislative assembly.[27]

The ukase was issued on 12 December; on the nineteenth Port Arthur fell, although the news was not public information for some days. Agitation for reform at once increased, reaching a climax on 22 January, ever afterwards known as "Bloody Sunday." Hardinge and Winifred (who arrived with Diamond on the Nord Express only on the twentieth) were only observers. His job was to provide as much accurate information as possible—no easy task in a "city of lies"—and he was criticized for sending only what he knew.[28]

As he drove to church, Hardinge himself saw the striking workers moving toward the Winter Palace to present their petition and walking back, cavalry shepherding the crowds and blocking their entrance to the palace. "Just as I got to the Embassy about one o'clock, the soldiers began to try to prevent the strikers coming over the Troitzka Bridge, just in front of the Embassy, and as the crowds continued to collect, I could see from the windows the soldiers firing into the crowd." Two hours later, the order was given to fire into the crowd near the palace; the official figure was 130 dead, but Hardinge estimated 300. Three independent English witnesses gave him the details.

> There seems to be no doubt that the troops fired without provocation on a quiet and unarmed crowd, which had come into the town with the peaceful intention of presenting a list of their grievances to the Emperor. It is difficult to explain the callous indifference of the Russian military authorities in the taking of the lives of quiet and orderly workmen, who were unarmed and showed no signs of aggressive action.[29]

Hardinge had not a little sympathy for the workers' aims, although he thought they went too far in their specific demands. The tsar, who was at Tsarskoe Selo, in Hardinge's view missed a magnificent opportunity to win popular support; when he finally received thirty-four workmen with a deputation two weeks later, it was too late. The whole incident, reported Hardinge to Lansdowne, "will have created a deep gulf, which will not be easily bridged, between the Emperor and the working classes who have hitherto been the most loyal subjects of the throne, and a blow will have been struck at the autocracy from which it will be difficult to recover."[30]

Hardinge had to intervene personally to protest against posters placarded about Moscow that English and Japanese funds had been responsible for the troubles, and to arrange for his military attaché to go to Warsaw to investigate an incident in which the British consul general was beaten up by soldiers. Meanwhile, he predicted more trouble to come. The resignation of Sviatopolk-Mirsky and the assassination of Grand Duke Serge Alexandrovitch, governor of Moscow, boded ill for the future. Hardinge had no love of revolutionary movements, nor of assassins, but he blamed the government for discouraging liberal moderates. With the tsar isolated at Tsarskoe Selo and the conservatives in control, the regime in its current form was committing suicide.

"It is an anachronism existing now only in semi-civilised and barbarous states, and must inevitably be modified to meet the requirements of the great advance made in Russia during the past 20 years."[31]

A committee of ministers appointed to apply the reforms could not be expected to alter essentials; officials, "most of whom have at one time or another been guilty of abuse of their position and influence," certainly would not limit their own power. The connection between those agitating for reforms and the demand for peace was intimate, for reformers knew nothing major could be done while the war continued. The Caucasus was in chaos, Finland disaffected, the universities closed, the railways working fitfully at best, and thousands on strike. The government procrastinated, hoping for a miracle victory in the Far East. Meanwhile, the ministers quarreled among themselves, while Witte waited for the chaos to reach such proportions that the tsar would have to appoint him head of government. Hardinge always appreciated Witte's ability but never trusted him: "I know for a fact that he was in favour of war with us over the Hull incident merely in order that he might rise to power from the ruins around him." And even Witte might not be the answer.

> In the midst of the prevailing confusion and disorder one seeks in vain for a remedy which shall be at once effective and reinvigorating. The Russian Government have now arrived at a stage where they appear neither able to make peace nor to wage war with success. To make peace at the present moment, and to face the danger of bringing home a defeated and discontented army requires an act of heroism of which this Government are not capable.[32]

Yet another serious military defeat was suffered at Mukden in March, but still there was no sign of a major peace movement; on the contrary, Hardinge reported, life went on as usual, with St. Petersburg's opera, ballet, and restaurants overflowing. Witte, however, was worried, and, now a strong supporter of peace, he used Hardinge to try to move the tsar to act. In a long conversation, Witte outlined the terms he himself would make in peace negotiations, including final withdrawal from the Manchurian venture and recognition of Japan's position in Korea, and suggested that perhaps a peace overture from King Edward might break through the barrier of silence surrounding Tsar Nicholas.

Hardinge knew how serious a step this would be and replied to Witte only that he would think it over. He would not even promise to transmit the suggestion to London. In his report to Lansdowne, he could not make a specific recommendation: the tsar was so isolated that "it is impossible for me to judge, even from hearsay, of His Majesty's frame of mind on the question of peace, not is it possible for me to foresee how such a step on the part of the King would be received by the Emperor," to say nothing of Britain's Japanese ally. All he could say was that many ministers favored peace and that the war and peace parties were engaged in a mighty struggle around the tsar.[33]

Lansdowne, probably wisely, decided that while peace was very desirable, a premature attempt to intervene would be ill advised. No direct peace overtures were made through the spring, as Russia continued to hope against hope for a military victory. Hardinge at least was able to keep in close touch with Russian relations with Japan, passing, for example, the text of one Russian note home to Lansdowne "thanks to the courtesy of a gentleman who had access to the document in question."[34]

Hardinge returned to England on 19 April for a month's vacation, leaving Cecil Spring Rice, his first secretary, in charge. The Hardinges gathered for an enjoyable rest spent mostly at Crichel. In his memoirs, Hardinge recorded that his principal object was to urge Lansdowne to strengthen the Japanese alliance, then under renegotiation: "I pointed out when I got home that the best and surest way of coming to terms with Russia after the war would be by making an agreement with Japan which Russia would recognize as making impossible any aggressive action against British interests in Asia. I am glad to say that my representations carried some weight." He also stayed at Sandringham and was able to discuss affairs with Knollys and the king. On 29 May he and Winifred were back in Russia.

On the twenty-seventh, the Second Pacific Squadron, ex-Baltic fleet, was annihilated by the Japanese at Tsushima. The news arrived late and was released slowly. When it was generally known, Hardinge reported St. Petersburg felt the consequences of the war for the first time, becoming a "town of mourning and sadness." Many of the fleet's officers had come from the leading families of society, while few aristocratic officers had served in the Far Eastern land battles, where the Guards had not been used.[35]

Although the tsar still opposed peace and hoped for some military miracle, reformist pressure increased, and Hardinge believed that there was still a strong possibility that "quite a fairly good constitution" would emerge from all this. In that sense the war was a blessing in disguise, "for the country has made more progress in reforms during the past year than during the last forty years." The scheme of an elected assembly, or Duma, proposed in March but still unimplemented, was to have been scrapped by the minister of the interior had the Russian fleet been victorious. Only the combination of continued internal disturbances—the *Potemkin* mutiny in the Black Sea, for example—the concurrent Moroccan crisis and resignation of French Foreign Minister Delcassé (leaving Russia very isolated indeed), and the face-saving intervention of President Theodore Roosevelt permitted the negotiations for peace at Portsmouth, New Hampshire.[36]

Even then the Russian official attitude was most disdainful, as if the war could be continued indefinitely. After considerable maneuvering, Witte, who at least had no fear of responsibility, was appointed chief Russian plenipotentiary. Announcement of the peace negotiations had demonstrably relieved public opinion, Hardinge reported, but the crucial moment would come when the Japanese stated their terms. However moderate these were, the military party might well demand that Russia fight on. The question would then be whether Russia would save some Far Eastern possessions by making peace and probably paying an indemnity, or continue to fight and see them all conquered by Japan—and thus have to pay an even heavier indemnity for Japanese withdrawal.[37]

Meanwhile agitation continued, despite the best efforts of government and reactionaries. As Hardinge saw it, turning back was no longer a possibility:

> The Russian people, ignorant as they are, have at least learnt by combination their power and irresistable weight, and have succeeded in extracting from an unwilling Emperor and Government promises of wide-reaching reforms, of which in due course they will insist on the execution. It may be truly said that a very remarkable change is passing over this country, and that the Russian of today is no longer the patient, long-suffering creature of only six months ago. The disorders and outbreaks which have occurred are characteristic of the efforts of a down-trodden race to acquire greater liberty, and to shake themselves free from a regime of arbitrary oppression, and these efforts, which have so far met with a considerable measure of success, have been regarded by intelligent onlookers as unlikely to lead to any general upheaval, so long as the military forces remained loyal to the Emperor and the Government.[38]

As the *Potemkin* mutiny demonstrated, there was a question of that loyalty, but Hardinge thought that such troubles had shown many the real internal dangers; so long as great care was taken to prevent another Bloody Sunday in the capital, there would be no revolution.[39]

Still, the situation was grim enough, and it was hardly lightened by a new round of pogroms; the Jews were an easy scapegoat given their prominence in the revolutionary movement, a prominence not surprising to Hardinge: "That justice may yet be done to this numerous and oppressed race is the wish of all those friends of Russia who are sufficiently enlightened to appreciate the advantages to be obtained from a loyal and contented people, and from the active cooperation in all branches of the Government service of a singularly gifted race."[40] The Russian government condemned the pogroms officially, but the violence continued through the summer of 1905, further undermining the stability of the regime.

In August, the procedures for elections to the Duma were outlined. Hardinge at first hoped that the regime's critics would realize the magnitude of the concessions and accept the promise inherent in an Assembly; but by the end of the month it was clear that the electoral scheme was manipulated to weight representation in favor of the conservative peasantry and against the urban and mercantile classes. The public would not be admitted to the Duma, and nothing guaranteed that its debates would be published, or indeed that any measure it passed would become law. In the end, Hardinge predicted, hopefully, that the demands formulated by the zemstvo leaders, who had met again in Moscow, would be agreed to, "for the institution of a National Assembly to which Representatives of the people are to be elected would be a farce if freedom of speech and discussion and the right of public meeting were to be denied to the people."[41]

A more ominous note was sounded by Kaiser William's attempt to make further capital from Russia's troubles and isolation. The Moroccan crisis was not Hardinge's immediate worry, but he like others in the Foreign Office in London took this German maneuver as a direct test of the newly forged entente. In the general context of world power relationships, Russia's defeats could be seen in two ways: they reduced Russian military strength and thus limited the Franco-Russian counterweight to Germany, or these Japanese victories helped solve the problems in the Far East. Hardinge leaned to the latter view, particularly given the August 1905 extension of the Anglo-Japanese alliance, which made it operative against one power rather than two and brought India under its aegis. The strain upon the British navy was also relieved, and after Tsushima five battleships were moved from China to Europe. Hardinge had certainly been aware of the implications of Russian affairs in Anglo-German relations, but to state, as George Monger has done, that "it was probably the truth" that Hardinge, "whose main concern was Germany," wished to avoid war because it would be to Germany's advantage alone, is misleading. Hardinge was always concerned with Germany, but even had Germany not existed, the disadvantages of an Anglo-Russian war were sufficient unto themselves.[42]

Hardinge, like Lansdowne, shied away from general analyses of policy. But there was no mistaking the danger that Germany might yet upset a peaceful solution particularly when Kaiser William arranged a surprise meeting with Tsar Nicholas at Björkö in Finland. William aimed at no less than a continental coalition against the Anglo-Japanese alliance. Hardinge's usually excellent sources served him poorly this time; he soon gathered that the tsar had not consulted Lamsdorff—gravely ill after several heart attacks—or anyone in the Ministry of Foreign Affairs from which Hardinge received most of his information, and he therefore had to rely on the French embassy. William had done his best to encourage the tsar to continue the war; fortunately Nicholas stipulated that France must agree, and France did not, so the Björkö agreement never came into effect.[43]

Soon Japanese concessions at Portsmouth made peace possible, and Hardinge was surprised and relieved. He had feared that the tsar, encouraged by the tsarina, would hold out to the last, relying on a tissue of false reports and hopes from Manchuria. Although the Treaty of Portsmouth aroused little enthusiasm in St. Petersburg, Hardinge hoped that no time would be wasted in reopening the Anglo-Russian discussions on a wider rapprochement. Lamsdorff in fact made such an overture himself in replying to Hardinge's note of congratulations on the peace, and Lansdowne had already written privately in that sense. Hardinge had thus a friendly and cooperative message to convey when he informed Lamsdorff of the terms of the renewed Anglo-Japanese alliance.[44]

The reception was calm, Hardinge thought. Firmness and successful arbitration of the Dogger Bank claims had created a more favorable general attitude towards Britain. Russian press criticism had declined, thanks in part to French cash. By September relations were more friendly than at any time since the outbreak of the war, but it was a critical moment, since the Japanese treaty in its new form was a useful lever with which Germany could excite Russian distrust.[45]

Hardinge's task was to smooth the road for further Anglo-Russian discussions. Late in September, he had a detailed discussion with N. Hartwig, director of the Ministry of Foreign Affairs First Department, and particularly influential in Asian affairs. As Lamsdorff's right hand, Hartwig had the minister's confidence—"but not entirely mine," Hardinge reported. The ostensible issue was Russian removal of a bothersome Bombay consul, but the discussion ranged over Balkan and Asian affairs. Both men agreed that with a little moderation on both sides an agreement could be reached. When Hardinge pointed out that such an agreement migh disrupt the smooth course of Russo-German relations, Hartwig responded that at least in the Ministry of Foreign Affairs they well knew the true value of William's policy. The outlook was encouraging.[46]

Hardinge's discussion with Hartwig was one line of attack. In London, Benckendorff and Lansdowne agreed that while friendly relations were desirable, it would be an error to move too fast: Lansdowne was concerned that any discussions should proceed one issue at a time. Benckendorff promised to sound out Lamsdorff more fully in November and then resume conversations; he saw no reason why an agreement could not be reached, even on Persia and the Gulf, provided that it was not conceived in a spirit of hostility to Germany; and, finally, he hoped that Lansdowne would authorize Hardinge to speak in a similar vein to Lamsdorff. Lansdowne, however, did not yet share the same sense of urgency felt by Benckendorff and Hardinge.[47]

Hardinge, meanwhile, was dong his best to counteract the influence of the suddenly pro-German Witte, freshly returned —with swelled head—from his successes at Portsmouth and a hospitable reception at Berlin.[48] Bompard, eager for Anglo-Russian discussions to go forward and ever fearful of another

Russo-German agreement, also talked to Lamsdorff. The foreign minister was even frank on the hostile content of Britain's rewritten Japanese pact but admitted that an important factor was the spirit of the treaty as much as the words, and that would take time to judge. By the end of October, as Hardinge prepared to return to London on leave, Lamsdorff seemed to be cooperative and even Witte had modified his enthusiasm for closer German relations, largely, as Hardinge saw it, from simple opportunism: only a small clique at the court actually advocated a German alliance.[49]

It became clear to Hardinge on arrival in London that he was to be the next permanent under secretary in the Foreign Office. His tour in St. Petersburg was thus over, save for a week in January to pack and to bid farewell to government officials and friends. Arriving on the sixth, he found Lamsdorff upset by an imaginary Anglo-Chinese covention on Tibet. The canard was useful, for Hardinge was able to ask Lamsdorff to exercise extra caution on such reports when he, Hardinge, took up his position in London. Hardinge also talked to Witte, and, in a private audience, to the tsar and tsarina.[50]

He departed for Paris on the twelfth with tokens of Russian esteem, both verbal and material: the tsar had given him a diamond-inlaid snuffbox, which he could hardly refuse under the circumstances.[51] With a G.C.V.O. from King Edward in hand as further recognition of his success, and an important promotion, Hardinge could be pleased—and pleased as well that he had done a good job of helping to steer Anglo-Russian relations through a dangerous passage, and had left those relations in considerably better condition than when he had arrived. Hardinge was, in fact, an excellent professional ambassador, establishing serviceable sources of information; providing comprehensive data on local events and conditions; advising his superiors on the best line of approach; representing his own government fairly to his hosts; and, above all, taking such independent action as was required by the circumstances. He had faced hostility, tension, even the prospect of a major war, and surmounted them all. The position of permanent under secretary, however, was likely to be even more demanding.

Hardinge's promotion to the permanent under secretaryship surprised many and doubtless annoyed some, for at the age of forty-eight he was a good many years junior to the other under secretaries. He was well informed of the internal politics of the Foreign Office and staff, however, for he had never lost touch through the tensest hours in Russia.

In the spring of 1904, when Hardinge moved to St. Petersburg, several goals were as yet unattained. Bertie had not yet been given Paris and Villiers remained in the Foreign Office. Hardinge regarded Villiers as absolutely useless, and hoped to see him ousted before February 1906, when Sanderson would retire at age sixty-five. Lisbon was the likeliest possibility, but neither Hardinge nor Bertie felt that Villiers was suitable for even that rather backwater post.[52] A further complication arose when Sanderson's failing eyesight forced him to take a leave in midyear, returning in December 1904 to finish out his term; fortunately, from Hardinge's viewpoint, it was Bertie, not Villiers, who meanwhile filled in.[53]

But who would be Sanderson's permanent successor? By the end of 1904, Bertie had reached the conclusion that Hardinge himself was a possible Diplomatic Service candidate for the post, junior as he was. He said nothing to Lansdowne, but he did tell Arthur Balfour that Hardinge would probably accept the job on suitable conditions.[54] With Bertie now closer at hand in the Paris embassy (settling in by the New Year), and Gorst, a possible rival, having proved to be a bad choice for the Foreign Office, Hardinge's chances were real enough and by midyear he felt that he was seriously in the running. He had stipulated that he would take the job if he were to receive £1,000 per annum personal allowance as a rough equivalent to his ambassadorial allowance; he felt that the permanent under secretary should be able to entertain foreign personages. Also, his time in the Foreign Office must count towards his ambassadorial pension of £1,700 (the Office pension was only two-thirds of salary, a difference of nearly £200). He would be taking a considerable financial loss in the appointment and could hardly be expected to add financial worries to the obviously demanding work load. Of course, he admitted privately to Bertie, he might not be offered the post at all—and if he were offered it without his conditions, he might take it anyway.

A further uncertainty was introduced by the declining fortunes of Balfour's Unionist government and his replacement, in December 1905, by Sir Henry Campbell-Bannerman. Bertie felt that Hardinge's chances were still good, whatever party was in office, but that he should be cautious in asking for special allowances other than his ambassadorial pension: his position must really be made by his own ability. As for the £1,000, the other departmental permanent under secretaries would naturally demand similar grants. Perhaps, instead, Winifred ("Cousin Bena" to Bertie) might have a palace apartment assigned to her as a Royal Woman of the Bedchamber. Bertie was now earning £9,000 plus £2,000 allowances, so it was easy for him to give such advice; but Hardinge rather enjoyed his St. Petersburg scale of income, and it alarmed him to have to take a cut from £7,800 plus £2,500 to a salary of £2,300 with no allowances:

> I hate all questions connected with money and all I want is to be able to live comfortably and like a gentleman, and now for the first time for many years I am able to live comfortably within my income and entertain &c. properly. However you may be quite certain that if Lamps' post is offered to me I shall not make many difficulties although I shall keep a stiff upper lip on the subject of my pension in view of the fact that I should only have a little more than a year to serve for it.[55]

A rumor that Lansdowne would continue Sanderson for another year—on the grounds that he should let the new government fill the post—was worrisome. Yet another concern was

Hardinge's own successor in St. Petersburg, mainly because Hardinge's favored choice, Arthur Nicolson, had stiff competition. It would help, however, that Lady Nicolson was also Lady Dufferin's sister.[56] Lansdowne was well aware of these maneuvers and of Hardinge's conditions, for they were put to him by no less a person than King Edward.

It was only when he returned on leave in October that Hardinge heard definitely from Lansdowne that the job was to be his. The impression given by his memoirs that the question only arose at this time is misleading: "the factor which decided me to accept the post was the wish expressed by King Edward that I should do so, His Majesty having invited me to Sandringham for the celebration of his birthday and to express to me his wishes." Once again, "I had always realized that the only way to get on in the service was to disregard material advantages and seek only for power," but it helped to have the firm support of King Edward.[57]

Once accepted, other decisions followed. Villiers was out, and Hardinge agreed that he was to go to Lisbon, regarding the matter somewhat more charitably than Bertie (the remark in *Old Diplomacy* that "I urged that a good post abroad should be found for Sir F. Villiers" is disingenuous). Louis Mallet was recommended to Grey in December as his private secretary, while Barrington was given the vacant under secretaryship for the eighteen months remaining before his own retirement, at which time Mallet, eventual trainee for Hardinge's own job, would move into the assistant under secretaryship. Nicolson went to St. Petersburg, and Hardinge hoped that Spring Rice, who had done such a good job as first secretary there, would return to the Foreign Office in Villiers's position.[58]

Some of these appointments could not be made—Spring Rice, for example, went to Teheran—and others required time and effort to accomplish, but by the end of 1905 Hardinge and Bertie could take pleasure and satisfaction in the fact that the permanent under secretaryship, Paris, and St. Petersburg were all under the direction of like-minded and trustworthy men. Even the matter of salary had come out in Hardinge's favor. On Lansdowne's advice, he had accepted the position without any promises save that of his ambassadorial pension, but he did not give up the fight for a special allowance. Hardinge saw a letter from a Treasury official to a mutual friend, congratulating himself on having "landed a big fish on very favourable terms," which stiffened his resolve enormously, and "that official soon found his fish was still capable of running out a great deal of line. I finally secured the suport of the King, Balfour and Ld. Lansdowne & I goaded the latter to further action by asking whether it was the Govt. or George Murray [Treasury under secretary] who governed the country." The result was £500, not £1,000, and it was an exception, not a precedent, but this was a victory nevertheless.[59]

The Hardinges now settled down in London, purchasing a house in Bryanston Square. Much paperwork was required to pay the initial £4000 cost, which depended upon Arthur Nicolson paying for Hardinge's St. Petersburg furniture, which depended in turn upon the Treasury paying Nicolson's outfit allowance—a typical transaction for this profession. But once more Russian winters had been left behind, and Hardinge had quite definitely traded salary for "power." He also had objectives clearly in mind, at least regarding Anglo-Russian relations, and a new and relatively inexperienced foreign secretary to guide and advise. If the appointment as ambassador to St. Petersburg placed him among the elite of his country's service, the appointment as permanent under secretary gave him even more—the chance to influence importantly his country's foreign policy.

IV Triple Entente

Hardinge took up his post as permanent under secretary on 1 February 1906, the first ambassador to be appointed to that post since Addington (1847–54). He was worried to the end that he might be called in to help Sanderson in the last few days in an awkward condominium, as "Lamps'" eyesight gave him more and more trouble, but Hardinge would be sole occupant of the position for five important years. The period can be divided into rough halves: the first two hectic years, dominated by the Moroccan crisis which tested the Anglo-French Entente and the Anglo-Russian Accord which completed it; and the second half, in which Foreign Office attention was centered upon the Balkan crisis of 1909 and its aftermath—with the naval race and relations with Germany always as counterpoint to these themes. Hardinge's role in the formation of British policy in these years was significant, perhaps critical; although he would be permanent under secretary again for an equal period (1916–20), his influence, like that of the Foreign Office in those war years, would never be as great.

The Office itself was undergoing substantial changes. In the first place, it was now under the control of a new foreign secretary, Sir Edward Grey. Grey was a senior Liberal Party leader and had a reputation as a foreign policy expert in the House of Commons. He was a perplexing, rather enigmatic individual, whose image still remains blurred about the edges despite the best efforts of his biographers. He was certainly a self-contained man, elusive, shy, a solitary figure with the perfect mentality for the hobbies of bird-watching and fly-fishing which he pursued zealously. His experience abroad was minimal, and he had little interest in repairing this lacuna. His command of foreign languages ranged from weak to nonexistent, and his knowledge of modern non-British history was scarcely better.

And yet he was much admired. To nearly all observers, he was hardworking, sincere, earnest, forthright, with a sense of detachment which kept him from passionate politics. He had his critics, more for policy than personal reasons. Only later would questions be raised about the degree to which his personal convictions led him to violate his own apparent code, as for example in the extent to which he informed his cabinet colleagues of the details and deeper meaning of the Anglo-French Entente. It is not the task of this book to render a verdict upon this question; suffice it to say that Grey had for better or worse considerable freedom in the execution of foreign policy, in part because Prime Ministers Campbell-Bannerman and Asquith and most Liberal cabinet ministers took little direct interest in this area, in part because Asquith's Cabinet was split between the "Liberal-Imperialists" and the "Radicals." Grey was not necessarily a spokesman for the former faction, but he did not wish to see the control of foreign policy in the hands of the latter.

There are two relatively simple views of Grey as foreign minister: first, that he was a man who was willing to consult his senior advisors, the trusted professionals, but a man who took a close and absorbed interest in his work (particularly so after his wife was killed in a carriage accident, news of which tragedy arrived on the day Hardinge took up his appointment), and who made the final decisions himself. The other interpretation of Grey is that he was "a weak man and easily affected by the atmosphere in which he worked, [who] had little opportunity of asserting himself in his own right,'' meaning that he was dominated by Hardinge and the other top Foreign Office officials.[1]

In fact, Grey had clear principles, enunciated at the time of his appointment. Put simply, these were that Britain's security rested upon the continuation of the Anglo-French Entente, continued friendship with the United States, and, though Grey was somewhat less enthusiastic about this, the renewed treaty with Japan. The latter was a potential obstacle to any Anglo-Russian accord, but for the time being Grey believed these principles to be so important that he was not prepared to sacrifice them in pursuit of the will-o'-the-wisp of German friendship.[2] He was anxious about Germany, it is true, but anxiety is not necessarily hostility, a generalization which applies equally to Hardinge.

Grey's relationship to Hardinge was complex. It might have been awkward: Hardinge was a last-gasp Conservative appointment under a new Liberal master. But Grey did listen to his most important subordinate. Hardinge after all was able, experienced, even older (by four years). The two men shared mutual respect and confidence, Hardinge not least because Grey's view of the role of the permanent under secretary was very similar to his own. Nor did Grey wish to share in the royal limelight, so long as Hardinge did not abuse his position. More important was a shared basic approach to world power relationships. In return for the freedom to advise Grey on major essentials of policy, Hardinge returned strong loyalty (as always, not uncritical). In his memoirs, he contrasts working with Grey to working with Lansdowne's ''very reserved and rather jealous nature'':

> With [Grey] I was able to discuss everything with the utmost freedom, more as two equals than as Chief and subordinate, and he allowed me the greatest liberty of action. Had it not been for the complete absence in him of any feelings of petty jealousy, my relations with the King during the following years would have been a source of difficulty between us. I always look back to those five years of work

> and co-operation between Sir E. Grey and myself as five of the most fruitful and happiest years of my life. They were ceaseless sunshine without a shadow.[3]

Grey seldom disagreed with Hardinge on major appointments in the Office and abroad, and this too was an important area of influence, with a considerable impact upon policy. When Hardinge arrived, the three assistant under secretaries were Gorst, Campbell, and Barrington. The latter, who had not yet taken up his position, replaced Villiers. But in April 1907 Gorst was moved to Egypt, and Barrington retired in June, leaving two important openings to be filled. Barrington's was given to Walter Langley, a specialist in the Americas who had come up through the Office ranks and was in Hardinge's view a very efficient head clerk (he left the Office in 1908). Gorst's position went to Louis Mallet. Mallet's abilities as précis writer to Lansdowne had caught Hardinge's eye; as a strong supporter of the Entente, he would in time have the reputation of being the most ardent Germanophobe in the Office (he ended his career as last British ambassador to the Ottoman Empire). Hardinge recommended Mallet to Grey, who chose him as his private secretary in April 1906, and, when Gorst moved to Egypt, promoted Mallet to the under secretaryship where he and Hardinge worked closely on Eastern problems.[4]

Some of the lesser appointments were also to prove important. Mallet's replacement as Grey's private secretary was William Tyrrell. Tyrrell had a varied career which included Bonn University, private secretaryship to Sanderson (1896–1903), secretary to the Committee of Imperial Defence (1903–4), and second secretary at Rome (1904–5). He became very close to Grey, first as précis writer (1905–7) and then as private secretary. Known for his wit and humor, he was neat, dapper, and clever, expressing his shared distrust of Germany more often in verbal than in written communications (his later career would include the posts of permanent under secretary, 1925–28, and ambassador to Paris, 1928–34).[5]

Another key promotion was that of Eyre Crowe, a second Office professional with extensive experience of Germany.[6] Son of Sir Joseph Crowe, British consul general in Saxony, he was born in Leipzig and educated in Düsseldorf. Tall and reticent, he had few close friends and was in some ways isolated from his colleagues. Crowe had come up the ladder slowly; born in 1864, he joined the Office in 1885 and became senior clerk, on Hardinge's recommendation, only in 1906. He was another with a reputation for strong hostility to Germany, due most notably to some strongly penned warnings against German policy. Precisely how much influence his memoranda had is a moot point. However, his promotion raised him out of the herd, and Crowe, too, would be permanent under secretary (1920–25).

These appontments, together with those made and yet to come in overseas posts, such as Bertie in Paris and Arthur Nicolson in St. Petersburg, insured that most key positions at home and abroad were filled with congenial types, and in time won for Hardinge the label of leader or mentor of the anti-Germans whose appointments he supported.[7] This interpretation requires caution. While "sound attitudes" certainly mattered, suspicion of Germany had grown upon many diplomats, and if those conservatives who represented the Sanderson-Villiers school on procedures are removed, together with all those worried about German intentions, very few able and willing senior men would have remained for promotion in this small cadre, a fact which too often has been forgotten.

Grey's trust for Hardinge in appointments and procedures was only one aspect of the new Office atmosphere—part of a general Liberal trend to "modernization" and "efficiency," although Hardinge had not been motivated by party politics.[8] The altered procedures themselves insured that a rather haphazard system became a fairly clear-cut organizational pyramid which Crowe trimmed into shape. Hardinge moved very quickly to take advantage of this and to insure that he himself was kept well informed of all pending issues. On 3 February, he told the under secretaries how the new system would work:

> Important questions have often trivial beginnings, and the difficulty has been pointed out to me of deciding what is or may develop into a question of political importance. It seems to me therefore best that *all* the work (except in cases of pressing urgency) should pass through me to the Secretary of State, a mere glance at the dockets being in many cases sufficient.

Six days later, another minute ordered that all papers connected with the interdepartmental Committee on Imperial Defence, an increasingly important body, be kept by his own secretary. It is not clear whether Grey approved these instructions before Hardinge assumed his appointment; Grey had not yet returned to the Office after his wife's death, so Hardinge may have acted on his own.[9]

By the end of February, Hardinge had altered even the hours kept in the Office. By 11:30 A.M., Grey was at work (leaving at 6:00 P.M. when Parliament was in session; he maintained a heavy work load in the House). When he arrived, he wished to deal at once with all important telegrams of the previous night, meaning that the whole process from receipt and registry to arrival on Hardinge's desk had to be completed by noon at the latest. The Office closed at 6:00 (5:00 in summer), and Hardinge ordered that clerks must arrive by 11:00 A.M. It was difficult to whip juniors into line, and he was still working on this two years later. Nor was it the only problem. Hardinge minutes discussed the undesirability of the members of a department closing down that department in effect by all lunching at once, or the equally undesirable practice of running up large bills with the in-house caterer; his attention to such details was part of the altered tone of the Office.[10]

Apart from diplomacy itself, Hardinge's work was extensive and varied. He supervised secret service expenditure (details are still secret). He handled a considerable portion of relations with the press. He battled the Treasury for salary increases in the Office and the Diplomatic Service; he had special reasons for taking pride in raising Nicolson's pay to £8,000 a year (in fact, he was one of the few permanent under secretaries to keep in view a balance of the Office and the Service salaries). He watched over the posts and appointments overseas. He supervised the entry of younger men into the Office, writing for example to both Villiers and Nicolson about their sons' performance; after 1907, he presided over the Board of Selection when the nomination process was taken away from the foreign secretary. He appointed the king's messengers ("it is only right that I should point out that [x] . . . has [had] the bad taste quite recently to marry an actress. I venture to express the opinion that it is hardly intended that the post of King's Messenger should be filled by persons of that kind") . He arranged for Foreign Office officials to be present at court levees to see the king and to shepherd his foreign guests about (a practice previously restricted to the secretary and permanent under secretary); he arranged which foreign representatives the king should see, aside from personal friends of the sovereign—and which he should not.

> Supposing The King were to invite to luncheon or dinner the Argentine Representative, the Brazilian and Chilian Ministers would immediately take offence, and, were all three Ministers to be invited, the Venezuelan, Guatemalan and other Ministers would all be annoyed if they did not receive similar treatment and finally The King would be reduced to inviting the Haytian Minister, which would be quite impossible.[11]

In the final analysis, however, the new system must be put down as his main contribution to the working of the Office. It never functioned quite as the model proposed and was again inadequate by 1914, but it produced a notable increase in efficiency and was certainly an important step in modernization. Hardinge himself settled down to administer it from the top. A survey of the documents on a particular country in any one year shows, in fact, that the permanent under secretary saw and initialed the important papers on each issue of note and on many lesser problems. Hardinge only occasionally minuted the dockets, and Grey did so even less frequently, but the initial "H" is present often enough to demonstrate the permanent under secretary's work load. The key dockets, those few which had become the vehicle for a debate upon policy (not necessarily closely related to the specific document under that cover), always were passed to Grey if he was present: Hardinge had views and goals, but Grey was the responsible cabinet minister. In the same way, Hardinge always passed to Grey his own important private correspondence with ministers abroad, since such correspondence existed by virtue of his position.[12] No record survives of verbal discussions between the two men, which were the main means of working out a particular policy. It is therefore only from such sources as the docket minutes and private letters that Hardinge's views and influence can be discerned.

Grey was suspicious of Germany; Hardinge, and his closest colleagues, shared that suspicion. This is now the generally accepted interpretation of Hardinge's position, and on the whole it is accurate. But the feeling that Germany should be regarded as a hostile power was not something which stemmed from close experiences of a German university or personal antipathy to German philosophy. It had grown upon Hardinge gradually, born of his experience of German foreign policy, with the Boer War, intrigues in China and Russia, the Baghdad Railway, Björkö, and the continuing snarling over Morocco. Nor should it be overlooked that Germany was now the strongest potential enemy Britain might have to face. It is the task of military and diplomatic planners to prepare contingency plans—and after the Russo-Japanese War, Germany, with her growing fleet, was the contingency.

The difficulty of Anglo-German relations was that there were few precise issues which could be discussed or arbitrated like Newfoundland fisheries or Persian concessions: it was as much a question of attitudes as specifics. Morocco was one specific, however, and its resolution did not contribute to Anglo-German friendship. In September 1905, after long and acid discussion, France and Germany agreed upon an agenda for a conference. The conference opened at Algeciras on 16 January, with Arthur Nicolson speaking for Britain. Germany's attempt to extract a price for French domination of Morocco was a test of the Entente, and the result was that secret Anglo-French military conversations had begun by the time Hardinge reentered the Office. Hardinge did not comment upon that delicate subject in his memoirs, but he soon knew as much about these talks as Grey or Sanderson—which is to say, a great deal more than the Cabinet.

Hardinge's direct introduction to Morocco was in Paris on 15 January on his way home. Visiting Bertie, he took the opportunity to talk with Foreign Minister (and Premier) Pierre Rouvier (1905–6). The French position was a firm one: Germany would obtain no foothold in Morocco. Two main means of influence were at issue, a state bank with its financial power, and control of the police; France would resist any proposal which permitted a chance of German control of any part of the force—even at the risk of war.[13]

The German claim for some voice was fairly strong, and their case against exclusive Franco-Spanish police control seemed reasonable, particularly given their willingness to make large concessions on finance if France was cooperative on the police. Rouvier claimed, however, that France had little to fear from Germany; as Hardinge reported to Spring Rice, chargé in St. Petersburg, if they continued to hold out, "in two or three years time the Kaiser will be thinking of something else and. . .they [the French] will gradually get a free hand on Morocco." France was nevertheless feeling less secure than she appeared at Algeciras:

> By the bye. . .the French have exploded a bombshell by asking Grey point blank whether we will join them in the event of war with Germany. No reply has so far been given but our Military & Naval Auth[oritie]s have been instr[ucte]d to concert joint measures with the French. It is

> difficult for a liberal Gov[ernmen]t to say definitely & without knowing how war breaks out that they will join France but Grey told [German Ambassador Count] Metternich that in the event of an unprovoked attack on France by Germany or of hostile action by Germany arising out of our agreement with France he must expect to find us on the side of France. If we were to give to France an ~~unconditional~~ assurance it would be necessary to obtain from France that nothing should be done in this Morocco Conference without consultation with us & that in the event of our being at war with Germany for any other reason France would maintain an attitude of benevolent neutrality and would prevent any other Powers from chiming in.[14]

It was a very delicate issue, as Grey knew well. A warning to Germany, clear enough if they cared to heed it, was easier than a commitment to France. Hardinge did not mean in the remarks quoted above that a Conservative government would have entered where Liberals feared to tread; he knew that no government could do more. When the same assurances, more carefully phrased, were given to France in encouragement as had been given to Metternich in warning, it was as much as could be done.

> This is of course very secret, but it is as well you should know. Of course no Gov[ernmen]t could make a defensive alliance with France without taking Parliament into their confidence and in this instance only Grey, C.B. [Prime Minister Campbell-Bannerman] and Lord Ripon [Privy Seal and leader of the House of Lords] have been consulted. Cambon seems fairly satisfied and as we are warmly supporting the French at Algeciras they are convinced of our good faith & of our resistance to German blandishments, which are unremitting.[15]

Even the limited assurances could be read as a commitment or at least a "moral obligation," and carried with them the danger that France would only stiffen its backbone at Algeciras: hence British concern that France fulfill its promise to consult on any maneuver at Algeciras.

In early February, as Nicolson supported the French position on the Moroccan police—that only France and Spain should run the force since only they had the experienced professionals near at hand in other North African possessions—Hardinge wished to make it clear that if the conference broke up on this issue, it would not be Britain's responsibility, a difficult enough role to play since Britain had really given France a free hand. This tightrope act was largely Hardinge's, for in early February Grey's tragedy made Hardinge in effect acting foreign secretary.[16]

Typically, he remained calm—for calm in a crisis was one of his more striking attributes. Careful study of all the evidence showed that Germany was not really preparing for war, although sheer exasperation could always produce a confrontation. The existence of the conversations with France would serve as a further check upon Germany, because, as he wrote Nicolson,

> These facts are sure to come to the knowledge of the Germans and are bound to have a pacifying influence. They dare not risk the loss of their sea trade for any advantage to be gained from Morocco. In my opinion, if we can only keep the peace without making concessions for the next year the situation in Europe may be entirely changed by the reoccupation & reappearance of Russia on the European stage. All depends on whether the present tranquility can be maintained.[17]

Grey, when he returned to work, had a solution to the police question: a mixed international force with a French inspector. Hardinge was surprised that Paris did not reject it out of hand. That France must not come to think Britain capable of disloyalty was a Foreign Office fear which would grow steadily under continued cultivation. Hardinge suggested that Nicolson could put forward Grey's plan as a private suggestion. Germany had also to accept the proposal, and Hardinge's friends in financial houses in the "city" (notably the Rothschilds) reported that Germany would be satisfied with nothing less than a port in Morocco, probably Mogador.[18]

Grey was willing to run the risk of giving Germany a port if that was the price for avoiding war, always provided the Admiralty said the risk was acceptable from their standpoint. For if war came, France would clearly expect British support. If Britain chose to stay out, Japan, Russia, and the United States all would sneer at British perfidy and search elsewhere for friends current or potential. Worse, Germany could then exploit the situation to her own advantage, as for example in stirring up trouble in Turkey, where there was even then an irritating incident over Sinai peninsula frontiers that some thought was German-inspired (Hardinge was at first, but only at first, skeptical).[19]

Hardinge strongly disagreed with Grey over a Moroccan port for Germany, apparently the first major divergence between the two men, unfortunately on a basic issue and less than a month after Hardinge had become permanent under secretary. Grey wanted both to uphold the Entente and to pry concessions from France, which seemed to Hardinge dangerously inconsistent. In a rare counter-memorandum (it was normal for the foreign secretary to have the last word), Hardinge stressed that it was not certain at all that Germany would force war over Morocco, for if she did Russia would have to come in. The important thing was that if Germany understood that Britain stood solidly with France, "without any limitations as to whether action by France in Morocco is aggressive or not, such knowledge would almost certainly deter Germany. . . ." But if France were left in the lurch at this juncture,the inevitable result would be for both France and Russia to become part of Germany's satellite diplomatic system. Germany had already made such offers to France, and important people in Russia—Witte, for example—favored the same sort of surrender out of fear.[20]

France did object to the proposals on the police, and Grey did not press his plan. He also agreed with Hardinge's recommendation to reject an idea from St. Petersburg (from Lamsdorff via Spring Rice) that Britain should make representations at Berlin to persuade Germany to accept the latest French proposal. Hardinge drafted Grey's answer: any British representations were unlikely to be effective, since Britain was bound by her treaty agreements to support France in Morocco. In any case, Germany was definitely not consulting Britain on the whole Moroccan problem.[21]

By the end of the month there was little to show for all the discussions at Algeciras save irritation. As Hardinge was careful to point out to Lascelles in Berlin, this feeling had even reached King Edward, who believed the kaiser to be the direct cause of Germany's hostility. Unless Germany altered her attitude, having already won the fall of Delcassé and substantial concessions, the conference would fail and tension be all the greater. "It is almost too much to hope that anything will come out of the Conference now beyond rancour & spite."[22]

March, however, saw a German reversal brought about by a feeling of isolation, engendered in turn by the intervention of President Roosevelt on the side of a fairly reasonable set of Austrian proposals. The basic plan put Spanish police in some ports and French in others, with Casablanca under a Dutch or Swiss neutral who would be inspector general for the entire force. To Hardinge, German acceptance of this proposal was complete justification of Delcassé's "policy of resistance to German bluff." Now it was the French who were obstinate, holding out for full control, and Hardinge feared that they might "sacrifice the substance to the shadow, and we find ourselves with them in a hopeless minority." The French were missing an excellent opportunity for a diplomatic victory over Germany, simply to gain the last small point (Casablanca in this case). More ominously, Britain would be forced to support France no matter what action France took. Again Hardinge argued with Grey, this time against completely unqualified support of French intransigence, for Grey had gone to the other extreme.[23]

Wisdom prevailed, and when the Algeciras Conference finally adjourned in April, a settlement had been reached which solved

Moroccan problems not "for the next seventeen years," as Hardinge remarked in his memoirs, but at least until the next major Moroccan crisis.

Hardinge, no doubt with relief, now had time to turn to other affairs as he and Grey moved to pick up the threads of the Russian negotiations. The resignation of Lamsdorff and the initial caution of his successor Isvolski blocked any meaningful advance, but the British position was prepared to the point even of conceding passage of the Dardanelles if need be as part of a general arrangement. Hardinge, eager to get on with the negotiations, suggested that King Edward visit St. Petersburg in July, but the king would make no commitment.

There were other projects, too, as Hardinge outlined to Spring Rice.

> Grey and I have many plans in our head which I hope will come off amongst them being a defensive alliance with France so that France may devote her shipbuilding money to her army on the Eastern frontier & if we pull off an agreement with Russia our position ought to be a good one. This also is *most private* as we have only talked of it together. It will be a revolution in the ideas of our politicians but Grey thinks he will be able to convert them by the possibility of reducing our own armaments in the event of these arrangements being made.

The defensive alliance was not to be, and perhaps it was for the best, but the letter is interesting as showing the drift of thought of both Grey and Hardinge in the aftermath of Algeciras.[24]

Hardinge was off in April for another of the king's Mediterranean cruises, having first heard of the idea from Knollys in March. Grey offered no opposition, although he doubted the legality of the king's argument that Hardinge qualified as minister in attendance by virtue of his ambassadorial rank and his privy councillorship. The party was to join the royal yacht at

Marseilles for a three-week cruise, with stops planned for Greece and Italy. The principal problem was to persuade the king not to meet the kaiser if he, too, should be visiting the Mediterranean. The king, having written to the kaiser to that effect, held to his intention despite the pleading of Knollys, Grey, and Hardinge alike that there would be a great outcry in France. Fortunately, the kaiser did not appear, and the voyage proceeded without Anglo-French incident. It was a pleasant Easter holiday and a chance for Hardinge to work upon the king with respect to the St. Petersburg visit.[25] He was also able to make some useful suggestions to the Greek government on the troublesome issue of international administration of Crete, once again showing the utility of having a professional diplomat on hand during royal travels.[26]

Far more important was King Edward's mid-August visit to Kaiser William at Cronberg on his way to Marienbad. Relations between king and kaiser had improved somewhat since Algeciras, and after a British initiative Berlin had passed an official invitation to the king. Edward apparently planned at least by mid-July for Hardinge to accompany him. He and Hardinge played Grey cautiously so as to arouse no opposition, but Grey in fact was only worried that Hardinge, who had been unwell, might get overtired and break down—and incidentally force Grey to miss his own much needed vacation.[27]

After dinner on the first day at Cronberg, Hardinge had a conversation with Heinrich von Tschirschky, German minister for foreign affairs, whom he had known and cordially distrusted as councillor of the German embassy in St. Petersburg, where he had been notably hostile to British interests. "An odious man!" Hardinge commented years later, with a rare exclamation point. The conversation ranged widely, but the principal subject was French distrust of Germany, which Germany wished Britain to help remove. Hardinge replied that the suspicion was very comprehensible given the direction of German policy in the Moroccan crisis. On the other hand, British friendship was something of which Germany could be assured—so long as no new surprise intervened to challenge the Entente or to threaten Anglo-Russian negotiations and thus disrupt the course of improving relations. Of particular interest was Tschirschky's reply: Germany quite understood Britain's desire to settle outstanding issues with Russia, and she herself had no political (as opposed to commercial) interests in Central Asia or the Persian Gulf.

The conversation lasted an hour, and almost immediately Hardinge was sent for by the kaiser. William was in a militaristic mood, speaking forcefully and at length on the need for a strong German army, ready to crush France if necessary. Disarmament was a chimera, and the approaching Hague Conference was great nonsense. If issues needed to be discussed, they should be discussed among the great powers with the lesser perforce following suit. Hardinge dodged a suggestion that Britain and Germany work out a common preconference position: Britain had not yet decided upon her own position at The Hague.

Once again, many subjects were touched upon, from Kiachow to Algeciras to visits of British ministers to Berlin. Hardinge reported to Grey that both the kaiser and Tschirschky "now seem at last to realize that friendly relations with us cannot be at the expense of our *entente* with France, but that if they are to exist at all they must be co-existent with our *entente*." To Knollys he was less diplomatic. "I think that I probably spoke to them much more straightly than Lascelles ever speaks to them, & they cannot say that there was any ambiguity in what I told them." To Bertie and Mallet, the meeting had gone too well, and Hardinge was being lulled by honeyed words. Grey, however, thought Hardinge had been quite correct in his responses; it was this that mattered, not a charitable appreciation of Germany's leaders.[28]

Hardinge's presence had been useful, above all to the king, who was not saddled with a cabinet minister yet could restrict his own remarks on foreign policy to pleasant platitudes. The pattern set at Cronberg was to be repeated more than once, giving Hardinge several excellent opportunities to tell plain truths to the Germans. These journeys were not accomplished without criticism at home that there should be a minister responsible to the electorate with the king—and some disgruntlement from the bypassed local ambassadors (Lascelles in this case).

The fall of 1906 was characterized by bothersome affairs of greater or lesser magnitude. The Hague Conference was one such headache, but one which could be prepared for in advance. Hardinge was convinced that it would be better if the conference never took place. As he wrote to King Edward, who fully agreed, other powers were certain to raise the claim that merchant shipping shoud be immune from capture by an enemy; once that principle was accepted, "the chief danger to Germany from a war with England will have been removed." Hardinge, like Crowe and Mallet and others, now viewed such questions from the aspect of Anglo-German relations, present or future, though not necessarily with the inflexibility or single-mindedness some would assign him.[29]

The conference was some months off, however, and Hardinge had other matters to deal with. The Russian negotiations, lethargic in the summer, came to life in the fall when Isvolski proposed a joint loan to Persia and Grey agreed (fearing that Russia would otherwise turn to Germany) so quickly that he was unable even to consult his prime minister. He hoped, correctly, that this cooperation would be rewarded by progress on negotiations, for Isvolski now set forward Russia's Persian claim: the northern half of Persia from a line running from Bandar Abbas to Birjand, thus including both Seistan and Persian Baluchistan. Hardinge and Grey agreed that Britain must have controlling influence south of this line, but Hardinge, more concerned than Grey to defend existing British interests on the northern side and in the Gulf ports, advocated the establishment of a middle ground open to general or common interests and urged that the loan money not be paid until Russia had recognized Britain's specific interests. When Russia seemed to hesitate, Hardinge was worried; failure to recognize Britain's suggested sphere would prove Russian aggressive designs against India, for which Seistan would be a necessary step. "In that case further negotiations would be useless."[30]

Hardinge's nerves were showing a bit, but the negotiations were vital. Britain was therefore prepared to grant the Turkish Straits to Russia, once the Committee of Imperial Defence concluded that this would not fundamentally alter the balance of power in the Mediterranean. Hardinge argued that Russian opinion would be so impressed with this achievement that small attention would be paid to Afghanistan and Tibet. Nothing was settled by the end of the year.[31]

The possibility of a concession on the Straits involved the Foreign Office in questions of naval strategy. The Mediterranean balance depended upon the presence there of the British Mediterranean fleet, but in the latter part of 1906 the Admiralty preferred to concentrate its main naval elements in home waters to meet the growing German naval threat. That threat was well understood in the Foreign Office, but there were other costs, notably the resulting inability to use naval detachments for diplomatic purposes. Hardinge was at the heart of this controversy, both as permanent under secretary and as friend of the king, for it was the sort of very specific issue the king became excited about.

Admiral John Fisher intended to keep a half dozen each of battleships and cruisers from overseas stations in a "nucleus" fleet at Portsmouth for reasons of economy and to strengthen the Home Fleet. Hardinge pointed out to Lord Tweedmouth, First Lord, that this was all very well if Germany ever attacked, but how would the navy be able to respond to the periodic troubles at Zanzibar or Suez, or Crete, or the Persian Gulf? "If we are to find that ships are to be no longer available as in the past we shall be sacrificing Imperial intersts to the problematical danger of an attack by Germany which we have been led to believe that our Home & Atlantic fleets are more than strong enough to repel." It was an argument that Hardinge could not win, but a year later the crisis he had foreseen arose in Chile. Naval protection for British interests was requested, but the entire naval strength in the Americas was a cruiser at Montevideo on the wrong side of the continent, and a useless sailing brig at Vancouver. To Hardinge it became a pet grumble, but Grey would not press the matter.[32]

Since it was also a pet grumble of the king's, here, too, Hardinge was on the receiving end of complaints, always the other side of the coin of royal friendship. King Edward could be most persistent, and he expected satisfactory answers in big as in little matters. It was Hardinge, for example, who had to fend off a very annoyed monarch when a bemused Grey arrived at a royal reception in an ordinary suit. "It is true that I did not tell him to come in uniform," pleaded an exasperated Hardinge, "but I could not conceive the possibility of his coming otherwise than in uniform." Nor was Hardinge exempt from Queen Alexandra's sudden and personal interests in foreign affairs, usually concerned with Greece or Denmark. She was not above calling Hardinge to Sandringham for discussion of something Prince George of Greece had written to her. "I am afraid the Queen does not realise how much work I have to do," Hardinge complained to Knollys after one such command performance, "and how extremely difficult it is for me to suddenly go away for a day without upsetting the whole of the work of this office."[33]

The tone of some of Hardinge's letters and comments of this period show him to have been under strain. He quarreled even with Bertie in Paris, when Bertie complained of a misdirected telegram from the Foreign Office. "I know that you are a model of perfection and never make mistakes," Hardinge wrote, and Bertie was offended.[34] Hardinge's frame of mind is partly to be explained by another of King Edward's interventions in diplomatic appointments—this time to send Hardinge to Washington as ambassador to succeed Sir Mortimer Durand. Hardinge favored Gerald Lowther, but the king objected that his wife was American. Hardinge was always concerned with the image projected by any diplomat's wife, but in this case the lady had a reputation for charm and attractiveness, and Lowther was wealthy and outgoing, just the sort of man to get on with President Roosevelt. The king suggested Sir George Buchanan, largely because he admired Lady Georgina, but Hardinge objected that Buchanan's ability was considerably less than Lowther's and he had no private means. There were few first-class candidates, however, and Hardinge settled on Maurice de Bunsen, ambassador in Madrid, although he did not quite meet Hardinge's rigid standards.[35]

The king, meanwhile, had decided that Hardinge was "the most desirable and efficient person for that particular post, which has now become one of great importance." No doubt Hardinge would be missed at the Foreign Office, the king told Campbell-Bannerman, but Grey was doing well and the staff gave him considerable support—and for Hardinge it would mean a peerage. Lady Hardinge was clearly in the king's mind as well. She had done well at St. Petersburg and would be appreciated in Washington: "Besides having great charm of manner she is very intelligent."[36].

Hardinge was not seriously alarmed, and he soon recruited Knollys to help smother the idea. He had much to do yet at the Foreign Office in the way of reform and Russian rapprochement and he was happy working there. The financial aspect was also important, for Hardinge could not afford the cost of the Washington post (all available funds had just been committed to the purchase and furnishing of a London house). Also, it was essential to be a good speaker in Washington, and throughout his career he distrusted his own abilities in this regard and found public speaking an odious burden.[37]

Despite opposition, the king persisted. Grey entered the lists with the simple but persuasive argument that Hardinge could not be spared, aside from the fact that he did not want the appointment. It would be the second major change in his career in less than a year, which meant moving from service to service and thousands of miles. After King Edward had written a second letter, Campbell-Bannerman called Hardinge in, but did not press the matter, advising Hardinge to speak directly to the king. Hardinge spent the night at Standringham and the king was persuaded, but only if Hardinge would suggest an acceptable alternative. After considerable thought, Hardinge turned to Lord Bryce, who was close to retirement age but had a charming wife and also enjoyed making "long and rather dull speeches on commonplace subjects which I knew to be a trait that would be popular with the American masses." King Edward thought Bryce a good choice and put his name forward as his own selection. Bryce got the job and proved to be an excellent representative.[38]

It was with some relief, therefore, that Hardinge spent Christmas at Crichel in a large party that included King Edward. Nor were the first months of 1907 as harrowing as Algeciras. But problems remained, and curiously the Foreign Office was just then concerned with two somewhat similar issues on the fringes of Europe, namedly Spain and Scandinavia. Like all problems at the time they were inevitably related to Germany, not perhaps with the sense of clear hostility expressed in Crowe's memorandum of 1 January, famous among diplomatic historians as a statement of irreconcilable rivalry, but related nevertheless.[39]

The concern with Spain was twofold. The less important issue was the king's desire to visit Spain again, a proposal which alarmed friends like Hardinge for security reasons. More dangerous was German pressure upon Spain. Germany asked first for a cable concession to the Canary Islands, the main object of which was taken in the Foreign Office to be the desire to land a branch cable on the Moroccan coast and thus secure a basis for further claims, and then proposed to construct warships in Spain for the Spanish government in return for control of the docks and arsenal of Ferrol. The French advised Madrid that they would in turn expect similar facilities at Cartagena, and for the time being that killed the proposal.[40]

France also suggested that Britain, Spain, and France should guarantee each other's possessions in the Mediterranean. Because Spain and France were not overly friendly, some persuasion would be necessary; much depended upon whether the proposal took the form of a tripartite treaty or separate Anglo-Spanish and Franco-Spanish notes. Spain preferred the former because it looked less like some sort of protectorate arrangement; Britain, following a Lansdowne proposal of 1905, preferred the latter, hoping that Germany would be less likely to misinterpret it. As Grey pointed out to Campbell-Bannerman, the Spanish if left to themselves might be forced to give way to German blandishments to avoid a closer French embrace. Spain would gain confidence if Britain guaranteed her islands and Moroccan coast, and in return Britain would gain security for Gibraltar. For that reason he and Hardinge opened negotiations with the Spanish ambassador in London.[41]

Discussions did not go particularly well, and Grey favored the king's visit as a way of approaching Spain. The journey was set for April. This time Grey objected to Hardinge's going, ostensibly because Hardinge would lose touch with Office matters, but more likely because Hardinge's travels had resulted in growing criticism of Grey, and this time important negotiations were involved. King Edward argued that overseas matters required a professional, but that he, the sovereign, could choose whether foreign secretary or undersecretary would be his companion. In any case, other cabinet ministers would not be up to the sort of work required. Hardinge provided some of the arguments through Knollys and spoke strongly himself to Grey when Grey at last brought the subject up. Grey submitted once again.[42]

Hardinge journeyed out with Queen Alexandra, joining the yacht at Toulon on 6 April and arriving at Cartagena on the eighth. Hardinge had with him the text of the proposed agreement which he had drawn up and which Grey had approved, but he was not overly optimistic. Spain had made a counterproposal that Britain should guarantee Spain's coast in return for the use of Spanish ports, a most undesirable obligation. Since a tripartite agreement would be seen by Germany as further tightening of the noose and might produce some hostile reaction, and since Spain's proposal was equally unacceptable, Hardinge's solution was to exchange notes that Britain and Spain would not cede, lease, or otherwise part with territory in the area concerned without consultation (presumably France and Spain would follow suit). This format would meet the requirements but give

Germany no technical cause for complaint.[43]

During two days of formalities at Cartagena, Hardinge, like most of the party, never went ashore; the Spanish royal party was similarly established on a royal yacht. Hardinge had trouble at first in discussions with the minister for foreign affairs, but direct talks with King Alfonso XIII and Prime Minister Antonio Maura, neither of whom wished to mar the royal visit, opened the way to agreement. Maura accepted Hardinge's draft and the notes were formally exchanged in May; the European powers were informed confidentially of their contents, which were received "with approval at Rome and Lisbon, with coldness at Vienna and ill humour at Berlin," as Hardinge put it years later.[44]

On his return in April, Hardinge's attention was directed to the northern edge of Europe. Late in 1906 Norway had raised the possibility of a treaty of guarantee for her neutrality and integrity, which would involve Britain, France, Germany, and Russia (essentially to replace a treaty of 1855 which was not abrogated by the separation of Norway from Sweden). King Edward, under the guidance of his son-in-law King Haakon VII who had just become king of independent Norway, favored the idea. The Foreign Office was not opposed, but caution was in order regarding the attitude of both Germany and Sweden. In the latter case, the issue was whether Norwegian integrity could be guaranteed without guaranteeing that of Sweden as well. A further complication was Norway's desire to depart from her declared neutrality should Sweden or Denmark be attacked; the inclusion of Denmark, in particular, so widened the proposal as to give it quite a different character.[45]

Hardinge was sympathetic to King Haakon in this, his first diplomatic venture. But the draft stipulation requiring British armed aid to protect Norwegian neutrality meant that Norway really had the power to initiate war by stating that her neutrality had been violated, and careful negotiation—and probably a mutual treaty among the guarantors—would be required to obviate this possibility. Other aspects suggested that Britain should not rush into signature, despite sentiment towards the king's son-in-law and even the Norwegian plea that their current government would fall should Britain not cooperate.[46]

Fortunately, this complicated issue was not raised at the midsummer Hague Conference in any important way. Other suggestions were put forward, including a separate conference on Scandinavia (it never took place), or adding Sweden to the guarantor powers (unacceptable to Norway). Britain, France, and Norway signed an agreement early in November 1907 which recognized Norway's integrity but made no pledges to defend her neutrality. This was not the end of the affair for Britain, as alarming reports arrived at year's end that Russia and Germany were conducting independent negotiations on the Baltic and the Aaland Islands. Secret discussions continued in 1908, eventually resulting in a multiparty agreement on the maintenance of the status quo in the Baltic and North Sea which meant little from a practical standpoint.[47]

A third series of negotiations was far more important for Britain: 1907 was the year of the Anglo-Russian Accord. The negotiations had been proceeding throughout the early months of the year, despite a series of setbacks and mutual suspicions. By 1907 the accord was needed to check Germany, not specifically to improve Britain's Asian position. For example, one problem was Russia's policy in Persia, of which Spring Rice, now minister in Teheran, complained loudly. But even if every report were true, Hardinge argued, once agreement was reached even the most obstreperous outlying lesser officials would be brought into line—a pious hope but a necessary one in this case. Hardinge and Grey agreed that the best policy in Persia was nonintervention, despite the extensive disturbances associated with the Persian revolution, in progress since the end of 1905.[48]

Hardinge kept the main goal in sight. He was particularly responsible for drafting the Afghanistan section and from the start was willing to concede direct Russian discourse with Afghanis on local issues; by late February he could "see daylight ahead." Individual points still presented difficulty, particularly a dangerous claim by Russia for a sphere of interest in Persia which would adjoin the Afghan frontier and which even Hardinge thought undesirable. Indeed, when it began to appear that Russia would intervene directly in Persian affairs, Hardinge advised that the Admiralty should prepare for a demonstration in the Persian Gulf, although there was little direct danger there.[49]

Hardinge was Grey's main adviser in the negotiations which followed through spring and summer. Frequent letters (always shown to Grey) exchanged with Nicolson in St. Petersburg tell the story in considerable detail, which there is no need to follow here. No apparent disagreements between Grey and Hardinge are revealed in the correspondence, official or private. The principal conflicts in fact were between the India Office and India on Persia and Afghanistan, and between Spring Rice and London. The more agitated the minister in Teheran became at London's indifference to local, Persian interests, the more impatient Hardinge became, and Grey had to write at least one soothing letter: "Hardinge hasn't got a gift of circumlocution & I have come to the conclusion that anyone who had would be intolerable in the F.O.; there isn't time for it." Hardinge not only had much to do; he also had his own view of the place of Persia in the larger scheme of things, which differed from Spring Rice's ideas. His own knowledge of Persia was useful in working out detailed Persian clauses.[50]

One problem which did concern him was the issue to Russia of a future railway concession to the Gulf coast. Even if such a railway should be purely commercial, Germany would doubtless claim the same rights. A German terminus on the Persian side would seriously complicate efforts to block the Baghdad Railway project; while the proposed Turkish line could be halted through Britain's financial position in Turkey (and Britain's lien on Kuwait), the same power could not be exercised to the same degree in Persia. The answer was to obtain a Russian pledge to support the status quo on the Gulf littoral, which might also silence Indian criticism. Unfortunately, Russia was disinclined to meddle in a dangerous area where others had interests, even as quid pro quo for freedom of the Straits. In the end, Grey made a unilateral declaration to the same effect. As finally drafted, the whole Persian section seemed advantageous:

> we obtain an unrivaled position in the Seistan triangle where the Russians renounce all idea of forming a base for the attack on India. Moreover they give up all idea of an outlet in the Indian Ocean which has been their dream for years. These advantages outweigh in my opinion any criticisms that may be offered by captious persons who do not realize that we have not the means to hold, in the event of war, the Southern half of Persia which has been the dream of Anglo-Indians for the last 50 years.[51]

"Captious persons," however, included more than liberals who felt that the Persian Constitutionalists, who had heretofore looked to Britain for succor, had been betrayed. The Persian government was equally alarmed that their country was to be sliced into zones, despite Hardinge's and Grey's assurances to the Persian ambassador that the agreement was a self-denying ordinance which specified the integrity and independence of Persia.

Persian worries could be explained away; Russian internal problems were more difficult to manage. In June Russia's second Duma was dissolved under the pressure of conservative court circles, and the electoral law was altered in a conservative direction. Hardinge spoke clearly on this: "I do not think that what goes on in Russia should be allowed to stop our negotiations so long as there is a Gov[ernment] with whom to negotiate. To do otherwise would certainly be regarded as an act of partizanship & might even be regarded as interference in Russian internal affairs." Hardinge had not lost his sympathy for the Duma, but "foreign policy based on sentiment can only end in disaster." On the other hand, sentiment had to be taken into account—and the Persian Gulf statement was aimed, in part, at disarming some of the critics who objected to dealing with the government which had shut down the Duma. Ironically, it was equally important for the conservative opposition, who were already claiming that Britain was giving too much away.[52]

By the end of August Russia had at last signed, and Persia was divided into spheres of interest: Russian in the north, British in the south, and a middle neutral ground. Britain's role in Afghanistan was recognized, and both parties agreed to a hands-off policy in Tibet. Nothing was said about the Gulf, but Grey declared in the House of Commons that Russia took note of Britain's predominant interest, which was very nearly the same thing. Hardinge's later summary is a fair one:

> As regards the Treaty itself it was not so much its text as the fact of its existence that was important, and though its terms might have been more advantageous to England in certain respects the Treaty served its purpose and maintained peace and friendly relations for ten years. That was the aim in view and it was worth some sacrifice to secure.

Peace and friendly relations—and there was also considerably less likelihood that Russia would join Germany in any hostile coalition.

Grey acknowledged the help of all concerned, and Hardinge got his share of praise for "his knowledge both of the Russian Gov[ernment] & of Persia & his clear view as to the good policy of an agreement." Hardinge in his turn was quick to thank Nicolson for his aid in the achievement of this grand project, "of which the realisation has been my dream for the last four years." For this, in part, he had left St. Petersburg for the Foreign Office, and after all the work and negotiations, not only with Russia but internally with the India Office and other interested parties, it was hard to think of it at last signed and sealed. Hardinge was also honest in his praise of King Edward's persistent support, and indeed the king had played a definite role, not least in supporting the appointments which made the negotiations so successful. As Hardinge put it to the king, many changes had occurred in Britain's world relationships since Edward had come to the throne only a few years earlier. Now, of course, much depended upon how Russia lived up to her bargain, but Hardinge was confident that Isvolski would remain loyal.[53]

Time alone would tell, but Hardinge could take considerable satisfaction in this agreement—the final accomplishment, on paper at least, of the Triple Entente. It is not the place of this work to decided whether the existence of the Entente made war more or less likely. It is clear, however, that Hardinge had pursued the Russian accord with single-minded determination throughout, although Grey and others agreed with him on the desirability of the treaty, and he certainly did not accomplish it alone. Naturally the accord had wide repercussions, but even viewed merely as a resolution of many outstanding Asian issues, it was useful in smoothing the path of Anglo-Russian relations. Hardinge knew from firsthand experience how close the danger of war between the two powers had been, and could be again if neither reined in its aspirations across Asian frontiers—all the more a danger as Russia turned away from her Far Eastern humiliation.

Hardinge had contributed to the Entente in other ways, as for example in the Spanish agreements. It was in Morocco, however, that his role was greatest, for here he was a consistent supporter of France, for better or worse, in Grey's first real test. Naturally Hardinge wished to avoid Anglo-French disagreements for their own sake, but in this case it was a question of German pressure, and Germany was not only the greatest military danger but also appeared to wish to prod and provoke on all sides. Hardinge differed from both Grey, who at times would have given Germany more elbowroom, and Crowe, who thought Germany utterly implacable. From the German standpoint, policy had been predicated upon the unlikelihood, indeed impossibility, of Britain reaching an agreement with her worst enemy, Russia, but that very calculation had resulted in an overconfident forward policy in Morocco and elsewhere, and now Britain saw Germany as a greater threat—in Morocco, in the Baghdad Railway, in the German fleet. The Entente existed not to resolve such conflicts, but to defend France and the European balance of power.[54] Hardinge was not the man to spell out such thoughts in lengthy memoranda for Grey or the Cabinet, but it was the sort of calculation which must have passed through his mind as issue added to issue in the Anglo-German and Anglo-Austrian relations which were to be the focus of his last prewar years in the Foreign Office.

V Triple Alliance

Hardinge's concern was first and foremost the conduct of Britain's foreign policy. But "foreign policy" is a multifaceted crystal which reflects, in the best of circumstances, basic themes predominating over time in a nation's history. One such theme in the years in which Hardinge was permanent under secretary was Britain's naval supremacy and the challenge presented to it by the construction of the German fleet. The Foreign Office was directly involved only with diplomatic ramifications, but no member could be other than disturbed by this growing rivalry, which preceded Hardinge's return to London. There were other aspects of Anglo-German relations: Morocco, Björkö, the Baltic, Turkey, Egyptian finances, even the tone of press reports all mattered. But to Hardinge, as to many, the naval race was the heart of the matter. As he put it more than once, "if Germany would place some limit on her naval construction scheme suspicion of Germany's intention would soon evaporate on this side of the channel." His suspicion was not that Germany would attempt to invade, but that Germany would use the fleet as a weapon of pressure when Britain was otherwise occupied.[1]

It behooved Britain, therefore, to look to her own interests and allies and to be cautious about overt demonstrations of Anglo-

German friendship and solidarity which might alarm France and Russia. One problem was the normal exchange visits between king and kaiser. Edward visited Kiel in 1904, and William had not been in England since a private visit to Sandringham in 1902. A proposed invitation in 1906 was dropped due to the Moroccan crisis, but in the spring of 1907, King Edward revived the idea. Before the kaiser could visit, however, King Edward, once again accompanied by Hardinge, was off to Marienbad in the summer, meeting William and Chancellor Bülow on the way at the palace of Wilhelmshöhe near Cassel.

Hardinge had only one serious conversation, wth Bülow, whom he had known well at Bucharest. He had the feeling that he was the sole auditor to a prepared speech. In an hour's meeting, Bülow disclaimed any aggressive intention toward France. Even in Morocco, Germany only desired that her commerce should not be excluded and should receive fair treatment. Nor did the Anglo-Russian Accord jeopardize any German interests. It was all diplomatic and polite, and Hardinge responded in kind—although not without pointing out some discrepencies between Bülow's words and the actions of the German minister at Tangier. Hardinge went away with his views unchanged: "The impression he made on me was that he wishes to be friendly, but I confess that I have never felt much confidence in anything that he said to me. He has always struck me as very cunning and clever."[2]

After a day of ceremony and talk, the king and his party left for Ischl, meeting Emperor Franz Josef on the way. The contrast was striking, for the Austrians offered no military display and no dull reviews, but rather a quiet and well-prepared reception. "The German Court was in fact a vulgarly flamboyant Court," as Hardinge put it, and King Edward, too, found the Hapsburg emperor more pleasant company. Hardinge had a lengthy discussion with Baron Aerenthal, Austrian minister of foreign affairs, whom he had known when they both were ambassadors at St. Petersburg. It was in general an exchange of platitudes, and Aerenthal said all the right things on the Anglo-Russian Accord,

German errors in Morocco, and the need to maintain traditional friendships; but there was little agreement on Balkan problems, above all Macedonia. The kaiser's visit eventually passed off without notable difficulty; the Balkans were less transient.[3]

Early in 1908 supporters of the Anglo-Russian Accord like Hardinge and Nicolson could be satisfied that it was apparently working well. The Baltic negotiations were worrying, but Isvolski seemed to be playing up well in Persia, where both countries were alarmed at growing German interests. Isvolski was also displeased with German attitudes on the Baltic and the Baghdad Railway; in Hardinge's opinion, he would not soon get over these annoyances and should therefore be supported by Britain and France. On the other hand, Russia was increasingly angered by Austrian advances in the Balkans, notably the proposed railway through the Sanjak of Novi Bazar towards Salonika, whose obvious purpose was to separate the Slavic and increasingly anti-Hapsburg states of Serbia and Montenegro. "The struggle between Austria & Russia in the Balkans is evidently now beginning and we shall not be bothered by Russia in Asia," minuted Hardinge with relief if not satisfaction, and, as the tension increased, "the action of Austria & Germany will make Russia lean on us more & more in the future. In my opinion this will not be a bad thing."[4]

A project to solidify the Triple Entente by a royal visit to Russia had been in the air since at least the previous November, when Hardinge had urged it upon the king while discouraging a visit to Berlin. Going to St. Petersburg was inadvisable for security reasons, but the king could visit the tsar on his royal yacht at Reval as he had visited the Spanish monarch at Cartagena. The king set a tentative date for Whitsuntide. The visit depended, of course, upon peaceful conditions in Russia (he could not go should there be another Duma incident) and in the Balkans, where the powers were considering a separate proposal by Grey for the administration of the several Macedonian districts.[5]

Hardinge in the meantime was occupied—in addition to the

normal concerns of the Office—with answering a series of questions on British defence put to various departments by the Committee on Imperial Defence. Most interesting was the query whether "a German invasion as a 'bolt from the blue' during normal peaceful diplomatic relations [was] reasonably conceivable?" Crowe's answer, aside from pointing out obvious problems in defining "normal peaceful diplomatic relations," was yes, given strained British relations with some third power and German conviction of success. Hardinge's redraft saw the possibility as less realistic:

> It is of course possible that the leaders of an absolutist country such as Germany should lose all sense of moral & international obligations and perpetuate an act which, even if successful, would be condemned by the whole world and by future historians as an infamous aggression. It is however hardly conceivable that such an idea should be seriously contemplated by a civilised Power at a moment of profound peace. It presupposed also the friendly neutrality of Germany's powerful neighbours, France & Russia.
>
> The reply to this question should be 'It is conceivable but not reasonably so.'[6]

Once again, it was a difference of emphasis, the fine line between suspicion and hostility, even phobia. Hardinge's views were obviously important, and for that reason it is worth recording one of the few lengthy statements he made on the subject, in a letter to Lascelles (it should be borne in mind that Hardinge throughout thought that Lascelles's determination required stiffening):

> I very much fear that the suspicions now held here can only increase with time and the increase of the German Navy. When one comes to think that, as the Germans admit, their navy is being built at very great sacrifices in order to impose their will, it is quite conclusive to us that it is only upon us

that they wish their will should be imposed, for their fleet is already strong enough to impose it on other Powers. We fully realize and acknowledge the supremacy of their military position in Europe: they recognize our actual naval supremacy at present, and they know the existence of England as an independent country. Nevertheless they wish to contest that supremacy, and it is evident that they are extremely anxious that the contest should not take place for some years to come—that is to say until they are ready. The only means by which that day can be indefinitely deferred is by the construction of a very large number of battleships in this country by which the supremacy will still be maintained. To build these battleships will cost a great deal of money, and we must look forward in this country from next year to a very considerable increase in our taxation in order to meet the demands of the Admiralty. Our people will suffer in consequence and they will ask: 'Why is it necessary to build this enormous number of battleships?' and when they realize that it is solely on account of Germany's desire to contest our supremacy at sea, the man in the street will say: 'Damn those Germans!' So long as our taxation is increased to build our fleet against the German fleet, so long will the hostility of this country continue towards Germany. . . . I am very despondent about our future relations with Germany. There is no innate hostility to Germany in this country, not such as we know to have been preached and inculcated in the German youth. For many years we have regarded Russia as our great enemy, but the moment that we realized that Russia has no longer any intention to attack us in Asia, the hostility felt in this country towards Russia has developed into a sentiment of almost friendship. If we only knew for certain that Germany had no intention in the future of attacking us, there is absolutely no reason why our feelings towards Germany should not be the same as they are now towards Russia, but the fear is always present and will remain so long as the German Navy League persists in its present intentions.[7]

Such general evaluations did nothing to settle the question of a visit to Russia, and Hardinge urged Grey to speak to Asquith (Campbell-Bannerman had resigned in April). The time was ripe. Hardinge feared that both Grey and Asquith would give in to Liberal Party extremists, and he asked Nicolson, home on leave, not to make alarmist noises to Grey on conditions in Finland or on the future of the Duma. "If the visit can take place we shall in my opinion have scored our success whatever may take place later. . . ."[8]

By early May, Hardinge knew he was to go to Reval. He was therefore closely involved in the detailed preparations, and the need to settle disagreements over Macedonia in advance of the visit, by last-minute concessions if necessary. At the end of the month, the question of Hardinge's presence in the Russian party was raised in the Cabinet. Grey argued that not only did the king not wish to have a regular cabinet minister in attendance, but that the idea that one must be on hand when the king interviewed a foreign sovereign or minister was simply out of date. Hardinge would be there as a direct link with the Foreign Office and policy control, almost as a special ambassador. This defense silenced criticism (though not of the royal visit itself) for the time being, but Grey was prepared to face the same objections in the House.[9]

In the first week of June the *Victoria and Albert* sailed for Kiel, arriving on the seventh. Only Hardinge and Queen Alexandra had the stomach to face meals on a very rough passage. The two, joined by a weak Ponsonby, were taking tea when suddenly the queen was thrown, chair and all, into the corner, pursued by teapot, hot-water urn, and plates of tea cakes. Luckily she was unhurt, and Hardinge, thrown against the table, rescued her from the mess. The queen had her faults, but as usual she took this incident in her stride. At Kiel, the yacht was met and escorted by Prince Henry of Prussia and a large body of troops, some of whom galloped along the banks during the passage. Hardinge noticed that work was being done on the canal and was told by a German officer that it was being doubled so that ships could go both ways at once, and that the job would be finished in five years. None of the British officers on the yacht or the two escorting cruisers had noticed this, "and when I reported the fact on my return to London, the Admiralty was sceptical and had to send an officer to verify the fact before they were convinced."

The yacht reached Reval on the ninth, in much better weather. The tsar, tsarina, and members of the Russian imperial family were on hand already on two royal yachts and the cruiser *Almaz*, sole survivor of the fleet that was destroyed at Tsushima. Two days of ceremonies and banquets were enjoyed by all, but for Hardinge there was serious work in conversations with Isvolski and Prime Minister P. A. Stolypin. Much time inevitably was spent on Macedonia, where Isvolski, for all his professed admiration for Grey's suggestions, had to walk carefully to insure that the recent improvement in Anglo-Russian relations did not produce a countervailing deterioration in Russo-German relations: he knew well that Austria opposed Grey's plan. Hardinge outlined a position nearly word for word the same as he had written to Lascelles. When a crisis came, as it well might in seven or eight years, Russia would be in a critical position as the "arbitor of peace," and for that reason, and for their shared and mutual interests, Britain and Russia should stand side by side.

Persia was another important topic. Hardinge pressed for Russian collaboration in a trans-Persian railway. Isvolski was all for railways, but his proposed railway linked with India's system (Hardinge saw that idea as premature), while Hardinge's ran only to the Persian Gulf and thus would, in Russia's view, open up north Persia to commercial competition from other states. Afghanistan, Crete, and other issues were also discussed. On the whole it was another useful conversation; Isvolski, Hardinge reported, "struck me as very able and adroit, but extremely timid." Hardinge also had several friendly talks with the tsar, who was obviously highly pleased with the royal visit. Everything went "almost better than I had hoped for."[10]

The trip was beneficial in solidifying Anglo-Russian relations, the main objective. Hardinge was subject to some criticism because the king had spontaneously made the tsar a British admiral of the fleet (which was unconstitutional without prior Cabinet approval)—the theory being that a minister in attendance might have avoided this. It was unfortunate personally, but Hardinge was more concerned professionally to disarm the inevitable suspicions in Berlin and Vienna, and to persuade Isvolski to move on the issues discussed at Reval, above all Persian railways.[11]

Unfortunately, events in Persia reflected badly upon the accord, for in late June Mohammad Ali Shah with the help of the Cossack Brigade (and the backing of the Russian legation) overthrew the constitution, closed down the Assembly, and removed many of the liberal leaders. Martial law was declared in Teheran and an army sent against Tabriz, where the populace had revolted against the government. There was little Britain could do except to give sanctuary to some opposition leaders. Pressure at home mounted against a policy which sacrificed Persian liberals for closer association with autocratic Russia. Hardinge and Grey remained firm, refusing to make demands or complaints in St. Petersburg which would anger Russia and undermine the efficacy of the Convention.[12]

Macedonia was another worry, but here conditions had suddenly changed dramatically. Early in July the Young Turk revolution began in Salonika, inspired partly by fears, generated by Reval, that the powers were about to take total control in Macedonia. Time alone would show the validity of the Young Turks' reformist promises, but by the end of July the Constitution of 1876 had been restored and the Young Turks established in power. Gerald Lowther was the newly appointed British ambassador to the Porte, and before the month was out Hardinge had come to think that it was a splendid opportunity for him and for Britain, perhaps a chance "to entirely reverse our attitude and policy towards Turkey of the last few years."[13]

Hardinge was elated: German influence in Turkey should

decline owing to the many German contacts with the discredited sultan, and the Young Turks appeared to want to take the responsibility for Macedonian reforms. The specific issues which had clouded Anglo-Turkish relations over the years, and which resulted primarily from the maladministration of such provinces as Macedonia and Crete, might now, he hoped (too optimistically), be resolved. Meanwhile, Hardinge had another trip to Germany to make.

King Edward's annual visit to Marienbad seemed to both the king and the Foreign Office a good opportunity to meet the kaiser again, and to discuss the general state of Anglo-German relations and the specific and immediate issue of who was to succeed Lascelles as British ambassador in Berlin (the kaiser had objected to Sir Fairfax Cartwright, minister in Munich and Britain's first choice). Such a deliberate use of the king by the Cabinet was unusual. Edward liked the idea of the meeting, and of raising major issues—but not of doing the talking himself, so Hardinge as usual went along.

Grey provided a long memorandum for the king, repeating Britain's arguments on the naval race which were already quite familiar to the Germans. His principal objective was the reduction of German naval expenditure. If Germany would cut, Britain would cut, even without any formal agreement. But Germany should understand that if she lost her fleet, her army would remain in being; if Britain lost her fleet, she lost everything. Hardinge had the same instructions, with orders to talk to the kaiser if the king did not.[14]

The king and a relatively small party arrived at Cronberg on 11 August. King Edward spent the morning with the kaiser and told Hardinge that the conversation had gone well, but when he had mentioned the navy question and the fact that he had a paper on it, William had neither asked to see it nor inquired about its contents. After lunch, William called Hardinge up to speak to him. "It was a trying moment for me to carry out my instructions as the Emperor's numerous suite together with Sir F. Lascelles formed a group about ten yards distant, and I could see the King sitting in a corner of a small summer-house smoking his cigar and watching me from the corner of his eye."

The kaiser was in an expansive postprandial mood, but Hardinge was not satisified with platitudes and went to the point at the first opening. Genuine apprehension was felt in England about Germany's underlying intentions. If her program continued, in a few years' time, Germany would be superior in first-class battleships. The rivalry carried on in this manner would eventually so embitter relations that a critical situation would probably arise. The kaiser replied in some anger that the British would retain a large superiority. Hardinge's lengthy official report, written without notes, only hints at William's fury:

> This programme was not a new one; it had been passed by law; and it had become a point of national honour that it should be completed. No discussion with a foreign Government could be tolerated; such a proposal would be contrary to the national dignity, and would give rise to internal troubles if the Government were to accept it. He would rather go to war than submit to such dictation.

Hardinge replied that discussion was hardly dictation, but German figures on British ships were simply incorrect. The kaiser sent for official statistics; Hardinge tried in response to direct the conversation to the general points of Grey's memorandum, but a reference to the possibility of German invasion once Britain's fleet had been defeated only angered the kaiser further. "The Emperor replied with some warmth that the talk of invasion was sheer nonsense. . . ." He himself directed German foreign policy," and was it likely that he would ever tolerate such an idea for an instant?" And so it went, without any resolution.

For the remainder of the afternoon Hardinge was badly treated by the German suite, "who were almost lacking in ordinary civility and would hardly speak to me. To me it was a matter of supreme indifference as the King expressed to me his warm appreciation of the manner in which I had tackled the Emperor.'' The ''supreme indifference,'' however, dates from many years later. Two hours passed, and Hardinge had a second conversation with Herr Martin von Jenisch of the German Foreign Office (Wilhelm von Schön, the foreign secretary, was ill), which was much the same. This time Hardinge caused some consternation by warning that public opinion might force the cancellation of a proposed royal visit to Berlin in 1909 if the race continued.

In summary, Hardinge wrote:

> Although it is to be regretted that the German Government have assumed such an uncompromising attitude towards any discussion or modification of their actual programme of naval construction, it is as well to know the worst and to be prepared for it.
>
> What strikes me forcibly in the attitude of the Emperor and of the German Government is their unreasoning fear that any reduction of the German programme may be regarded by their countrymen as due to the dictation of a foreign Power, more especially of England. . . .

At dinner Hardinge was still being cold-shouldered but later, to the surprise of all, William, obviously in a better frame of mind, called him over and talked to him for more than an hour on many topics. At the end of the conversation, William made his main point: '' 'The future of the world is in the hands of the Anglo-Teuton race. England, without a powerful army, cannot stand alone in Europe, but must lean on a Continental Power, and that Power should be Germany.' '' In other words, Britain would be better advised to choose Germany over France and Russia. For Hardinge he had a special token—the Order of the Red Eagle, Second Class (offered and declined, on the king's advice, the previous year), which Hardinge accepted as an outward sign that their quarrel had not been serious.[15]

William's account of the discussion, made also without notes (but reconstructing it sentence by sentence), puts it in stronger language. In his version, after he had said (in English), "then we shall fight, for it is a question of national honour and dignity," Hardinge turned red with embarrassment and apologized for his regrettable lapse. As Gordon Brook-Shepherd has remarked, the truth lies somewhere in the middle: Hardinge may well have apologized for giving the kaiser the wrong impression, but the kaiser's account, ringing true enough on his own words, has Hardinge talk in much the same language and then humble himself as if he were a plainspoken but loyal German subordinate, not a professional diplomat in a delicate situation.[16] In both accounts, however, the meaning was clear: the quarrel had been and continued to be serious.

As on the previous journey, King Edward left on the night train and arrived at Ischl on the following morning to be met by Franz Josef, Aerenthal, and the Austrian party. Again, the atmosphere was a pleasant change. Hardinge had a long talk with Aerenthal on Macedonia and the Sanjak railway, both men making suitable pledges of friendship. Hardinge was certainly serious in this, for, as he reminded Goschen, "as difficulties with Germany are likely to grow more acute in the not far distant future, a friendly Austria will be a very convenient check on her ally." Although Austria held firmly to her alliance with Germany, Aerenthal admitted that if Germany persisted in her naval construction, a very critical situation might arise.

If Hardinge had wished to sound Austria on the possibility of direct intervention in Berlin to ease the naval race, he must have been disappointed. But there is no evidence to suggest that an overture of this sort was planned, let alone made, despite the accusation that King Edward's diplomacy aimed at the division of the Austro-German alliance. In the light of recent worries over the Sanjak and Macedonia, the first and necessary step was to restore friendly Anglo-Austrian relations. If Austria did speak to Berlin, well and good, and better still if this "softened" the alliance, but this was, at best, a secondary or tertiary objective of Hardinge's last meeting with Aerenthal, a man he liked but regarded as "ambitious and therefore dangerous."[17]

Interestingly, Aerenthal had given Britain a hint of the coming Balkan crisis which would forever end the "spirit of Ischl." He began by asking if Britain had any intention of modifying its regime in Egypt in the light of the Young Turk revolution. The question was important to Austria with her analogous situation in Bosnia and Herzegovina. Hardinge

> replied that it might prove necessary in the near future to extend the basis of Government in Egypt, but that it was premature at present to decide what measures, if any, should be taken. He [Aerenthal] remarked that, Bosnia and Herzegovina being contiguous to Macedonia, the Austrian Government could hardly avoid making some sort of political concessions to the inhabitants of these two provinces.

The form of the "concession" was to be annexation, but that was some weeks off.[18]

King Edward continued on to Marienbad, and Hardinge returned to London. Both King Edward and Grey praised his necessary stand before the kaiser, although Grey played down his role to the Cabinet in order, as he explained, not to raise the old question of a cabinet member being present at such meetings. The king was also pleased, no doubt because he had been spared the awkward responsibility of "belling the cat." Grey, in summarizing the discussions, looked for some ray of light: "I do not think the prospect of some slackening of German Naval expenditure is hopeless." Aerenthal had told Hardinge to focus upon an undercurrent in Germany which would prefer to ease the naval race, and Grey had similar indications from the German embassy in London. This lead would be followed, and there was always hope. "I must add that the instruction I gave to Sir C. Hardinge was carried out under difficult circumstances in a way which I entirely approve."[19] The Cabinet had to think over the situation; Hardinge for his part had a few days' rest, but the end of September and early October saw the development of a crisis of the first magnitude.

In mid-September, Isvolski and Aerenthal, meeting at Buchlau, agreed that Russia would not oppose the annexation of Bosnia-Herzegovina (occupied by Austria since 1878), and Austria would accept the opening of the Straits to Russian warships. Details of the agreement remain obscure, but both men were worried about the effect of the Young Turk renaissance upon the areas of their immediate concern. Isvolski now set out on a European tour to obtain the necessary agreement of the several powers to a changed regime for the Straits. By the end of the month he had obtained conditional German and Italian approval and headed for Paris. Meanwhile the Bulgarians seized the Turkish "Orient Railway" in Eastern Rumelia, encouraged, Hardinge believed, by Austria.

The possibility that Prince Ferdinand might declare independence was clear to all. He had visited Budapest on the twenty-third and perhaps received Aerenthal's approval of such a declaration (Hardinge in later years came to believe that the Austrians simply deciphered all the Bulgarian dispatches, but collusion was inferred by many). Lowther wisely asked what to say to the Turks if Ferdinand did act. Hardinge advised him, with Grey's approval, to tell Turkey to protest formally and submit the matter to the signatory powers of the Treaty of Berlin. The progress of the Young Turk regeneration should not be jeopardized by adopting warlike measures which would only play into the hands of reactionaries and, at best, be a useless pursuit of the shadow of sovereignty. The best plan, as Hardinge pointed out to Nicolson, was to act in concert with Russia, hopefully in such a way as to give Bulgaria no pretext to declare independence, for if that happened Greece and Serbia would demand compensation and Austria might find it a convenient moment for the annexation of Bosnia and Herzegovina—all too accurate a prediction.[20]

When reports of Ferdinand's intention to act arrived, Hardinge was in charge of the Office with Grey away. Hardinge knew Britain would be criticized if nothing were done, and at once sent orders to the ambassadors in Berlin Treaty capitals to urge those governments to warn Sofia that any such step would have the most serious consequences. It was little enough, but Britain really had no power to block Ferdinand's declaration. On 3 October Count Mensdorff, the Austrian ambassador, gave Hardinge a letter from Aerenthal, dated 28 September, announcing the decision to proclaim annexation of Bosnia and Herzegovina. Hardinge was surprised and worried. As he wrote to Grey that day, the annexation was very ill timed and would probably produce a declaration of Bulgarian independence. "It is depressing to see the applecart upset by those stupid Austrians, & I feel convinced that Aerenthal has initiated this to compensate for his many failures." Isvolski, of course, had doubtless worked out the details with Aerenthal, the only issue being the actual timing, but "Aerenthal's falseness is beyond all depths."[21]

Independence was declared on the fifth and annexation the next day, but Hardinge had already taken the unusual step of calling Grey back from Fallodon: "I think the S. of State, who is after all responsible, should be in town at such an important juncture." He now advised Grey that Britain should move very cautiously on an immediate Russian proposal for a conference, to insure that it would not simply be used for the further dismemberment of Turkey or the overthrow of the Young Turks. In Hardinge's mind was the conviction that "Germany is of course an accomplice with Austria in encouraging any action likely to deal a severe blow to the Young Turk party," and thus to British influence at Constantinople, while Isvolski had only the cherished Straits in mind.[22]

Hardinge clearly was angered. "Of course we shall evidently have to recognize both the annexation of Bosnia and the independence of Bulgaria," he explained to Bertie, but neither without due compensation. Particularly annoying was the obvious collusion, "a deep-laid plot on the part of several Powers, which has been studiously concealed from us." Moreover, Britain had been in the midst of attempting to smooth Bulgarian-Turkish relations on the railway matter, with some hope of success. Worse of all, Aerenthal had told Goschen only days earlier that he did not believe in the rumors of a forthcoming Bulgarian declaration. Whatever the actual degree of Austro-Bulgarian collusion, Hardinge took Aerenthal's lie to Goschen as a personal affront.[23]

In the following days Grey and Hardinge worked closely together, Grey obviously agreeing fully with the policy Hardinge had recommended. Practically speaking, there was little choice. All the statements in the world that Turkey would need to have adequate compensation would bring no useful result unless the powers agreed, and Russia was most unlikely to cooperate unless given free passage of the Straits. Yet if Russia achieved this goal, as Hardinge pointed out, there would be a great outcry in Britain, unless something really substantial was done for Turkey which would both strengthen the Young Turks and show that the Entente powers supported them. Tyrrell, in this context, proposed that the Entente powers guarantee an international loan to Turkey for internal reforms. Grey preferred to consult first with Isvolski who was in London.[24]

Predictably, Isvolski wanted the Straits, but there was confusion and disagreement on what this meant: would "freedom of the Straits" mean that they would be open to all nations, or only to Russia? Grey and Hardinge could agree to the idea of a conference, a small diplomatic point for Isvolski while the Russian had gotten himself into a mess, he had in Hardinge's view been thoroughly cheated by Aerenthal, and as he himself pointed out, if he were completely discredited he might be thrown out of office (and Stolypin along with him).[25]

Passage through the Straits was another matter. Although Asquith and Grey would have accepted Russia's proposals, the rest of the Cabinet would not. On the twelfth, Isvolski dined at Grey's with Hardinge, Benckendorff, and Secretary of State for India Lord Morley, the five men trying to find a way out of the dilemma. Isvolski suggested that perhaps the Straits might be opened to belligerents if Russia was at war—an idea which at least contained the element of reciprocity the Cabinet demanded.[26]

Much time was spent in the ensuing weeks in the futile attempt to get the concerned powers to the conference table.

When Isvolski left for Russia, Grey and Hardinge were certain that he believed in Britain's good faith. To that extent, if Austria and Germany had intended to undercut the Entente by raising the question of the Straits in the worst way they had failed. Even Persia was not allowed to disrupt relations, although Russian officials continued to work unchecked in the interests of Russia and the Persian conservatives. The same dinner group, Morley above all taxed Isvolski with such Russian intrigues, but there was a problem with local agents. "We have had to suppress the truth and resort to subterfuge at times to meet hostile public opinion," Hardinge told Nicolson. "This is entirely owing to their lack of control over their officials." On the other hand, Hardinge still had faith in Tsar Nicolas, and he was instrumental in obtaining a letter from King Edward praising Isvolski, which Nicolson presented in a rare audience with the tsar.[27]

Fortunately, no armed Turko-Bulgarian clash occurred to test further international relations. The longer peace lasted, the more likely it was that some permanent settlement could be reached. Hardinge was to spend much time and energy in the next months trying to reconcile the widely diverse figures of what Turkey asked and Bulgaria (and Austria) offered in compensation. In January, however, an Austro-Turkish agreement was reached, considerably strengthening Aerenthal's position, and in April, Turkey recognized Bulgarian independence.

Another aspect was the proposed loan to Turkey. From the start this was to be a private rather than a government proceeding, and Hardinge suggested to King Edward that he might encourage Sir Ernest Cassel to take up the British third of a £1,500,000 loan. Hardinge had no hesitation about using Cassel's financial reserves but he despised the man personally, since he had seen Cassel bargain with Grey for a G.C.B. in return for a loan to the Bank of Morocco to support British interests in that beleaguered country. Hardinge recorded the incident in *Old Diplomacy,* but struck his real opinion from the final draft:

I was horrified at the sale of this greatest of English rewards

> to a German Jew financier for a sum of money however large, and I upbraided Grey for it and told him that he had depreciated the value of the honour. It is only right to say that Sir E. Grey had no appreciation of the value of honours and despised them.

Hardinge turned down a K.C.B. a few months later, with a disparaging reference to Cassel, but accepted the G.C.B. when he left the Foreign Office for India in 1910. When Cassel offered him the post of head of a newly formed National Bank of Turkey at £3,000–4,000 per annum, Hardinge refused and advised H. Babington Smith, who took the job, to hold out for no less than £10,000, which he did and successfully—"This little transaction gave me great pleasure as a set-off to Cassel's G.C.B." Hardinge also went out of his way to point out to Knollys that there had never been a case of a naturalized British subject like Cassel being made a peer, and "I hope there never will be!" Obviously, all was not sweetness and light in the royal circle of shadow advisers.[28]

Ambassador Metternich hoped at Christmas that there might be some slackening of the German naval program for economic reasons. If true, this good news was due in Hardinge's view to persistent British promises—notably by the prime minister—to continue to adhere to the two-power standard. In fact, he reasoned, if the Liberals had said this since they first came into power, the naval race might have eased already. But Britain would have to remain cautious in negotiations, for good reason.

> It is far more essential for us to have a good understanding with Russia in Asia and the Near East, than for us to be on good terms with Germany, and, since it is highly improbable that there can be any real improvement in the relations between Germany and France, it is absolutely vital to us to continue to support France, and to maintain what is now called the 'Triple Entente'.[29]

But at least one major crisis had been surmounted, and despite worries over alliances of both friends and potential enemies, the year had not gone badly. Grey in particular had played up well, and Hardinge was much more confident in his chief's knowledge and decisiveness than he had been two years earlier.[30]

Aside from necessary attention to the growing Austro-Serbian tension, the first weeks of 1909 were spent in planning a royal visit to Berlin for early February. The Foreign Office as usual thought first of the effect upon the Entente. Hardinge urged Nicolson to use every chance to tell Isvolski that in Britain's eyes the Entente came before even a reduction in the naval race—"urged" because Grey had not yet approved this suggestion, but Hardinge was convinced that he would.[31]

Hardinge was not sure until the end that he was to go himself, for the Cabinet insisted that a minister be in attendance. Grey did not wish to go, and since he had avoided previous journeys, his going would have attracted far too much attention. The party was a large one, including a reluctant Queen Alexandra but not Winifred, on duty as lady-in-waiting but with no desire to return to Germany. The trip was in some ways a nightmare, marred by a series of small incidents and accidents from the time the Channel was crossed 8 February. King Edward was feeling ill and longed for Biarritz; an alarming bronchial attack after dinner was passed off too easily by his doctor.[32] No major conversations were planned, but the king did discuss the naval question briefly with the kaiser, and Hardinge had his usual talk with Bülow, which covered much ground, especially on detailed Balkan issues and on the recent Franco-German incident at Casablanca in Morocco. The real issues, the naval race and the Baghdad Railway, were not discussed at all.[33]

When the trip was over, Grey and Hardinge were both concerned and annoyed at reports that Isvolski was suspicious once again. This predictable response not only irritated Entente relations but jeopardized the chance of perserving Austro-Serbian peace just when it seemed that Bülow might be cooperative on the Balkans. Without definite German assurances, all that could be done was to try to persuade Vienna to be reasonable, hope Bülow would cooperate, and then urge Russia to push Serbia into line. It was all very complicated and delicate, for Britain dared not risk a rebuff from Aerenthal or more suspicion from Isvolski.[34]

To make matters worse, when the test came Bülow said that action must be taken at Belgrade, not Vienna—meaning that his assurances to Hardinge were useless. By the end of February the situation was alarming, and Isvolski was no help.

> It is really too childish. If we only could get Isvolski to tell the Servians categorically that it is of no use for them to put forward claims to territorial compensation, there is very little doubt that we should be able to finish off this Balkan question within three weeks or a month. Unfortunately we cannot bring him up to scratch and, if any suggestion of that kind is made to him, he at once declares that he has been abandoned by France and England, and that he may in the future have to make other arrangements. If he could save his skin by doing so, I have no doubt he would; but he is in such a hopeless position that I think [he] will have to fall anyhow, unless he is able to assume a bold front and to face the Pan-Slavists.[35]

That Hardinge's comments from these weeks are sometimes quarrelsome or petulant can be explained in part by a serious bout of influenza which sent him to bed for nearly two weeks, and in part by his frustration over the Cabinet's decision to lay down only four capital ships in 1909. Hardinge, a staunch defender of naval supremacy, vented his spleen on Grey in a letter to Knollys:

> I always told you that Grey is a weak man. I thought that success had given him confidence & even strength, but as regards the latter characteristic I was mistaken. I expect that nothing can ever make a weak man a strong one and that it

> is a great mistake to ever think otherwise. The outlook is gloomy[.] Sir W. Churchill is the one man in the Cabinet who knows what he wants and how to get it.

The remark was atypical; of Churchill's many characteristics, Hardinge admired only his drive and determination, while he soon returned to a calmer appraisal of Grey when the foreign secretary suggested a compromise which would allow the construction of more ships if needed. In mid-March Hardinge returned to work, concerned to keep Grey in the midst of the fight, above all to hammer home the lesson of past British overtures for discussion of the naval race which Germany had so clearly rejected. Ironically, Hardinge was attacked for running Grey, but nothing shows Grey's independence of mind so clearly as this major problem.[36]

Hardinge also returned just in time for the temporary climax of the Balkan crisis. Bülow had acted at last, but in such a way as to force Russia—demonstrably unprepared for war—to abandon its encouragement of Serbian claims and to recognize Bosnia's annexation. Britain favored discussing several different proposals, but Isvolski had surrendered to what would come to be seen as a German ultimatum, on the condition that Britain did. Since it was impossible to be more royalist than the tsar, Britain agreed; Serbia in the end of March was forced to recognize the annexation and in effect to abandon its claims. Austria had won a victory, but a pyrrhic one, including as it did

> undying hatred from Russia, and possibly from Servia; unpleasantness with England and France; annoyance of German-Austrians at having two millions of Slavs added to the Slav majority in the monarchy; a wrangle with Hungary as to the future of the annexed Provinces—and possibly difficulty with Austrian Slavs. . . .

and all in return for the addition to the empire of two provinces which were Austrian to all practical purposes before the annexation, and the humiliation of Isvolski. Anglo-Austrian relations survived the Bosnian crisis, and in fact improved in the months that followed; on the other hand, the separate alliance systems had been that much more solidified by Austro-German and Anglo-Russian cooperation, whether Anglo-Austrian tension be seen as the result or the cause of closer ties between Britain and Russia.[37]

Even at that, Hardinge was worried by Isvolski's surrender to the implied threat of force.

> Do you not think [he wrote to Nicolson] that people who reflect will say to themselves: 'Is it not better for us to come to terms with Germany and Austria and leave France and England alone?'—or will they be farsighted enough to see that the loyal support which we have given them throughout this recent crisis may be of inestimable benefit to Russia if repeated at the time when she is engaged in a death struggle with Germany and Austria?

His own conclusion was that there was too much Germanophobia in Russia at the moment, but he was concerned for the future, above all if Isvolski fell and a more reactionary government came to power.[38]

If such government asked whether Britain would aid in a war against Germany and Austria, what should Britain's answer be? Hardinge recorded his own views on a question that might well become more than academic. France was weakened by internal struggles; Britain had made it clear that she would give Russia no more than diplomatic support in the Balkans; Russia had hardly recovered from the Japanese War; and German ambitions for dominaton in Europe remained unfulfilled. Thus if Russia asked for aid and was refused, "it is almost inevitable that Russia would be compelled by her military weakness to come to terms with Germany and to modify her attitude towards the aims of the Central Powers." Nor could France then stand isolated on the continent when Germany demanded a guarantee of neutrality in any Anglo-German war.

A possible alternative, which inspired Hardinge's memorandum in the first place, was a firm alliance with Russia, for firm alliances with France and Russia would certainly obviate the risk of total British isolation. Even then, so long as Britain's naval defenses remained intact, there was no cause for alarm. But it was very clear that British public opinion was not prepared for such an alliance and would not be so long as Russia remained under reactionary rule:

> it must not be forgotten that although from time to time there may be a reactionary wave in Russia the Russia of the future will be liberal and not reactionary, and it would be a mistake to prejudice future Anglo-Russian relations by an alliance between England and a reactionary Gov[ernmen]t in Russia which would not be regarded with sympathy in either country while the position of the necessity for a strong combination of Powers a few years hence to resist an attempt to create the permanent hegemony of Germany in Europe overshadowed the general political situation. Moreover public opinion in this country which is in complete sympathy with the liberal and constitutional development of Russia does not yet sufficiently grasp the danger to Europe of Germany's ambitious designs, though undoubtedly anxiety on this score is gradually growing. . . .

For these reasons, Nicolson, who steadily urged closer Anglo-Russian relations, was told by both Grey and Hardinge that an alliance was impossible. As Hardinge admitted privately, a return to power of the Conservatives might produce a movement towards Russia. "I naturally cannot say this to Grey & Asquith but I thought I would tell you privately what has been one of the determining factors to my mind in answering the question. . . ." For the time being, however, not even the term "Triple Entente" was to be used in any correspondence which might some day be published.[39]

What of the opposite possibility, an alliance with Germany? Britain had recently received an overture from Baron Kiderlen-Wächter, the German minister in Bucharest, close to Bülow and temporarily working in the Berlin Foreign Office. Kiderlen-Wächter suggested to Ambassador Goschen that both countries bind themselves not to make war on each other or join a hostile coalition, and to observe benevolent neutrality in case of war by either against a third party. Hardinge saw this as a simple trap, for while the agreement was in effect, Germany would be extending her hegemony over Europe. Then would come England's turn.

> if, relying upon a profusion of friendly assurances from Germany, which public opinion is always too ready to believe and to accept as genuine, England had in the meantime neglected to maintain an absolutely predominant naval supremacy, she would richly deserve the fate which would inevitably await her, and compel her for the first time in history to take her place amongst the satellites of the German constellation.

The very announcement of such an agreement would leave Britain totally isolated. Hardinge pronounced himself unworried that any British government "should ever be duped by such a transparent proposal," but it was as well to make the danger very clear: as he put it to Goschen, the German overture had "a delightful *naïveté*."[40]

Grey, Asquith, and the king all thought that Hardinge had made an able response, and he had no real fears that the offer would be taken up. Enlarging the British fleet was another matter, but Hardinge realized that Grey's cabinet position had been adopted to avoid a rupture; when the critical decision was made in July, Grey would indeed argue the absolute necessity of unquestioned naval security. Hardinge's failure of confidence had been only momentary. Meanwhile, when Germany returned to the proposal, she was told very plainly that no agreement was possible without a reduction in the German naval program (although the short-term excuse of a pending general election was also cited for putting aside the proposal for the time being).

A more difficult problem to deal with was Germany's attempt to drive a wedge between Britain and Russia. The kaiser and the tsar were scheduled to meet at Reval. William had issued the invitation, and Nicholas had not refused. "Were it not that I believe the Emperor Nicholas to be perfectly loyal to us, there would, I think, be great danger to the equilibrium of Europe from the impending visit"—Hardinge felt Isvolski's suspicions of British visits to Germany in reverse. Should the unlikely happen, however, "we shall simply revert to that position of isolation which some stupid person calls 'splendid,' and which is not dangerous to us provided we are really strong at sea."[41]

Hardinge's mind was also full of German plans for the invasion of England, Committee on Imperial Defence (C.I.D.) subcommittees on espionage (Hardinge, as permanent under secretary, supervised the expenditure of £40,000 a year on secret service), and the ever-present irritant of the Baghdad Railway; he was hardly likely to advocate negotiation of an Anglo-German treaty without the essential preliminary. As he wrote to Grey in August, "an agreement on naval affairs *must* come first. As a matter of fact anything further is really superfluous," a position which both Mallet and Tyrrell supported in separate letters to Grey and which Grey himself had already adopted. It was Hardinge, however, who saw to it that Russia was told of the German overtures:

> [I]t was a step upon which I insisted, although Sir Edward regarded it as a breach of confidence which would not be perpetrated in private life. I am quite confident, however, that, had we kept the matter absolutely secret, without telling the French and the Russians, as the Chancellor wished, the Emperor would have chosen the first opportunity to tell the French and Russian ambassadors at Berlin that we were negotiating with Germany behind their backs.

> When dealing with people of this kind one must have rather a different code of morals, and I think that the risks that we ran were so great as to amply justify us in the steps which we have taken.[42]

In the fall of 1909 Bülow's successor, Theobald von Bethmann-Hollweg, pursued a naval understanding with considerable zeal, but in the negotiations he and Foreign minister von Schön offered little more than a pledge not to speed up Germany's program; even that concession would have to be linked to a political agreement. But even the weakest general formula recognizing the staus quo was dangerous, for as Crowe put it, France would not regard it in a kindly manner if it meant the status quo in Alsace-Lorraine. Germany appeared willing to concede British naval supremacy—but as Hardinge pointed out in an important minute, Britain intended to preserve this in any case, and hardly needed to pay Germany for her recognition of a fact of life.

Nevertheless, no definite offer could be refused without submitting to the charge of insincerity. The best that could be done, as Grey told Metternich, was to await specific German proposals. When the proposals came at the end of October, they proved to be disappointing, for Britain would still require a vast building program merely to keep up a three to two ratio in dreadnoughts: "the vaunted concession is in reality no concession at all." The more Hardinge considered the offer, which he had to dissect for the Cabinet on Grey's behalf, the less it seemed to him that any useful result could come of it. If anything, his opposition was even stronger than it had been in the spring, above all to a political agreement which required Britain to stay neutral while Germany established her supremacy over Europe and which "would be a derogation from the honourable role which Great Britain has played in Europe for more than three hundred years and which has greatly contributed to the peace of the world."[43]

On the other hand, Hardinge had no objection to continued negotiation on the Baghdad Railway. Britain was in a strong position here, for she had the power to disapprove the customs duty increase which would be necessary to fund kilometric guarantees for the builders. Although the idea of a competitive concession in the Euphrates valley was seriously discussed, the better solution was to try to obtain control of the Persian Gulf end of the line, which would insure that the railway terminus on the Gulf would never be a threat to Britain. In the light of the continued inability to resolve the naval race, it also seemed wise at least to attempt a settlement with Germany on this other outstanding issue.[44]

The Baghdad Railway issue had complicating ramifications. The very fact of Anglo-German railway discussions aroused suspicians in St. Petersburg, for Isvolski had counted on Britain to block, not facilitate, the railway. Hardinge toyed with the idea of a rival line from Mohammera at the head of the Gulf to Khurramabad in western Persia, but he became convinced that the Baghdad line would be built, and better with Britain than without, if only from the viewpoint of finances and improved communications with India. Russia, with her own eye on future railway schemes, was not so easily persuaded. Yet another factor was future control over the oil fields of Mesopotamia, suddenly of real importance as the Admiralty converted from coal to oil-fired ships. The Foreign Office was as reluctant to see Germany control this resource as it was to see Germany develop the irrigation or port facilities of Iraq.[45]

Persia, too, was increasingly connected with the Baghdad negotiations, as Germany increased her commercial and political activities—not a difficult task since influential Persians found cooperation with Germany less contaminating than with Russia or Britain after the 1907 accord. Britain's policy since that time was simply to develop her own sphere and pay as little attention as possible to what happened in the north. "We have no desire to do anything to weaken or undermine the Russian position in the North of Persia. All we want is that their action should be in conformity with out agreement and with the principle of the independence & integrity of Persia." But these words of Hardinge's were for Isvolski's consumption. It was really not so easy to ignore the Russian invasion to relieve the siege of Tabriz in March 1909, but it was necessary to make the best of it. Russia could be asked to leave, but only politely; as Hardinge put it, they would leave in time, and if they left too soon, under pressure, and more disturbances occurred, they would simply march back—all the more likely to stay. Concessions to Germany, however much Germany might ask only for the open door and commercial equality, were another matter. The Foreign Office saw that at a minimum such concessions should be linked to German concessions on the railway, but even these would not persuade Britain to join in some general agreement.[46] By the time Hardinge left the Office in mid-1910, nothing had been agreed. The railway problem alone was settled on the verge of the war.

The year 1910 was, for Hardinge, one of fewer large-scale diplomatic problems, but considerable personal change. It began with an important election campaign, fought on issues of the budget, the powers of the House of Lords, and Irish Home Rule. Hardinge was not a political man, and for him the important result of such an election lay in the field of foreign policy. In that sense, the election did not worry him. He admired and worked well with Grey, but he had no fears that Balfour would accept the German offer should the Conservatives return to power. Hardinge preferred that the Liberals stay, but with a diminished majority which allowed them little leeway in foreign affairs: "This, I think, is the most desirable solution at the present time." As the election progressed, another fear occurred to him: if the radical wing of the Liberals commanded too much power, more conservative politicians would refuse office, particularly Grey, who professed indifference as to whether or not he stayed in the Cabinet. The real issue was not the German agreement, but constitutional matters, and Asquith would have to choose between Grey and Lloyd George; if it was the latter, Grey told Hardinge that he would resign ("He is full of brave words at present!" Hardinge wrote Knollys).[47]

Hardinge was disappointed, however, by the postelection Liberal surrender to the Irish nationalists on the question of reducing the power of the House of Lords. Again, Hardinge personally was inactive, but as a naturally conservative man he opposed any change in the basic constitution. Grey had not resigned, "squared," Hardinge felt, by references to the legitimate power of decision by an elective chamber as opposed to one which was hereditary. Hardinge had hoped that Grey, Haldane, Morley, and Crewe, the moderates, would hold out, although "I never expected much of the Prime Minister, who is an opportunist of the worst kind." Now the country was in for unicameral government. One of the worst aspects of the whole situation was dragging the king in to name the Liberal peers, if necessary. "The lack of patriotism amongst these party politicians is absolutely deplorable. Their whole aim is to stick to office, no matter at what sacrifice. I think I shall have to go and live in Greece, where they have at length realized that single chamber government is a farce and a fiasco."[48]

Even more disheartening was the illness and death of King Edward. In March the king went to Biarritz as usual, where he had time—despite persistent bad health—to write a long letter to Hardinge on the detailed plans for the reception of President Roosevelt in June. He returned at the end of April and fell ill at once, dying on 6 May. The effect on Hardinge was great, according to Margot Asquith. At Hardinge's house she encountered both Grey and Hardinge, who were "white with sorrow."[49] The king on his return had sent for Hardinge, but was too ill to see him.

It was a considerable wrench. Edward's friendship and support had been of great importance to Hardinge's career, and Hardinge had repaid him with loyalty and very close contact with the doings of the Foreign Office. The king was useful to Hardinge, but the relationship was reciprocal. Grey had not minded this link; it relieved him of a task he preferred not to shoulder—as long as Hardinge kept him informed. "I always took the greatest care to tell him of everything that passed between the King and me, unless it was a matter outside the interest of the Foreign Office which the King had told me in confidence.'' On the whole this was an accurate recollection, except where it was a question of influencing Grey himself. At the very last, for example, Hardinge was trying to persuade the king to see Grey, for Edward disagreed with Grey's constitutional position: Hardinge hoped that Grey would be persuaded, but it was also undesirable that there be any public display of coldness between king and minister.

The king and Hardinge often corresponded; when Edward was abroad, he expected Hardinge to write him weekly, and rarely failed to reply. At home, Hardinge was sent for once a week, often for a tête-à-tête breakfast at Buckingham Palace. Hardinge had his disagreements with the king, but they were occasional storms in a normally sunny atmosphere. Hardinge and Winifred both got on well in court circles and had close friends there in the queen, Princess Victoria, Knollys, and even Alice Keppel, whom Hardinge admired as much for her good influence and complete discretion as for her beauty and vivacity.

> There were one or two occasions when the King was in disagreement with the Foreign Office, and I was able through her to advise the King with a view to the policy of the Gov[ernmen]t being accepted. She was very loyal to the King and patriotic at the same time. It would have been difficult to find any other lady who would have filled the part of friend to King Edward with the same loyalty and discretion.

Hardinge had his disagreements with others of the king's close circle—Esher, Fisher, Soveral, Cassel—but there is no question that he missed the dead monarch, ''who had been so good to me, and whom I really loved as a man amongst men.'' Fortunately, Hardinge had much to do in the two weeks after Edward's death, with the arrangements for foreign missions coming to the funeral. Only then could he leave for a fortnight's trout fishing in Wales, "very glad to get away from London and all the gloomy association of the past fortnight."[50]

Hardinge was fortunate in another sense, for he was not to remain in London long. In the fall of 1910 he sailed for India with the rank and dignity of viceroy. The idea had first been brought forward by Knollys in January 1909, while Hardinge was staying at Windsor. Knollys, who knew Hardinge well and was no doubt familiar with his long-standing ambition to emulate his grandfather in India, asked him if he would like to succeed Lord Minto, whose term would expire the following year. Hardinge of course said yes, and Knollys put his name to the king. Edward was favorably disposed at first, although he was reluctant to lose Hardinge at the Foreign Office, "'but thought you would do India very well, and that you would *look the part*.'" Hardinge told only Winifred, for nothing was certain, "but I told her at the time, and never changed my opinion during the many ups and downs of my prospects during the following year, that I felt quite certain that I would get the post, and maintained my conviction at moments when things looked rather hopeless."[51]

As the months passed the prospects did indeed look hopeless, for by the new year Hardinge had an important challenger in Lord Kitchener, the hero of Omdurman and South Africa. Kitchener soon had his supporters, including the king, who was particularly persuaded of the need for a strong hand in India by the murder in London of Morley's political aide-de-camp by an Indian student. The Prince of Wales, Lord Roberts, and Lord Haldane at the War Office, who saw India as a good way to keep Kitchener away from Whitehall, agreed. Only Lord Morley took a strong stand against Kitchener. "Morley hates the *idea* of sending Kitchener out," wrote Sir Deighton Probyn, Keeper of the King's Privy Purse and a strong Kitchener man, "fearing people will say his (Morley's) policy has failed," and that Kitchener once there would take the bit in his teeth. More important, Kitchener would show India how Britain intended to rule in the future. Minto was another whose views might carry some weight, but Minto was careful not to take a clear-cut position.[52]

The king was Kitchener's strongest supporter and applied considerable pressure upon Asquith who, although opposed to sending the general, probably would have appointed him had Morley agreed. Asquith several times said that he intended to appoint Hardinge, but the king had decided that Hardinge was more useful where he was or, as second best, in the embassy at Paris that Hardinge would want some day. King Edward believed in a man sticking to his forte, and Hardinge was a diplomat, not an administrator. Asquith, according to Hardinge's own account, bowed to the king's request and said he would search for another name (Hardinge heard Sir George Murray of the Treasury mentioned). Edward's death, sad as it was, removed his opposition to Hardinge: after the funeral at Windsor, Morley—who had already made inquiries as to whether the viceroy could live on his salary—took Hardinge aside and asked him if he would like the job. When Hardinge said yes, Morley inquired if Hardinge was a "tariff reformer." "I was able to reply truthfully that, although owing to my official position I had never taken any part in politics, I was and always had been a free trader. Morley said that was the only point he wished to know, and that I might regard the matter as settled, but that for the time being I was not to tell anybody except my wife."[53]

Silence was required because Asquith had not made up his mind, or so Morley told Esher—an early supporter of Hardinge's and "absolutely the first to put the idea into J.M.'s head," but now a backer of Kitchener because that was the king's wish and Kitchener would know how to deal with nationalist agitation. But on 9 June, Asquith wrote to offer the job at last. Hardinge shared a congratulatory dinner three days later with Knollys, Soveral, and Esher, relieved that the tension was over. Kitchener had even passed him a message through Sir Walter Lawrence (Curzon's secretary in India) that a private income of at least £8,000 a year was necessary to do the job properly, though of course much depended upon the definition of "properly." Kitchener was hard hit by the news, having already appointed his personal staff; but Hardinge won, because his name was early in

Third secretary in Constantinople, 1882–84. (Dowager Lady Hardinge of Penshurst)

Winifred, Diamond, Alec, and Edd, December 1902. (Dowager Lady Hardinge of Penshurst)

House party at Sandringham, July 1895. Left to right: George, Duke of York; Princess Maud of Wales; Lady Hardinge (with violin); Duchess of York holding Prince Edward; Alexandra, Princess of Wales; Hon. Charlotte Knollys; Crown Prince Frederik of Denmark; Princess Victoria of Wales; Constantine, Duke of Sparta. (Royal Archives; reproduced by gracious permission of Her Majesty Queen Elizabeth II)

Reval, 1908. Central group, left to right: Queen Alexandra, Tsar Nicholas II, Lord Hardinge, King Edward VII. (Royal Archives; reproduced by gracious permission of Her Majesty Queen Elizabeth II)

King George V and Queen Mary leaving Delhi, 16 December 1911; Hardinge on right. (Royal Archives; reproduced by gracious permission of Her Majesty Queen Elizabeth II)

King George V and Lord Hardinge, Delhi, December 1911. (Royal Archives; reproduced by gracious permission of Her Majesty Queen Elizabeth II)

Viceregal splendor: Hardinge's record tiger and friends. (Dowager Lady Hardinge of Penshurst)

Delhi before the bomb; smiling Hardinges turn on to Chandi Chauk from Queens Gardens. (Dowager Lady Hardinge of Penshurst)

Delhi after the bomb, Lord Hardinge being lifted down. (Dowager Lady Hardinge of Penshurst)

Ambassador Hardinge (center) receives Lloyd George (third from right) in Paris, 1922. (Dowager Lady Hardinge of Penshurst)

Hardinge in retirement (left) with Caryle Hardinge (later 4th Viscount Hardinge, center) and Alex Hardinge (later 2nd Baron Hardinge of Penshurst). (Dowager Lady Hardinge of Penshurst)

the ring and because Morley would not have Kitchener on any terms.[54]

The usual letters of congratulation now poured in, including one from Joseph Wood, headmaster of Harrow, who gave the school a holiday at Hardinge's wish (Alec, down with measles, was unable to enjoy it), and Kitchener, who, nothing loath, hoped Hardinge would use his influence to assist Kitchener's appointment to Egypt. Grey's letter was typically touching. He was simply glad for Hardinge, "because you told me long ago that you would like it. . . .I do rejoice most sincerely as a friend, but I sigh as S. of S. for Foreign Affairs." Few of Kitchener's backers were seriously upset: King George V, who received Hardinge soon after his own accession, was typical, admitting that he had supported Kitchener but that he was now delighted with Hardinge's appointment.[55]

As was customary, Hardinge went to India as a peer, although he would have preferred to go as Sir Charles Hardinge, as his grandfather had gone as Sir Henry Hardinge, to be raised to the peerage as a reward when his term expired. The title was a problem, for Hardinge's elder brother was already "Viscount Hardinge"; Hardinge therefore took the style "Baron Hardinge of Penshurst." His brother suggested several alternatives such as Lord "Bidborough" or "Tonbridge," both locales of old family associations, for if Hardinge were ever raised to Viscount, there would be a problem of precedence. But Charles persisted, and "Hardinge of Penshurst" it was. One shock was a bill for £330 in fees for the creation, luckily waived by the Treasury under the circumstances.[56]

Far less personal was the matter of Hardinge's successor. His own choice was Sir Arthur Nicolson from St. Petersburg, and as soon as Hardinge had sounded him and found him willing though unenthusiastic, he pushed his name to Grey, who in turn needed little convincing since Nicolson had done so well in the Algeciras and Russian negotiations. But *The Times* had Nicolson picked as well, and Hardinge had to move circumspectly. It would be well, he urged Grey, to decide as soon as possible, "so as to prevent any attempts at wire-pulling from outside.'' Grey was annoyed at the press report: he had already obtained Asquith's approval but he had been unable to say anything to Nicolson until it was clear who would be viceroy of India.[57]

Nicolson took over on 1 October, but Hardinge was infrequently at the Office after Parliament rose for the summer. He had much preparing to do, and it was a quiet diplomatic season. He severed his connections with the Foreign Office with no assurance that he would return (though he still hoped for Paris some day). He could look back to a successful tenure—successful in enlarging and solidifying the Entente, for its own sake and to guard against what Hardinge was now convinced was German hostility: agreements conceived to avoid colonial clashes were now primarily to prevent German hegemony. It is difficult, of course, to separate Grey from Hardinge and Hardinge from the other principal staff members, for they shared many common attitudes and they worked together well in pursuit of common objectives. To Grey fell the responsibility for the political, internal side of foreign policy, as well as the major decisions themselves—Cabinet, Commons, public. Hardinge's task was the running of the Office, the administration of policy, and smooth relations with the court. It was a happy partnership and an important one, but Hardinge now had a completely different set of problems to face in India.

VI The Delhi Durbar

Hardinge never thought seriously of declining the appointment as viceroy and governor-general of India: "it is an absolute fact that twenty years before I went to India. . .my mind was made up that. . .my real ambition was to follow in the footsteps of my grandfather. . . ."[1] His grandfather was not the only Indian connection. His father had served and painted in India, and a good many other family members had Indian experience (typical of any large nineteenth-century English family with political and military links). His uncle, General Sir Arthur Edward Hardinge (cousin Arthur Hardinge's father), had been commander in chief of the Bombay Army, 1880–85. Hardinge was particularly proud of an even earlier association, commemorated by memorials in both Bombay and St. Paul's cathedrals: in 1808 his great-uncle, Captain George Nicholas Hardinge, R.N., in command of the frigate *San Fiorenzo* (thirty-six guns), had been killed at the age of twenty-eight in a lengthy but victorious struggle off Bombay against the bigger French frigate *La Piedmontaise* (fifty guns), terror of the Malabar coast. It was indicative of Hardinge's Indian dreams that he referred to the captain and his monument in his first speech in Bombay. India, in other words, was not simply another post abroad.

> I left England full of enthusiasm for my great undertaking and more than happy at the complete realization of my highest ambition. I appreciated fully the immense difficulties before me and the heavy responsibilities of the office I was to hold. I recalled that my own grandfather must have felt as I was feeling and that in the face of great trials and dangers he had achieved lasting success, and I hoped that I might have the strength, wisdom, and courage to do the same. I was fully aware of my own limitations and was very diffident, though not afraid. Had I known all that was to befall me before I set foot again on the shores of England, how different my feelings would have been from what they were on that November morning. What a mercy it is that the future is a closed book.

He expected that India would not be totally strange, as he explained in a speech at a banquet given him by the County of Kent:

> Surrounded as I have been during my youth by Indian works of art brought home by my grandfather and by my father, by books on India, and by pictures containing views of India and the ordinary episodes of Indian life, I cannot help feeling that much that I shall see for the first time when I reach India will be familiar to me, at least in imagination. . . .[2]

But India was no longer the India of his grandfather, and Hardinge, whose Indian experience was in negotiating with the India Office on spheres in Persia or influence in Afghanistan, had to deal with different problems than the Sikh wars—and deal with them in an atmosphere in which the power of the viceroy was considerably restricted over what it had been even a decade earlier under Curzon. The speed of telegraphic communications, the close attention of Parliament, even the history of Curzon's own viceroyalty had all combined to put much more power in the hands of the India Office and its secretary. Kitchener, for that reason, would have been a bad choice as viceroy: the independent commander of South Africa or the Sudan could not have used the same formulas in treating Indian nationalism.

The general situation in India in 1910 has been thoroughly studied by a number of able scholars, as thoroughly as the subsequent period from 1910 to the end of World War I has been neglected. Put briefly, the last years of the nineteenth and first of the twentieth century had witnessed the substantial growth of an educated class of Indians who felt entitled to a larger say in the governance of India and who were increasingly vocal in their criticism of the regime's failures to provide greater Indian representation in other areas as well. In the years just prior to Hardinge's arrival, for example, economic policies produced a steady increase of prices, mainly for the benefit of the manufacturing interests of Britain, or so it appeared to Indian commentators. An atmosphere of distrust began to prevail in Indo-European relations, not among the princes and rural magnates encountered by aristocratic Englishmen or in the still isolated preserve of the Indian army, but certainly among the political leaders of the Indian National Congress. Such leaders, and the politicians and lawyers who supported them, were viewed as "disloyal." Although they objected to the stigma, disloyal they certainly were if loyalty meant defence of unchallenged perpetual British rule.

Specific grievances had arisen which gave the nationalist movement increasing life, but none so rankled as Curzon's partition of Bengal, made primarily for adminstrative reasons. Except among adversely affected British business communities, the reduction of the administrative burden of Bengal by the separation of Bihar and Orissa would probably have caused little excitement. Not so the division of Bengal itself. Minto, Hardinge's immediate predecessor, upheld the partition, convinced that revocation would only be taken as a surrender to agitation—always a fear when the prestige of the "raj" was at stake. The result had been rapid growth of the nationalist movement, demanding *swaraj* (loosely, "self-government"), on the one hand, and engaging in an active terrorist campaign on the other.

Bengal, again, was the principal scene of *dacoitis* (violent gang robberies). But outrages which captured the attention of home and government circles could occur anywhere, even London. In 1908, the wife and daughter of a British lawyer were killed by a bomb thrown into their carriage in Muzaffarpur, and Sir Andrew Fraser, the lieutenant governor of Bengal, was wounded by an assassin; in mid-1909, Lt. Col. Sir W. Curzon-Wyllie, known to many as a friend of Indian students, was assassinated in London (Curzon-Wyllie was Morley's A.D.C.; it was this murder which particularly alarmed King Edward). In November, Viceroy and Lady Minto were bombed in their own carriage at Ahmadabad, near Baroda; luckily the bombs, made from coconuts, hit soft sand and failed to explode immediately. The next month a retired tax collector was shot in Nasik; in January 1910, an Indian deputy superintendent of police was shot dead in the Calcutta High Court.

The government's answer was threefold. With respect to terror, the policy was to repress sedition wherever possible. Police controls were expanded in the Seditious Meetings Act (1907, 1911), the Explosive Substances Act (1908), and the Indian Criminal Law Amendments Act (1908), which together allowed the government to keep tight control of political activity. Legislation was inaugurated or extended to permit suppression of inflammatory newspapers (Indian Newspapers Act, 1908; Indian Press Act, 1910). Unfortunately, jailed editors and closed newspapers hardly silenced a critical native press; they did create embarrassing legal cases and some minor martyrs. Nor did some liberals at home view suppression of a free press as the best of all possible imperial policies.

A second approach was to play upon the concern of Indian Muslims that their claim for adequate representation in appointments to government positions—as in Indian affairs generally—was going by default. In any case, the Muslims of Bengal were not offended by a partition which created a Muslim majority in the eastern province. In 1906 the All-India Muslim League was established in Dacca, and although the government did not officially recognize this body as representing Muslim opinion, it tended to lean in that direction. This policy was in part born out of sympathy for the Muslim cause, but the willingness to listen to Muslim representations surely stemmed from awareness, overt in some, unconscious in others, that one way to preserve the raj was to "divide and rule."

The third means of coping with Indian demands was to inaugurate a policy of gradual reform, sufficient to appease the legitimate and moderate demands of loyal India. To this end Minto and Morley had jointly authored a series of measures which went into effect in 1910. The reforms seem small enough in the aftermath of Indian independence, but at the time they were major, even revolutionary, acts. Most important in the public eye was the first appointment of an Indian to the viceroy's Executive Council—astonishing indeed to those who thought that no Indian could be trusted in a real test. Indians were also appointed to the less important Secretary of State's Council in London. More significant in the long run, however, was the extension of the size and extent of Indian representation in the several provincial legislative councils. The provision that such representation would be communal undermined for many critics the value of the concession, for it only applied the law of "divide and rule"; but the government had no intention of going further, particularly since an "official" majority (the device by which the government secured a majority in various councils through its own nominations and appointments) would be eliminated in the provincial—but no other—councils. Morley had promised greater Indian representation, but not the establishment of parliamentary democracy in India. Hardinge thus arrived precisely at a time when new and major steps had been taken, and it was his job to make them work—not to carry them further.

Hardinge was appointed by a Liberal goverment, but his views were conservative. He would have to see for himself, but he went to India, as he put it to Gorst who faced somewhat similar problems in Egypt, with no prior commitment to the view held by radical Liberals "in favour of self-government for all communities, whether they are capable of governing themselves or not." To his old friend Lord Crewe (who would replace Morley as secretary of state for India in November 1910), he explained that he looked forward to five years which "may be a period of consolidation of the great reforms bestowed upon the people by this Government, and of conciliation of all races and creeds."[3] Hardinge did have an ideal, however, stemming from his diplomatic experience—the undramatic one of finding equitable, quiet, useful solutions to real problems, for he believed that problems had solutions (a statement not necessarily true of all professional politicans). There have been worse ideals; but much would depend upon what he found in India.

There were of course arrangements to make and new honors to post—the viceroy was head of the Indian Orders, so Hardinge now acquired Grand Crosses of the Star of India and the Indian Empire (G.C.S.I., G.C.I.E.). But family and salary were both problems. For some time the Hardinges were reluctant to take Diamond, for the conditions were reported to be bad and her health was always delicate. Several doctors advised that she could go, however, and Lord Lansdowne said that his daughter, about the same age when he had been viceroy, had done well in India. The Hardinges accepted this advice gladly, for it was bad enough to leave Edd at Sandhurst and Alec finishing Harrow.[4]

The biggest headache was money, particularly after Kitchener's warnings. Curzon invited Hardinge to Hackwood and went over his own viceregal accounts (kept, typically, in Curzon's own hand). Curzon had spent a great deal but his expenses had included such unnecessary items as a complete retinue of nine hundred with bodyguard and a band at dinner every night. More reassuring was Lansdowne's advice that he had saved £20,000 during his term. As it happened, the Hardinges managed to live within their income (roughly £16,500 per annum after taxes), though not with Curzonian splendor. The early years were costly, with royal durbars and the like, but the latter were less so, not least because of the war. Hardinge never had reason to complain of the efficiency of his military secretary, Lt. Col. (Brig. Gen. Sir) F. Maxwell, who along with ceremonial life and tours managed all of the viceroy's household finances.[5]

Staff appointments demanded attention. Lord Errington, Hardinge's valued private secretary, stayed on under Nicolson in the Foreign Office. After considerable thought, Hardinge appointed as a replacement (Sir) James Du Boulay, then secretary to the Bombay government. The appointment proved a good choice and since the "P.S." handled the viceroy's time, papers, and interviews, it was an important one. Other staff included the necessary A.D.C.s, Hardinge's butler from St. Petersburg days, his valet of seven years, Winifred's maid, Diamond's nurse, and a French chef.[6]

August and September were months of vacation, but Morley traveled to the Hardinges' rented house near Penshurst to discuss Indian prospects. Minto had a running complaint against India Office interference in the details of Indian administration, but Morley assured Hardinge that "he had absolute confidence in me and that as soon as I am in the saddle in India he looks forward to throwing the reins on the horse's neck." Morley gave Hardinge the impression that he did not care much for Minto, and that he was annoyed that Minto claimed credit for the recent reforms. Perhaps the two did not discuss Morley's private correspondence with the several provincial governors—another grievance of Minto's and an issue upon which Hardinge had similar views—but they certainly did discuss King George V's desire to visit India. The king had wanted to return since his visit as Prince of Wales in 1905–6, and from the time of his coronation he wished to crown himself emperor at Delhi. In early September he spoke to Asquith, who advised that Morley must be consulted. Delays followed, and only after Hardinge sailed for India did the Cabinet approve the visit.[7]

October brought much packing and preparation, and two nerve-wracking speeches to Kent and the old Harrovians at the

Savoy. Further interviews with Morley, Haldane (regarding an Indian Cadet Corps), and Asquith (on the king's visit), a farewell dinner from the Foreign Office, a final luncheon with the king and queen (including Hardinge's new honors and the Order of the Crown of India for Winifred), and they were off, leaving London on 2 November. Hardinge nearly had his pocket picked, and because of the enthusiasm of friends seeing them off was actually left behind by the train, which had to return for him.[8] By the eighteenth he was at Bombay, landing at the Apollo Bundar for an official reception from the governor, Sir George Clarke.

Clarke had hoped to be named viceroy and, in his sixties, knew the chance would not come again. He was Hardinge's first conquest in India, although he still feared that the new viceroy would find "that the huge mountain of a gov[ernmen]t machine at Simla will effectively cut him off from me." But Clarke promised their mutual friend Valentine Chirol of *The* (London) *Times* to give the new viceroy all possible support, despite his doubts about Hardinge's untested administrative ability.[9]

On 21 November, after an impressive journey across India, the Hardinges arrived at Government House in Calcutta. "As I entered the great marble hall the first picture to catch my eye was that of my grandfather, who seemed to be looking towards me, and I felt this was of good omen." The Mintos did not leave for two days, a source of considerable embarrassment to Hardinge (Minto had a horse running in a race), but on the afternoon of the twenty-third Hardinge was at last formally sworn in and entered upon his duties as viceroy.[10]

Government House, their new residence, was an impressive building, well suited for official ceremonies but very awkward for daily life, with living rooms separated from reception rooms by long corridors. "I remember that I had to walk over 250 yards on the same floor to reach my daughter's room from my own bedroom." Golf and riding were available, although Hardinge discarded the custom of early morning exercise, preferring to relax in this way after work. Winifred was soon busy on the extensive charitable work expected of the vicereine, as much at least as frequent illness permitted, giving special attention to hospitals. Diamond had her own staff to keep her occupied: "She has one whose sole duty seems to me [to] give her dog its dinner! You will hardly believe me when I tell you that we have 500 servants in this house. What they all do beats me entirely."[11]

The work itself was never-ending. "I could work all day and all night if I wanted to, but I do not want," Hardinge confessed to Sanderson. "However I do my nine or ten hours a day and manage to get through it all." As always, public speaking was the grueling part of the job, but at least the reaction was favorable from the press, "who are unanimous in saying that I half told them nothing, which is exactly what I intended. I ought to be a finished orator by the time I return to England."

Much of the work was interviewing. "One has however to be very careful & astute," he explained to Bertie, "as the Hindus are quite unfathomable themselves & are always trying to catch you out. They are as clever as monkeys, but not really a nice race." Hardinge had years of experience at being diplomatic in interviews: to that extent his training was actually excellent preparation for the position of viceroy. He knew, however, that his sudden popularity might be short-lived. "Most people are rather a success in their first year as they have not had time to say 'no', but the time must come when 'no' has to be said & then popularity begins to wane. I do not think that would upset me but both Curzon & Minto writhed under it."[12]

The viceroy did not work alone, but had by necessity to rely upon an Executive Council, with members for finance, home affairs, public works, commerce and industry, education, and law, in addition to the commander in chief who oversaw military affairs. Foreign matters were traditionally the preserve of the viceroy himself, but he did require a secretary for the Foreign Department for administrative duties. Hardinge had little need of advice in the larger context of world affairs, but the Foreign and Political Department also controlled relations with the Native States. Hardinge's choice for this position was Sir Henry McMahon, Resident in Baluchistan, who knew the frontier and possessed a pleasing, gentlemanly personality, "but slow and not too bright." Hardinge was to be greatly surprised when McMahon was selected during the war as Kitchener's successor in Egypt—an appointment on which the viceroy was not consulted and which he afterwards put down to the simple misunderstanding in London of the function of the Indian secretary to the Foreign Department.[13]

To the extent that Hardinge had supervised a substantial government department with many lines of communication leading to his desk, his tenure at the Foreign Office was surprisingly good preparation. His first impression of the system reflected this, for he found the staff work to be reasonably well done, but economy was eminently desirable in the amount of minuting which various officials added to the files. He promised to set a good example himself.[14] It was an excellent principle, for the amount of work was great and would increase with the approaching royal visit and durbar.

The two days in Calcutta before Minto's departure had already introduced Hardinge to the outstanding internal problem of "sedition" and the government of India's policy of legal repression wherever possible. A series of trials was in progress as usual. "I began to feel that if only the trials . . . could be finished and set aside there might be some hope of peace." He certainly wished to end the agitation, which he blamed mainly on the much criticized partition of Bengal. Enemies of partition hoped that at the durbar the king might announce its reversal. Hardinge at that time, a year before the durbar, had not the slightest intention or desire for such a reversal—but the link between sedition trials and durbar was in his mind from the start.

In Hardinge's opinion, many of the prosecutions in progress would end unsuccessfully and should be brought to an immediate conclusion. His first Executive Council, in which he expressed these views, was properly noncommittal, except for Ali Imam, Law Member an sole Indian on the Council, who put up a paper asking clemency in sedition cases and thanked Hardinge for his views. The immediate problem was Sir Edward Baker, lieutenant governor of Bengal, and his legal advisors. Hardinge soon sent for Baker, "a nice little man but a firebrand & the cause of our difficulties," to explain to him his views, that "pacificiation is in the air and . . . it would be very fatal to miss the present opportunity." No further prosecution would be initiated without his own personal consent, a prohibition which Baker "received with an ill-grace." Hardinge found Baker hard to decipher: "a curious mixture, at one moment he is a friend of some Indians of doubtful reputation and the next moment he is burning to prosecute for some rather trifling incident."[15]

Hardinge would have preferred to make a clean sweep of the Bengal legal luminaries. Lord Crewe, who took over the India Office in November (Morley had taken the opportunity of the change in viceroys to retire), expressed similar views and even suggested that Hardinge exercise personal supervision over justice in Bengal. Natural conservatism made Hardinge resist both this and demands to investigate the Bengali police for brutality and incompetence. He thus found himself very quickly between conflicting pressures, but, like most viceroys, emerged more as defender of Indian bureaucracy to home authorities than vice versa.[16] In this case, consultation with Sir Lawrence Jenkins, chief justice of Bengal, did result in bargains with some accused culprits, who pleaded guilty and were released on good behavior.[17]

Hardinge's problems with Bengal were not over, but there were other ways of working for pacification. He was under pressure from the start to extend the temporary "Seditious Meetings Act," due to expire in March 1911. It had been passed in 1907 but was expanded to include all of India in 1910. This was an awkward situation, because Indian feeling was strongly against the act while all the local provincial governments wished to have it permanently in their arsenal. Hardinge felt it was an error to apply the act permanently to all of India when only the two Bengals were disturbed. In March, the act came before the Legislative Council (this body, more public and less powerful than the viceroy's Executive Council, had elected members as well as government officials). Hardinge argued that it was essential in the control of terrorism, and since the viceroy was chairman of this assembly, not surprisingly he had a cooperative official majority with which to override any opposition. He let it be known, however, that the act would come into effect only in specially proclaimed districts as needed, and in fact he did not have cause to make such a proclamation while viceroy.[18]

Bengal was a persistent worry, but Hardinge's most immediate concern in the short time between his arrival and his first official tour (April 1911) was the proposed durbar and its many ramifications. The ceremonial arrangements themselves would be enormous, and required much detailed attention. For this, Hardinge soon appointed a committee under the presidency of Sir John Hewett, lieutenant governor of the United Provinces, who was temporarily relieved of other duties; he kept in close touch by putting Maxwell, his military secretary, on the committee. Lord Curzon had been responsible for an elaborate durbar for King Edward's coronation in 1903 (the king had not been present in person), and Hardinge and others always had comparisons in mind.[19]

Most important was the inevitable "boon" or concession which in the old Indian tradition would be expected of the king-emperor. Suggestions poured in, but in the Executive Council any large projects which were mentioned met insuperable difficulties: remission of land taxes would be too costly; reduction of the salt tax would not really reach the lower class. Prisoners might be freed, more lands made available for military colonization in the Punjab, or famine loans renounced, but these were hardly the "big" idea expected in the king's name.[20] Crewe in London was also besieged with proposals, and was particularly afraid that the king was attracted to the idea of elevating Bengal into a presidency, similar to Bombay and Madras. It was not at all clear how this could be done without reversing the policy of partition.[21]

Hardinge agreed that Bengal was dangerous to meddle with. By early January (with the durbar set for early December), he had definitely settled on a large technical education scheme, originally proposed by Valentine Chirol, as the only feasible substantial concession yet suggested, and so he wrote to the king. The main point in its favor was that it would counter the argument that Britain merely exploited India without giving anything in return, an argument in which "there is unfortunately a certain amount of truth." He tried to let the king down gradually on Bengal, where there was not only the problem of reversal of policy: a governor in Calcutta might well be only a sinecure, overshadowed by the presence of the viceroy. To Crewe, he was considerably franker:

> I am sure it would not do. It would be a reversal of the policy of the last few years and would be regarded as a concession to noisy clamour. It would be a severe blow to the loyal section of the Indian people, which after all is by far the largest section, and it would convince them that it is only necessary to go in for sedition and crime to eventually obtain any object they may desire. . . .The best thing to be done is to allow the suggestion to quietly drop altogether.[22]

The king refused to let the matter drop, urged on, according to Crewe, by Sir Walter Lawrence, Curzon's private secretary at the time of partition and a strong opponent of the measure. Late in January the king asked Crewe again if the matter could be mentioned at the durbar. Crewe temporized but felt obliged again to ask Hardinge if there was any possibility of reverting to the "status quo ante Curzoneum," not perhaps in complete detail, but by establishing some federal enclave for the viceroy in Calcutta, much like Washington, D.C.[23]

Hardinge was difficult to persuade. Feeling about the partition, he responded, had nearly disappeared; "what we want is quiet, and any tinkering with what was done six or seven years ago would raise a terrible storm. I shudder to think of it." Nor did the idea of an enclave appeal to him; as he pointed out to Baker, rather prophetically, if ever a Bengal presidency was created, "the Government of India had better clear out and go elsewhere.'' The idea of transferring the capital from Calcutta was hardly new, and Delhi had been discussed as an alternative at least since the days of the Mutiny. It was once again in the air when Hardinge arrived.[24]

On the other hand, moving the Bengali government out of Calcutta really was impossible from every standpoint. Arguments in favor of the status quo are always ready to hand, and this case they were numerous, from the existence of that status itself for five and a half years, through the law courts and the university, to the fact that Muslims who had been pleased by the partition in the first place, and who had been encouraged in the development of provincial pride in Eastern Bengal, would now regard reversal as a Hindu victory.[25] Hardinge passed all the arguments home, and for the time being the idea was dropped. Unfortunately, it appeared that the authorities at home would not accept the substitute of education, or even another new proposal which Hardinge thought a bit ''thin''—that the income from cotton excise duties be used for education.[26]

Hardinge made one last appeal to the king. An educational boon ''is the only thing that would make a real and lasting impression, and it is what the extremists dread most as they think it would convince the waverers once and for all that we are treating India in a disinterested manner.'' He had a personal reason for this plea as well. As ex officio chancellor of Calcutta University, he had made an early morning surprise visit to student hostels and emerged badly shocked by what he had seen. One result was his insistence that the Eduction Department spend more on such facilities—''a very useful connection for me between cause an effect.'' He was equally discouraged by the ''futility'' of the education provided for many, based as it was on rote memorization of undigested data, unassimiliated because of linguistic inadequacy. Of the twenty thousand students in the Calcutta system, perhaps one in ten would get the government job to which all aspired. Technical education might do something to alter this system.[27]

But Hardinge was by mid-March mired in details of the durbar and of the Legislative Council, which kept him in the chair for long and often wasted hours while he had other work to do. Cost of the durbar was a particular worry; that expenses would be large mattered less than that they would be larger than Curzon's. "Curzon always tried to make out that his Durbar cost only £140,000, but the figures were faked and it cost more than half a million"—by "faked" he meant put under the heading of regular departmental expenses. The new durbar was likely to cost a crore of rupees (roughly £660,000), although £1 million had been allocated.[28]

But each detail presented some difficulty, particularly since the king wished to consider each point personally, and had the habit of asking anyone who had been to India for his view. The separate postdurbar trips for the king (shooting in Nepal) and queen (sight-seeing in Rajputana); the king's means of transport in the opening ceremonies (he unwisely chose a horse over an elephant, and, in his field marshal's uniform, was unrecognized by Indian observers); the site and form of the durbar amphitheater; the king's staff, his camp, his heralds, the decorations. . .this was too high, that too low, too many of these, not enough of those—it was a nightmare for all concerned, not least McMahon, master of ceremonies, in charge of decorations for individuals. "I shall not sleep comfortable until it is well over," Hardinge confessed to Chirol.[29]

A letter to Curzon from this period reflects Hardinge's temper:

> Some of the suggestions that I get from home are really quite impossible, and I wonder who the originators may be. . . . I do not go into the question of the expense of your Durbar, as from what I hear the expenditure on that occasion was debited in an entirely different manner as to what is now being done by the Finance Department. . . .

Curzon was taken aback (not a normal condition for him). "My dear Charlie . . . You are certainly very down on any suggestions about the Durbar, and I shall save my skin by making no more! . . . I really do not think we are all such nincompoops at this end as seems to be supposed. Some of us have even had some experience of a Durbar.'' Curzon was not about to give up, possessed of what Crewe called ''George Curzon's peculiar incapacity for understanding what is, and what is not, the proper occasion for interfering in other people's affairs,'' and viceroy and ex-viceroy continued to exchange politely hostile missives on a host of subjects over the next five years.[30]

By the end of March, many durbar details remained unsettled. Hardinge closed a tiring Legislative Council session fairly confident that he had done well in preserving the flow of debate (though seldom interfering directly), and managing successfully to navigate the shoals of Indian politics as represented by this body. The Seditious Meetings Act required all his talents, but he took new confidence from the experience, ''quite a rhetorical success such as I have never known before.'' His greatest relief was the absence of expected criticism of durbar expenses by nonofficial members.

Social responsibilities had been equally taxing, from his first levee of nineteen hundred people, which he finished sitting down, exhausted (this news prompted a letter from Curzon on the subject of how levees should be arranged). Two or three dinners a week, concerts for four hundred (Winifred played), garden parties for two thousand, entertainment for the visiting German crown prince which won him a fine portrait of the Kaiser by Laszlo, rather an embarrassment in years to come:[31] it was with considerable relief that Hardinge greeted the end of the session on 27 March; the next day he was off on a tour covering more than two thousand miles.

The first stop was Delhi, where Hardinge went over the durbar ground. He estimated that twenty thousand workers were already on the job, but directives had to be issued on several matters including the cleaning and repair of various buildings in the Red Fort, where ceremonies were to take place. From Delhi he was off to the Punjab to visit the battlefields so important in his grandfather's career. At Ferozeshah, where a costly victory had been won in 1845, he was treated to a magnificent reception from the Sikhs, including three grizzled veterans who had been at the battle as boys; in his official durbar he was presented with several trophies from the battlefield. At Lahore, Hardinge held another durbar in the audience chamber of Ranjit Singh, founder of the Punjab Sikh kingdom—the same reception room where his grandfather had declared the annexation of the Punjab. His frequent references to his grandfather's associations with the Sikhs apparently struck a responsive chord.

From Lahore (where Winifred stayed) Hardinge made for the frontier, visiting Quetta, where he held a great durbar in Sandaman Hall, full of Baluchi chiefs, and inspected the garrison and staff college. At the Afghan frontier itself, he "looked with curiosity, but without any envy" across into Afghanistan, and noted the preparations made for a rapid British advance to Kandahar in case of need. Karachi, the final major city on the tour, was unimpressive, but the victory opened the Hardinge Bridge, a substantial span of over fifteen hundred feet across the Indus. After the Sind Desert and Bahawalpur, Hardinge was happy to reach Dehra Dun for a fortnight's rest complete with a golf course, tigers, and stags—it was the place he liked best in all of India. The trip as a whole had shown him new areas of India, although his fifteen to twenty speeches (ten in four days alone) were the usual ordeal. In the first week of May, however, he was off to Simla, the summer capital, and work.[32]

The Hardinges found Simla very compatible, for Viceregal Lodge, new for Dufferin in the 1880s, was much like an English country house, with fine reception rooms to which Hardinge added extra bedrooms and a large room for the Legislative Assembly. The viceroy was truly king in this small official world, packed during the hot months with much of the all-Indian bureaucracy. When the Hardinges tired of Simla itself, they could retreat to a weekend lodge at Mashobra, seven miles and a thousand feet distant, with fine views of the Himalayas. Simla life was a mixture of holiday and office work; the government continued to operate, but there was also a gay social whirl, with nightly dances. "Fortunately I am not expected to go to them," Hardinge explained to Sanderson, "but I think it very hard for all the young men who are mostly clerks in Government offices and have to be in their offices at 10 in the morning." Hardinge, however, had much to do as usual and, also as usual, Bengal, and Bengali justice, was the principal concern.[33]

It was not simply a question of misguided prosecutions and obstreperous advocates. "The fact is," Hardinge reported to Morley, "there has been no Government of India during the last two years, and affairs have been allowed to drift in the two Bengals with the absurd idea that there should be no interference with the Local Governments." Members of the Executive Council persistently urged this principle, above all Sir Robert Carlyle (Public Works) and Sir John Jenkins (Home Member); Hardinge openly accused the latter of writing disloyal minutes, for which the man appeared properly chastened.[34]

To Hardinge, there was little point in having a "Governor-General in Council" if he, or they, could not interfere when necessary. By the end of May, the Council was more cooperative; "were it not for the maladministration of the two Bengals, and the Durbar, I could sit here with my arms crossed and have a very jolly time." The durbar could be dealt with by detailed attention, but the maladministration required constant hammering, including the establishment of a strong river police force on launches, increased subordinate police, more armed officers, and better communications—it was uphill work. Sir L. Hare (lieutenant governor of Eastern Bengal and Assam) and Baker in the west both had to be persuaded to take action, and Hardinge did his best within the limits he had set of not taking direct control. His words could be strong, for example to Hare: "I wish you and your officers to understand that we expect the Government of Eastern Bengal to pull itself together and to set work to restore order."[35]

Hardinge did interfere to order arrested but released dissidents to be watched openly, but this was a security measure for the king's approaching visit. In general his policy was to goad the authorities into action, while not himself rushing into precipitate and irrevocable decisions. He offered no radical solutions, but he rejected the obvious, easy alternative of fobbing off responsibility through accusations of incompetence against uncontrollable subordinates. Part of the problem was overcome when in mid-June Baker asked for a leave of absence which proved the preface to retirement.[36]

That such measures as a new governor and river police did not get to the heart of the matter was uppermost in Hardinge's mind, even when considering the durbar and the boon. He had not abandoned education; quite the contrary, there was a growing demand for free education at all levels in India, and the Education and Finance Departments agreed that such a gift would cost some £6.5 million (not high for 250 million people, when at home Britain then spent £18 million on 45 million). Obviously a scheme of such magnitude would take years to fund and establish (he would start with free but not compulsory elementary education), but to Crewe, now back at the India Office, he enthusiastically supported a memorandum on the subject from Harcout Butler (Member for Education). Unfortunately, there was no assurance that home authorities would accept elementary education any more than technical education—and opponents in India claimed that few people would really be affected by a measure which would give the government unwanted responsibility for every problem in the entire educational system.[37]

Hardinge was thus still searching for the grand gesture and for solutions in Bengal when in mid-June Sir John Jenkins suggested that the durbar proclamation announce the move of the Imperial capital to Delhi. Hardinge suddenly saw the light with this paper, for the linkage of this scheme—bombshell, really—with the reunification of Bengal, which had been discussed ever since Hardinge arrived, might kill two very large birds with one stone. Neither Delhi as capital nor Bengali reunification was Hardinge's idea, but it became "my scheme," as he called it in his memoirs while giving proper credit to Jenkins, by his linking of the two in one durbar proclamation and taking public responsibility for the decision. He knew there would be a howl of anguish from Calcutta's British population, and worried whether the shift to Delhi, the old Muslim capital, would sufficiently placate Muslim opinion to compensate for the loss of Muslim influence inherent in the return of eastern Bengal to dependence upon Calcutta. He was willing to face opposition, however, if the project were a wise one and the details of the reorganization equitable.[38]

Within three days he had prepared a lengthy note for the Executive Council setting out the proposal in detail. The change must be framed in such a way that it would not appear simply that the government had given in to agitation. The Bengalis did have real grievances, for example the fact that they were outnumbered by others in the legislative councils—Muslims in the east, Biharis and Ooryas in the west (an arguable point, actually, for it depended on how one played with numbers, titles, and religious affiliation.)[39] The requirements were fairly clear-cut: satisfy the Bengalis, provide convenient administrative units, and conciliate the Muslims. The best way to do all this was to restore the chief commissionership of Assam, the most backward area; create a new lieutenant governorship in Bihar and Orissa; establish a presidency in Bengal with a legislative council of its own (Hardinge did not need to state the fact that the central government was legally responsible for all legislation dealing with provinces without legislatures); and create a special imperial capital district at Delhi under the direct rule of the government of India. Even the cost had been roughly calculated, at some £4–5 million sterling, for moving the capital.

The Executive Council as a whole responded favorably. Hardinge was pleased; it helped that Sir Guy Fleetwood Wilson, Financial Member, wrote a private note to say that if the changes were effected, "it will make Your Excellency the 'biggest' Viceroy who ever came to India," and that the creation of a new capital at Delhi would demonstrate to the world that the British raj was in India to stay.[40]

Hardinge's plan was for the king to announce at the durbar that the transfer would be made, and that he, the king, had suggested to the government of India that it prepare a modification of partition so as to satisfy all parties in Bengal. This would allow for consultation of various vested interests after the fact and was a reversal of Hardinge's earlier position, as he admitted to Crewe, but such flexibility was one of the more useful aspects of Hardinge's character. Linking the two ideas together permitted this change of course. "It is a bold scheme that would be appreciated, even more in the future than at present." Hardinge passed home his memorandum, together with Council responses, in mid-July, adding that while the two declarations were interdependent it was the move to Delhi, above all, which was the larger need. (The correspondence was so secret that Hardinge copied out his own letters, and Diamond's nurse typed the Council minutes.)[41]

Crewe could only await the full details, although he was unlikely to offer instant opposition since he himself had proposed changes for Bengal in January—changes which included the separation of the government of India from that of Bengal. Broadly speaking, he approved the idea, but for the time being told only Asquith, Sir R. Ritchie (India Office under secretary), and F. H. Lucas (his own private secretary) and, somewhat later, the king, his secretary (Lord Stamfordham), and Morley. The Cabinet would be told only on the eve of Crewe's departure for India with the king. The king was enthusiastic, reminding Crewe that he had asked the previous year whether something could not be done about Bengal. Morley and Asquith similarly were impressed, so that Hardinge encountered little opposition at home until the public announcement was made at the durbar and Curzon and others learned of the plan.[42]

Crewe asked for a formal dispatch from Hardinge which would be for ultimate publication, setting out the benefits to be gained. Hardinge had only to revise an existing draft, removing "some unflattering remarks about the Bengalis and other matters." This dispatch of 25 August, printed as a command paper, was notable above all for one remark, given as a justification for provincial self-rule and a superior, separate capital at Delhi—but taken by some as a surrender to Indian nationalist agitation:

> it is certain that, in the course of time, the just demands of Indians for a larger share in the government of the country will have to be satisfied, and the question will be how this devolution of power can be conceded without impairing the supreme authority of the Governor-General-in-Council. The only possible solution of the difficulty would appear to be gradually to give the Provinces a larger measure of self-government, until at last India would consist of a number of administrations, autonomous in all provincial affairs, with the Government of India above them all, and possessing power to interfere in cases of misgovernment, but ordinarily restricting their functions to matters of Imperial concern.

Hardinge would have been the last to argue for eventual Indian independence, and he meant no more than what he said: a gradual increase of participation at the provincial level. Provincial self-government was not at all to be confused with Indian self-government. His own views are quite clear, and were expressed several times. "All sensible people know that Colonial self-government for this country is absolutely out of the question," if self-government meant practical independence. Hardinge's principles were administrative decentralization, the admission of more Indians into some branches of the administration, and the permanency of British rule. That the latter might someday prove incompatible with Indianization does not seem to have occurred to him: what he did believe was that British rule was forever incompatible with "Colonial *swaraj*." The phrase "just demands," like "autonomy," could be taken as a defense of the nationalist agitation and became the focus of later controversy in the House of Lords. Hardinge's emphatic denials show his own intentions, which were to remain fixed for his remaining years, even when eventual self-government became the official policy of the government.[43]

Hardinge had different reasons for revising partition. His frankest explanation came in a letter to Sanderson after the durbar was over and the information public. Essentially, the partition should never have been made in the first place.

> It was a vindictive measure intended to break the power of the Bengali, and [Curzon] underrated the strength and character of the Bengalis since they have been absolutely persistent in maintaining their agitation for the redress of this grievance, which since the inauguration of the Legislative Councils has become even more pronounced than at first. It would have been a case of moral cowardice when one realised the legitimacy of their grievance and injustice of their treatment not to have taken some steps to remedy an evil of that kind.

Nor could Hardinge be accused of self-interest, since he gave up viceregal quarters in Calcutta and a beautiful country house at Barrackpore to which by this time he was devoted, in order to go to Delhi in the winter of 1912 to live in a small bungalow or even a tent.[44] There was more justice in the accusation that Hardinge would thus avoid considerable social costs, but that was hardly his major consideration.

The issue of cost was rather for the moving of the capital. For the moment the rough figure of £4 million sterling was accepted. Crewe, who had serious doubts whether this was enough, was careful to hedge in his official response by noting that the Indian government had not been able to go fully into the costs as yet. Secrecy was useful in this way, for the following months could be spent in working out the details, including expenses, rather than in countering the many possible arguments. In November, the Cabinet was at last told and gave its formal approval, although by this time it would have been very difficult to turn back.[45]

Meanwhile, Hardinge and the Executive Council had to prepare a comprehensive list of other, lesser boons which would be proclaimed as well. Hardinge was still working on education and saw to it that in the end a grant of fifty lakhs (Rs. 50,00,000 or £330,000) was made for this purpose. Other concessions were a salary bonus of a half-month's pay for all civilian and military employees; land grants for long-service soldiers; extensions of widows' pensions; release of selected prisoners and debtors (not including Bal Gangadhar Tilak, a well-known extremist nationalist leader, whose release had been urged by Ramsay MacDonald but who to Hardinge was "the only really dangerous . . . man in India"); and the extension to Indians of certain honors and awards, above all the Victoria Cross (the first awards of which, therefore, were made in World War I).

The general list found favor at home, although the question of commissions for Indian officers had not yet been resolved. Crewe in particular was impressed that India had found the necessary money for these boons. The sum for education was regarded in India as inadequate for the occasion (Curzon in his time had given Rs. 85,00,000)—but even fifty lakhs would be useful as one of the few boons which would have meaning for all of India in a way that moving the capital and reuniting Bengal would not. By November, both the list of general boons and the special declarations on Delhi and Bengal were ready.[46]

On 9 November, the king and his party left England on H.M.S. *Medina*. Hardinge was to meet the royal party at Bombay, but he passed through Delhi for last-minute inspection and a disastrous durbar dress rehearsal. Sir John Hewett, chairman of the durbar committee, threatened to resign because Hardinge altered some of the arrangements in a way he disapproved; "I sent him word that it was I who was responsible for the Durbar and not he, and that he could do as he liked. I heard no more of his threat."[47]

It was too late to do very much (in the actual performance, the ceremonies went well enough), and Hardinge was off for Bombay to superintend the royal arrival on 2 December. At the proper time, the governor-general (Hardinge was no longer viceroy with the sovereign present in India) went on board in full uniform to be received by the king's staff in casual clothes—the first inevitable ruffle in an inevitable series. The king, however, was in full uniform, and Hardinge's annoyance was replaced by astonishment when he heard the king tell the queen, for the first time, of the movement of the capital.

A large full-dress dinner on board had to be endured in heat exceptional for December, and the next day the king and queen disembarked for an official welcome. While they visited Bombay, Hardinge raced ahead to be on hand when the king, using the viceroy's special train, entered Delhi on the seventh. The state entry was impressive, all but the king's unnoticed presence to those who expected a royal elephant in full regalia. "As I passed along," Hardinge recalled, "the people cheered and I could hear them say, 'There is the Lord Sahib, but where is the King?'" In every other way, however, the entry went well, and the durbar assemblage took up residence in an astonishing canvas city of twenty-five square miles housing over two hundred thousand people, complete with roads, sanitation, polo grounds, and the medical and security measures upon which Hardinge insisted.

The ceremonies themselves had been carefully planned in advance. Hardinge spent much of his time returning visits from the various chiefs to the king. These visits were doubly important because Curzon had not had time to make them in 1903. One Foreign Department staff member who accompanied Hardinge recorded (no doubt apocryphally) the sort of problem encountered with this swarm of princes: "'Does Your Highness not find Delhi rather warm?' 'Sir, I have been shivering ever since I left Travancore.' 'Does Your Highness not find Delhi rather cold?' 'Sir, the heat is somewhat exhausting compared with Chitral.'"[48] Hardinge had rather more to do than recover from the lashings of betel, or jasmine, or tea mixed with yak butter offered in these marquees. He closely supervised the special camp section, called the "Press Camp," which was in strict quarantine while it printed up the announcements on Delhi and Bengal in complete secrecy. At least the Hardinge family was united: the two sons arrived in October for the durbar, Edd bound for the Fifteenth Hussars and Alec for Cambridge, as did Winifred's brother Lord Alington (whose visit resulted in his near death from typhoid). Winifred was not only in the camp but also gave the address to Queen Mary from the delegation of "Indian ladies."

On 12 December came the actual durbar ceremony itself, which has been elaborately described, not least by the official historian, Sir John Fortescue, whose account includes much detail (and not a little carping criticism). In a hollowed-out amphitheater, 4,000 special guests, 35,000 troops, and 70,000 spectators witnessed (at least those close enough witnessed) a most impressive series of ceremonies, which included a procession of governor-general (the only one privileged to kiss the king's hand), Council, governors, chief officials, ruling chiefs, and princes, marred only by the apparent rudeness of the Gaekwar of Baroda, who appeared in plain clothes and then turned his back on the king (he later apologized to Hardinge).[49]

After the homage ceremonies, Hardinge read out the series of lesser boons conferred upon the people of India. Then the surprise was at last sprung as Hardinge handed the special announcement on Delhi and Bengal to the king, who read it out in a voice loud enough to be heard by most of the four thousand durbaris. The surrounding crowd only learned by word of mouth and the printed copies now distributed by government officials. The camp and press, and soon all India, were fully occupied for days with discussion of this event. Since Bengali Hindu leaders were pleased with reunification, they were less critical of the movement of the capital than they might have been, and only the European community of Calcutta was completely hostile. For them Hardinge now was the main enemy, and their motto became "H.M.G.," meaning "Hardinge must go!" The Calcutta *Statesman* led the charge, and Curzon, Minto, and Lansdowne soon joined in at home—but the changes were there to stay.

The ceremonies were not over, however. Perhaps the most glittering display in a short-lived ceremonial world created only for display was the state investiture, which took place the evening of the fourteenth in an enormous *shamiana* or marquee, with a thousand seated viewers (and many more standees) crowded in to watch honors being awarded. Hardinge, as Grand Master of the Order of the Star of India, was intimately involved. As a surprise and at his suggestion Queen Mary was invested with the Grand Cross of the Order. There was also a moment of unexpected drama, as Fortescue records:

> the ceremony was about half-completed, when suddenly the fire-alarm was heard without, and a strong smell of burning became evident to every one. The electric light at the same time flickered up and down, threatening to go out at every moment, and continued to do so for two or three minutes. Presently some one cried out "Fire," and two or three hundred people rose to their feet. . .the assembly was within a hair's-breadth of a panic, and might have succumbed to it, had not some gentleman in the body of the tent sternly growled out "Sit down," whereupon the timid reluctantly resumed their seats.

Hardinge's account identifies the gentleman: "The alarm spread to the audience, who began to leave their places, but I stopped this at once by shouting out, "Sit down! Nobody is to leave his place!" There was indeed a fire, clearly dangerous in a tent city, which destroyed Lucas's tent after a messenger had propped a bicycle with a lighted lamp against it.[50]

This was the only serious danger, and the week of ceremonies, parades, military reviews (one of fifty thousand troops) and tattoos, visits and return visits, investitures, polo matches, garden parties, and dinners was a striking success. On the fifteenth, the final day, the king and queen laid the foundation stones of the new city of Delhi, although the actual site had not been picked and the stones eventually had to be moved. On the sixteenth the durbar camp was broken, with the king going off to Nepal to shoot tigers (and the criticism that he preferred the fixation of hunting to visiting his domains, since he never approached south India at all). The Hardinges returned to Calcutta and Barrackpore, to catch up on the ordinary work of government and to prepare one more reception for the king and queen when they visited Calcutta after Christmas. On the thirtieth the king and queen arrived, and Hardinge again was the main supporting actor in a grueling official role. "These were ten of the most strenuous days of my life, as I had to supervise and provide for every moment of the day for my royal guests, but everything passed off without a hitch and to Their Majesties' complete satisfaction." Hardinge's last major speech of the visit—proposing the royal health at the state banquet—went well (nervously, he had asked Crewe to go over the text). His reward was royal thanks, silver pieces for his table, and a diamond and ruby pendant for Winifred.[51]

On 8 January the royal party left for Bombay, passed in another train by Hardinge so he would be on hand to receive them for the final farewell. Hardinge obviously betrayed something of his relief, for, once on board the royal barge headed for the *Medina*, the king remarked, "You seem very pleased, Charlie, to be getting rid of us!" to which Hardinge made the necessary diplomatic reply. After a last luncheon on board Hardinge returned to the shore, saluted—at the king's order, he felt, to repair the lack of six weeks earlier—by the escorting British cruisers.

More than a ceremonial coronation and a display of the might and majesty of the British raj had been at stake. It remained now to implement the major and significant decisions announced at Delhi, not least the beginning steps of the creation of a capital for a land of 250 million people. Hardinge therefore returned to Calcutta with relief, but fully aware of the work ahead. It was "my scheme" now in his mind, and his was the responsibility of making it work.

VII Last of the Old Raj

Hardinge's first year as viceroy was dominated by the problems of the durbar and unrest in Bengal, his second by the repercussions of the durbar announcements. The work of the viceroy, however, was never-ending, and there were other important concerns to which Hardinge had been giving attention for some time. One of these, related directly to both durbar and the creation of a new capital, was finance. Although there had been a brief depression in India shortly before Hardinge's arrival, he was fortunate that the first years of his regime corresponded with a time of general prosperity resulting from bountiful crops and general trade growth. Even in 1910–11, India had a revenue surplus of £5.5 million, allocated to education, municipal development, and the floating debt. On the other hand, the future could never be certain—above all in India, so dependent upon the monsoon—and there were other aspects of finance that took a considerable amount of any viceroy's time.

A particularly vextious issue was the fluctuating exchange rate of the silver rupee relative to the gold-backed pound sterling. That the rupee's worth (and thus the real income of every employee of the Indian government) depended less upon the state of the Indian economy than it did upon reserve holdings of bullion or silver in both England and India had become a public issue by the time of Hardinge's appointment. The wheels ground slowly: a Royal Commission on Indian Finance and Currency was appointed in 1913 and reported in 1914, just in time for the whole matter to be put in abeyance until the end of the war. Of much more immediate concern were anticipated extraordinary expenses: the durbar had been allotted £1 million (it cost two-thirds that sum); the move to Delhi would require £4 million by conservative estimate. Income, however, would fall in one important area: an Anglo-Chinese agreement of 1910 already had begun to limit sales of opium to China, and revenue from this source would drop from £5.1 million in 1912–13 to £1.6 million in 1913–14 in a total budget of £50–55 million per annum.

The solution was clear to Hardinge from the time of his arrival: cut military expenditure, then running some £20 million a year on British regular army units stationed in India and British-officered Indian Army components (not including the colorful irregular units maintained by the several Native States). As Morley had foreseen, the Anglo-Russian Accord had eased Russian pressure in the direction of India, and there was now little reason to continue the heavy expenditure and elaborate organization planned in the Curzon-Kitchener era. Afghanistan, frontier tribes, even China might become worrisome, but none would require manpower on the scale of a potential conflict with Russia. Hardinge would not cut British troops, only less efficient Indian regiments. In January 1911, he pushed the question in his Executive Council, and the commander in chief promised to report on possible reductions. Hardinge hoped that at least ten thousand, perhaps twenty thousand men could be cut from the Indian forces, although for the time being he avoided figures except in his private remarks to Crewe and to Wilson, who supported him. The army numbered over a quarter of a million troops; as was pointed out in discussion, the figure was too large for ordinary police functions, but too small to quell a genuine revolt by the Indian masses.[2]

The months passed, and Hardinge concluded that the military authorities would not cooperate. Sir O'Moore Creagh, commander in chief, seemed willing enough but had not the forcefulness to make his staff toe the line. The general staff, in fact, was attempting to obtain the support of the British press in its fight against reductions, on the grounds that Kitchener's excellent system should not be trifled with. Hardinge disagreed entirely. The army according to its own figures would be eighty thousand rifles short on mobilization, to say nothing of inadequate artillery. It was not the perfect system Kitchener's admirers imagined, but was shot full of deficiencies such as expensive and useless barracks, and regiments unfit even to stand guard duty (Hardinge had personal experience with the Eighty-eighth Carnatics).

General Haig, chief of the Indian General Staff, answered Hardinge's arguments with a long memorandum and violated normal practice by sending a copy to the War Office. Hardinge discovered the source of the leak by tracing each of the twenty numbered copies of the document, and then complained to Creagh. Since Creagh seemed unwilling to act, Hardinge sent for Haig, dealt him a "severe reprimand," and saw to it that for his "inexcusable behavior" Haig was rewarded in the durbar with a K.C.I.E. instead of the much more restricted and therefore coveted K.C.S.I.: petty retaliation, perhaps, but not in that world and at that time—and there were few ways that Hardinge, or any viceroy, could keep the army in line.[3]

Wilson, who had little respect for Creagh either, suggested that a committee of experts be appointed to help prod the army into more than the petty cuts they suggested of fifty lakhs (£330,000), less than one percent of their budget. Hardinge agreed and in September 1911 told Creagh that if the Army Department did not make the economies, the Finance Department would. Reluctantly, Creagh agreed to the committee, which was established under Field Marshal Lord Nicholson late the following year. The commission, promising at first, became internally divided, and was to be of little real help. Meanwhile the picture was grim: "In fact the administration could hardly be worse. It makes me feel very nervous as to possible revelations in the event of a serious military crisis or emergency. Nobody seems to be able to attach responsibility to any person or persons. . . ."[4]

It was not only a matter of the reduction of forces and expenditures. The basic conception of the future use of the army in India was at stake the instant Hardinge associated the proposed reductions with Britain's international position. Hardinge naturally followed foreign policy developments as closely as possible while in India, and regular private correspondence with Nicolson, Tyrrell, and others kept him well informed. However, his official voice was restricted to the areas of traditional Indian concern—Turkey, Afghanistan, and Persia. A major goal, for example, was to maintain British influence at Kuwait in the Persian Gulf in light of the possible completion of the Baghdad Railway. If necessary, Hardinge would have resisted with force Turkish attempts to revitalize or extend long-dormant influence in the gulf.[5]

Such action would be local and limited, however, and this view shaped Hardinge's conception of the potential use of the Indian army. A strong memorandum of August stressed the limited nature of such operations as justification for the necessary cuts (and the committee to suggest them).

> It is hardly necessary to discuss possible eventualities connected with Germany, Turkey, and other Powers which the General Staff are of opinion 'may necessitate in the future an increase in the Army in India.' Beyond minor operations in the Persian Gulf, there is no likelihood in the immediate future of any operations against Foreign Powers in regions not coterminous with the frontiers of India. . . . Such eventualities are almost as improbable as 'an increase of the Army in India.'

In Persia, it was the home authorities who wished to extend responsibilities and India which offered resistance; the railway which Hardinge had supported in London he opposed in Simla on the ground of expense. Even war against Turkey would be limited to operations in Mesopotamia, "and I have the further authority of the late Director of Military Operations in London for saying that they are impossible." Kitchener's overall dispositions, designed to meet a Russian invasion, were as out of date as the large expenditure they entailed; the army had not absorbed the effect of the Anglo-Russian treaty or the revised Anglo-Japanese alliance. The whole situation, Hardinge concluded, had to be met "with courage."[6]

But in England the military had different views, at least about the possible use of Indian troops in any European war. The Committee on Imperial Defence discussed just this eventuality in late August—but without Crewe's presence and without informing the India Office of the details. Crewe justifiably complained to Haldane, but as he advised Hardinge, the Cabinet was unlikely to give its approval: "Asquith said that he would never, in any circumstances, agree to such a use of Indian troops. It is therefore an impertinence for the soldiers to make plans for this contingency. . . ." Communication between the General Staffs in India and London was only an academic exercise.[7]

Hardinge was annoyed nevertheless, not so much with the principle of sending troops to Europe as with the making of decisions over the head of the viceroy and the India Office. With Crewe's authoritative statement in hand, Hardinge told Haig to destroy the plans made in collaboration with the War Office. Creagh agreed that the mission of the Indian army was the defence of India, and Haig had little choice but to obey, ostensibly—but the plans were merely pigeonholed, to emerge for a useful purpose in 1914.[8]

Hardinge had more control over plans for the new capital at Delhi. His first thought was to keep the project out of the hands of India's Public Works Department, for which it was too demanding a challenge. He preferred to establish a small committee of first-class men to supervise the planning, and talked of competition among the leading architects. The Executive Council agreed to get expert advice from England, and Hardinge telegraphed for help in laying out the town (architectural designs of buildings would come later). Hardinge made it clear that he intended to supervise the planning process closely.[9]

On Wilson's recommendation, early in 1912 Hardinge chose Malcolm Hailey (later Lord Hailey) as chairman of his advisory committee with the title of "Chief Commissioner of New Delhi." Suggestions for experts arrived from all sides, although they were for architects rather than the much rarer species of town planner. Edwin Lutyens had several supporters, including the president of the Institute of British Architects; H. V. Lanchester, who had worked in India for Scindia and Gwalior, was another. Hardinge was rather drawn to Swinton Jacob, who had done some major buildings in Lahore. Hardinge had ideas on the question of style as well: from the start he believed that something more than simple Western Renaissance or classical patterns were required; the new capital of India would require buildings with a "distinct Oriental touch." Crewe from London pressed Lutyens —whom Hardinge thought "more of a country-house architect"—and a compromise was for Crewe to appoint Lutyens, Brodie (a sanitary engineer from Liverpool), Capt. G.S.C. Swinton, vice-chariman of the London County Council, and Lanchester, but only on Hardinge's insistence, in a temporary and advisory capacity.[10]

Meanwhile, Hardinge faced mounting criticism both in India and in Britain. He knew, of course, the sort of reaction he could expect from Calcutta, and friends in England kept him informed of the line of attack that such obvious opponents as Curzon—who had partitioned Bengal in the first place—would take.[11] Curzon was told of the durbar pronouncements only the day before they were made in Delhi, however, and he did not get his day in Parliament until late February. In a sense he had too much to struggle against, dissipating his effort on both Delhi and Bengali unification. Clearly he was hurt personally by the failure of the government to consult him in advance. The responsibility for this fell upon the Cabinet, Hardinge ("I speak of him with respect because he is a personal friend—who had only been in India a few months. . . ."), and Crewe (also only a few months at his post). Curzon's most telling arguments were those which criticized the cost estimate of £4 milion, if only because of the rise of land values at Delhi which the announcement would inevitably produce, and the estimate that the basic construction work would be completed in three years. To Curzon, eight to ten years and £12 million were safer bets.[12]

Hardinge's plans survived Curzon's worst. He came quickly to the conclusion that at least in India only moderate damage had resulted, due largely to Curzon's "intense unpopularity in India," where many wondered how an ex-viceroy could indict a policy already pronounced by the king. Indeed, Curzon, Minto, and Lansdowne could do little more than irritate, for the decisions were permanent. Their opposition, like Calcutta's hostility, would simply have to be borne. Hardinge at least was soon to leave for his spring tour, Simla, and eventually temporary quarters at Delhi, and Calcutta's attitude may have helped him decide not to keep Government House as the viceroy's Calcutta residence, even though the king had urged him to do so. In any case, Hardinge had few regrets—as he departed with English-language press comparisons with Siruj-ud-Dowla (nineteenth-century Nawab of Bengal and author of the Black Hole tragedy) ringing in his ears.[13]

On the other hand, the reaction from those favoring reunion, like Bihar and Orissa, was heartwarming. By mid-February he reported that even in Calcutta agitation had died down save for a few diehards. "The fact is Calcutta merchants are far too busy making money to interest themselves much in political affairs." Many, he reported to Crewe, regretted their first hostile outburst. Thankfully, much of his own attention was devoted to details of the new administrative districts. Some aspects of the proclamation required only formal notification by the viceroy or the secretary of state in Council, others needed legislation in India, but parliamentary legislation was required to grant powers to the new governor and council of Bengal.[14]

Hardinge's spring tour of 1912 included Patiala, Peshawar (where he stayed with Sir George Roos-Keppel, famed master of the northwest frontier), the Khyber, Landi Kotal, Malakand, the valley of the Swat River, and Kohat, and he managed to have a look over the Afghani plain of Jellalabad in the process. After ten days on the frontier he returned to open the Upper Chenab Canal, a massive irrigation project which had taken seven years and £2 million. The experience of starting the water on its way to provide abundant crops in desert lands was exhilarating, but Hardinge admitted private doubts to Wilson: "From what I saw I am quite convinced that in some parts we are doing too much canalisation, and the country is becoming absolutely water-logged," an interesting observation in the light of increasing salinization half a century later. Ten days in camp with Du Boulay and two A.D.C.s provided rest and shooting; Winifred, who was along, enjoyed the trip as well, although she had been ill on the frontier.[15]

As usual, Hardinge was refreshed by his tour, and he found the atmosphere at Simla less heated than Calcutta's in several ways. Delhi once again occupied the bulk of his attention. He had no clear ideas, but like anyone who "knows what he likes" in art or architecture, he had a general standard in his mind: "a pure Oriental style of architecture adapted to meet the exigencies or the requirements of a western administration," as he put it to Chirol, was his goal, but it was self-contradictory, for once modified it could hardly be "pure Oriental."[16]

As Hardinge was writing this, however, Lutyens was approaching Delhi for his first look, unimpressed by the heat, the dust, or anything he had seen of British Indian planning ("made 40 times more difficult by past mistakes, false economies & want of imagination") or Moghul style ("cumbrous ill constructed buildings covered with a veneer of stone or marble—& very tiresome to the western intelligence"). Lutyens's first meeting with Hardinge at Delhi at the end of April went well, and Lutyens found Winifred very friendly and amusing, thus establishing an important relationship for the future, since she was to serve as important intermediary between two strong-minded men.[17]

The immediate problem was not style, but location. The committee had still not even rejected the durbar site north of Delhi as the location for the new town, although there was little room for expansion on that side of the old city, crowded between the Delhi ridge and the Jumna River, waterlogged and malarial. Hard negotiations followed, but by the end of May Hardinge was pleased to report that the north side had been rejected; the new capital would be somewhere to the south of old Delhi, though much controversy would follow over its precise location.[18]

Hardinge never doubted that the city should be to the south side—but it was his one conviction. At Simla, once again he found Lutyens more congenial than he had expected (the feeling was still mutual), and he gave the architect the task of sketching designs for the viceroy's house. Both Hardinges liked his first rough drawings, already including the central dome and portico which so dominate the final building. Hardinge was ready to give Lutyens the contract for this building; he was startled, however, when Lutyens told him its cost would be £530,000 (scaled down a day later to £200,000)—for one building, only days after Curzon had again attacked his £4 million estimate for the entire city. The very uncertainty of the figures added to Hardinge's worries.[19]

In July, Lanchester arrived for consultation on the town layout. Hardinge got on well with him, but not his first plans. After two hot days at Delhi, Hardinge was convinced that the first designs for a city in the plain east of the ridge were far too spacious for the town and buildings it would encompass. Vast parkways, avenues lined with princes' houses, 240-foot-wide roadways. . .Lanchester was told to draw up a new plan. Hardinge in his memoirs recalled suddenly fixing upon the hill at Raisana (the current site of Government House, the viceroy's residence) as the only proper location; in fact, for some months he vacillated between several possible schemes.[20]

Nothing, in any case, could be decided until the Committee journeyed back to India at the end of the year and met Hardinge in December. Crewe in London faced numerous pressures himself, not least from the king and queen who both took close interest in the proceedings. Until the Committee chose a site, Crewe could not give Lutyens a contract. The secretary was nervous about appointing a single architect for such an edifice in any case, and in the end sent out Herbert Baker with Lutyens in November, promising a contract if the two men could agree.[21]

In retrospect, the decisions about the new capital of Delhi appear to be the most important of 1912, but there were other sensitive and significant matters. One particular concern was a commission proposed by Crewe and established under Lord Islington (former governor-general of New Zealand) to investigate conditions in the Indian Civil Service. Hardinge was unimpressed by comembers Ramsay MacDonald, of the Labour Party, and Lord Ronaldshay, a parliamentary critic of Hardinge. The appointment of Chirol, on Hardinge's recommendation, and the greater representation of the I.C.S. for which he also asked, helped a bit, but Hardinge thought the commission would have its knife out for the I.C.S., the "back-bone of the administration." To Clarke in Bombay he expressed his real feelings, obviously still smarting from criticism of his "autonomy" dispatch justifying the transfer of the capital in 1911:

> I consider that the question of the future autonomous development of the Local Governments is really a trifling question compared with that of whether the Government of India are to be allowed to govern India for the benefit of India or the benefit of a few faddists and of the interests of certain communities and factions in England. It is a far more serious question than that of local development, and I do not know how it is ever going to be settled without some tremendous crisis. Morley, owing to Minto's weakness, did an infinity of harm, and the India Office have not yet learned wisdom. I do not at all approve of the composition of this Commission, but I congratulate myself that I have succeeded in considerably strengthening it from an Indian point of view.[22]

Hardinge had stated more than once that Indianization was a basic principle of is viceroyalty, but what he meant was the admission of more Indians to the subordinate services—the separate provincial cadres and some of the all-India technical branches such as education and public works—not the higher executive level of central government administration normally staffed by the I.C.S. His great fear was that the Islington commission would make drastic recommendations at that level, and would dip into the Political Service which staffed foreign, frontier, and Indian States posts, and which Hardinge was convinced could not encompass non-Europeans.[23] No ruling chief, no Persian ruler, would recognize an Indian as representative of the government of India. The commission had some two dozen services to consider, however, and Hardinge could hope that the Political Service might not be touched; meanwhile Chirol kept him well informed.[24]

On the other hand, the commission might provide a means for recruitment to the I.C.S. from provincial services, the assumption being that Indians thus promoted would have already proven themselves at a provincial level. Also the recruitment age might be lowered, for Indians generally required more years of preparation, given the lower level of education in India and the need to master so many aspects of an essentially foreign culture, and indeed to travel to that culture's center for the examination. Hardinge believed that the effort was not only worthwhile, it was a necessary part of the selection process, and he and others opposed simultaneous examinations in England and in India.[25]

The commission finally made its recommendations in the fall of 1914. In late 1915 the report went to Hardinge for signature. It was published in 1917, but action on the rather lengthy document was postponed until after the war, when it became linked with larger issues of postwar policies and thus passed out of Hardinge's purview. The 1917 pronouncement by Edwin Montagu, then secretary of state for India, that official policy was to increase participation of Indians in every branch of administration made Hardinge's views on the services somewhat irrelevant.[26]

The future of the I.C.S. was a significant issue, but it was only one of many. The procession of problems requiring the viceroy's advice or decision was perpetual: the status of indentured Indian labor in several British colonies, affiliation of the new Muslim unversity, a gold coinage for India, repercussions of Turkey's troubles in Italy and the Balkans, the breakdown of the Anglo-Russian entente in Persia, constant official receptions and appointments. A surprising amount of time was spent with the Native States, for the problem of succession here, mismanagement of finances there, or the advantages of disadvantages of a royal marriage alliance not only involved much paperwork, but also social obligations when Hardinge invited the rulers concerned to Simla or Calcutta for resolution of the question. Baroda had to be given a second chance after the durbar; Jodhpur a regent for a minor ruler; Scindia, maharaja of Gwalior, made a poor selection of fiancée, and so on.

Hardinge took a close and personal interest in the Native States, and his policy in general ran counter to that of his Political Department, which preferred to assume control of a state through the Resident in the case of a minority. Hardinge valued and respected the native aristocracy—a natural bulwark, after all, against radical Indian political agitation. For this reason he strongly supported the establishment of a special college for rulers' sons and the formation of a politically effective Chamber of Princes. Hardinge's inclination in this regard was to use his diplomatic abilities and the art of persuasion to win some excellent lifetime friendships, the reward for which was to come in part in the response of these same Indian princes to the empire's needs in World War I. It was not entirely fortuitous that these friendships enabled Hardinge to indulge in his favorite pastime of hunting (including forty-six tigers, one a record eleven feet five and a half inches).[27]

In mid-October, Hardinge set off on an official tour to Kashmir. He was impressed with the ceremonies, including a state entry by water complete with a flotilla of old barges and costumed retainers, and by the hospitality of the maharaja, whose grandfather had been placed on his throne by Hardinge's grandfather.[28] From Kashmir the viceroy moved on to pay official visits to Indore, Udaipur, and Jaipur, memorable for a nasty fall at pigsticking, followed by food poisoning—the perils of a viceregal tour. Such trips could be most exhausting. On one noteworthy day in Jaipur, he rose at 5:30 A.M., drove to visit the Nawab of Tonk sixty miles away, arriving at 9:00 for an official durbar, returned at 2:00 P.M., was received by the maharaja at 4:00, inspected Imperial Service troops at 4:30, attended a garden party from 5:00 to 6:00, and finally left Jaipur at 10:30: "At the end of the day I felt half dead especially as I had had a bad headache."[29]

Bikaner, Bhopal, Delhi for military maneuvers (an unusual and much appreciated viceregal attention to military affairs), and finally Bhurtpore in the central provinces concluded the tour. At Delhi he rode over the ground of the new city with Valentine Chirol, who agreed that Hardinge had chosen the best site, even though it was three miles from Old Delhi. The final stage of the tour was planned as a state entry into Delhi, as the government of India officially moved to its new capital. An official durbar would follow the entry, but as Hardinge was careful to explain to the king, it was only to be on a local scale, of some three hundred people, to mark the ceremonial changeover (the government of India had actually administered the Delhi enclave since 1 October).[30]

On 23 December, in beautiful weather, Hardinge arrived at the main Delhi railway station just before noon, and was met by the ruling princes of the Punjab and an address of welcome from the municipality. Outside the station the Hardinges mounted a large and gorgeously decorated elephant for the procession which passed south through the Queen's Gardens, from which the public had been excluded, and then turned east into Delhi's main street, Chandni Chauk, heading for the durbar in the Red Fort. Hardinge had a presentiment of evil, he later recounted, but Winifred replied that, "It is only that you are tired and you always dislike ceremonial." They had gone no more than a few hundred yards when there was a shattering explosion. The danger of assassination had become a reality.

The procession arrangements had been made by Hailey as chief commissioner. As always when security breaks down, the man in charge was blamed. Hailey anticipated no unusual trouble, given the recent quiet and the enthusiasm over the durbar announcements, but he had consulted C. R. Cleveland, head of the Criminal Investigation Department, who came twice to Delhi. Security was actually at minimum because Hardinge himself had impressed upon Cleveland the need to take the fewest precautions possible on viceregal journeys, an instruction which put Cleveland in an invidious position. As a result no special measures were taken for the state entry. Some two hundred police guarded the route, along with mounted lancers on police duty; householders along the way had each signed a document making them responsible for the good behavior of those present; hotels and rooming houses (but not private houses) were searched in advance; troops lined the route at intervals of four paces, mainly as a crowd control device.[31]

Elephants are slow and distinctive targets, and Hardinge was on the largest. General Creagh had suggested that he go on horseback, as the king had at the durbar; the government of India had no state elephants, and it would be embarrassing to have to borrow them from various princes. But Hardinge chose elephants for the symbolism and there were more than a dozen in the midst of the procession, preceded and followed by various official formations. The eighth elephant carried the Hardinges, twenty paces behind one with McMahon and Du Boulay, twenty paces ahead of another with Creagh's staff.

Hardinge's elephant carried five people, including the mahout. The howdah was a heavy wooden structure, ornamented with silver; Hardinge sat in front on the right with Winifred by his side. Behind on the right sat Jemadar Mahabir, bearing the state umbrella, and on the left was Hardinge's personal servant, Jemadar Ghugru. Only viceregal "dignity" had prevented adding Diamond to the group. Security was not entirely neglected; riding on all four sides of the elephant were four armed police officers.

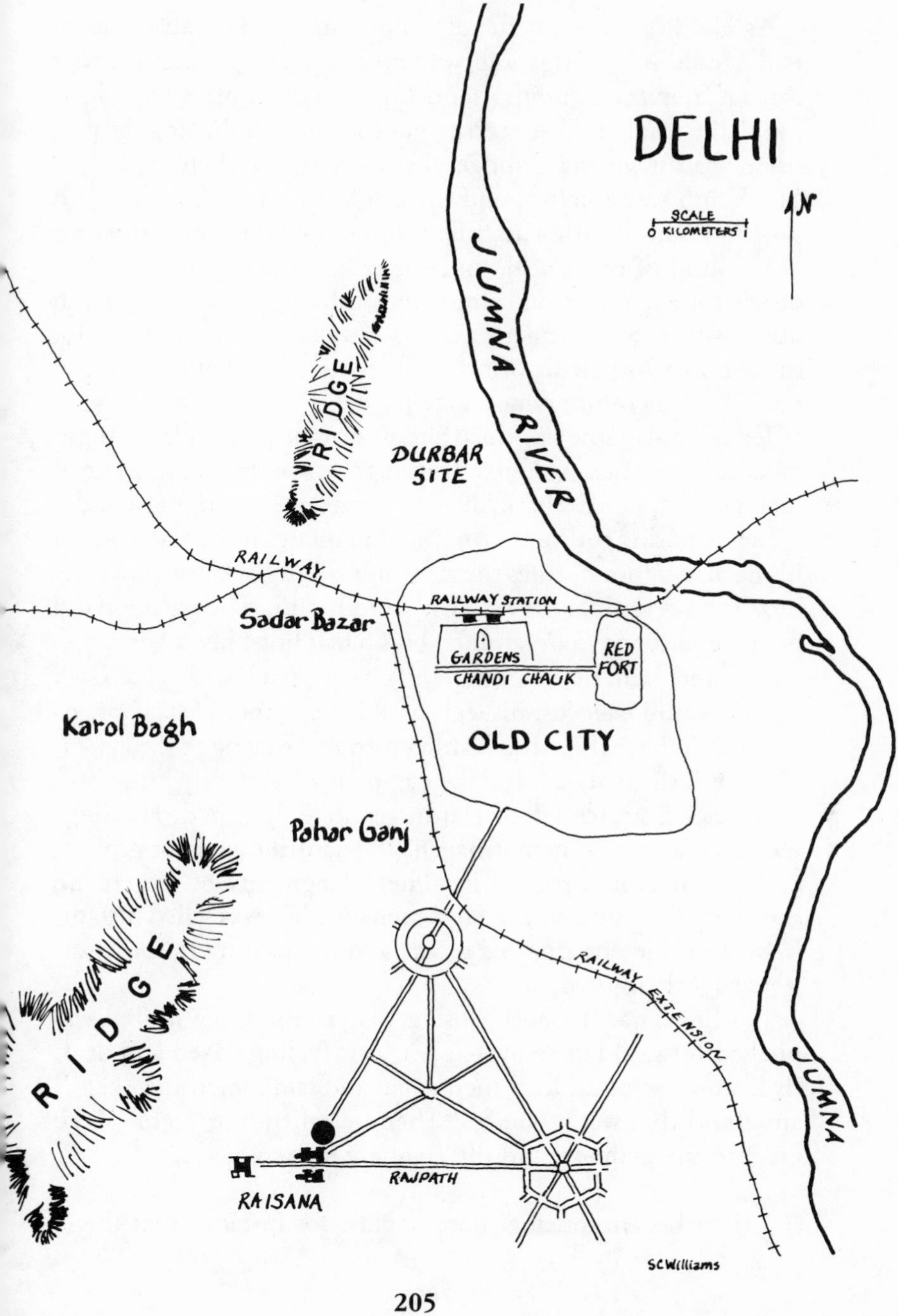

DELHI
SCALE
0 KILOMETERS 1
N
JUMNA RIVER
RIDGE
DURBAR SITE
RAILWAY
RAILWAY STATION
Sadar Bazar
GARDENS
CHANDI CHAUK
RED FORT
OLD CITY
Karol Bagh
Pahar Ganj
RIDGE
RAILWAY EXTENSION
JUMNA
RAISANA
RAJPATH
SCWilliams

As Hardinge's elephant came opposite the Punjab National Bank Building, a large and warren-like structure, a bomb was thrown from the building, probably from the roof: it passed between the front and back sections of the howdah, hitting the partition against which Hardinge's back rested, and there exploded. The bomb was a half-pound Wills tobacco tin, reinforced with iron and bound with wire, filled with one-half to three-quarters of a pound of picric acid, and either fused or equipped with a detonator exploding on contact (possibly even both). It was, in other words, a particularly vicious device—all the more so for containing what the reports term "needles," probably the metal darts used then for gramophone needles.

Jemadar Mahabir was killed almost instantly; Jemadar Ghugru had only superficial wounds. Hardinge was hit by a large piece of metal that ripped his back for eight inches over the right shoulder blade, exposing the bone. Another fragment hit the right side of his neck and four needles the right side of his back just above the hip. The strength of the howdah saved his life. The partition did not extend to the floor, and the bomb had burst just against it—a bit higher, and he would certainly have been killed; a bit lower and he would have lost his legs, with little chance of survival. As luck would have it, he was leaning forward, waving to the crowd. Winifred, the mahout, and the elephant all were very lucky, suffering not a scratch. Both Hardinges were deafened, Hardinge seriously, as his ear hemorrhaged (the eardrum was not broken, and the deafness passed in time). Fragments of the bomb showered the crowd nearby; one teenaged boy was killed instantly by a needle entering his brain, and a dozen more spectators were slightly injured.

Hardinge was in shock, losing blood rapidly. Winifred was pitched forward but recovered her seat, feeling dazed and deaf. By her own account, he turned to her and said something like, "I am afraid that was a bomb." Then he called out "aghi" ("go on") to the mahout, and the elephant started again.

I then began noticing more details, for instance that the

> howdah back had gone, and that the Viceroy looked pale. I said to him: 'Are you sure you are not hurt?' He answered: 'I am not sure. I have had a great shock, but I think I can go on.' A few seconds afterwards I stretched backwards to be able to see him from the back, and through a slit of the uniform near his right shoulder (the furthest), I could see flesh appearing. Then I thought: 'Shall I tell him he is wounded, which will frighten him, or take the risk the harm of the jolt of the elephant may do him?' I looked round again, and noticed the legs of a man who was hanging backward and dead. Then I quietly said: 'Do let me stop the procession, as I fear the man behind is dead.' (We had moved a hundred and fifty yards.) He said: 'Of course, we cannot go on under these circumstances.' I stopped the elephant and signed to Colonel Maxwell on the elephant in front. He ran up, and the Viceroy said: 'Can you do anything for the poor man behind?' And I said: 'I would like Colonel Roberts [Lt. Col. T. R. Roberts, I.M.S., Hardinge's doctor] to come. I think the Viceroy's shoulder is hurt.' Just then the Viceroy had a little convulsion, and he was rapidly losing consciousness. On regaining consciousness, he gave all instructions for the full carrying out of the ceremony.[32]

The accounts of all observers, including Winifred, naturally differ, for it all happened too fast. Winifred recalled, for example, that Hardinge's pith helmet was blown off, and she said to him, "You cannot go out in India without a topee," or some such banality (the helmet, badly torn, was blown into the road). Wilson, two elephants behind, remembered Hardinge sinking down, "as ice does when it melts at the base," until nothing was to be seen "but the back of his somewhat balding head and his two white gloved hands lying limply over the two seats of his howdah." The agonizing problem now was to get Hardinge down; Winifred could not lift him, the jemadars were dead or injured, and the elephant had been chosen specifically for its size.

Fortunately, the nearest elephants carried not senior councilmen but younger staff, who could slip down and run to help. Most of the procession remained in place, and those on elephants remained conspicuous targets if there were more bombs at hand, a thought which occurred to several. Most of those nearby were mainly concerned to help the injured. Only Khan Bhadur Shaikh Abdullah, deputy superintendent of the C.I.D., riding on Hardinge's left, dismounted and ran into the bank building at once—but it contained at least 150 people on two stories and the roof.

Meanwhile Maxwell, McMahon, and others struggled to erect a sort of scaffold from packing cases to reach the badly shattered howdah. Motor cars had to be found and brought up, no easy problem since the street had been cleared and there were none in the procession. Hardinge was lifted down on a charpoy (native bed). Winifred who had shown amazing coolness to this point, nearly collapsed, thinking he had been killed. A dose of brandy from a nearby St. John's ambulance brought her round, and she saw Hardinge into a car. By this time he had momentarily recovered his senses with the doctor's help, and he ordered Wilson, the senior councilman, to take the procession on. Wilson, who had dismounted and come up, was asked to deliver Hardinge's speech, crumpled and bloodstained, to the durbar.[33]

Winifred hurried ahead with ten minutes' start to get things ready at Viceregal Lodge, which was virtually empty as all the staff had gone to attend the ceremonies. It was now about 4:00 P.M.; by 6:00 Hardinge was under chloroform and the doctor was operating to cut out bits of metal—but it was clear that he would recover. As all witnesses testify, Winifred's courage was great: she said afterwards in explanation that Bucharest, Constantinople, and St. Petersburg had accustomed her to bombs.

By now the procession had arrived at the Red Fort, to be received by a very nervous crowd which had heard only rumors of disaster: the many wives of officials in the procession were naturally thoroughly alarmed. Upon entering the reception chamber, Wilson announced that Hardinge's injuries were slight, but that poor men doing their duty had been killed or maimed. He was certain that all loyal citizens would abhor the incident, but his immediate thoughts turned to the Mutiny of 1857.

> It ought to appeal to all loyalists as amounting to a sacrilege on such an occasion and I hope that everyone of them here will make it clear to his countrymen that such an attempt checks all progress. It puts the clock back it may be for fifty years, and remember what happened here fifty years ago. Thanks to Almighty God the attempt has failed.[34]

The formal, prepared speeches were then read out as if nothing untoward had occurred, and the return procession was accomplished without incident, but with a detour that avoided the actual scene of the explosion.

At the site, the police had now carried out a thorough search, but so long after the act that there was little chance of finding the culprit or culprits (if the bomb was fused, one to light, one to throw). The search was much criticized later, but the police did their best under the circumstances. This witness had seen a suspicious woman (an excellent disguise) on the roof; that one had seen a hand wave and a trail of smoke; a third saw something from the other side of the road altogether. Not a trace was found, and the C.I.D. had reluctantly to conclude that the bomb had been thrown by persons unknown to the building's occupants. A reward was soon posted of Rs. 10,000, to which ruling princes and individuals added amounts to an eventual total of one lakh (1,00,000 or £6,660, a considerable fortune), but no information was forthcoming.

In fact the bomb had been thrown, as the police guessed from its type, by a group originating in Bengal, not the Punjab. The precise criminals were unidentified for some time. They were Rash Behari Bose, a young man who had belonged to a small terrorist organization operating out of Chandernagor (a French possession in Bengal which often served as a refuge for such elements), from whence he had moved to Dehra Dun to organize northern provincial activities. As head clerk at the Imperial Forest Research Institute, he had an excellent "cover." His associate, also in his early twenties, was Basanta Kumar Biswas, an employee (under an alias) of the Popular Dispensary at Dehra Dun. Rash Behari Bose (not be confused with the Congress, and Indian National Army, leader Subhash Chandra Bose) had organized the plot and had brought the bomb from Calcutta. Which man threw the bomb is not known, but after the explosion Rash Behari returned to Dehra Dun, and according to some accounts even organized a sympathy meeting for Hardinge.

In late 1914 the arrest of a third man, Dina Nath, who had introduced Rash Behari to Punjabi terrorists, led to Bose's trail. His movements of 1912 were traced, and it was discovered that he had been on leave from the Institute at the time of the explosion and had now disappeared. Basanta Kumar Biswas, however, was arrested for another terrorist crime, found guilty, and sentenced to transportation; the government, on appeal, triumphed, and he was hanged in May 1918. Rash Behari went underground in Lahore, Delhi, and Banaras, and was active in an abortive plot to foment revolution among Indian soldiers in 1915. The plot was revealed by an informer, and he fled the next year to Japan, where he wrote voluminously for the Indian independence movement in the interwar years. He emerged briefly to play a minor role in the Japanese-backed Indian National Army in Thailand in World War II but, too old and ill, he returned to Japan in 1942 and died in 1945.[35]

At the time, of course, none of this was known. The Executive Council, under Wilson's leadership, discussed the possibility of quartering troops on the buildings in Chandni Chauk. It was a response of panic, but Wilson backed it: "in my opinion, the time has come when a city must be held responsible for what occurs within it," even though innocent victims would suffer. Council members were uncomfortable; several argued against the measure, and the rest were noncommittal.[36] Fortunately, the idea was not pursued, nor was a later one that the bank building be pulled down. Hardinge vetoed this vindictive measure, but was not above some feelings of revenge—he was glad in private when Delhi trade suffered as the alarm spread to the surrounding area. On 26 February Hardinge resumed the reins of authority; luckily, no special punishment had been inflicted upon Delhi. (Wilson was left bitter because he had received only Hardinge's thanks and not the peerage he thought was his proper reward.)[37]

When Hardinge resumed his duties, he was not yet fully recovered. The wounds were more serious than most people knew, and Crewe even suggested that Hardinge might step down and take six months in Europe. The worst part, Hardinge wrote King George, was "the 'trying to forget.'" The bomb was a severe shock, challenging his success and popularity in his own mind. His doubts were offset, however, by the wave of sympathy expressed in thousands of messages from India and England. A few hostile letters were to be expected: one Bengali youth wrote to say he regretted that the bomb had only injured the viceroy. Muslims blamed Hindus, and vice versa. Some sympathizers wished to give money, and a new fund drive was organized to accommodate them: their money went to a teaching hospital in which Winifred had been active. At Chirol's suggestion, Phyllis Clarke in Bombay organized an all-India address from the women of India for Winifred, which included three hundred thousand signatures and was presented in an engraved elephant tusk on 20 June, Hardinge's birthday. Another smaller fund, eventually some £12,000, was used to treat children in Indian hospitals.[38]

Recovery was its own reward as well. By the end of January, Hardinge was able to open the Legislative Council in Delhi, the first session in the new capital—but he did so only with the help of doctors and drugs and with his arm still in a sling. In his speech he expressed his thanks for the sympathy, admitting that he himself had discouraged excessive security precautions. "If it was an error, it is an error that I am proud of, and I believe it may yet prove not to have been an entirely mistaken confidence, for out of evil good may come.[39] The effort was a strain, and he left for a fortnight's rest at Dehra Dun, ironically close to his attempted assassin. Continued pain resulted in an x-ray revealing unremoved bits of needle points, metal, wood, and clothing, and on 30 January he underwent another operation. By 20 February the bandages were off for the first time, and a week later he resumed full control from Wilson.

The ordeal was over, but it might happen again, and various authorities now insisted upon greater security precautions when the viceroy moved about. Nor was it over in Hardinge's or Winifred's memory, or opinion at home. In March, the king's speech at the opening of Parliament made reference to the tragedy and a unique mention of a female private citizen, Winifred:

> In my Indian Empire, on the 23rd December, at the ceremony of the State Entry into Delhi, a wicked attempt was made on the life of my Governor-General and Viceroy. Through the mercy of Divine Providence the plot failed in its full extent, but I deeply regret that innocent lives were sacrificed and that the Viceroy was gravely wounded. The fortitude of the Viceroy and Lady Hardinge and the disciplined courage of all the officers of Government have my warmest admiration. I gratefully acknowledge the expressions of sympathetic loyalty which the crime has evoked from the Ruling Chiefs and from all classes of My Indian subjects.[40]

The little work Hardinge was able to do in January principally concerned Delhi, for the assassination attempt had forestalled a reunion with the experts, and the viceroy was too weak for major decisions throughout January and February. Lutyens, who had remained in India through the summer, killed time by visiting Bombay and Agra (the Taj was beautiful by moonlight, "but it is not architecture"). In March, however, Hardinge and the Executive Council had approved the committee's final site recommendation, and Lutyens and Baker had sent in their common suggestions on the precise location and alignment of the secretariat.[41]

The secretariat was Baker's: parallel double buildings facing the approach to Lutyens's Government House. Comparisons must in the end reflect value judgments, but it is Government House which most observers find the greater achievement. Hardinge fought some of Lutyens's later sketches, mainly quarreling with facial decorations ("Are not your semi-circular arches very commonplace? They strike me as such and are to be seen everywhere in England. . . ."), the height of the dome, and similar points. Lutyens replied in polite tones (commonplace features were good or bad depending upon their setting), trying to educate Hardinge and ease him away from pet "oriental" concepts.[42]

Lutyens and Baker returned to England to work on their plans, but traveled out to India once again in November 1913. Hardinge by this time was an admirer of Lutyens, not even raising the question of his favorite pointed arches. Hardinge did wish to cut down the dome of Government House, but Lutyens was prepared to accept this. "He flew a small balloon 300 ft. up in the air to see how high it would look. My dome is only 180 feet or so!! So he said it was too high. It is all very mad." Cutting down in scale, to reduce costs, was agonizing to Lutyens, now lost in what he called "Bedlampore," but he did it nevertheless.[43] Finance was still the primary consideration, for Hardinge's estimate of £4 million had been premature. When Lutyens left in March (travelling on the same vessel as Winifred and her stepmother, Lady Alington), Government House estimates were £520,000, all government buildings £3.5 million, and £5 million for the whole project. But much of the detail of cost and financing had to await the future, for World War I was about to interrupt the construction of Delhi.[44]

After Lutyens had left, Hardinge was optimistic. It was more than the plan: two years after the government of India had left Calcutta, Hardinge was convinced that it had been the right thing to do. The government was more accessible and independent than ever before; a quite different and truer perspective of India was possible away from the domination of Calcutta. Now he only wished to push on, to begin building as soon as possible before his customary five-year term was over.[45] It had been a considerable struggle, but two years and a half after the announcement the site was picked and the plans were made, and Lutyens and Baker in the coming years would be responsible for the creation of a remarkable capital complex and monument to the raj. Lutyens's Government House was a triumph. Its design owed little to Indian antecedents, but Hardinge had insured that Lutyens saw, and perhaps absorbed, some of the tradition which is reflected in decorative motif and, above all, in adaption of the building to its general Indian setting and its local environment at Raisana. It was Lutyens's triumph, but it owed something to the patron-artist relationship, to Hardinge's determination to see the project on to, and off of, the drawing board before his own departure. Since that departure came in the midst of World War I, delays would have pushed the completion of New Delhi into the 1920s, and quite possibly the limbo of other hopes which died in the war—preventing that was Hardinge's triumph.

Hardinge was certainly correct in the wider outlook possible from Delhi, and it was an act of farseeing statesmanship, though of course not unique to him, to be an early convert. But moving to Delhi had one drawback: it was all the more difficult to find solutions to Bengal's continuing problems. In December 1912, five days before the attempt upon Hardinge's life, there had been another bomb outrage at Midnapur. This was a minor affair, but Hardinge was incensed to find after his own recovery that Carmichael, the new governor, had visited Midnapur in January and made a temporizing speech that wiped the slate clean for the future (or so Hardinge understood it). "This sort of weakness really plays the devil, and I cannot help thinking that the chaos that prevails in Eastern Bengal is largely due to his dislike of doing anything that might be unpopular with the masses."[46]

One difficulty was that the problems in Bengal were inevitably caused at least in part by economic conditions, but Hardinge, with Chandni Chauk fresh in his mind, believed in different origins:

> the movement is a conspiracy with ramifications stretching over large areas of which the object is to render Government ineffectual and so to promote revolution. Nothing could be clearer than this, and what I want to know is whether the Government of Bengal realise the danger of the situation and whether they are taking steps to cope with it.

Carmichael had held out the olive branch, but this was the wrong approach: "It is absurd for anybody to imagine that he can be on friendly terms in Bengal with Loyalists, Extremists and Dacoits at the same time."[47]

Hardinge searched his own mind and those of his advisors for suggestions. Further represssive legislation was not the answer. Until the legislation already in being was effectively applied, more laws would merely make extremists out of moderates. The Press Law had proved useful to Clarke in Bombay. Another idea which Hardinge recommended to his Council was to send two native regiments to serve in various guard positions in Eastern Bengal and thus release an equivalent number of regular police for other duties. From Bengal came the proposal that general autumn army maneuvers take place there to impress local dissidents.[48] These and other measures to some extent alleviated the trouble in Bengal, but no measures would pacify the province while there was economic hardship.

Bengali troubles at least were primarily restricted to Bengal. In India as a whole, a greater worry was the growth of Muslim agitation caused by the troubles of the Ottoman Empire, divisions within the Indian National Congress, and even British policy itself. Muslim League spokesmen advocated common cause with the Congress, but Hardinge believed that Muslim leaders were too shrewd to become Congress pawns. He wished to show Indian Muslims that he, as viceroy, had urged the authorities at home to give diplomatic support to Turkey in her hour of need, but Crewe vetoed an open declaration and Hardinge had to be satisfied with general remarks in the Legislative Council.[49]

When a specific grievance arose, Hardinge was in a position to intervene directly and in person. Such an incident occured in mid-1913 at Cawnpore. A new road constructed in the town managed to pass round both sides of a Hindu temple but required the removal of a Muslim mosque's ablution area (a very unholy shed which also included a privy), which extended into the road. Local authorities had ordered the shed, condemned since 1909, moved from one side of the mosque to the other, and there was no objection until it was discovered that the Hindu temple, originally marked for destruction, was to be preserved. A mob of angry Muslims marched on the spot and began to rebuild the partly dismantled shed. The police who attempted to turn back the Muslims were stoned, and, in the typical escalation of a crisis, force was met with force. In serious rioting the next day (4 August), twenty-three rioters were killed along with one policeman (by a police bullet). Local authorities stood firm, and the affair quickly became a rallying point for Muslims throughout India. In the end, an appeal to the viceroy brought his personal appearance in Cawnpore, a compromise settlement (the washhouse was built above the street as an arcade—the mosque itself was above street level), and release and amnesty for the prisoners.[50]

Hardinge was glad to have resolved the crisis and cooled tempers, especially since some of the legal cases against rioters might not have stood up in court. "How difficult it is to get local officials to act with any sense and with a little foresight! They seem to suffer dreadfully from lack of breadth of view." Hardinge had not accomplished this alone; Ali Imam (a Muslim) had spent three hours persuading local Muslim leaders to accept the settlement. The issue had become so deadlocked that even the best-intentioned local officials could not have reached a settlement by this point.[51]

In India the popularity of Hardinge's action, as demonstrated by the telegrams that arrived, showed him that local officials were not properly sensitive to Muslim opinion. Since he had intervened to accomplish a solution that he had suggested to them three months earlier, it is hard not to conclude that his patience had been considerable and his action, when it came, timely and appropriate. As he wrote to Lord Willingdon, newly installed governor of Madras with whom he had discussed the matter before going to Cawnpore:

> Now could you conceive anything that would create a worse effect throughout India than the knowledge that twenty-three men had been killed and over a hundred people imprisoned for six weeks in attempting to retain possession of a bit of ground which the local Government claimed illegally to have acquired? Of course this is very confidential, and it is not a thing that can be said openly.

His deeper feelings could be explained to Sanderson in England:

> What some Anglo Indians do not understand is that the days of government with a big stick are over and that justice is a safer basis than prestige for British rule in India. I assure you I simply hate the word prestige. Out here it means that if you do a wrong thing, you must stick to it and everybody must support it.[52]

Hardinge was a conservative viceroy, happier without the need to interfere in affairs such as Cawnpore, just as a diplomat thrives on smooth relations between nations. But at times he had no alternative, not only to prevent tragic consequences but also from a sense of justice. Hardinge's imperialism, never spelled out in formulas or generalizations, was of that variety in which fairness meant both means and justification. As has been pointed out, he had no vision of the voluntary future end of the empire or the grant of self-rule to India. Constitutional changes might be necessary to meet changing times—a new provincial council here, a princes' conference there. To the suggestion, made by Mohammad Shafi at an all-India Muslim League meeting at Lucknow, that the Legislative Council be altered to include a nonofficial majority, Hardinge registered only scorn; at that point, "the Viceroy had better pack up his traps and leave the country. His position would then be lacking in dignity."[53]

Dignity was an important component of Hardinge's philosophy. Cawnpore offended his sense of fitness of things, and fairness required intervention. His fall 1913 tour—in which Cawnpore was the first stop—was temporarily distracting. He set off in the viceregal train (normally ten cars), and his carefully orchestrated travels took him to Mysore and back; each hour was carefully accounted for, all laid out in a leather-bound volume with maps and diagrams. "At 8.37 . . . the Special conveying Their Excellencies halts for eight minutes at the French Rocks Station. Here the First Assistant Resident and the two Principle Officers of the Mysore State meet His Excellency," and so on through each elaborate and tiring day. For formal splendor and the panoply of the raj, the fall 1913 tour was the end of an era as much as was the broken howdah in Delhi.[54]

At Madras, however, an even greater problem with far wider ramifications than Cawnpore caught up with him: the status of Indians in South Africa. Hardinge had watched this problem since his arrival in India, for even then there was a longstanding grievance about the treatment of Indian immigrants into South Africa, and particularly about indentured labor in Natal. There was no guarantee, for example, that immigrants would be granted citizenship once their indenture expired. At that time, South African authorities suggested that the best solution was for India to end emigration to Natal. In 1911 a resolution to this effect was passed in the Legislative Council, but it could not affect Indians already in South Africa. Indian authorities could only take notice of the objectionable features of South Africa's Immigration Bill and trust that the Union Government would adhere to its assurances on the rights of persons domiciled in

South Africa.[55]

Unfortunately, the affair simmered on and by 1913 had become an issue of considerable importance among Indians, not only in South Africa but in India as well. Natal had imposed a head tax of £3 on indentured laborers who remained when their contract expired, and in 1913 a court ruling seemed potentially to invalidate all non-Christian marriages. South African authorities rejected Indian requests to modify their position, and Cape Colony officials refused to receive an unofficial Indian delegation to discuss the now closed immigration. That Indians in South Africa had organized their own efforts with the assistance of Mohandas K. Gandhi perhaps inspired Hardinge to take action. A call by moderate nationalists for a special session of the Indian Legislature had even more effect on him. But the method Hardinge chose was directly due to press reports of police brutality to strikers, death by flogging, and mass meetings in South Africa, which were creating the worst possible effect. He took the very unusual and technically wrong step of protesting directly to the governor-general in South Africa, Viscount Gladstone.[56]

Hardinge followed this with a strong telegram for Crewe to use at cabinet level. To the king, as to Crewe, Hardinge called for a full and impartial inquiry, although he doubted that the Cape Government could be relied upon to do this. The basic issue was simple: "no educated Indian can realise that there is any justification for Indians not enjoying in other parts of the Empire the same liberty and rights as any others of Your Majesty's subjects."[57]

On 24 November Hardinge made a strong public statement in response to addresses from various bodies in Madras, so strong that it jolted opinion in India, England, and above all among angry officials in South Africa. Most important, Hardinge rose to the defense of the strikers against legal discrimination:

> They have violated, as they intended to violate, those laws, with full knowledge of the penalties involved, and ready with all courage and patience to endure these penalties. In

> all this they have the sympathy of India—deep and burning—and not only of India, but of all those who like myself, without being Indians themselves, have feelings of sympathy for the people of this country.

The blame was clearly upon South African authorities for taking measures which, if the allegations were true, "would not for a moment be tolerated in any country that claims to call itself civilised."[58]

The speech was immensely popular, and as one historian has commented, "almost overnight made Hardinge into perhaps the most popular British figure ever to serve on the subcontinent." In justification, Hardinge pointed out that this public statement, associating the government of India with the agitation, had come just in time to stop what might have become a dangerous radical movement in India itself, where the only target must have been the government of India. As Hardinge admitted, India—governmental or private—had no real means of retaliating upon South Africa. Crewe protested mildly against Hardinge's missive to Gladstone and noted that the Madras speech "has somewhat fluttered the dove-cotes," but he was sympathetic.[59]

Within a few days, the Cabinet discussed the speech, and several members were critical of Hardinge's language (a view the king shared). It was generally recognized, however, that silence on the viceroy's part would have been misunderstood in India. Crewe had more trouble defending direct communication to Gladstone. The Cabinet agreed to disagree, and took no collective stance on what was now a quarrel between two parts of the empire. Hardinge, for his part, regretted only the passage quoted above which extended his sympathy to illegality. Once again, he opened his mind to Sanderson:

> India has been extraordinarily patient under a sense of deep provocation, and this I believe has encouraged the idea in the minds of South Africans that India is a negligible quantity for whom nobody, not even the Government of India,

> would stand up and fight. It is a feeling that I have long had. . . .

The speech, moreover, had "an almost magic effect" in calming agitation that many considered very serious indeed. After all, India only asked fair and proper treatment of Indians living in South Africa.[60]

In the end, a three-man South African commission (including no Indians) agreed to cancel the requirement for licenses to remain in the colony and to permit Indian priests to act as marriage officers empowered to solemnize (monogamous) marriages in accordance with the religious beliefs of the parties concerned; for those already married, one wife and child would be permitted to enter South Africa.[61]

It was not a perfect solution, nor did it pledge full legal equality, but it was enough for the time being. Muslims, embarrassed by the South African refusal to recognize any marriage in a religion which permitted polygamy, at least would be permitted one legal wife. Hardinge announced in March 1914 to the Legislative Council that these new steps, if fully carried out, were "a very complete and satisfactory attempt to arrive at a final solution of the difficulties that have arisen in South Africa. . . ."[62]

This conclusion was an exaggeration, but, as with Cawnpore, Hardinge's personal intervention had played an important role in the temporary solution obtained. Cawnpore, however, was important only in India; South Africa had larger imperial ramifications, and Hardinge had acted with decision when all other possible approaches seemed to have been exhausted. These crises, like the planning of Delhi, had not the attention-winning drama of the great durbar of 1911, but they had demanded close attention and the exercise of both patience and decision. The year 1914 was to provide tests sterner even than the bomb in New Delhi.

VIII India and the War

By the spring of 1914, Hardinge could take pride in his accomplishments as viceroy in a complex variety of matters. Although he had alienated vested interests from Calcutta's European community to South Africa's governor-general, he had won many friends in India. In the normal run of things, he could soon expect to rest upon his laurels; strong tradition limited the viceroy's term to five years. He began to think about returning home, but not for reasons of ill health as rumored. Since his arrival in India, he had never lost touch with various changes in the Foreign Office and the Diplomatic Service; a top opening in Berlin would be available just when Hardinge returned from India (aged fifty-seven), although he preferred Paris above all.

Winifred's health was another concern. Late in 1913, she had decided to return to England in the hot weather of 1914 for six months of rest and visits to family and friends. Hardinge accompanied her to Bombay in late March—his first visit since 1910 and an opportunity to open the port's new docks, the finest in India. He admitted to Sanderson that he was going to miss her very much, particularly since viceroys led a very isolated existence. Such correspondence as remains says nothing of her health, but she was very ill and must have been worried. Hardinge returned to Simla, where he found social obligations a burden, although Diamond was some comfort. He was hardly in a frame of mind receptive to the idea then in the air of extending his term.[1]

On her arrival in England, Winifred took medical advice on symptoms of intestinal pain and indigestion. Several opinons and x-rays confirmed that she would have to undergo two operations for uterine hemorrhage and a tumor, diagnosed as malignant. The first operation (27 June), in a private Park Lane hospital, went well. The second, two weeks later, was more serious; after the operation, she began to fail. Knowing she was dying, she gave farewell messages to the doctor and to her sons, who were present, and her heart stopped.

All who knew her were shocked at this sudden and totally unexpected loss. Hardinge received the news by telegram; sadly, for some weeks he still received hopeful letters from her and friends, delayed by sea mail and wartime conditions. As *The Times* pointed out, it was a tragic irony that she should survive the Delhi bomb only to die in a London nursing home. A small service in London was followed by a memorial in the Chapel Royal at Windsor: more than two hundred people crowded in, and hundreds of wreaths testified to her wide circle of friends. Hardinge in India was deluged with telegrams of sympathy, including one from the kaiser, but it was Queen Alexandra's which was most moving on his "overwhelming sorrow and irreparable loss of your beloved darling Bena. . . ."[2]

There would be no need to belabor the loss to Hardinge, except that his reputation as a rather cold and reserved man has persisted—"Capability Hardinge." As with many such individuals, however, his small circle of friends and family was very close. Shortly after Winifred's departure from Bombay, Hardinge had written to Chirol that her health was one major objection to any extension of his term, and she "must always be *the* paramount consideration, for it is to her that I owe almost everything," adding that he could not again face a long separation. Chirol explained to his editor, Geoffrey Robinson, who also admired Winifred (Robinson wrote the editorial leader in *The*

Times on her death, a very rare intervention), that he had written to Hardinge and offered to go out to India; he had received a very touching and grateful acceptance (the outbreak of war prevented the journey).[3] Hardinge went on with his work as usual, but as Du Boulay remarked, it was "a melancholy household."[4]

Hardinge's personal blows were not over for the year, however. The Fifteenth Hussars (the king's), Edd's unit, was one of the first to be sent to France. In an early action, he was seriously wounded by machine-gun fire during a reconnaissance (his display of courage won him the D.S.O.). Invalided home, he made a smooth recovery, and by December he made definite plans to leave for India early in 1915 to spend four months' sick leave with his father. Hardinge received encouraging reports from Queens Mary and Alexandra, Chirol, and Crewe—everyone who visited Edd. In the same room was his cousin, Gerard Sturt (eldest son of Lord Alington), who eventually died of severe wounds.[5]

Once again, Hardinge was swamped by telegrams, and he reported to King George that India was taking a close interest in Edd's progress. He was relieved to hear that his son was doing well, but he had little choice but to release his own A.D.C.s for service in France, and before the year was out, two were dead. That Alec, Hardinge's second son, intended to join the army with Harrow and Cambridge friends was news which brought mixed emotions.[6]

Suddenly Edd took a turn for the worse, and before Christmas he was dead, swept away by a virus. Crewe and Chirol and Queen Alexandra did their best to express their sorrow, but it was a terrible second blow within one year. Hardinge could take only small comfort from the fact that Winifred had not had to suffer Edd's death. "His death has made me still more sad and unhappy than I was," he wrote to the king.[7] There was Alec, who would survive the war, and Diamond, and friends like Chirol—and the tragic but inescapable fact that far too many others were suffering similar losses. And, of course, there was the war itself.

Hardinge was warned of the imminent outbreak of war only six days before England's declaration on 4 August. He rushed to Simla from Dehra Dun to implement existing plans for steps to be taken in the empire, steps well known to Hardinge who had earlier chaired the C.I.D. subcommittee which prepared them. They included such measures as seizure of German ships in Indian ports. Hardinge, as viceroy, signed the declaration of war on India's behalf—rightly assuming that there could be no protest (if indeed the question occurred to him), an assumption made on far less certain grounds by another viceroy in World War II.

India, and Hardinge, had rejected the idea of sending troops to Europe in 1911, and the Nicholson Committee had stated that India had no obligation to keep troops for possible use outside India. By 1913 Hardinge's attitude had altered, at least to the point that he preferred sending troops to Europe in some future crisis to paying a larger immediate share of Britain's naval expenses. "We could send troops to Europe in an emergency," he explained to the king, "on a much larger scale than it would be possible for any colony to do. . . ." The emergency had now arisen, and for overseas service India was quick to offer up to three divisions of infantry and one brigade of cavalry out of a total of six divisions in India (the remainder was the minimum needed in case the northwest frontier exploded and Afghanistan turned hostile). The troops were ordered to Egypt, Malta, and Gibraltar, but Hardinge protested that they should be sent to France: it would be a slur upon a fine body of troops if they were barred from France while the French had Algerian and Senegalese troops in the lines. The protest, combined with the desperate need in France, was effective; the Third (Lahore) and Seventh (Meerut) Divisions were rushed into battle and soon held one-third of the British line. Five Victoria Crosses were awarded to Indians in France.[8]

By the end of August, sixty thousand men had been sent overseas, six hundred officers had been kept for European service (most British officers took home leave in hot weather), and forty-six thousand rifles and fifty million rounds of ammunition had been supplied—when eighteen thousand men to China was the largest expedition India had previously fielded overseas. Hardinge credited his general policy of "sympathy and conciliation" which "is now bearing fruit and has amply justified itself. I write this in no boasting, but in a deeply thankful spirit." But it was great satisfaction to enjoy "what few people ever enjoy during their term of office, a vindication of my policy and administration."[9]

Part of Hardinge's thankfulness came from the loyal response of the Native States, fully the equal of that of the British community in India. Twenty-seven states maintained Imperial Service Troops, and all were offered to the government. Hardinge sifted through them and accepted the dozen best, including the famous Camel Corps of Bikaner. The rulers of Bikaner, Jodphur, Patiala, and other states served with their forces.

In British India the response was equally enthusiastic, from British and Indians alike. One of the first proposals was to expand, by the inclusion of Indians, the European volunteer companies existing in the major port cities. Hardinge warmly supported the request of Indians to join, but except for Ali Imam, the Executive Council refused to support the viceroy—his only such substantive defeat.

> I always said that these civilians see no further than the ends of their noses and are as narrow in their conception and ideas as possible. Many of them retain the ideas of the days following immediately the Mutiny, and fail to see that in time of emergency the people have an inherent right to defend their own shores, and that they can be trusted to do so.[10]

Seemingly of minor importance at a time of hectic preparations, the question of volunteers was the first of many measures which dampened enthusiasm for the cause. To his credit, Hardinge realized this.

For the same reason, Hardinge complained—to little effect—about rigid censorship ordered from home (identical rules applied in England) and the failure to use the Indian troops in Europe at once. If Indian feelings were offended, "the whole situation may quickly change and we may have a sullen and discontented people to deal with." Hardinge willingly offered in return to denude India even more of her limited military strength. "I can only assure you," he wrote to Crewe,

> that it is our one aim and object to cordially cooperate in every possible way with the military authorities in England, and we have spared no effort to do so, running even a certain amount of risk by the depletion of our stock of rifles, ammunition, &c., for the sake of the cause. As long as I am able to keep the people of this country in good humour by showing them that their co-operation is valued at home, I would even be ready to take greater risks than at present should the necessity arise.[11]

A particular problem would be Muslim sensibilities if war broke out with the Ottoman Empire. Hardinge laid plans to educate Muslim opinion in India, and he impressed upon authorities at home how essential it was to make Turkey take the aggressive step which would lead to the break. Meanwhile he asked permission to issue an assurance that the allies would make no attack on the holy places in Arabia or Jeddah (the main pilgrim port) if the Turks did not interfere with Indian pilgrims. The declaration was made in November. War with Turkey would be a test, but Muslims had already demonstrated their zeal, and on 8 September, when the Legislative Council convened, private members of all faiths vied in their expression of loyalty.[12]

Hardinge wished to keep these feelings alive, but it was difficult to make efficient use of them, particularly when military authorities remained uncooperative. However, he had no further ideas and must share in the blame for using only such enthusiasm as was immediately handy. L. F. Rushbrook Williams's criticism is an apt summary:

> Indians, however, were left without much guidance. In

> consequence, the astonishing outburst of popular emotion was allowed to exhaust itself almost fruitlessly in proportion to its magnitude: until, at a later date, it had to be artificially revived to meet a domestic danger and to sustain the unprecedented war effort of 1918. The authorities seemed to rest content with the knowledge that India was safe from revolution: it appeared scarcely to occur to them to enlist in the cause of the commonwealth even a proportion of the energy and devotion so freely proffered. Offers of service were courteously acknowledged: some few were accepted, others were pigeon-holed. But no attempt was made to set up any organization which might be capable of coordinatng them, and turning them to the best account.[13]

The demands of London were far more efficiently regular. In September a mixed division was sent from India to East Africa. Further requests followed through September and October, as Hardinge struggled to keep three divisions intact on the northwest frontier, for if war broke out with Turkey and a jihad was proclaimed, that minimal line of defense might become critical—and to weaken it might inspire panic. By the spring of 1915 nearly all British regular units had left (forty-three of fifty-two battalions, and forty-four of fifty-two artillery battalions), soon to be replaced by Territorial Army troops with little training and less equipment. Hardinge insisted only that for every British battalion that went overseas, an Indian one went as well, "for after all it is only Indian troops that are in a position to become a military danger," as he explained to Gen. Sir Beauchamp Duff, the commander-in-chief.[14]

Had Hardinge insisted upon dangers on the frontier or of internal security, he might have reduced India's commitment. His thinking was simple: if the empire fell, India would fall, no matter how many troops were kept back. Meanwhile, public opinion was critical for the preservation of stability in India, and this explains Hardinge's repeated insistence that home authorities not commit the blunder of using Indian troops merely for garrison duties. Hardinge, like many others, believed that the risk would be short in duration: a European war could not last more than four or five months.[15]

By the end of October, the growing tension with Turkey necessitated preliminary preparations for a landing at the head of the Persian Gulf to secure the oil pipelines at Abadan and the port of Basra. War was declared on 5 November; on the sixth, British forces landed in Turkish territory. Hardinge feared the possible effect among Muslims and the potential drain of Indian resources. If the Turks brought up reserves in strength after Basra was taken, a full division would be necessary from India—and it could only come from the frontier or the troops designated for Europe. The latter proved to be the case, and the sixth (Poona) Division was diverted from its destination in France to the Gulf.[16]

How far the force should proceed into Ottoman territory was a moot point, and Hardinge offered no initial opinion. His nervousness is clear from (verbal) orders to give out as little news as possible on Gulf and Mesopotamian operations. A public remark by Asquith at home that this was the chance to oust the Turks from Europe in Gladstonian "bag and baggage" fashion was disturbing, although Hardinge shared this view in private. From his vantage point, restlessly awaiting the response of the amir of Afghanistan to news of the war, such open expressions were misguided.[17]

Operations at Basra went too easily, and the temptation to advance was irresistible. Baghdad was an obvious long-range goal, but Hardinge knew the long line of communications would require a larger force of at least two divisions in Mesopotamia. Duff was eager to move on if the troops could be found, and Duff was the professional. Sir Percy Cox, chief political officer with the expedition, wished to declare the permanent occupation of Basra: this could not be done publicly, but Hardinge did ask Crewe for private assurances to that effect. Clearly Hardinge was an early victim of success, and Crewe had now to cool his ardor. Hardinge at least had no desire to conquer all Iraq: a long frontier with Russia (promised a healthy slice of Ottoman territory) and unwanted governing responsibilities meant that Basra, and the permanent security it would provide for Britain's Gulf position, was enough for the time being.[18]

London refused to go so far, and Hardinge urged his views on anyone who might have influence—the king, Crewe, Nicolson, Chirol, Wingate in the Sudan. He did much of this work by himself: McMahon, his foreign secretary, had been kept in London on leave and then, to his own and Hardinge's surprise, named high commissioner in Egypt; A. H. Grant, his successor, was only just settling in. Hardinge received enough encouraging responses to tell Cox by private telegram to proceed on the assumption that Basra would be permanently occupied, although this advice ran counter to his official orders from London.[19]

But Basra, the town, became Basra, the Ottoman province. The advance upriver was sanctioned piecemeal, first to Qurna, fifty miles up the Tigris (it fell on 9 November), then Amara, sixty (air) miles beyond Qurna, where in January orders were issued to consolidate, since troops were in short supply. Hardinge felt awkwardly placed to judge the situation, and he wanted to see for himself. The urge to get away from India was great; he received the news of Edd's death on 17 December, and on the twenty-eighth he cabled to ask Crewe for permission to visit Mesopotamia. On 25 January he left Bombay for the Gulf.[20]

Grim as the cause might be, the trip was refreshing. Alec had returned from England as an Indian army reserve officer to serve as A.D.C. to the viceroy, and with Chirol he met Hardinge at Bombay. Family reunion, new places—Crewe had approved the trip partly for this reason. Hardinge would gain personal experience of the situation and, as Crewe explained to the king, "an interval of change and distraction from his anxious post in India and his great personal sorrows."[21]

On 31 January Hardinge arrived at Kuwait, his first stop, where he exchanged visits and honors with the rulers of Kuwait and Bahrain. He then visited the oil works at Abadan and traveled up the Karun River in a launch. At Mohammera, he invested the Shaikh—an important figure in prewar Gulf diplomacy—with the K.C.S.I. Hardinge had once opposed involvement in the oil operations, but now he delighted there was so large a British stake in this area, "since it makes it absolutely certain that we can never give up Busrah [sic] which I regard as the key of the Gulf."[22]

At Basra, Hardinge was greeted with full military honors. He investigated the situation of the sick and wounded and found them cheery and the hospitals well run, but the Mesopotamian force had not yet suffered the severe losses of later stages of the campaign. Altogether he was impressed with the arrangements; an advance was not far from his thoughts, but for the time being the winter rainy season and overflowing marshlands made immediate action impossible.[23]

It was on the whole a useful trip, for Hardinge had never before seen either Basra or the Gulf, areas on which he spent so much effort in correspondence. He returned to Delhi even more enthusiastic about the possibilities in Mesopotamia, and that picture stayed in his mind well after it had come to differ substantially from reality. His main conclusion was that the enclave had to be enlarged and secured from all Turkish influence, which objective required occupation of Nasiriya on the Euphrates and Amara on the Tigris. The future of Baghdad was also in his thoughts. As he put it to Curzon,

> I do not want to go to Bagdad unless forced to do so, but when the time comes to make peace with Turkey, Bagdad, Busra, and perhaps even Mosul must be lopped off, and while we remain at Busra some kind of protectorate over the rest of Mesopotamia must be established.

But to hold what Britain had it would be necesary to advance (an old story in Britain's Asian history). Hardinge prepared a "Note on the Future Status and Administration of Basrah" which he sent home and which discussed the potentialities of trade, irrigation, and petroleum development, and the impossibility of returning Iraq (not merely Basra) to Turkish rule. The Basra vilayet (province) would be sufficient, if the control was complete and permanent.[24]

Unfortunately, home authorities, far from relinquishing troops for Mesopotamia, asked more for Europe from a wary and weary India. Hardinge now began to drag his heels, for the three divisions sent early in the war had become nine, as India called upon all available reserves and recruits, and the three divisions of territorials sent in return were an inadequate substitute. Some of the early euphoria had evaporated, and there were increasing internal security problems, principally related to food supplies—although Hardinge reported that the problem was more inflationary prices than physical shortages. He had already urged the prohibition of any grain exports: it was important not to provide the opposition with the argument that India was being starved to feed Europeans. By the end of February, his protests were taking on a more determined note: "We feel we have not been treated fairly, and that no effort is being made by the military authorities to meet our needs. It is the old story of treating India like a milch cow, and this creates a deplorable impression here."[25]

Hardinge's arguments would have been more persuasive had he been appealing for troops for India rather than Mesopotamia. Crewe and others did not appreciate arguments that Basra, which all thought was secure, was in danger of being outflanked by the Turks unless reinforcements were sent—reinforcements which were simply not available. In any case, future policy towards Asiatic Turkey, seemingly a useful preliminary to running further risks in that part of the world, was completely undecided. A committee was soon established at home to discuss exactly this problem. Meanwhile Hardinge did his best to urge his increasingly ambitious views: permanent transfer of Basra; cession of the Baghdad vilayet, to be established as a native administration under British control; the Baghdad Railway to pass to British ownership; undetermined concessions elsewhere to persuade

Russia to relax her grip on northern Persia—even to withdraw if possible—or partition of Persia if that undesirable alternative were forced by Persian participation in the war on Turkey's side. To help the process along, Hardinge supported the appointment of a new commander, General Sir John Nixon. The previous commander had done well but was not senior enough to command the thirty thousand men in Mesopotamia at the time.[26] Nixon arrived in early April, and it was soon clear that he was not the man to sit quietly in Basra.

For his part, Hardinge had to give increasing attention to affairs within India. As time passed, enthusiasm cooled, news was scanty, and uncertainty was aroused in some Muslims by the fighting against Turkey. Individual officials went home to serve, plans were put in abeyance, and the government of India began to be seriously concerned about security problems made more threatening by the depletion of British and Indian troops. Attention focused upon several individual issues, such as a clash between the government and Sikh emigrants which cost a number of lives but was not really dangerous; the individuals concerned were simple working men, far from their home villages.[27]

More alarming was the Ghadr Party, a Punjabi Sikh revolutionary group, about three hundred of whose leaders and sympathizers Hardinge ordered detained in early 1915 at the request of Sir Michael O'Dwyer, lieutenant governor of the Punjab. Because of this movement in the Punjab, general insecurity in Bengal, and dangers on the frontier, the government of India, with Hardinge's approval, decided to introduce a law on the lines of the British Act for the Defense of the Realm (DORA), which gave exceptional discretionary powers to the goernment.[28]

The DORA was introduced in mid-March. There was considerable outcry at a bill which was more drastic than the British equivalent, and several Legislative Council members told Hardinge they would have to oppose the bill. In fact it passed unanimously after lengthy debate and a few minor amendments. Hardinge's frank remark that it would be more pleasant to do without the legislation, and the fact that Parliament had passed the British equivalent without a murmur, may have influenced some members.[29]

Hardinge felt more than justified in this measure, in part because of a new level of Hindu nationalist agitation. In December 1915, more extremist leaders established the Home Rule League at Poona, challenging less effective moderate Congress leadership. Tilak and Annie Besant, leaders of separate but similar movements, toured India in a whirlwind campaign of 1916 to inspire demands for home rule. Hardinge was urged to step in, but he preferred to let these leaders, particularly Besant, speak.

More immediately dangerous was Muslim separatist and pro-Turkish feeling. There was trouble in several Muslim regiments and agitation against Britain's assault upon the caliph (the Ottoman sultan); the former was suppressed, the latter quieted for the time being by the internment in a Hindu village of the principal leaders, the Muslim brothers Mohamed and Shaukat Ali. Further incidents occurred, however: for example, the arrest of a revolutionary emissary with a load of bombs in the lines of a cavalry regiment at Meerut, and the repulse of several thousand Afghani tribesmen from a frontier post. Fortunately the Amir Habibullah adhered faithfully to his pledge of neutrality, encouraged by a series of letters from Hardinge, and frontier incidents were just that rather than any sustained campaign. But there was more than enough need for security measures, whether the DORA or Hardinge's reluctant acceptance of six thousand Nepalese troops to be used as a striking force in case of trouble. By the end of May Hardinge could report that the situation was reassuring, a distinct and pleasant change from the tense weeks of February and March. Special tribunals, operating under the DORA, proved particularly effective in the Punjab.[30]

Less satisfactory was the extension of Hardinge's own term, for he had looked forward to coming home. In January, Crewe raised the prospect that his return might be delayed by the war.

Crewe felt that once extended, Hardinge's term should last the duration of the war. The king and Asquith agreed that changing horses in midstream was dangerous, especially where "the stream is deep and rapid," as Lord Stamfordham explained it, "but the horse knows the danger and can be trusted!" Continued work would keep Hardinge busy, and when the war was over Kitchener could be sent out. But Crewe was afraid that the strain might be too great and Hardinge break down, which would be a disaster for India. If the war continued into 1916, as Crewe personally felt it would, Hardinge would probably have to stay on for two or three more years to deal with its immediate aftermath. Chirol too was worried about Hardinge's health but told Crewe he saw nothing wrong with a temporary extension, for, say, six months.[31]

As the time for decision approached, Hardinge was bombarded with telegrams and memorials asking him to stay on. He was worried that any successor might not view Indian aspirations as sympathetically as he felt he would himself—but five years was enough. Authorities at home could always say that he was needed there for consultation on foreign affairs. The knowledge that Nicolson had decided to retire and not move on to Paris after the war (when Bertie would definitely be leaving) was another spur.[32]

In May the cabinet coalition was restructured, and Crewe became Lord President of the Council. The desirability that there not be at once both a new viceroy and a new secretary of state increased Hardinge's chances of staying. Hardinge was sorry to lose Crewe, an old friend since Harrow days, although "absolutely ineffective in defending in the House of Lords the policy of the India Office and the Government of India." Austen Chamberlain, his successor, was a good choice in Hardinge's mind, and he was quick to ask him for a decision. It was not merely anxiety to get home; as he admitted to his friend Ronald Graham in Paris, "I am not a bit happy here, where everything reminds me of my loss and how irreparable it is."[33]

Chamberlain and Asquith weighed the advantages and

dangers of extensions and decided to accept Chirol's plan of a short term while hunting for a successor. Hardinge was asked to stay on until the spring move to Simla in March 1916. He accepted at once, and the news was made public.[34] Unfortunately, the last part of Hardinge's term coincided with disaster in Mesopotamia.

The arrival of General Nixon in April 1915 altered the situation in Mesopotamia, because Nixon gave wide interpretation to his orders (from Duff, not Hardinge), which instructed him to hold such portions of neighboring territories as affected the security of Basra. He soon ordered an advance on Amara. Crewe approved, rather after the fact, if Nixon was certain he could hold the newly added territory, and Chamberlain saw no reason to reverse Crewe's decision. Hardinge, like Crewe, had been given little notice of the advance. Amara fell on 3 June and Nixon soon announced, this time with Hardinge's support, that Nasiriya was the next step: it fell on 25 July.[35] The Turks now concentrated at Kut al-Amara, 90 miles north of Amara (125 by river), only 100 (air) miles south of Baghdad. Nixon was eager to press on, although those in India were worried by the ever-lengthening lines of communication.[36]

When Kut fell in September, Baghdad glittered all the more as a potential prize, possession of which would insure both Iraq and Persia's friendly neutrality. By mid-month, Hardinge was thinking even of a possible raid in force upon Baghdad, and would have pushed for it "if it were not that in the East one must never go back having once advanced," and that an advance would require a reserve of troops in Egypt on which Mesopotamia could draw if necessary against a Turkish counterattack.[37]

By October a decision was necessary, for Nixon said he could take Baghdad. His subordinate, Major General C.V.F. Townshend, disagreed, although Nixon did not forward his objections to India and later denied that he had received them at all. The War Office and Admiralty alike urged caution, and Chamberlain was already uneasy at a note of doubt which had crept into Hardinge's letters. Asquith was uncertain enough to establish a special interdepartmental committee—with little authority and less military expertise—to consider an advance. Predictably, the committee advised that Baghdad was desirable if it could be held, and somehow this lent legitimacy to a decision which was too tempting to refuse: it promised a bold victory, at least in propaganda, very much on the cheap compared to France or Gallipoli. In meetings of 14 and 21 October the Cabinet discussed Baghdad at length without making a decision, but Chamberlain telegraphed privately that unless India regarded the chance of eventual withdrawal as decisive, the advance would be sanctioned. The extra division of reinforcements which India had listed as an essential preliminary would arrive only later, as Indian units fighting in France were released for Mesopotamia.[38]

Hardinge, now moving from Simla to Delhi for the last time (and thus suffering the first of a lengthy round of farewell speeches and dinners), was by now a convinced advocate of advance, assuming that the home authorities provided the reinforcements—and also assuming, quite logically, that his military advisors knew their subject. Hardinge was not a trained soldier and cannot really be blamed for believing Nixon and Duff. His assessment of Baghdad was political, and it was correct: the value in Near Eastern eyes of its capture would be great, with a most beneficial effect on Arabia, Persia, and Afghanistan; in short, "a very suitable ending to what has been so far a most satisfactory campaign." It was fatally easy to take pride in the capture in advance. As he put it to Stamfordham, "My little show in Mesopotamia is going strong, and I hope that Baghdad will soon be comprised within the British Empire."[39]

Hardinge still wavered between permanent occupation and lightning raid, while Duff urged that it was better to stay. Hardinge believed that London would make the decision, while Chamberlain was leaving it up to the viceroy. Nixon meanwhile acted on his own, sending Townshend onto Azizyah, halfway to Baghdad, and insisting to Delhi that he could go on without more troops until the Turks tried to recapture the city. Hardinge offered no negative arguments to Chamberlain or the Cabinet, and in that sense was as blameworthy as any other nonmilitary enthusiast who succumbed to Baghdad's allure. He would have required strong evidence to overrule the army, and he had no such evidence—and little desire to search for it. Townshend might have furnished it, but it was not Hardinge's responsibility to circumvent Nixon and consult his subordinates. There can be little question that the principal responsibility was Nixon's: After giving Chamberlain a last chance to say no, Hardinge ordered Nixon to advance, stating clearly that he expected the necessary reinforcements to be sent as soon as possible.[40]

At first the advance went well. In mid-November, however, Townshend's force fought a difficult battle at Ctesiphon, twenty miles south of Baghdad. Townshend was sufficiently mauled and overextended to find it necessary to fall back on Kut to rest and await reinforcements. He had lost forty-six hundred killed, wounded, and missing, and the involuntary "raid" had not even reached Baghdad. By early December, the rest camp at Kut had turned into a trap.

Hardinge, meanwhile, was thinking of the long-range future, prompted by what appeared to be a promise to Arab leaders from McMahon in Cairo that Mesopotamia would be part of some future Arab state—not at all Hardinge's intention for the area, certainly where Basra was concerned. The pledges contained in McMahon's correspondence with Amir Hussein, the sherif of Mecca, did in fact reserve British interests in Mesopotamia, but Hardinge did not find this reservation satisfactory, particularly since India was not consulted in the first place. Annexation of Basra was still his minimum goal, but McMahon's words appeared to rule this out. To Hardinge, the promises simply asked for trouble from some future Arab administration and jeopardized potential revenues and room for Indian immigration and commercial expansion.[41]

When it became obvious that the Gallipoli operations would be discontinued by evacuation, suddenly the sweet prospects of Mesopotamia had soured. Hardinge cabled Chamberlain to warn of the loss of prestige evacuation would produce; it might well decide the Persians to come in and, like a tumbling house of cards, the Afghanis and the frontier tribes with them. More Turkish troops would be released for Mesopotamia and Aden; the troops promised from Europe were more than ever needed, and British units remaining in India should be brought up to full strength. The capture of Baghdad would not offset these disadvantages, because without Gallipoli to worry the Turks, the risk of Baghdad being retaken by them was considerably greater—an ironic argument, since one reason for marching on Baghdad had been to make life easier for the British forces at Gallipoli.[42]

The defeat at Ctesiphon, and the final arrival of Townshend's personal reservations, were far more shocking. Hardinge reported that Townshend's force had been ten thousand effectives, not the twenty thousand he had thought. Hardinge and Duff agreed at once to send two territorial brigades (and one of artillery) from India's scanty resources, since the promised force from Europe was still not in sight. For the moment Townshend seemed safe enough in Kut, but there were other problems. Chamberlain from home sent alarming stories of a breakdown in the medical arrangements which had seemed adequate the previous spring. When Hardinge heard, it was too late. All he could do was report that the principal medical officer in Basra had been replaced, and complain about the drain of medical officers in Europe. The breakdown required far more desperate measures: hospital facilities, doctors, above all transportation arrangements down river from the battlefield were entirely inadequate for a force the size of that in Mesopotamia and the number of wounded suffered at Ctesiphon.

The question was how to remedy the situation. Chamberlain could do little in London; Hardinge was rather closer in India. But the obvious course for Hardinge was to pass warnings and complaints to Nixon and urge him to do something. It was also the better part of wisdom to suggest caution to Duff, even now planning a new advance—but overruling Duff was a major step which Hardinge would take only with the greatest reluctance (clashes between viceroy and commander in chief in the past were not always resolved in the viceroy's favor, as Curzon had found with Kitchener). Hardinge had learned a hard lesson about the campaign in general, however: "To divert our troops from the decisive point in Flanders is to play the game of Germany, and, in my humble opinion, this policy has been far too often pursued during the present war to the great advantage of the enemy." After Christmas, his optimism revived; there was still hope of relieving Townshend, defeating the Turks, and holding Baghdad as a base, as soon as a large enough force was concentrated on the Tigris.[43]

Hardinge tried to calm worries at home about Townshend's safety in Kut. Nixon was to blame for completely failing to obtain aerial reconnaissance of unexpected Turkish troop concentrations (this was particularly aggravating to Hardinge, for he had obtained the few airplanes in Mesopotamia only by repeated appeals to London). Nixon was out, however, and Hardinge reluctantly accepted Duff's choice of successor, Lieutenant General Sir Percy Lake (Duff's chief of staff and already in his sixties); there seemed no immediately available alternative. Hardinge told Lake before he assumed command that future operations would largely depend upon the information Lake provided on local conditions, flood levels, and enemy dispositions. In other words, the viceroy hoped still for the relief of Kut.[44]

As spring, and Hardinge's return to England, approached, that hope dwindled. Very late in the day, the decision was taken to put Mesopotamia under the War Office. Under the circumstances, Hardinge agreed. Only the fall of Erzerum to a Russian advance stood in the credit ledger in the Turkish war; Hardinge now begrudged Russia nothing if it improved the situation in Iraq. All attempts to relieve Townshend failed, and after Hardinge's departure, the entire army at Kut surrendered.

Perhaps Hardinge would have intervened more decisively had he not been uncertain about his own term for six months and then found it extended for only a few more. There was little he could have done about the advance on Baghdad without a detailed intervention in military affairs which would not have been possible from Delhi (as Duff found to his cost), and Hardinge believed, as he wanted to believe, in Duff and Nixon. He could have given more energy to forcing action on the medical situation when he was first urged by Chamberlain to do so. He acted with as much alacrity as Duff would allow, which was not enough. When the first reports arrived, Surgeon General MacNeece was sent to investigate but did not travel north of Basra, pleading insufficiency of time. Horrors multiplied, and by late February Duff had agreed to send another mission to look, this time seriously, under Sir William Vincent, I.C.S. from Bihar, and Major General Alfred Bingley, fresh from Egypt.[45] Their report would await a new viceroy. Hardinge spent two days in Bombay on his way home, and he did his best to inquire there about medical conditions, turning up little new information. It was now up to his successor, but more would be heard of Hardinge's role in the Mesopotamian campaign.

Mesopotamia was only one of the most worrisome problems of Hardinge's last months in India. If long-range plans for Turkey were a concern, long-range rewards for India equally demanded attention. Hardinge had been considering this question since late in 1914, when he had responded to an inquiry from King George as to what concession he proposed for postwar India (it must be remembered that all thought the war would be of short duration). Hardinge replied with a list of preferred points: enrollment of Indian volunteers, permission to Indians to carry arms (they required licenses, as Europeans did not), and regular commissions for Indian soldiers (the Islington commission had recommended immediate announcement of this point, but Hardinge objected that it would undercut postwar concession announcements). There would, he realized, be demands for more Indian participation in the government, but he had not altered his views on this: "It is most necessary that other aspirations directed towards self-government of some kind should be carefully controlled, otherwise chaos may supervene." Provincial autonomy, as defined in 1911, was a legitimate goal, and he now added greater freedom from interference by authorities at home—a standard demand of terminal viceroys.[46]

Hardinge had good cause to complain. In the spring of 1915, he was particularly incensed when a bill authorizing the establishment of a provincial executive council for the lieutenant governor of the United Provinces was rejected by the House of Lords (Curzon, again), mainly on the grounds that the provinces had not sufficiently advanced. That a few peers could reject a bill proposed by the governor-general in council, approved by the secretary of state and his council, and recommended by the Cabinet, only proved his point. Hardinge was publicly critical in a speech at the close of his Legislative Council on 25 March, noting his "profound regret" that a vote of forty-seven to twenty-six (from a total membership of nearly 650) enabled a handful of peers "who perhaps hardly realise the rate of progress made in this country during the past few years" to throw out the bill. Hardinge was criticized for this remark, but it was, as he said to the king, simple justice:

> progressive concessions must be made to India at the end of the war, not as a price for her loyalty, a phrase which most Indians would deeply resent, but as justified by her progress and advance in civilisation, by her valued cooperation in the war, and by the important position which she occupies in the family of nations composing Your Majesty's worldwide Empire.[47]

Hardinge was even more annoyed shortly afterwards Parliament rejected a proposal for a High Court in the Punjab. Both were fairly small issues; both would come in time; but rejection of both would bring increased agitation in India.

> What seems so foolish is that people do not understand that India can be kept perfectly quiet and contented if small concessions, inevitable in the future, are, with a little fore-

sight, made from time to time instead of waiting for the moment when concessions will be wrung from the Government almost by force.[48]

Hardinge had other, more tangible recommendations to make as the months passed. In August 1915, for example, he proposed that army pensions be increased by fifty percent and pay raised generally. The effect would be immediate, but it was the long term that concerned Hardinge. The army had to remain contented, "especially at a time when the educated classes of India are likely to be disappointed in many of the political concessions that they hope to receive." Individual suggestions such as this were better linked to a comprehensive plan of the postwar direction of the government of India, and through the late summer and early fall Hardinge encouraged various provincial governors and Executive Council members to express their own views. The result was a considerable debate on such issues as provincial self-government and commissions for Indians; but in general the correspondence discussed, with approval, Hardinge's own earlier list.[49]

Hardinge's specific proposal in the case of provincial councils was to increase the number of popularly elected representatives. His experience showed that Indians did not always vote with Indians and against the government, and in any case the Legislative Council at the center, which Hardinge would change only by making equal the numbers of official and nonofficial members, had the power to nullify provincial legislation as, of course, did the viceroy at the top. "Justice" required such representation—as always, not the same thing as Indian self-rule—just as it required more equality for India in the councils of the empire. By this Hardinge meant that Indians should receive fairer treatment in Canada or South Africa, representation in the colonial conferences equal to that of the self-governing dominions, and such public and outward signs as the appointment of Indians to Privy Council membership. The net result of altered policy in these areas would be to satisfy some of the legal aspirations of "the more thoughtful and loyal Indians." Authorities at home would have to reach a fuller comprehension of the progress of India, and the fact that "it is useless and even dangerous to regard India from the standpoint of ten or more years ago."

The question of the future financial position of India was another sore point. India was running a heavy deficit owing to the war and the inflation in its wake, and was therefore very reluctant to eliminate any source of income or add sources of expenditure—hence Hardinge's rejection of a Cabinet suggestion that India take over the entire cost of Mesopotamian operations. In this context the excise duty on cotton products from India was annoying: although the duty was in the interest of British manufacturers, it was hard to forego any important source of income. Chamberlain, however, had the last word in such issues, and the most he would offer for the future was the possibility that the estimated one percent rise in customs duty might not be fully extended to the cotton excise. Wartime financing was extremely complicated, and as always in the hands of the experts; details need not be entered into here, but Hardinge's hope, as a "free trader," to end the excise was not realized during his tenure as viceroy beyond a promise from London to consider the matter when the opportunity arose.[50]

The treatment of indentured labor had already aroused Hardinge in South Africa, but there were other areas, such as the Fiji Islands, where workers were mistreated. Shortly before leaving, Hardinge took considerable pleasure in ending this system altogether: "the one thing that I wish to see done before I leave India," although the five-year delay which colonial authorities insisted upon was far less pleasing.[51]. Abuses, not the system itself, irritated Hardinge, but the end effect was the same.

Hardinge's successor was Viscount Chelmsford, but Hardinge had little role in his selection. Hardinge had heard Chelmsford's name mentioned as a possible candidate, and it was clear to the viceroy that Chelmsford, who had done well as governor of Queensland and New South Wales, was wasted as an officer in the territorials guarding a wireless station a few miles from

Simla.[52] But Hardinge still had no information, nor was his opinion asked, by the end of the year. "I cannot help thinking," he confessed to Butler, "that it is going to be K[itchener] and that the Government at home dare not say so." At the new year, however, Chelmsford was offered the post by Asquith and accepted readily. Hardinge thought it a good choice, and was relieved that a successor had been found—he had offered to stay another six months if necessary—but he himself was still without future employment. He expected Paris some day, but Bertie would be unlikely to leave while the war continued.[53]

Many regretted his departure, "and without boasting I think I may say that is the general impression throughout the country." The king honored him with the Garter; although this was a standard reward for a retiring viceroy (either that or a marquisate), it was the only English knighthood Hardinge did not yet possess and one not before given to a holder of lesser rank than a viscount. To Chelmsford he recommended some of his ablest servants for honors: Du Boulay, J.B. Wood, his political secretary, and others.[54]

Hardinge's last months were physically tiring, and for the first time he suffered attacks of fever. Nevertheless he maintained a heavy schedule. In February he opened the new High Court for Bihar in Patna, a considerable satisfaction given the role he had played in establishing the new province. At Banaras he laid the foundation stone of the Hindu University, receiving the warmest reception he had seen since 1911—marred only by a public reference by Gandhi to the possible justification of violence and bombs. At Delhi he opened the Lady Hardinge Medical College and Hospital for women which Winifred had inaugurated. At the end of February, he invested the maharaja of Jodhpur with full powers in open durbar before a gathering of Rajput notables.[55]

It was his last such visit, the sort of thing—for all his dislike of public speaking—that he had much enjoyed. He returned to Delhi, also for the last time, to pack and make his farewells. Many friends had gone, and it was a "land of regrets" (Hardinge's phrase to Chirol) for more than Hardinge alone.[56] The last major ceremony in Delhi was his farewell speech, which summed up his hopes of the last five and a half years:

> It has been my endeavour to fulfil the dream of my boyhood, the ambition of my manhood—not merely to be Viceroy of India—but to follow in the footsteps of the procession of the great men who have gone before and to leave India happier, more self-confident, more prosperous and higher in the scale of nations than I found her.

Whether India was happier, of course, is arguable, although there was less of both extremism and terrorism from the middle of his term until well into the war. How self-confident India was would only be seen when the war ended. The war itself was an awakening for India just as it was the world over, and Hardinge, for all his conservative, gradualist views, felt something of this, just as he knew that India had changed considerably in the last prewar years. It was that basic sympathy which won for him the respect of so many Indians and the distrust of a fair sampling of bureaucrats.

One of his frankest statements in this regard was made to a European audience at the United Service Club in Simla in October 1915:

> England has instilled into this country the culture and civilization of the west with all of its ideals of liberty and self-respect. It is not enough for her now to consider only the material outlook of India. It is necessary for her to cherish the aspirations, of which she has herself sown the seed, and English officials are gradually awakening to the fact that high as were the aims and remarkable the achievements of their predecessors, a still nobler task lies before them in the present and the future in guiding the uncertain and faltering steps of Indian development along sure and safe paths. The new role of guide, philosopher and friend is

> opening before you, and it is worthy of your greatest efforts. It requires in you gifts of imagination and sympathy, and imposes upon you self-sacrifice, for it means that slowly but surely you must divest yourselves of some of the power you have hitherto wielded. Let it be realized that great as has been England's mission in the past, she has a far more glorious task to fulfil in the future, in encouraging and guiding the political self-development of the people. The goal to which India may attain is still distant, and there may be vicissitudes in her path, but I look forward with confidence to a time when strengthened by character and self-respect, and bound by ties of affection and gratitude, India may be regarded as a true friend of the Empire and not merely as a trusty dependent. The day for the complete fulfilment of this ideal is not yet, but it is to this distant vista that the British official should turn his eyes, and he must grasp the fact that it is by his future success in this direction that British prestige and efficiency will be judged.[57]

That Hardinge's own proposals could hardly be equated with more pronounced Indian desires should not obscure the fact that he was even then well ahead of most of the ruling structure beneath him. He had come a considerable distance from his prewar remarks on eventual self-determination. To the Imperial Legislative Council, however, he advised caution and discouraged "extravagant hopes and unrealisable demands." It was indeed "guarded liberalism."[58]

Perhaps Hardinge was not a "great" viceroy whose name echoes down the corridors of history—but then much depends upon the criteria of "great." Surely he was a successful viceroy, "a wise and imaginative statesman, fully alive to new developments in India," as one Indian historian put it.[59] He made enemies, and many found him cold to overtures and sudden to anger. His success was more with Indians than with the bureaucracy, against whom he seemed to direct his intervention in Bengal, or Cawnpore, or South Africa. Nor was he beloved by the independence movement, or the terrorists of Chandi Chauk. But he was respected by moderates for his wisdom in reuniting Bengal and in developing provincial autonomy. The move to Delhi which he supported so strongly was a bold stroke, signalling, in a larger context of world history, that India, linked by administrative ties as much as by railroads, was no longer merely a mysterious hinterland behind selected foreign-held seaports. It cannot be shown that the response to the war would have been less under another viceroy, but Hardinge had won friends and respect by his policies as much as by the bomb that jeopardized his life, and surely these played a role in 1914, above all among the princes whom he called his friends: that thirty-five of them journeyed to Bombay to bid him farewell is testimony enough.

But perhaps no twentieth-century viceroy could be "great," given the tight controls of Parliament and Cabinet in the age of the telegraph. The viceroy was surrounded by splendor and immense bureaucracy, with a salary nearly double that of the prime minister but with little real power. His superiors in London made most critical decisions: "Every decision that he made, they could unmake; every appointment that he advised, they could query; every honor that he sought to grant, they could refuse."[60]

In early April 1916, Hardinge returned to Bombay. He sailed on the third, the day of Chelmsford's arrival, thus keeping his promise not to repeat the embarrassment of his own reception by Minto. The S.S. *Maloja* carried home a considerable party, including Alec, the Du Boulays, and Maxwell, on his way to a battlefield death in France. After the brief stay with McMahon in Cairo, Hardinge arrived in England on 22 April, to a reception from the mayor of Dover and a party of friends at Victoria—an unemployed ex-colonial governor.[61]

IX The Foreign Office and the War

Hardinge was without enthusiasm, but not without prospects. Nicolson had already mentioned to Grey the possibility of Hardinge resuming his old position as permanent under secretary, unusual as that might be. Hardinge was given no official indication of this, but he must have thought of it since Nicolson was to retire and there was no obvious successor in the Foreign Office. Grey made no immediate decision, but Nicolson told Stamfordham, who told the king, who told Crewe, and so on—soon Hardinge's friends had mobilized to influence Grey's choice. Hardinge himself, on arrival, simply requested his Foreign Office pension of £1700 a year, which was granted retroactive to the day he left India.[1]

On the same day, Prime Minister Asquith wrote to ask him to chair a cabinet subcommittee on postwar commercial and industrial policies, a task which Hardinge estimated (and Asquith agreed) would require a year of hard work. This offer forced Grey to decide, and he chose to bring Hardinge back, promising Paris at the end of the war or whenever Bertie left if he himself was still foreign secretary. Asquith understood that Hardinge could not also take on the industrial committee, but clearly Grey had not consulted him on Hardinge's future.[2]

Asquith had another sensitive assignment, which he did not think would delay Hardinge's return to the Foreign Office: that of chairman of a royal commission to inquire into the Easter Rebellion in Dublin which had nearly coincided with Hardinge's arrival in England. The commission was to investigate the causes of the outbreak from the standpoint only of the degree of responsibility of the Irish excecutive, civil and military, in the sense of negligence or inadequate security precautions. Hardinge was given as colleagues Justice H. Montague Shearman (King's Bench) and Sir Mackenzie Dalziel Chalmers, formerly Home Office under secretary (1903-8), both men with the requisite legal and administrative experience. Hardinge as always took the responsibility seriously.

> It is no whitewashing business, for I and my colleagues are finally determined to go as closely as possible into the matter and to state freely our conclusions whether palatable or not to the Gov[ernmen]t. . .as far as I am able to judge nothing can exceed the fatuous incompetence of the Irish executive, and no excuse can be made for Birrell's 'laissez faire' policy. He was hardly ever in Ireland.

The choice of Hardinge was immediately criticized in the House of Lords by Lord Donoughmore on the grounds that as viceroy he himself was the probable subject of a forthcoming inquiry on Mesopotamia. Hardinge was annoyed, particularly since his official position prevented him from replying, but the commission soon went to work, in May holding hearings both in London and in Dublin. Interviews were conducted with officials like Augustine Birrell, chief secretary at the time of the rising, and Sir Matthew Nathan, the under secretary, both of whom had soon resigned, Lord Wimborne, the lord-lieutenant of Ireland, and others. Hardinge left much of the questioning to his colleagues, but no new information altered his scathing opinion of the Irish government.[3]

The commission was back in London in early June and by the

end of the month delivered its report. The general system of government received its share of criticism ("anomalous in quiet times, and almost unworkable in times of crisis"), but the policies pursued took the heaviest fire:

> the general conclusion that we draw from the evidence before us is that the main cause of the rebellion appears to be that lawlessness was allowed to grow unchecked, and that Ireland for several years past has been administered on the principle that it was safer and more expedient to leave law in abeyance if collision with any faction of the Irish people could thereby be avoided. . . .Such a policy is the negation of that cardinal rule of Government which demands that the enforcement of law and the preservation of order should always be independent of political expediency.

The belief that the government would remain supine encouraged the Sinn Fein. The military and above all the police—both the undermanned Royal Irish Constabulary and the unarmed Dublin Metropolitan Police—had given adequate warnings, but they had not been taken seriously enough. Above all the report condemned Birrell, who had primary responsibility for the policy which had failed. Nathan, his main aide when Birrell was absent from Dublin for long parliamentary sessions in England, had not impressed enough upon Birrell the need for watchfulness, but Nathan had only been appointed in September 1914.

The government thought the affair was over, although the Irish had other views. Hardinge, with his usual efficiency, had performed the task he was given—a thankless task, literally, for Hardinge recorded that it was the only royal commission that he knew of which had not been thanked by the government. For his own part, he was just as glad that the "wretched Irish Commission" had not included the "hopeless and absurd system of government, or rather misgovernment, in Ireland," for he could now get back to the Office, assuming his duties formally on 20 June, his birthday, a week before the Irish report was completed.[4]

Hardinge found a very different atmosphere from that of six years before. Although he had kept in touch with personnel shifts, he had not witnessed the tremendous growth in work load, nor had he known, save in broad pattern, the actual policy decisions of the last months; Foreign Office prints, freely supplied to the viceroy in peacetime, had been cut off during the war. The staff, formerly 150, was now near 500, dealing with three hundred telegrams a day. Considerable areas of responsibility had been placed under Robert Cecil in a separate but overlapping Contraband Department. Hardinge was relieved not to be responsible for this immense and complicated subject, dealing as it did with much of Britain's wartime trade, but the overlap was undesirable and Hardinge had to work with Cecil in smoothing out conflicts. The secret service work had increased proportionally, and before the war was over the Office, under Hardinge's direction, was spending £1 million a year on this work, "of which I had to render an account to the last penny."[5]

The demands on Hardinge himself were too great. In the first place, his relationship with Grey inevitably was not as close: "We both had grown older during those six years and both had suffered." Grey was set in his own ways (by 1916, his tenure as foreign secretary was one of the longest in British history). He had become estranged from Nicolson and was now used to making decisions alone or with others of his staff, leaving the permanent under secretary to administer the mushrooming department. Also Grey's own energies were failing. He went off every Friday afternoon and was gone until Sunday evening; Hardinge found it necessary to remain in London until Sunday afternoon to insure that the work did not pile up at impossible levels—and it was not worth leaving London merely for a free Sunday afternoon. The result was that he returned daily to his house on Portman Square, a quiet house, with Diamond at Queen's College and Alec in France with the Grenadiers. By Christmas, with ten days free, he was feeling unwell.[6]

Nor was the system itself working. Nicolson had found Hardinge's prewar concentration of authority virtually unmanageable under the flood of war work; the system had been designed for quieter times and could not be altered now save by drastic partitioning of responsibilities. As Bertie put it in late 1914, Hardinge's design had proved an "egregious failure," the result being, in Nicolson's case, "that he neglects what he is supposed to do and accepts without inquiry what others suggest. . . .There is no discipline and the tail wags the dog."[7]

Finally, Hardinge was worried about the next permanent under secretary, for he assumed his own stay would last only until Bertie retired for good. No clear heir had emerged, and Hardinge brought Ronald Graham home from Egypt with this in mind. No one in the Office could do the job, he explained to Graham: "All the F.O. admit this." Graham, however, had serious doubts about his own administrative ability. Not only did he prefer diplomacy, but he had also been absorbed by the Egyptian internal situation for years, and had not kept up with foreign developments. After some persuasion Graham came. Once again there was factional division within the Office: Hardinge found him invaluable as a sort of understudy and did not consider anyone else competent to fill in even for a few days, but Crowe and his friends objected to Graham being brought in from the outside.[8]

If the Office had more work, it also had less responsibility. In part this was the inevitable product of the war. It is, after all, the normal function of diplomacy to prevent war, and to that extent the old diplomacy had failed. Grey himself had contributed to the decline of the Foreign Office, believing that it should take a back seat to the generals once war broke out. There was still much work in dealing with neutrals (including the United States), the lesser powers, trade, passports, and the like, but the larger relations with allies were the responsibility primarily of the Cabinet or the military. As Bertie had warned, the Foreign Office was now primarily a "pass-on" department, passing on instructions to others, "often without considering whether such instructions are advisable or feasible and sometimes in ignorance seemingly of what has already been said and done by some other Department of the Foreign Office."[9]

This situation was reinforced when the government was reconstructed in December. Asquith, Grey, and Crewe among others were out of office, and Lloyd George became prime minister. The more important appointment to Hardinge was that of Arthur J. Balfour as foreign secretary. Balfour was always friendly and charming, but by the new year Hardinge had found him not up to the daily grind:

> it is of no use to close one's eyes to the fact that he is growing old, that he is incapable of real hard work and that it is distasteful to him, largely owing to reasons of health. Still his mind is as clear as ever, and he will, I think, be extremely useful to this Office in preparing really first class State documents while I run most of the business as I am now doing. I am careful, however, to leave to him the final decision on all questions of policy.[10]

The change of superiors, in other words, only increased Hardinge's load. One innovation which contributed to this was attaching Hardinge, Admiral John R. Jellicoe, and Field Marshal Robertson as permanent experts in their fields to advise the daily sittings of the "War Cabinet," Lloyd George's new guiding body. Hardinge had attended the earlier "War Committee" with Grey when Foreign Office matters were discussed, but daily participation was a waste of each morning. Since afternoons were spent in interviews with ambassadors and others, ordinary business often had to be conducted in the late night hours. His patience wore thin and, as he put it to Butler, his cabinet experience "makes me despise party politics more than ever."[11]

Hardinge was also not fond of the unofficial diplomats under Lloyd George's aegis, such as Lord Esher, well known from King Edward's time, who had attached himself to the British military representatives in Paris, "wearing a military uniform of his invention as Governor of Windsor Castle," for which the only suitable adornment would have been a field marshal's baton. His function was as obscure as his insignia.

> It was understood that he kept Lloyd George and Winston Churchill informed of his impressions of events in Paris and at the front and that he passed on to Sir Douglas Haig all the information and gossip that he received from sources in London and Paris. At the same time he could not help retailing his gossip and information whether good or bad to his lady friends who spread all over Paris canards of Esher's or some other person's invention. Altogether he made a good deal of mischief without doing any apparent good and was no doubt a thorn in the side of Lord Bertie. . .especially on account of his pessimistic reports of the state of feeling towards the war in England, which Bertie was doing all he could to refute.[13]

The "dog at the fair" (Hardinge's and Bertie's long-standing nickname for Esher) was only one example. Another was Mark Sykes, already known to Hardinge from Near Eastern affairs and above all the Sykes-Picot Agreement which had partitioned Turkish Arab territory between France and Britain.

> These amateur diplomatists are to my mind most dangerous people and Mark Sykes in particular owing to his lack of ballast. Still they are all the vogue at the present time and I am not sure that we may not see the civilians yet occupying high military and naval posts merely because they are amateurs.[14]

If the problems of war and the "new diplomacy" and Hardinge's own duties were not enough, there was also as yet no escape from the repercussions of his days in India: a constant stream of petitions and memorials pursued him for months, in the erroneous hope that he could intervene. He did preserve his interest in the important questions, managing in 1917 with

Chamberlain to get cabinet approval of Indian representation at imperial conferences and an increase of cotton import duties.[15]

Delhi seemed his vulnerable spot. Curzon had no intention of discontinuing his attack simply because Hardinge had come home, putting up a memorandum to the Cabinet suggesting that "a luxury such as Delhi" was certainly out of place in wartime. It was a poorly timed stroke; few cabinet members wished to revive the controversy, and Asquith made Curzon modify his language before the document was circulated. Curzon saw Hardinge daily but said nothing to him about his memorandum: "He had evidently been plotting this stab in the back for as soon as I had left India, and in the hope that he could influence the Cabinet without giving me the opportunity to replying to his attack." The Cabinet, as Hardinge anticipated, did nothing, and early in 1917 it was Hardinge, not Curzon, who became a member of the New Delhi Advisory Committee (with Crewe, Lady Minto, and Sir Thomas Holderness of the India Office) to advise on matters of style. Hardinge never abandoned his interest, and he had already pledged to see the finished city someday, despite a tradition which prevented ex-viceroys from returning.[16] The war, however, allowed little attention to the new capital, in India or in London.

The Foreign Office's main responsibility during the war was to keep old and win new friends for the allied cause. Aside from the initial entente alliance and its associates of 1914—Belgium, Serbia, Montenegro, and Japan—the main addition was Italy, which declared war on Austria in May 1915. Hardinge had no part in the negotiations, but Nicolson soon sent the terms of the London Agreement (April 1915) to India. Hardinge thought them bad. Italy would provide little meaningful military aid, and promises which sought to keep Austria from the sea and assigned Asia Minor territory to Italy only built up trouble for the future. To Ronald Graham he added his real conviction: Italy should have been bought in on Britain's terms, not Italy's.[17]

Unfortunately, further wartime agreements such as the promise of the Turkish Straits to Russia (Constantinople Agreement, 1915), whetted Italy's appetite for more territories in Asia. Hardinge's frequent meetings with ambassadors (particularly "that ass Imperiali," Italy's representative) often concerned this subject, although there was little he could do to avoid what was going to be a Franco-Italian struggle for Turkish provinces. Resolution of this conflict, as he pointed out, would depend ultimately upon whether or not there was going to be a Turkey after the war. His position on this matter, stated in 1915, remained constant throughout many tribulations until it was more than vindicated at the Lausanne Conference of 1922–23: he felt that the ten million highland Turks, a martial race which he admired even in the midst of war against them, should be left to themselves. Such a diminished state would require an exit to the sea, "and this could only be obtained in the Aegean and at Smyrna." In any case Smyrna, where British and French interests predominated, should not be given to Italy. Hardinge would have treated Italian claims with frankness, but Russia and France preferred to hold back the details of inter-allied partition plans. Since Italy intended to claim the entire coast from Smyrna to Alexandretta, Hardinge knew there would be trouble: "It is clear that the Italians intend to open their mouths very wide," and the wider they opened, the more preposterous Hardinge thought their appetite.[18]

Lloyd George, however, proved willing to give the Italians all they asked at Saint-Jean de Maurienne in April 1917, largely because Britain and France had bitten off large pieces for themselves in the previous year's Sykes-Picot agreement, and it was hard to deny Italian claims for compensation. Smyrna was designated a free port at Hardinge's insistence, but it was included in Italy's zone, and even more was promised if Turkey was to be further carved asunder. Lloyd George, in his "astounding ignorance history and geography hardly knew where Smyrna was," and old interests of Britain had thus been sacrificed. "The only consolation to me," Hardinge wrote Bertie, "from the surrender of our interest is that it will probably never take place, and

I trust that at the end of the war we shall wipe the slate clean.''[19]

In the Balkans, some states took sides before Hardinge returned to England. Bulgaria joined the Central Powers in October 1915, leaving only Rumania and Greece uncommitted. If Hardinge had little enthusiasm for Italy's participation, he had less for Balkan allies—although there came a time when every diversion of the enemy was useful. By the summer of 1916, he advocated an effort to detach Bulgaria from the opposite side and, more important, did his best to keep negotiations going to bring Rumania in with the allies. Rumania's decision was delayed by her large territorial appetite and the issue of future relations with Russia.

But Rumanian matters were decided in the Cabinet, and it is difficult to evaluate Hardinge's influence upon this body, although he was present at discussions. To the very end he was sure that Rumania would keep wriggling, for, as he put it to Buchanan in Petrograd, Prime Minister Ion Bratiano was ''one of the most evasive fellows, and always had been.'' This could have been a most embarrassing phrase, affecting the negotiations themselves, for the letter was captured, published in German newspapers, and read out in the House of Commons by an Irish representative in March 1917—by which time Rumania's war effort had come and gone (more embarrassing personally was a reference to Reginald McKenna, chancellor of the exchequer, as ''narrow-minded and pedantic,'' which required a written apology).[20]

In August 1916 Rumania joined the war against Austria-Hungary, ill prepared for what followed. Austrian, German, and Bulgarian forces overran the country before the year was out. British diplomacy could not be blamed for this disaster, but Hardinge found it very discouraging: ''it is most unfortunate that every little Power that receives the support of the allies seems to go to the wall. I look upon the overwhelming of Roumania as a standing disgrace to the Allies, and particularly to Russia,'' whose forces seemed unable to give Rumania any assistance whatsoever.[21]

Greece was a more complicated tangle. At first it remained neutral, and pro-allied premier Eleutherios Venizelos, in power since 1910, was forced out, as King Constantine decided against foolhardy intervention. Constantine henceforth was written off as pro-German, but when Venizelos returned to power in mid-1915, the king gave secrect approval for an allied landing at Salonika (September-October). He refused to depart from neutrality, however, and Venizelos soon resigned again to organize a revolt in the Aegean islands and a separatist movement in Salonika. Hardinge watched the progress of allied intrigues with Venizelos and against Constantine from his seat on the War Committee, but Greece was more a scene of French than British activity, and the permanent under secretary's advice was easily overriden in any case since he was not a cabinet minister.

Lloyd George, Curzon, and Bonar Law all seemed to relish the possibility of establishing a Venizelist republic in Athens. Aside from his own personal preference, Hardinge, like Grey, worried about the effect this might have on Russia, attached as it was to the Greek monarchy and, at another level, doubtful about the future value of the Dardanelles if they were to be closed by an Anglo-French dominated Greek republic. The tsar might well be driven to the conclusion that only Germany and Austria were left as defenders of monarchism. "I live in fear and trepidation at hearing that the French have done something awful at Athens," he admitted to Bertie. With Grey on leave and Crewe in charge, the Foreign Office voice was particularly weak. Hardinge drafted orders to Britain's man in Athens not to support a republican revolution, but the War Committee canceled his draft when Crewe presented it.[22]

Hardinge's royal connections meant that he could not simply leave Greece to others. He spend the weekend of 3 September at Windsor and got a good going over from the royal family, naturally interested in the fate of the Greek ruler. Hardinge listened patiently to the king's defense of "Tino," but he himself believed that "the German Military attache has been living in King Tino's pocket all the time," and that the Greeks, if they intervened, "would open their mouths very wide and complicate matters in the final peace negotiations." He preferred to leave them in the lurch, to recover their lost cities in Thrace as best they could from the Bulgarians. Meanwhile he would publish the Constantinople agreement on the Straits, as Russia wished, for this would undermine reactionary court circles in Petrograd who were trying to discredit the allies' good faith. Interestingly, Hardinge knew that publication (which did not come to pass) would upset Indian Muslim sentiment, but he was no longer responsible for presenting India's views, and the larger need of continued Russian cooperation in the war came first.[23]

The Greek surrender of Kavalla to Bulgarian forces incensed many, including Hardinge. He now proposed, with Grey's support, that Greece should make her position very clear by a public declaration of war, although he still had a low appreciation of the value of any Greek war effort. This new position, however, was apparently in response to Grey's considerable anger, for Hardinge preferred to be quit of the whole business, particularly since it increasingly appeared that France would be Greece's new protector. The allies demanded the surrender of the Greek fleet and other war material and the expulsion of German and Austrian agents. Greece refused, and the allies responded with a short-lived landing at Piraeus, a longer blockade, and recognition of Venizelos's provisional government in December. In the following year Constantine was forced to abdicate, Venizelos became premier, and Greece entered the war on the allied side. This was largely a French operation, with which Britain had little to do, but Hardinge believed that a secret bargain had been struck by Lloyd George—a free hand to France in Greece for the right to pull British troops out of the dead end of Salonika. No part of the Greek story inspired Hardinge with respect for allied, or cabinet, high diplomacy.[24]

There were other problems by the end of 1916, such as the "Arab Revolt." Hardinge now admitted that India could have taken a "broader line" on this in the first instance, although he had not changed his mind about the future of Mesopotamia.

Similarly, relations with the United States were increasingly important, but they fell more to others like Cecil, and the American files for these months show little beyond generalities: "A firm, friendly and unaggressive policy without any sign of fear will probably keep American public opinion straight. . . ."[25]

Hardinge devoted far more attention to the United States when it became a question of American peace overtures. He found on arrival at the Foreign Office in 1916 that really nothing had been done to consider the question of war aims, a situation which he found astonishing and which he set out at once to remedy, his haste inspired by reports that Germany would probably ask for an armistice in the fall. As he saw it, Britain had no European demands to make save Heligoland. But the allies would want more: Italy had her promises, France would expect Alsace-Lorraine and Saar frontier rectifications, Russia Constantinople and eastern territory (and the thorny question of Poland had not been touched), Asian questions would have to be settled. In fact, as he wrote to Bertie, there was some feeling of being left out in the inevitable scramble.[26]

In mid-December 1916, President Woodrow Wilson made his first definite proposals, asking first for the various belligerents' terms of peace. Hardinge suspected that this superficially simple proposal was meant to divide the allies—for how else could one regard a request which would produce separate lists of demands from each power without reference to the claims of others? Hardinge at bottom was not in favor of peace in late 1916, for if it were concluded on the basis of the status quo, nothing would have been settled. On the other hand, phrasing the answer to Wilson was a delicate matter, and Hardinge, kept out of it by illness (a week in bed) at the crucial point, thought Britain's answer unwisely seemed to shut the door on future negotiation.[27]

Not surprisingly, Hardinge was a strong critic of Wilson, his diplomacy, and his phrases: "too proud to fight" would prove as memorable as "scrap of paper." The president, he concluded, preferred public diplomacy because it enabled him to be disagreeable to each set of belligerents in turn, and thus stay out of the war as long as possible. Hardinge was more directly involved when it was suggested that Spring Rice, now ambassador at Washington, should be augmented or replaced by some august personage who might exercise more influence. Hardinge as usual opposed such unprofessional procedures, but in 1917 Lloyd George selected Balfour himself for the task. When Germany's declaration of unrestricted submarine warfare brought the United States to sever relations with Germany, Hardinge breathed a sigh of relief.[28]

The alliance was thus augmented by the United States, but it ran the danger of losing Russia. In March 1917, troubles in Petrograd brought the establishment of a provisional government and the abdication of the tsar. Allied relations with the new government were unclear. The War Cabinet attempted to suppress press reports on the Petrograd revolution, hoping that Russia would go on with the war; Hardinge, with Buchanan's pessimistic dispatches in mind, thought this the wrong decision.[29]

Aside from a tentative and futile peace overture from Austria-Hungary, which showed that the enemy was tired too, the signs were not promising, particularly after Lloyd George's surrender at Saint-Jean de Maurienne. The prime minister's amateurism had cost much, and without the framework of any definite policy. As Hardinge put it to Chirol,

> In fact the lack of direction and of seasoned thought on matters of foreign policy are to me very depressing. We live from hand to mouth with a policy of make-shift, and really I think it is almost all the present Government are capable of doing. The one man with a well balanced mind and a real knowledge of his subject is Balfour, and he has been sent, much against his will, on a futile expedition to America on a job for which he is totally unfitted, while his knowledge and experience on this side would have been quite invaluable. The War Cabinet as at present constituted is, to my mind, not a satisfactory form of Government.[30]

The trials inflicted upon the Foreign Office by Lloyd George were only a part of Hardinge's burden. There were always personal worries (he could take secret relief in the trench foot which brought Alec home from France, where he won the Military Cross)—but in the spring and summer of 1917, the Mesopotamian campaign became both personal and public concern.

Soon after his voyage home, Hardinge had worked over a précis of events in Mesopotamia sent him by Chamberlain. He was sensitive to the fact that the search for scapegoats might attempt to saddle him with responsibility for the advance, when in fact he had only accepted Nixon's view. He asked Chamberlain to delete a reference which seemed to say otherwise. As it was, if papers on Kut were published, it would be hard to justify the attempt on Baghdad without relating it to dangers in Persia and Afghanistan, but that would be most impolitic to say publicly. Hardinge believed that he and Duff should still emerge safely. Nixon would be sacrificed. He was a gallant soldier, guilty only of "one of those mistakes or rather miscalculations of which similar instances have been the means of creating the British Empire as it now is." He only hoped, he told Chamberlain, that enough information would be given out so that people realized, "in spite of shortcomings in Mesopotamia, how much was achieved with how little in hand." Chamberlain, who objected to forcing officials to defend themselves in the midst of a war, agreed to the creation of a Mesopotamia commission only with the greatest reluctance, when it appeared that the government might be defeated in the House. He did not fear for his own reputation, however: "For myself as for you I believe that full inquiry can be only to our advantage."[31]

As the commission went to work, it was soon clear that neither Chamberlain nor Hardinge was exempt from criticism. Above all they were attacked for their frequent communication by private telegram or letter. Such documents were not officially put before the viceroy's Executive Council or the secretary's council at home, the implication being that neither official had consulted his council on such crucial decisions as the advance upon Baghdad. Crewe answered with the need for secrecy, above all in India. The commission still felt that the Executive Council might have objected, for example, to so denuding India of troops and military supplies.[32]

It was not until December 1917 that Hardinge was called before the commission. He first laid out his views in a lengthy written statement. He was concerned to show how much India had contributed to the war effort—on that there was little question—and also to show how the advance upon Baghdad had been decided upon, step by step. It had been a miscalculation, but an intelligible one.

> Having private information that the Gallipoli expedition was not going well, and bearing in mind the views of the Cabinet upon the 'great political and military advantages of the occupation of Bagdad,' the Commander-in-Chief and I came to the conclusion that General Nixon was in the best position to judge as to the number of troops that he would require to attain his objective, and that under the circumstances of the moment the Government of India would have placed themselves in an invidious position, and would have exposed themselves to the criticism of having ignored the demands of the Empire if at a critical moment they had overriden the opinion of the General in command in the field, and had vetoed the advance to Bagdad.[33]

And India had its own justified complaints, at direct War Office communications with the Indian commander in chief, at the failure to reciprocate India's provision of essential items (airplanes above all). Medical arrangements had broken down, and MacNeece had not done the job of investigating he should have—but then Hardinge and Duff had sent Vincent and Bingley. Hardinge ended on an upward note, with a spirited defense of Nixon's grit and Duff's loyalty, handicapped as they all were throughout by the system inherited from Kitchener.

In some four hours of mainly desultory conversation, it was clear that Hardinge could not be blamed for the advance on Baghdad. He had not seen Townshend's reservations; the responsible commander, Nixon, said he could do the job. In general, the only area where Hardinge was really open to serious criticism was in the matter of private communications and his failure to consult his council officially on the various stages in Mesopotamia. As the commission concluded, an official dispatch from Chamberlain to Hardinge listing all the available evidence on the medical breakdown would have forced the council to respond formally, and perhaps as a result more might have been done sooner to repair deficiencies.

By mid-May the commisson's report was finished and circulating, although it was not yet published, nor was it certain that it would be. High officials of the government soon knew that the commission condemned Nixon, Hardinge, Duff, Barrow (military secretary at the India Office), Chamberlain, and the War Cabinet in that order (aside from subordinate officers criticized for specific blunders on the medical or transport side). The actual wording of the final charge against Hardinge was mild:

> To Lord Hardinge of Penshurst, as Viceroy, belongs the general responsibility attaching to his position as the head of the Indian Government, to which had been entrusted the management of the expedition, including the provision of medical services. In regard to the actual medical administration he appears to us to have shown througout the utmost goodwill, but considering the paramount authority of his office, his action was not sufficiently strenuous and peremptory.

Other sections condemned Hardinge for the private correspondence and other, lesser matters—but not, save for a minority report by Commander J.C. Wedgwood, for specific responsibility for the errors that led to Kut.[34]

Hardinge's reaction was predictable. The document was "unfair and narrow-minded," leaving the impression that Mesopotamia was India's sole effort, criticizing everybody and giving credit to nobody in the process. The Cabinet's concern, however, was what to do with the report. Pigeonholing it would anger the House; court trials for the civilians mentioned, like courts-martial for the officers, would require the leveling of specific charges. Neither would be easy; as in Hardinge's case, the commission had been critical but specified no crimes as such. Lloyd George gave over to a committee of Curzon, Chamberlain, G. N. Barnes and Lord Derby the task of making recommendations. The decision was to do nothing about Hardinge, who had erred mainly in trusting his military advisors and in altering one specific telegram (this accusation, specifically mentioned in the report, was in fact erroneous). Duff and others were to be asked to resign (second thoughts would alter that decision, for a man so requested could ask for a court-martial). For Hardinge, the report was condemnation enough.

> It was further pointed out that while the Committee was called upon to decide on the life, fortune and honour of the senior officers in India referred to in the Report of the Mesopotamian Commission, the publication of the Report would—in such a case as that of the ex-Viceroy—in itself be a punishment to those whose conduct had been thus exposed, and that it would be very damaging to their reputations and future careers.[35]

Hardinge felt the recommendations of Curzon's committee on the military officers were "drastic and cruel," when men were thrown out without a pension, as if they had committed a crime beyond incompetence. "It makes my blood boil," he wrote to Chirol, "to think what a callous brute Curzon must be, living as he does in the lap of luxury and yet making such a proposal. . . ." It was soon clear that Parliament would force a debate upon the report itself, and Hardinge requested permission to participate. He drafted a statement which Crewe and Chamberlain went over in advance, making minor suggestions—for obviously it would be hard to refuse him permission to speak, unusual as that might be for a civil servant.[36]

On 3 July, Hardinge made his defense in the House of Lords. He attempted in a speech of nearly an hour to answer all the various charges in terms similar to his written and oral evidence to the commission but which had not yet come before the public. The general reaction to his defence was favorable, more so perhaps because it was Hardinge's maiden speech in Parliament. He had not convinced his audience on all the charges, but most recognized that his culpability was on a different level than that of the military authorities.[37]

Letters of sympathy now arrived in considerable numbers, but Hardinge's trials were not over. The Cabinet had already decided to move against responsible parties, and Hardinge was a responsible party. Some members (Bonar Law, for example) felt that anyone condemned should be asked to retire. The Cabinet did not actually wish to make such a request, but a strong hint should be enough. Lloyd George delayed a few days, and then asked Curzon to make such a suggestion to Hardinge. Curzon, perhaps worried by his mission, told Balfour of it on his way to see Hardinge; Balfour at once sat down to compose a protest to Lloyd George.[38]

Hardinge had already offered his resignation to Balfour on 30 June, three days after publication of the report, in what was apparently an oral exchange. Balfour refused to accept it, but Curzon's request raised the question once more. Curzon based his appeal on the need to ease the government's situation and to forestall future hostile criticism of the Foreign Office.

> He spoke without interruption for about twenty minutes, while I was growing angrier every minute. When he stopped I let fly and told him that his action could hardly be described as that of a friend when he came as the emissary of a craven Cabinet to ask me to "ease the situation" for them

> by my self-sacrifice when they ought to be upholding the honour of and defending their faithful servants, and that if they had had the courage to do so they would have had public opinion at their back.

Hardinge could not accept the implied censure of the Cabinet and gave Curzon a frank expression of his views of Cabinet and Curzon alike. "He slunk from my room like a whipped hound."

Hardinge went to see Balfour, who advised him not to resign before Thursday's debate, and Stamfordham, who reported to King George (then in France) that Hardinge felt the end of his career had arrived. Stamfordham then went to Lloyd George, confident that the king would deprecate Hardinge's resignation, making the strongest case he could for Hardinge.[39] Lloyd George explained that Hardinge had been the rough equivalent of the prime minister of India and had to assume responsibility for those beneath him. The country was at war and impatient at failure—and Lloyd George added a clear warning to the king not to interfere. It was equally clear, however, that the Cabinet had passed no formal resolution on Hardinge: individual members had only agreed that it was desirable to ask for his resignation. Lloyd George hoped for Hardinge's quiet removal without resistance, but it was not to be.

Hardinge saw both Asquith and Lansdowne, but he did not decide upon a course of action until he read in the evening papers that Bonar Law was to announce the formation of a judicial inquiry in the House on Wednesday. That same evening he wrote to Balfour again:

> As I do not wish to be thought to have been driven into my resignation by anything he may say I think it best to send it to you at once. I cannot tell you how thoroughly disgusted I am at being driven into this course after a lifetime of service to our country. . . .

The resignation, in a separate letter, said simply, "In view of the message conveyed to me yesterday by Lord Curzon from the War Cabinet I have no other course open to me but to tender to you once more my resignation for you to deal with as you think best.''[40]

Balfour received the resignation the next morning but did nothing with it. That day the Cabinet decided to establish a court of inquiry, as the papers had predicted, and Austen Chamberlain resigned as a result, feeling that he could not continue to act in the Cabinet or defend his subordinates when he himself would be on trial. His resignation freed Chamberlain to speak more openly in the two-day debate in both Lords and Commons that began that evening.

Few new arguments emerged in the debate, but several members of both Houses went out of their way to defend Hardinge completely or in part. Curzon, on the second day, was his most effective critic in the House of Lords, this time keeping to the constitutional question and the rule of India by ''a kind of concealed duumvirate.'' And yet Curzon finished as a defender of Hardinge, oblivious apparently to his own role as poison-bearer:

> the Viceroy who in the first year of this war, in the state of terrible tension that then prevailed kept India quiet, assured its loyalty, and poured out in such abundant streams its contribution to every aspect and theatre of the war not only ran great risks, but rendered great and resounding service to the State.[41]

But the public eye was on Commons. Chamberlain managed to work a defence of Hardinge into his own self-justification. His most effective argument was his reference to the military controversy of Curzon's day: the system installed by Kitchener was precisely designed to give the viceroy one stream of military advice, and as a result he could hardly be blamed for taking it (fortunately, Hardinge's role in Duff's original selection was forgotten). The debate in general was favorable to Hardinge, the main defense coming from Balfour. The foreign secretary described his double refusal of Hardinge's resignation, adding that Hardinge was badly needed in the Foreign Office. "Even if he did not do his duty in India," he remarked in a backhanded compliment, "in my opinion that is no reason at all for telling him that he is not to do something else that has nothing to do with India." Hardinge really was a lesser issue in a wide-ranging debate, though he did come under serious attack from Irish representatives, who had not forgotten his Irish commission. At the end of two days' fruitless discussion, Lloyd George reached the obvious conclusion that the debate had little to do with winning the war.[42]

Hardinge was pleased, writing quickly to thank Balfour for his support and "the most generous tribute to his services to his country that any man has ever received."

> I knew beforehand with what chivalry you would champion my cause in the House and out of it, but your splendid speech coupled with that of Chamberlain has brought peace to my mind for I have been very unhappy during the last few days over the prospect of the severance of my official connection with you and the Foreign Office. For the last three days I have done no Foreign Office work, but I propose to resume my duties on Monday if you think that is right.
>
> I cannot tell you how grateful I am to you.[43]

A new court of inquiry was to be established, and the government would have to await its decision before accepting Hardinge's resignation. The last public struggle followed when Dillon of the Irish Home Rule party moved for adjournment on the issue. Once more, Balfour spoke up: "So long as I am responsible for a Department I am not going to permit what I conceive to be a gross injustice being done to any one of my subordinates." On that basis, if Hardinge was out, he himself was out; if Hardinge was guilty, moveover, then the whole government was guilty. The opposition could not bring down the coalition government on this issue, but for Hardinge drama nearly ended in farce, and he might have wished to save himself from his friends at the remarks of Admiral of the Fleet Sir Hedworth Meux:

> I have known Lord Hardinge since he was a boy; we were at school together. I was the clever and lazy boy, and he was the industrious one, and look at the way he has got on! There is no man in this country who has spent a finer life than Lord Hardinge. You can talk about his society influence and riches, but he was a very poor younger son, and to be a poor younger son is to be very much worse than to be a well-to-do working man. . . .[44]

A rather un-rich Hardinge could take comfort in the fact that the motion failed, 81 to 176, against a combination of Irish nationalists, pacificists (against Hardinge's anti-German stand), and "a few Anglo-Indian reactionaries & other cranks." He had survived a struggle in which his career and reputation were at stake, the latter, as he had often said, "dearer to me than life."

> The War Cabinet, who had been as frightened as hares, could only think of the clamour of the wolves for blood, and banished from their minds all ideas of justice and right, and had I been so weak as to listen to their suggestions my fate would have been sealed.

Hardinge admitted to being battered by the most grueling ordeal of his career. His victory, however, made it difficult for the Cabinet to proceed with formal inquiries against Duff, Nixon, or virtually any other responsible officials. Hardinge knew how much he owed Balfour for his survival, and his thanks were deepfelt. He also knew that Balfour's loyalty took into consideration Hardinge's constant insistence upon formal, judicial inquiry, which he had every confidence of withstanding.[45] But as Balfour had pointed out, Hardinge shared the guilt which fell upon the entire government. He had supported the parsimonious prewar attitude which served India's soldiers ill in Mesopotamia; he did not intervene effectively enough to cure the medical problems; for too long, he was blind to Duff's faults; he failed to consult his council, and circumvented the meaning if not the law of India's constitution. But his guilt was hardly the sort for which he could be tried, and as many fair-minded people realized, his contribution to India's war effort, considering the loyalty which he called forth in the first instance and the sacrifices he subsequently made for both India and himself, was substantial indeeed, far outweighing his fault in listening too willingly to his military advisors.

Hardinge had little time for foreign affairs during the Mesopotamian crisis of June and July. For several days he had not even been to the Office, but nothing had changed regarding Lloyd George's proclivity for private diplomacy. Labour leader Arthur Henderson was sent on a mission to Russia; since he knew nothing of Russian affairs, it was a notable failure.[46] Spring Rice had been bypassed by special missions to Washington, and Arthur Hardinge was under pressure in Madrid.[47] Finally, in April 1918, Lord Derby—possessor, in Hardinge's view, of "the brains of a tomtit"—was sent to Paris as a special representative, with greater powers than Bertie possessed.[48]

Not only ambassadors were victims of the "new diplomacy." Hardinge had for some time been fighting a proposal put to the War Cabinet by Robert Cecil (and strongly supported by his brother, Lord Edward Cecil, longtime veteran of Egyptian administration) that would hand over control of Egypt and Sudan to the Colonial Office. In Hardinge's mind this would have been a disaster, for it would imply annexation and thus alienate all moderate Egyptian opinion, cause the fall of the Egyptian government, and endanger Britain's position in the Muslim world. Egypt was too advanced for colonial status and too backward to be a self-governing dominion—the only two categories under Colonial Office responsibility. The day was far off when Egypt could stand on her own feet, and when it did come, the Foreign Office would have to negotiate the end of the capitulations and the international legal tribunals and settle its international frontiers: "the introduction of another link in the chain would be to add a fifth wheel to the coach," concluded Hardinge in a fortunately rare mixed metaphor.[49]

At stake as Hardinge saw it was the Curzonian concept of "sacrificing everything to efficiency in dealing with Eastern peoples. Orientals prefer to rule themselves with less efficiency than may be in acccordance with our ideals, and I am not sure that they are not the happier in doing so," he wrote to Wingate. His language was that of a dying age, but his seldom-articulated sympathy for the differences among cultures was what had won his Indian popularity, and what, in the last analysis, made him so different a viceroy from Curzon.[50]

Over the new year Balfour was away from the Office for some time, and Robert Cecil was temporarily in charge. Hardinge was unhappy with this appointment, regarding Cecil as "a creature of impulse with little if any knowledge of foreign affairs. The result is that he accepts any wild scheme put before him by any outsider. . . ." (This was at least more favorable than a description of 1920: "a sanctimonious crank of the worst description—impulsive and without balance.") The two men had numerous conflicts, of which the control of Egypt was only one.[51]

A bigger question was that of the future amalgamation of the Diplomatic Service with the Foreign Office.[52] Hardinge approved this change in principle, but differed substantially with the Treasury (and with Cecil) on the terms by which it might be achieved. Long discussions at least provided a basis for formal union when the war was over. Less could be done about reorganization of the Office itself, although with the enormous growth of its responsibilities, regularization was essential. It was no longer a small and familiar cadre of gentlemen; by war's end there were five hundred clerks in the Office alone, not counting subordinate departments not housed in Whitehall. The vast crowding was most inconvenient; thirty worked in one room alone, from heads of departments to the lowest-ranking typists.[53]

By the end of the war the Office dealt with over a quarter-million dispatches annually, nearly half in the Contraband Department of the Ministry of Blockade, which for all its separate title and eighty-seven employees was still closely attached. If anything, the Office was oversupplied with information, as a 1918 report pointed out, and there was much waste and duplication of effort. Hardinge, technically in charge of much of it, could do little to make corrections. He had never been overly sympathetic to the massive expansion of Foreign Office commercial responsibilities, for they would become quite unworkable without the different sort of recruitment of which he also disapproved.[54]

In this sea of scurrying clerks and circulating files, inevitably some issues captured particular attention. One such was control of Middle Eastern affairs, which once again pitted Hardinge against Cecil. By mid-1918, Cecil was no longer minister of blockade, but assistant secretary of state in the Foreign Office in a new position designed to relieve Balfour of some of his work. Cecil's responsibility included the Middle East, although Hardinge had managed to keep Egypt out of his hands, and all decisions on high policy went to Balfour. Open disagreement came on the appointment of the head for the new subdepartment on the Middle East. Hardinge favored Graham; Cecil backed Crowe. Balfour heard out the arguments and chose Crowe. Hardinge had lost a campaign which he had not conducted well. It was an important struggle in the succession to his own position, for Crowe would eventually get the job, not Graham. Egypt was also given to the new department, but since events in Egypt were changing very rapidly, and since it was still under the Foreign Office, this made less difference.[55]

Such controversies were debilitating, and Hardinge found himself more and more involved in them. Gone were the days of leisurely consultation with Grey on decisions of high policy. The twentieth century had caught up with both the Foreign Office and its chief administrator. Hardinge did have opinions on the events of the last year of the war, however, and—almost suprisingly—occasional influence.

Nothing was more alarming to the allies than the progress of events in Russia. By the end of 1917 the provisional government had fallen and the Bolsheviks had taken power. The immediately visible consequence was an appeal to all beligerents for an armistice and negotiation of peace. In December, Russo-German negotiations began at Brest-Litovsk. In March the treaty was signed, costing Russia all of Poland, the Ukraine, and non-Russian border areas; meanwhile the civil war had begun. Western diplomats could do little. Hardinge was particularly frustrated by dual foreign policies, "one of the Foreign Office and the other 'amateur,' running side by side," he told Buchanan. "We never quite know what is in the air and surprises are frequently sprung upon us. . . ."[56]

Hardinge did his best, despite the prime minister, and was in fact considerably more flexible than many inside and outside the Foreign Office, both as to the parties to be supported in the Russian struggle and as to the method of support. He was quite willing to compete with Germany in the use of bribery (as controller of secret service funds, he was in a position to do so), if it could be done successfully—"although it is not a pleasant thought," he added for conscience's sake.[57]

By mid-December, however, the energy and brutality with which the Bolsheviks approached Russian problems were more obvious, and the certainty of their fall less sure. Still Hardinge believed the other parties of the provisional government to be in a majority; when the inevitable famine hit, the demand for efficient administration would be on the increase. Meanwhile, the best policy lay in "bolstering up all that is most stable," meaning for example the Cossacks and the Caucasian states, and in watching Britain's own interests, but it was hard to know how to put this policy into practice.

The end of December saw the division of Russia into spheres of allied responsibility, in part upon Hardinge's initiative, and a conference in Paris (Milner and Cecil representing Britain) took a stand against interference in Russian affairs, while advocating specific policies in various fringe areas which did exactly that. Conferences and discussions at home, in some of which Hardinge took part, accomplished just as little.

Many aspects of the Russian situation were beyond Britain's power to control, such as Japanese intervention in Siberia (the Cabinet had little choice but to approve this allied action). More opportunities were provided in Asia Minor, for the collapse of Russia opened the Black Sea to allied intervention in this area and the Caucasus. The policy, as decided by Milner, Cecil, Hardinge, and the military chiefs, was not to engage in an anti-Bolshevik crusade, but only to support the border states—in other words, the same contradictory policy.[58]

Hardinge seldom contributed to decisions in the early winter: a bad fall in his garden produced a broken shin bone which kept him out of the Office for six weeks, on crutches through November, and lame until the end of January. By mid-November his minutes reappeared in the files, just at the time when proposals for peace discussion came from the Bolsheviks. Hardinge was convinced that the allied decision to recognize an anti-Bolshevik government at Omsk made any compromise most difficult, and it would not be easy to persuade the Bolsheviks not to attack the Ukraine, Finland, or other border states. A compromise, in any case, "can only be at the price of our withdrawal from Siberia & Archangel, & that would seem to be too heavy a price to pay." No bargain was reached, and Russia remained a problem for the peacemakers at Paris.[59]

In Britain's relations with other allies, too, Hardinge had an uphill struggle against unorthodox diplomacy. He had always opposed special missions, and he was particularly aggrieved when Lord Northcliffe was sent to the United States and Spring Rice recalled. His judgment in *Old Diplomacy* that Northcliffe had gone simply for his own glorification is unjust; Northcliffe was certainly unorthodox, but his task was to awaken the United States to the meaning of the war, and this he did. In the larger sense, however, Hardinge, although hopeful of American entrance, had not the semimystical view of the "Atlantic alliance," more fully developed after the war, that Balfour, Cecil, and others shared.[60]

Hardinge, as a traditionalist, preferred traditional alliances. France remained constant, and Russia had disowned her former ties. There remained Japan, although there were dangers in Japanese strength in Asia. It was clear that Japan had to be humored during the war (although as viceroy Hardinge had always opposed the possible use of Japanese troops in India or the Middle East). Afterwards it would be necessary to arrive at a distinct understanding on respective interests in the Far East. He had particularly in mind Japan's associations with Indian revolutionaries, as an example of the danger—not one of military threat, but rather of insidious propaganda or commercial infiltration.[61]

His attitude towards Japan was that of old diplomacy: allies were allies, but power was power, and professionals did not make free with grandiose pledges for the distant future and sweeping references to "democracy," a word which "began to stink in my nostrils." It is no surprise that Hardinge opposed, for example, the Balfour Declaration of 1917, which promised a national home to the Jews in Palestine. He did possess a streak of anti-Semitism, not uncommon in his age and class, such as emerged in his relations with Cassel; on the other hand, he could be sympathetic to the Jews in distress, as he had shown in Russia in 1905. Similarly, he found no difficulty in moving among Jewish financial circles in London and Paris. The main issue here, however, was that he distrusted such general pledges. Graham and Sykes were friends of Zionism, and Hardinge heard out their arguments. But the implications bothered him:

I cannot help feeling that this Zionist movement and its

> consequences have not so far been sufficiently considered. It appears that it is inseparable from a British Palestine, and this seems at present [April 1917] unrealisable. Are we wise in giving encouragement to a movement based on a condition which we cannot enforce? Failure, when it comes, will be laid at the door of the F.O., and not without reason.[62]

Hardinge did not press his opposition, for Graham, Balfour, and Cecil all favored the declaration.

It was a typical frustration to Hardinge of these last war years. He suffered from personal attacks in the press and Parliament, for little reward. His influence upon foreign policy was minimal compared to the prewar Grey years. The massive increase in administrative responsibilities was one cause. But the war killed the old diplomacy, as much by President Wilson's promises of a new world of open negotiation as by Lloyd George's preference for his own "private" diplomacy. Hardinge, as a preeminent practitioner of the old diplomacy, could not be expected to admire the Welsh wizard and his conduct of policy. He detested Lloyd George; Lloyd George disdained him. One conversation which Hardinge recorded and on second thought struck from his memoirs says much about their respective attitudes. The occasion was an official dinner at Lancaster House given by the government for the president of Portugal. Hardinge was placed next to Lloyd George to act as interpreter in French.

> A servant whispered to Lloyd George that an air-raid [by zeppelin] had been signalled at which he got very excited and said to me, 'We must all go down to the cellars.' I protested and said that the risk was very small and it would be better to stay. He said, 'Look at those French windows; could anything be more dangerous if a bomb fell into the garden?' I impressed on him that to show alarm would create the worst possible impression and that he would find that most people would not go down into the cellars.

> He said nothing but was evidently frightened. The air raid was quite abortive, but after dinner I heard him telling people that a raid had been reported to him but that he said nothing as he had felt that there was no real danger and he did not want to alarm people! He posed as a lion but in truth is only a rabbit. At this dinner and during a calm moment he mentioned Curzon as 'a typical aristocrat.' I replied that I could mention two real aristocrats, but of two entirely different types, viz: Lord Lansdowne and Mr. Balfour. He would not have it but said that the ordinary British public considered Curzon as a 'typical bloated aristocrat' with a 'high stomach,' great pride of self and a luxurious standard of living. He said that Curzon was hated by the populace and that if there was a revolution in England Curzon would be the first to adorn a lamppost![63]

Lloyd George, in Hardinge's view, knew not what an aristocrat—or a gentleman—was. What Lloyd George thought of Hardinge would become clear at the Paris Peace Conference.

X Paris and Retirement

By October 1918, Hardinge had a plan prepared and ready for the inevitable peace conference, the detailed work of Alwyn Parker over many months. It concerned conference procedures, staffs, and secretarial responsibilities, not peace aims. The arrangements had been made unobtrusively, but with Balfour's approval. Hardinge naturally assumed that such preparations would be the responsibility of the Foreign Office. He was no doubt pleased at the prospect of a renaissance of old diplomacy as practiced at Vienna century before. By December all the details had been filled in, including the choice of Graham to stand in for Hardinge while he was in Paris (assisting Curzon, who would be acting for Balfour in London). Hardinge assumed, quite logically, that he himself would be administrative head of the delegation.[1]

Positions on the many diplomatic issuses were generally prepared by the Political Intelligence Department, which produced a series of memoranda and handbooks quite useful to those who bothered to read them. Hardinge had little direct role, although occasional minutes show some of his own views —distinguished, as usual, by practicality and realism coupled with a belief in integrity as an essential attribute of sound diplomacy. Germany, for example, could not be partitioned simply to please Poles or Lithuanians or others. Nor could Germany be kept from uniting with the Germans of Austria: French fears were intelligible, but the best road to peace was to avoid forcing the German empire into radical measures such as a constitutional assembly. Italy would be a problem, but Britain had little freedom of action: "We stand pledged to our word, & it is not for us to suggest any modification of our engagements, except of course in the case of a decision by the Contracting Powers to take them into reconsideration." On the League of Nations, Hardinge distrusted utopian proposals, agreeing with Crowe that commitments might be made "which in our hearts and in our sober judgment we know ought to be rejected as dangerous make-believe," in a desire to flatter and placate President Wilson. But it was necessary that ministers understand this as well as Foreign Office professionals: "I am afraid the new system will present many disappointments in the future."[2]

Hardinge was fearful of more than "the hungry appetites of France and Italy who seem to want to grab everything." President Wilson would be capable of many surprises: particularly serious was the prospect of a conflict over freedom of the seas, on which Britain was unyielding. "I really think that it is rather impertinent of a University Professor to wish to lay down the law on such a subject to a country that has policed the seas for the last 150 years." Even worse, the president's views on Egypt, India, even Ireland were unknown.[3]

The formal arrangements were not as settled as Hardinge hoped. Lt. Col. Maurice Hankey, in the cabinet secretariat, had himself been thinking of how to organize the conference since mid-1917, and he had his own tables of organization and lists of delegates. Lloyd George preferred Hankey to supervise. At the end of November Hankey and Hardinge worked out a compromise. Hankey, who had asked Lloyd George to name him secretary-general of the British delegation, would supervise that delegation outside the conference; Hardinge would manage all conference arrangements on Britain's part. The arrangement still required Lloyd George's approval, and as Hankey put it in his diary, the prime minister "does not much like Hardinge."[4] Nevertheless, this was the understanding when Hardinge and the main Foreign Office party left for Paris on 8 January to take up quarters in the Hotel Majestic (the nearby Hotel Astoria was used for offices).

Hardinge's first task was to sort out the carefully chosen Office delegation of eighteen (so small it was the only one not to be subsequently reduced) including under secretaries Tyrrell, Mallet, and Crowe: a relatively small segment of the total British delegation of over two hundred (four hundred, if clerks, typists, and the like were counted). Invidious comparisons were made to the handful representing Britain at Vienna—but two or four hundred was small compared to the initial American total, when everyone from ambassadors to telephone operators was counted, of thirteen hundred. The task of supervising the whole delegation was not small. It was winter, and wartime shortages were still in evidence. Catering was taken on by the manager of Midlands Hotels ("vegetables at last" or "everything horribly boiled to death," depending upon viewpoint); logs had to be purchased for coal-burning hearths in the Astoria. Influenza soon ran through the staff, killing several—including Mark Sykes (for whom Hardinge had considerably more respect in the last months)—and the top floor of the Majestic became an impromptu hospital.[5]

Lloyd George still had not confirmed Hardinge's arrangement with Hankey. On the eighteenth he made his decision: Hankey would be the British secretary of the conference and Hardinge would be official head of the British delegation, ostensibly on the grounds that Hankey's cabinet secretariat experience better prepared him to coordinate the various departments and dominion representatives at what approximated the cabinet level. Balfour had already asked Lloyd George to make Hardinge the secretary; Hankey now asked to be excused from the order, remarking later, "I would rather return to London than let down

Hardinge.'' But Philip Kerr brought a peremptory demand from the prime minister. Hankey, after a mind-clearing walk in the rain, found a face-saving solution: Hardinge would be ''organizing ambassador,'' in charge of the whole elaborate organization at the Astoria, while Hankey would be merely British secretary. The solution gave Hardinge only an empty title, but he offered no resistance, even though the decision meant that Hankey now assumed charge from his office in the Villa Majestic of the British secretariat of the conference, which included mainly Foreign Office personnel (as distinguished, to add further confusion, from the British imperial delegation, which was composed mainly of War Cabinet staff).[6]

Hankey recorded that Hardinge was charming about his displacement, and indeed there seemed to be little friction and no grudge. At least one British delegate took the decision badly, for Hankey had no diplomatic experience, but there is nothing to show that had Hardinge been in Hankey's place as the ''Gentz of Paris'' or ''Secretary of the Cabinet of the World'' he would have been any more successful at prodding the Supreme Council of the conference to deal with the major issues before it, or to maintain effective liaison between the various conference and delegation sections. The result, however, was that Hardinge had little meaningful role at the conference. Lloyd George could graciously record that Hardinge's ''calm, clear, and unprejudiced judgment. . .gave to his advice an authority which was invaluable,'' but he relied upon his own staff and Hankey, as Balfour relied upon his private secretaries and Crowe, who was responsible for Germany above all.

Crowe and some others, and occasional juniors like Harold Nicolson who were put into positions of considerable responsibility on various committees, had much to do, while Hardinge oiled the wheels and stoked the furnaces. He soon tired of administrative trivia: ''Sometimes I feel almost a Bolshevik when these questions come up to me. However, it is no good making oneself miserable over trifles.'' As Lord Riddell (essentially an outsider) observed, ''all the important work seems to be done by

Hankey and his staff, supplemented by Kerr. It looks as if the Foreign Office had prepared an enormous amount of material that is of no use, or at any rate is never used.'' This was too simple a picture, but Foreign Office influence was less than it should have been, less even than it might have been.[7]

On the whole, internal organization of the British delegation functioned smoothly, and Hardinge had no major crisis on his hands. Diamond was along, serving in the delegation secretarial pool, and Hardinge found a congenial companion in a certain Mrs. Walker, assigned as his driver, who would remain a close friend for many years. He visited the battlefields; he saw his son Alec, on leave from the occupation force in Germany. But his inevitable frustration was visible to some: ''Neglected Hardinge turned nasty in his ivory tower, always an uncomfortable residence,'' recorded Robert Vansittart, adding that ''he need not have pouted for even Foreign Secretaries played small parts'' (Vansittart's main contribution to the conference was an elaborate memorandum on Cyprus, returned to him with an equally frustrating ''H'' and nothing more). Hardinge's work involved more than ''issuing permits for people to dine at the Hotel Majestic,'' but the incongruity of his title and responsibilities understandably gave rise to sarcasm, as in this verse by Ian Malcolm, Balfour's private secretary:

Who chaperones typists and watches their morals;
   Who orders our motors and shares our meals;
Who changes our furniture, settles our quarrels
   And patiently listens to all our appeals?
'Tis HE! whom Delhi and far Calcutta,
   Paris and Petrograd, all adore.
HE! whose cognomen 'twere treason to utter;
   Our Superintending Ambassador. . . .

The impression of Hardinge's elder statesman remoteness is reinforced by a letter of Harold Nicolson's to his wife: ''Today Hardinge sent for me solemnly & cursed me for going to a dance in day clothes. 'It brings us into disrepute! ! ! !'", or his unhumorous reaction to T.E. Lawrence boyishly cascading toilet paper down the stairwell of the Astoria upon Lloyd George, Balfour, and Hardinge.[8]

Obviously, Hardinge was not at his best at this conference. Overwork on unimportant matters coupled with discouragement at the methods and aims of the new diplomacy brought him, as he admitted later to Butler, very close to a breakdown. And yet his presence surfaces now and again in the files on issues in which he was interested, such as Turkey. Before he was superseded by Hankey, he was particularly active. For example, a few days after arrival Hardinge heard that Venizelos—"in many ways by far the cleverest man at the Peace Conference"—was talking as if Britain's cession of Cyprus to Greece was a certainty. Hardinge's immediate response was to organize a meeting of various British departmental representatives to discuss the matter, recording a strong common negative vote.[9]

Such initiative was less necessary on substantive matters after Lloyd George's decision on conference responsibilities. To the contrary, the prime minister soon suggested that Hardinge go off to the Turkish island of Prinkipo in the Sea of Marmora to represent Britain at a meeting of all parties concerned in the Russian civil war. The proposal was a faint hope from the beginning, for rightists refused recognition of the Bolsheviks, and the Bolsheviks were suspicious of any negotiations. Hardinge quickly declined; nothing would be served by this "most fatuous decision of modern times," since probably only the Bolsheviks would appear—and only to spread propaganda. At a dinner at the Majestic Lloyd George asked him to suggest another representative: Hardinge proposed Robert Cecil.[10]

Turkey was another matter. Hardinge's own views on the future of Turkey and Smyrna had not changed, and he attempted to guide the delegation to the right conclusions. On the thirtieth, he chaired a committee of Foreign Office and military officials which decided that free passage of the Straits would best be insured by international control or mandate and that the presence of Greece in Smyrna was preferable to that of Italy. But these carefully reached conclusions seemed to have little effect: to Lloyd George, "such things as committees were childish inventions of the Foreign Office or of the devil." By late February the situation was fairly hopeless, "when our own Delegate cannot decide whether the Turk is to remain in Constantinople or not, and really upon this so much of the settlement of the Near Eastern question depends."[11]

The last disparaging comment was typical of Hardinge at Paris. He was little more than an observer. Curzon in London was frantic at his own lack of information, but Hardinge could do little to answer his complaints. Important decisions were made in private conversations of a very few people, with no record being kept; "consequently people like myself only know what happens to leak out in conversation or what Mr. Balfour happens to remember to tell me. All this does not amount to much." Hardinge asked Hankey to help. "He told me that although he would be quite ready to do all that he could to help, he himself practically knew nothing of what went on since he only heard bits of conversation which might be misleading as he had not heard the whole. I think there is some force in this." It was more than a question of Hardinge's isolation:

> Between you and me it cannot be said that the Conference is being conducted in a businesslike manner; in fact order and method do not appear to exist. This will mean, of course, immense delay, while at the same time making any organization behind the principal delegates a matter of extreme difficulty. We work here largely in the dark, as it is almost impossible to obtain decisions on many questions of first importance on which other minor issues may be dependent. . . .[12]

By the end of February committees were at last at work on German problems, and Hardinge was slightly more hopeful: president Wilson and the others now saw some need for experts.

A month later, a treaty was in sight—but it was taking too long, and little energy would be left for other problems. Hardinge still held this view when his personal connection with the conference ended in mid-July, as he returned home for two months' leave, his first long leave since going to India in 1910.[13]

Hardinge was now offered the embassy at Rome, on the assumption that Paris would be given to someone outside the Service. He refused at once: Paris should remain the reward for the head of the Service. Grey's earlier pledge was not binding upon his successor, but Hardinge hoped that Balfour and Lloyd George would still honor it when Derby left. A principle was at stake, for when posts like Paris and Washington were given to outsiders, the appeal of the Service was bound to decline.[14] For the time being, Hardinge remained in the Foreign Office. Crowe now replaced him as permanent British representative at Paris, but as "plenipotentiary," not ambassador, and he soon found the task equally frustrating.[15]

The Paris Conference was the low point of Hardinge's career, despite the substantial administrative burden of those months. Arnold Wilson, busy running Iraq, visited the conference in April and reported to Sir Percy Cox in Teheran that Hardinge was "now a nonentity."[16] The remark is an epitaph for Hardinge's role at Paris. Not unnaturally, he was bitter, as Vansittart and others recorded—but his bitterness was as much for the method by which the treaties were negotiated and the treaties themselves, which he regarded with scorn.

The greatest blame went to Lloyd George, but "the ignorance and ineptitude of the so-called 'Big Four'" together produced treaties which contained clauses "which anybody with any knowledge of foreign politics or of European affairs would have realized as being opposed to every principle of national life and existence." At a dinner in 1923 Hardinge finally told Lloyd George, no longer prime minister, what he thought of the treaties; Lloyd George, Hardinge recorded, "said nothing for about ten minutes and then remarked in a friendly way, 'If I had to go to Paris again I would conclude quite a different treaty.'"

Hardinge did not put on record how the treaties might have been improved, but he would certainly have argued that the experts should have been consulted with more regularity. Above all the methods were at fault. One final example of Hardinge's recollection of the "new diplomacy" is worth recording, on the all-important Treaty of Guarantee for French security:

> I went one morning at the usual hour of 11 a.m. to see Mr. Balfour, and while discussing with him various matters connected with the work of the Delegation, Mr. Philip Kerr, Lloyd Geòrge's Private Secretary, entered the room. He handed Mr. Balfour a paper saying it was a draft Treaty of Guarantee by England and America of French territory in the event of German aggression. Mr. Balfour asked who had drawn it up and by whose orders. Kerr explained that Sir C. Hurst, the Legal Advisor of the Foreign Office, had been called up out of bed at midnight by Lloyd George and received his instructions to draft a Treaty of Guarantee. He had done so and the text of the Treaty had been already submitted to President Wilson and M. Clemenceau, both of whom had approved it. Mr. Balfour bounded out of his chair asking Kerr if he really meant to say that a Treaty of Guarantee had been drawn up and submitted to President Wilson and Clemenceau without consultation with any other member of the Cabinet and even without the knowledge of the Secretary of State or Foreign Affairs, a treaty which might involve the whole British Empire in a long and disastrous war! Kerr said that this was so and that Lloyd George had only sent the paper to Mr. Balfour to put the phraseology into proper shape. Mr. Balfour took the paper and was soon so engrossed with its details that I left him feeling that his attention was already too fully occupied for other work . . . . I doubt if any treaty of such vital and far-reaching importance has ever been negotiated in such a thoughtless and light-hearted manner.

For Hardinge the last months of 1919 were a quiet contrast to the conference. As at Paris, important policy matters were discussed and decided upon at the cabinet level or among international leaders; the permanent under secretary administered the Office and the Service, where the volume of work scarcely decreased when the peace treaties were signed. Administration, however, still involved major issues, for example in the Near East where the Office was still responsible for Egypt. In Egypt, as elsewhere in the world, nationalism was at large—attributed by many, including Hardinge, to President Wilson's unfortunate belief that "self-determination" applied the world over. General Edmund Allenby, the victor in Palestine, had been sent to Egypt to deal with the unrest, but "when he got to Cairo he was evidently quite unfit to cope with the Egyptians and he absolutely climbed down and granted the Extremists everything they have asked for. It is really rather a miserable affair." This opinion dates from Paris, where the Egyptians embarrassingly requested a public hearing, but Hardinge's attitude on Egypt altered little over the years: the partial realization of progress which he absorbed in India did not extend to other possessions.[17]

Hardinge's attitude was shaped by Egypt's popular demonstrations and strikes; similarly, his view of postwar India was formed in the aftermath of Amritsar, where several hundred members of an unarmed assembly were massacred by General R. E. H. Dyer. Hardinge blamed Indian authorities for having no policy: it should never have come to this. Dyer himself was not particularly to be blamed, "except that he pumped too much lead into a defenseless crowd"; strong action was required when Englishmen were attacked in the streets.[18]

Weakness meant trouble, whether in Egypt or in India. New postwar reforms like those of Montagu and Chelmsford (which took the Minto-Morley changes one step further) were a serious surrender. Milner, sent to Egypt to make recommendations, suggested the practical elimination of the protectorate, and Hardinge, who read first of the proposal in *The Times,* predicted disaster.

How are we to prevent the Indians making similar demands

> upon us, and why should such demands be conceded to the Egyptians and not to the Indians, who are in reality more advanced and more able than the Egyptians? I feel very gloomy about it all, and it is a great misfortune that it is the views of idealists rather than practical men that are listened to now in higher circles.[19]

On the other hand, Hardinge was not adverse to using self-determination if it meant the effective achievement of Britain's aims where they might otherwise be unobtainable.

> The programme of 'self-determination' is in full swing everywhere, and we must make the best we can of it. It would on the whole, I believe, be advantageous to us to use the cry Palestine for the Palestinians and Mesopotamia for the Mesopotamians, as we are practically certain to have a mandate for Palestine and Mesopotamia, and under the mandate we shall be able to exercise such control over the administration as we may desire.[20]

Hardinge's cynicism, widely shared in British and French ruling circles, is an example of "old diplomacy" trying to find its bearings in the new; even the reality of power had to be disguised behind mandates or self-determination. As if to complicate matters further, in the fall of 1919 Balfour retired and was replaced by Curzon—"a disastrous blow," Hardinge recorded in *Old Diplomacy*. Hardinge's relationship with Curzon in the year he remained permanent under secretary was distinctly unpleasant from a personal standpoint. As Vansittart put it later, the two ex-viceroys detested each other. "Now the one sat as Secretary of State in the room above the other, a mere Permanent Under-Secretary. They were connected by a broad old speaking-tube, and when George blew down Charlie blew up."[21]

Curzon's appointment should perhaps be considered the crowning blow to Hardinge's London career. Yet Hardinge had a deep sense of loyalty to his profession and to the Foreign Office, and Curzon had the same loyalty, not to individuals, but to what he deemed the role of the Foreign Office to be. Already, when Curzon had acted as foreign secretary during the Paris Conference, it had become increasingly clear how many views the two men shared: on unconventional diplomacy, on Egypt, on the future of non-European Turkey, and so on—and in a professional context, this commonality was far more important than common viceregal postures. Above all, frustration at the seemingly irreparable loss by the Foreign Office of its traditional role put the two men in the same camp. Lloyd George managed diplomacy by conference (between 1919 and his fall in 1922, he attended thirty-three), seldom bothering to keep the high-stomached Curzon fully informed. At San Remo, in April 1920, a conference which among other decisions allocated Near Eastern mandates, Hardinge was reduced to hoping that Curzon would be allowed to attend, "not that he had any influence, but simply to be able to tell us afterwards what took place."[22]

The principal issues, aside from French security, were the Near East, where no settlement with Turkey had yet been reached, and Russia, where no coherent policy had yet been determined. Hardinge, as a member of the interdepartmental committee on Eastern affairs, was familiar with both overlapping areas. He and Curzon particularly would give Caucasian states such as Georgia and Armenia as much support as possible to stop the Bolsheviks (the larger question of intervention was more often fought out in the Cabinet with Lloyd George against, and Churchill for). The Foreign Office could argue its position, as it could argue that the Turks should be expelled from Constantinople and left in Turkey, but a year after the Paris Conference Hardinge had to admit that British policy was still unclear.[23]

Hardinge could only do his utmost to preserve Britain's Near Eastern foothold against War Office determination to withdraw, although he knew there was little answer to the argument of "no troops." Immediate disaster was avoided when the Allied Supreme Council at Paris, where Curzon represented Britain, decided to aid Georgia, Armenia, and Azerbaijan. For once,

Foreign Office views had some influence.[24] In the weeks that followed, Hardinge fought his strongest battle—but in the end a losing one—to keep the Caucasian states alive, writing to the director of relief missions to find the food which to his mind was one effective weapon against Bolshevism, interviewing visiting Caucasian dignitaries, attempting to define Britain's policy optimistically. At bottom, however, his realism forced him to the knowledge that Britain could ill afford to be compromised in the Caucasus.[25]

It was easier to make recommendations on Smyrna or the Batum-Baku road in the Caucasus than on the broader problem of Russia. Hardinge was a determined opponent of Bolshevism, perhaps little removed from Churchill on that score, but he was far quicker to see the impossibility of intervention on the scale necessary to defeat Russia's new masters, if they could be defeated at all. When Lloyd George opened trade negotiations with the Bolsheviks in the spring of 1920, a scornful Hardinge (Russia had no trade to offer) was only glad that the Foreign Office had given the Poles and the Baltic leaders the honest advice to make the best terms possible. By June, as the Poles withdrew from their brief hold upon Kiev, Hardinge for once agreed with Lloyd George on the impracticability of intervention; Curzon leaned towards Churchill's view, and on this issue—but not on the unattractiveness of Bolshevism—Hardinge and Curzon drew apart.[26]

Aside from minutes on the documents, however, Hardinge's influence on Russian policy, or any major policy matter, was slight. Much of his time and energy were spent on minor but vexing matters, such as the lengthy attempt to pry the kaiser from his refuge in the Netherlands in order to incarcerate him in some remote corner like the Falkland Islands. In the meantime, Hardinge's contempt for Lloyd George only grew by association: "He often spoke of places as men and of names as places. He did not know the difference between Silesia & Cilicia, and on one occasion when studying a contour map of Asia Minor he attributed the different colours to different races of men!" In short, he was possessed of colossal ignorance, but still, "he always had a singular charm and was, when he chose, a most delightful and amusing companion."[27]

Working with Curzon was no easier, despite harmony of viewpoint. Curzon faced his own frustrations, and in Hardinge's view was inclined to take them out upon the staff. "I speak feelingly and with knowledge since I saved more than one Foreign Office official from dismissal and ruin for some trivial fault during the year that I served in the Foreign Office under him." Curzon was a bully bullied, but Hardinge had experience in dealing with him. At one point, according to Hardinge's draft memoirs, Hardinge threatened resignation (the issue is not specified), "with an intimation that I would make public my reasons for doing so and in a few minutes he came with tears in his eyes retracting all he said and asking me to withdraw my resignation." Further information is wanting, but given their past relationship, it is surprising if there was only one such explosion.[28]

By the middle of 1920, with the peace treaties apparently as complete as they were likely to be, Hardinge was ready to leave the Office, presumably for retirement. Although healthy, he was tired; he had completed forty years of service and was ready to hand over to a younger man. Curzon's failure to consult him on some important midyear appointments only urged him on.[29] In July 1920, Hardinge was offered the Paris embassy, at last—almost a tainted gift, as he was afraid it had been made simply to get him out of the way. But Curzon could have waited to fill the post until Hardinge retired at the end of the year, and Hardinge had to admit, reluctantly, that Curzon had been gracious in offering it to him, particularly since Lloyd George doubtless objected. Hardinge was glad to go. It meant a more peaceful atmosphere, "and I am rather fed up with my last four years at the Foreign Office," as he put it to Graham.[30]

There were two difficulties. First, the heavy social obligation would be difficult for Diamond, only twenty and not particularly inclined to such activities. The other problem was the old one of finance: Paris was notoriously expensive. The salary was £2500 a year, with "frais de représentation" of £9000. Derby warned Hardinge that his own expenses had run to nearly £14,000 in the off season alone. After some hard bargaining, Curzon raised the allowance to £14,000, or a total of £16,500. Given the reduced level of social functions generally and their virtually complete absence during a long illness of Diamond's, he managed to spend only £13,000 in 1921–22. Any saving had to be offset against initial outfit cost of £5,000, reimbursement for which he was still waiting when he retired.[31]

For once there was little question about the next permanent under secretary. Crowe was the logical choice with Graham gone. Tyrrell, the other candidate, was still proving himself as assistant undersecretary and was the junior of the two men in any case. Hardinge recommended Crowe, considerably reversing his wartime position, and bade farewell to the Foreign Office in mid-October; a month later, Derby made similar farewells and left Paris. Hardinge and Diamond arrived on 27 November, ambassador at Paris at long last.[32]

Hardinge's reception was warm, both from the government and from old friends who had of course seen him during the Paris Conference. The embassy itself was badly in need of repair, and Hardinge spent months unable to entertain while workmen pulled down and rebuilt all the chimneys—but the hiatus was beneficial to Hardinge's budget. Furniture was also a worry. Ambassadors did their own decorating, and Hardinge was insufficiently equipped for Paris. Curzon viewed the embassy with relief after Hardinge had gone and Crewe had replaced him: "It was such a pleasure to see that beautiful house without tiger skins, the silver caskets, the elephant tusks and common photographs of Charlie Hardinge. Instead there were some quite good oil paintings, all portraits from Crewe House. . . ."[33]

Although repairs and the absence of a wife gave Hardinge a reasonable excuse to reduce the traditional social functions at the embassy, ambassadors had no escape from the normal round of affairs such as large luncheons given by the British colony ("very tiresome") or receptions by Madame Millerand, the president's wife ("a ghastly affair," in which Diamond, whose French needed practice, was placed next to the hostess, with a large circle of important ladies waiting on every word).[34] His professional responsibilities were also time-consuming, if not as demanding as in London. In addition to being ambassador to France, he represented Britain in the ambassadorial conference which saw to the fulfillment of the several peace treaties.

Nor was the situation in France at the end of 1920 particularly fortuitous. Hopes of some recompense for the tragic and disastrous losses in manpower and material property seemed increasingly unrealizable (save for the recovery of Alsace-Lorraine), although the great awakening would not come until the Ruhr crisis of 1923–24. The right-wing Bloc National was in power. Alexander Millerand (president for 1920–24), like Poincaré before him, attempted to play a major role; Hardinge found him congenial enough, and similarly got on well with George Leygues, premier from Hardinge's arrival until January 1921, and his successor, Aristide Briand. In January 1922, however, Poincaré became head of the government and remained so until Hardinge's retirement at the end of the year. Poincaré's policy was to squeeze reparations from Germany as effectively as possible, and the result was the occupation of the Ruhr in January 1923.

This desperate action lay in the future when Hardinge assumed his post, and French security and recovery still seemed possible. The twin problems of security and reparations dominated Hardinge's two years in Paris, reparations in fact arising on the same day that Hardinge drove in full ceremony to the Élysée Palace for his formal presentation as ambassador. That afternoon Leygues called on him and became quite excited when Hardinge observed that reparations were in a fair way to being settled (the scheme of reparations payments and distributions then in effect had been agreed at the Spa Conference of July 1920). Leygues disagreed, convinced that the allies should extract the entire cost of the war from Germany. Hardinge pointed out that English opinion was unanimously agreed that this could not be done, although he knew that the French government had not yet persuaded its own people: the difference in viewpoint typified the ensuing months.[35]

Hardinge had serious doubts about the treaty of guarantee for France as well: "no sane Englishman could possibly be tempted by the idea of being dragged at the wheels of the Chauvinism and pseudo-Imperialism of France. We would suffer more and have to condone more." On this issue, again, Curzon and Hardinge were in agreement. As Hardinge put it in his newly activated diary:

> Winston [Churchill] is entirely wrong in thinking that if there were an Alliance, the French would be easier to handle. My opinion is quite the reverse. We are a drag on them at present and I go so far as to say that if we had an alliance with them and if they could feel that they were perfectly safe from attack from the sea both at home and in their colonies, they would in course of time become a danger to Europe from the military view.[36]

As Hardinge knew well, more than the treaty of guarantee bedeviled Anglo-French relations. The situation in Greece, the terms of the Treaty of Sèvres, or Britain's sponsorship of Amir Abdullah in Transjordan, which seemed to France to jeopardize its interests in Syria—all required lengthy discussions with Leygues and Berthelot, head of the French Foreign Office and until Poincaré's return to power an influential figure in policymaking (Hardinge regarded him as both brilliant and Anglophobe).[37] Further hours were spent in the ambassador's conference, which met weekly (a bored Hardinge tried to spread the meetings to every ten days), where discussions tended to focus upon the conference's clashes with the still extant Supreme Military Committee at Versailles.[38]

On 12 January, Leygues fell. Hardinge predicted that Briand's new government would take a stiffer line on reparations and disarmament, since the temptation would be too great to play up to the public on these issues. Briand, however, had far more support in the Chamber and the country at large than Leygues, and he was generally credited with desiring smooth relations with the allies. For himself, Hardinge was quite pleased, for he found Briand "a very attractive man and most interesting. He has a charming personality, natural and a wonderful gift of language. . . .It will be a pleasure to do business with him for one can see at once that he is quick and original."[39]

Curzon, not Hardinge, dealt initially with Briand, for the foreign secretary and Lloyd George arrived in Paris on 24 January for a reparations conference. Hardinge was not representative (embarrassingly, since the French and Italian representatives in London had attended similar meetings there, and full knowledge of the proceedings would have made discussions with the Quai d'Orsay easier, as he pointed out to Curzon). Hardinge had little to do with detailed decisions, and he regarded the product of this meeting, a forty-year payment plan for Germany, with disbelief:

> It is inconceivable to me that anybody could ever imagine that such a scheme will be realised and that one should expect that the Germans 40 years hence, which after all means more than one generation of Germans, should consent to be still paying a heavy war indemnity.

But since all the participants appeared pleased, there was nothing more to be said.[40]

After seeing Lloyd George off, Hardinge himself returned to London for Alec's wedding to Helen Cecil, Lord Edward Cecil's daughter, on 8 February. Alec was now assistant private secretary to King George, and the wedding was a brilliant social occasion. Hardinge came back to France the proud possessor of a new Rolls Royce, for like King Edward VII, he had discovered the solace of motorcar travel. For the most part the chauffeur was so much luggage, as Hardinge piloted the vehicle at considerable speed and not without incident. On one journey his brakes overheated and, somewhat naive about machinery, he decided they needed oil-ing, with predictable results. On another occasion there was a collision with a red lorry on the road to Boulogne ("a good deal of talk on the spot as to the responsibility of the accident"), and, shortly before retirement, an altercation with a boy on a bicycle. His friend Mrs. Walker often joined in these trips, bringing her own car and chauffeur. At Easter 1921, Hardinge and Diamond drove to Madrid and back, 1,650 miles in five days, to spend an hour or two in the Prado, and were joined by Mrs. Walker at St. Jean de Luz.[41]

On the other hand, Curzon had a knack for spoiling Hardinge's pleasure, either by insisting he remain in Paris, or by giving him chores to do along the road—for example, to inspect a villa he wished to purchase near Cannes. It helped only a bit that Lady Curzon was a close friend and was not above pouring out her complaints, including many against Curzon's intolerable social manners, on her own visits to Paris. Hardinge listened with sympathy, but for all that his diary still recorded his faith in Curzon's ability.[42]

There were more important matters for Anglo-French negotiation than Curzon's villa, but with the English Channel so narrow in an age of conferences, Hardinge seldom had part in them except to attempt to smooth troubled relations, above all between Briand and Curzon, on such matters as reparations and Silesia. The latter was particularly irritating when a German plebiscite victory of nearly two to one in March propelled Korfanty, the Polish leader, into a rising (3 May) which encountered only slight resistance from the local French commissioner.[43] Hardinge had little trouble explaining basic French motivation:

> I have no hesitation in stating my conviction that the main impulse in the French nation, whether in its policy towards reparations, disarmament, Upper Silesia or the occupation of the Ruhr is inspired by fear, fear of Germany, genuine alarm as to the moral certainty of Germany's early recovery from her losses and defeat, and grave anxiety as to the possibility of the isolation of France in the not distant

future.

The easiest temporary solution was to cripple Germany, whether in the Ruhr or in Silesia. But the French knew they could not act alone, and there was now considerable discussion of the Anglo-French treaty which Derby had advocated the previous year. Hardinge had spoken strongly against the alliance then, but now he was less certain, at least about a defensive guarantee for France:

> The danger of being involved in hazardous enterprises through the ill-considered action of French politics is so obvious that it does not need to be developed. But I cannot help feeling that there is a good deal of force in the views of many Frenchmen that it is in the interest of Great Britain that Germany should be hindered in any aggressive designs against France, and that this might well be secured by the ratification by Great Britain of the defensive agreement concluded in Paris in 1919 to meet any aggression by Germany on the Rhine.

But any reconsideration would be on the clear understanding that the treaty would be part of "a comprehensive scheme of settlement of pending questions all over the world."[44]

Matters were not so quickly resolved in 1921. There were too many Anglo-French quarrels, and as Hardinge admitted the Chamber, which he thought did not really reflect public opinion, was not ready for the treaty. Hardinge was able to explain more fully when Curzon was in Paris on 20–21 June to discuss Turkey and Silesia. Curzon managed to obtain an agreement for the gradual withdrawal of opposing insurgent forces in Silesia and, more importantly, he did much to mend fences with Briand in three meetings at which Hardinge was present.[45]

On 8 August Curzon and Lloyd George "and their tag, rag, and bobtail" arrived for yet another conference on Silesia. Hardinge was worried by Lloyd George's combative attitude.

> It seems to me so stupid to run the risk of breaking up the

> Entente for a question on which we have no material interest whatsoever and on which our attitude is entirely in the interest of the Boches and nobody else, besides we shall not get what we want by quarrelling with the French. If they do quarrel at the Supreme Council, I suppose it will be left to me to repair afterwards les pots cassés.[46]

The conference lasted for a week but Hardinge attended only one meeting (with Curzon in Lloyd George's absence), which, considering the lengthy hours of talk, suited him just as well, as he watched with the cynical detachment of a professional diplomatist trained in another tradition:

> It is interesting to note that the phrase 'Rupture with the French' is being constantly used both by Lloyd George and Curzon. The idea seems to be perfectly familiar to them and presents no drawbacks from our point of view. I asked Lloyd George at dinner two nights ago, and Curzon afterwards, what they considered that a rupture implied. Both of them answered that they did not know. When I suggested to Lloyd George that it might mean the withdrawal of our troops from Silesia and possibly from the Rhine, he at once replied 'Not at all, there is no reason why they should withdraw.' When I said 'Then what does a rupture mean.' He replied 'I cannot say.' This only shows the levity with which these so-called Statesmen talk of a rupture with France, which can only have the gravest consequences for the two countries concerned and would mean the collapse of an edifice which has taken twenty years to build up. I was most unfavourably impressed by both of them in that they showed an absolute lack of imagination on a question which they both recognized to be vital.[47]

Whatever it might mean, a rupture was avoided by a last-minute suggestion by Britain that Upper Silesia be referred to the League of Nations. Lloyd George and Curzon departed on the fifteenth, the latter once again lavish in his praise of all Hardinge had done (but Hardinge once again glad to see him depart). Hardinge himself was off to Verdun, Coblenz, and Cologne, where he was officially received by the commander of the British garrison. Germany seemed prospering and the Rhineland booming. As he reported to Curzon, if only people would travel through the devastated regions and the Rhineland, they would be much harder on Germany respecting reparations. "One cannot help feeling that unless the Germans are made to pay up to the very utmost farthing, they will have certainly won the Peace." After a return swing through Belgium and two unauthorized days in England, Hardinge returned to a somewhat calmer Paris.[48]

With Silesia on the way to settlement, Hardinge found the Near East to be his main worry of the last months of 1921. Anglo-French quarrels there had not ceased since the armistice, although there were notable low points, whether in Britain's establishment of Amir Abdullah in Transjordan or France's secret agreement with Mustafa Kemal's representative in London for an armistice in Cilicia (signed during the London conference). But matters in Turkey were now coming to a head. Throughout the summer the Greeks had maintained an offensive in central Anatolia, but by mid-September they had been stopped before Ankara in a series of desperate battles. The road now was back to Smyrna and expulsion—and to destruction of the Treaty of Sèvres, but this still seemed a remote possibility in late 1921. The French, however, had sent negotiator Henri Franklin-Bouillon to Turkey to negotiate with Kemal. Hardinge, told the envoy had no particular mission, knew better from intercepted telegrams. An agreement which resulted in French evacuation of Cilicia was concluded on 20 October. Hardinge, for all his own distaste at this deception, correctly warned Curzon that there was little chance of French repudiation of the agreement, although parts might conceivably be altered through later negotiation.[49]

Hardinge's concern was the relationship to French politics. He knew that British opposition to the agreement might provoke

Briand's fall: the premier had many critics, and some felt his only utility was in preserving friendly relations with Britain. If he failed in this he was expendable, partticularly since he was already under attack for his policies at the Washington Naval Conference which began in mid-November. But Hardinge would not treat the issue mildly to save Briand:

> With Latin races it is essential to stand up to them, the only thing that really matters being the question of form. Further Briand though outwardly very friendly to us, has in my opinion been the victim of treachery on the part of an Anglophobe Foreign Office here, headed by Berthelot who is anxious to recuperate his position by a hostile act of chauvinism towards us. I see no good in being tender towards a Prime Minister who through heedlessness or weakness is the tool of a hostile Foreign Office and I am not at all certain that in some ways I would not prefer to have to deal with a man who is openly hostile.[50]

Briand indeed gave every appearance of conciliation, and during the fall several meetings took place on a possible Anglo-French defensive alliance. In January, however, Briand, wearied by bitter attacks in the Chamber and press, resigned; "he prefered to leave to others the difficult task of reconciling France's claims with France's needs."[51] Hardinge was unimpressed with Poincaré, who formed a new government—"a man of narrow views and with a mind entirely absorbed in detail"—but treaty talks continued.

In April attention shifted to the Genoa conference, which for the first time included both Germany and Russia in European negotiations. Although the conference broke down in mid-May over the Bolshevik refusal to recognize Russia's prewar debts, Germany and Russia made a separate agreement at Rapallo. Poincaré in his first postconference talk with Hardinge obviously had been angered by this union of outcasts, but this made the premier no more flexible on Anglo-French relations either then or through the summer of 1922, which culminated in the Chanak crisis of September.[52]

In August, the Turks had begun their counteroffensive against the Greeks. By early September the Greek army had broken. Brusa fell on the fifth and Smyrna on the ninth. Hardinge was not surprised, for he had opposed Greek operations in Asia Minor since the start of the war.

> It is very easy to say 'I told you so' but anybody who knows anything about the Near East, knows perfectly well that it was only a question of time for the Turks to throw the Greeks into the sea. People will not understand that the Greeks are a rotten nation while the Turkish common soldier is about the finest fighting material that can be found anywhere except in India. England has played a miserable rôle throughout. We have encouraged the Greeks all the time and given them no support. I expect that they will hate us in the future.[53]

Hardinge's responsibility was to negotiate French support for the position at Chanak on the Dardanelles, Kemal's obvious next objective. It was a thankless task, for the French had no intention of offering resistance to Kemal. Lloyd George appealed to the dominions, and Curzon arrived in Paris for direct negotiation with Poincaré on what was now a legitimate crisis. The first two meetings went reasonably well, although Curzon's references to French desertion were ill received. At the third meeting, on 22 September, Curzon made a long and tactless speech which produced an explosion of wrath from Poincaré. Curzon was most upset when the premier shouted and screamed, and Hardinge interrupted to say that Curzon did not feel well and the conference must be adjourned. After a quarter of an hour, Hardinge went to see Curzon,

> and found him stretched out, with his leg on a chair [Curzon was suffering from phlebitis], weeping and drinking

large gulps of brandy from a great flask at his side. He said 'I must go home, I cannot stand this any longer, he has insulted me very much, and I have never been treated like this before. If he does not apologize, I must go home.'[54]

Hardinge told him he would have to withdraw his remarks about French abandonment at Chanak; reluctantly, Curzon agreed. Hardinge saw Poincaré alone, and told him that he had forgotten himself as chairman and Curzon's host.

I said that he had spoken to Curzon just as though he was a naughty schoolboy and that sort of thing could not be tolerated. . . . The little brute refused at first to apologize to Curzon, saying that Curzon must come and tell him that he withdrew the sentence about abandonment. I stated that Curzon was too ill to come at that moment, but that he had charged me to convey this message to him. He refused to accept it from me, saying that he must give it himself. I replied that I, as British Ambassador, was the recognised channel for any communication to the French Minister for Foreign Affairs. . . .

Warned that the conference might break up, Poincaré changed his ground but insisted that Hardinge had to make the apology to the whole body: Hardinge only agreed to make it to Count Sforza, the Italian ambassador. In due course, the apologies were all made; once the participants had swallowed these doses of pride, agreement was soon reached. Curzon sent off a telegram which gave the Cabinet a rather different story, although he was most generous to Hardinge. Hardinge, for his part, had contempt for both men. Poincaré had behaved like a cad, but Curzon had presented a "most deplorable spectacle."

Instead of weeping, he should have stopped Poincaré at once and threatened to leave the room if he continued in that tone. Poincaré, who is a cur, would have caved in at

> once. But really the spectacle of Curzon, extended in another room, with tears pouring down his face and a brandy bottle by his side, speaking in maudlin tones, was a sight which I shall not easily forget, as it was so absolutely lacking in dignity and restraint.[55]

Curzon went home on the twenty-fourth, not without another brief scene when Hardinge lectured him on his rudeness in turning up late for every meal.

As before, however, Hardinge shared completely in Curzon's attempt to avoid war with Kemal at Chanak despite some eager cabinet colleagues, "lunatics who ought to be shut up." Poincaré fully agreed, but the battle of words was fought out in London—and very nearly with bullets in Turkey. Fortunately, an armistice was agreed upon with Kemal at Mudanya, and Hardinge wrote to send his congratulations to Curzon, both for the armistice and for asserting the role of the Foreign Office in diplomacy once more: "I trust that the Garden City of Downing Street will now have its wings clipped," referring to Lloyd George's own secretariat established in temporary huts on the Horse Guards Parade.[56]

Further negotiations on Turkey were not to be Hardinge's concern, for he retired in December. He had been thinking of this step since midyear at least. He enjoyed the work,

> but I doubt if anybody has any conception of the loneliness of my life here. I have any number of French society friends, but I cannot look upon them as real friends since there are none whom I would really miss if I were told that I would never see them again! I am devoted to my daughter but a girl of 21 cannot be a real companion to a man of three times her age and I frankly miss the companionship of my relations and friends. I find the solitude of my life here quite intolerable. When I was in India it was just the same during the 2 years I spent there after my wife's death, but I felt I was then doing war work. In England I am much

happier.

It would also be much better for Diamond. Hardinge was coming to feel that "unless she had a chance of meeting Englishmen in England she would never marry."[57]

By September, Hardinge had definitely decided to leave. His only worry was that his resignation might be taken as a disagreement with Lloyd George's policies. Hardinge did not believe in ambassadors agreeing or disagreeing with policy—it was for them to carry it out. For this reason he issued a communiqué that he would leave at the end of November for family reasons (technically he retired on 31 December, but he left early to collect overdue leave). Curzon now told Lloyd George, adding that he had tried to dissuade Hardinge earlier, "since he has filled the office with great success and carries much weight in Paris. We shall find it hard to replace him."[58]

Hardinge would need a successor. Crowe told him that the first offer Curzon made was to Vansittart. The Foreign Office again shuddered at the thought that Lloyd George might put in one of his own friends. But Vansittart hesitated and was lost; Crewe was given the appointment, and Hardinge turned over to his old friend the Paris establishment, complete with repaired Rolls Royce. Packing, a staff party, a last luncheon from President Millerand (and the Grand Cross of the Legion of Honor, to complement his Second Class of twenty years earlier), and he was off. Press coverage was warm, as were a number of letters from friends. Curzon's fulsome letter was impressive enough for Hardinge to quote it in his memoirs. "My feelings are very mixed," Hardinge wrote to close his diary, "as I am in many ways sorry to leave Paris but I am still more glad to get home." The rest was needed, however, for as he put it to Curzon, "I really think I found it more difficult from the point of view of actual diplomacy than any post I have hitherto occupied and I sometimes almost desparied of keeping things straight."[59]

Hardinge had one last mission as he returned to London. All

the signs of late December were that disagreement on reparations would send the French into the Ruhr. Hardinge warned Poincaré that this would shake the entente, but he knew that Belgium would cooperate with France. Hardinge's alternative suggestion was for France to exploit the mines and forests of the Rhineland. Poincaré agreed to consider this with certain provisos, but Bonar Law, who had replaced Lloyd George as prime minister, to Hardinge's surprise rejected the idea in a private interview on the grounds that English public opinion would not tolerate the exploitation of the allied-occupied Rhineland. Hardinge pointed out that the result would be exploitation of the Ruhr, which meant a full-scale invasion of Germany, but Bonar Law was not to be moved. No official record was made of this conversation, or of Hardinge's subsequent letter to Poincaré that Bonar Law had refused the plan, but in 1924 Hardinge wrote to ask Poincaré's secretary for a copy of the letter.[60]

It was unfortunate that this last might-have-been was on an issue of such magnitude. While there is no certainty that exploitation of the Rhineland would have satisfied France and avoided occupation of the Ruhr, it might well have postponed it, perhaps indefinitely, with incalculable consequences. In any case, Bonar Law's curt rejection was misguided on a suggestion which had already received limited French approval. Hardinge charitably attributed Bonar Law's attitude to his failing health (he died within a few months), but approval would have associated Britain, once again, with French intervention.

Hardinge now entered into retirement at Oakfields, a house he had purchased adjoining South Park, Penshurst, and considerable preoccupation with the work of his gardeners, the dogs, and a collection of tame pheasants of which he was very proud, on his Foreign Office pension of £1700 a year. Some financial associations in the city, an investment in greyhound racing, presidency of the local branch of the Conservative Association (Hardinge became a Conservative soon after retirement)—a mainly social position—and regular attendance at the House of Lords (but few speeches) kept him occupied.

Diamond married in 1923 and moved to Scotland, but her health never returned to full strength and she died in 1927, leaving a void in Hardinge's life that could never be filled. Alec remained assistant private secretary to the king and in 1936 became principal private secretary to King Edward VIII, well known for his warning to the king of the probable political repercussions of the royal association with Mrs. Wallis Simpson. Hardinge's reaction to the abdication crisis is not recorded. But divorce in scandal had been cause for dismissal among his own subordinates at Paris, and Alec had demonstrated personal courage and respect for monarchical institutions beyond the individual that were much like his father's. After King Edward's abdicaton, Alec stayed on in the same capacity with King George VI, working through the war years until forced to resign by ill health in 1943, a year before Hardinge's own death.[61]

Hardinge's attention was now focused on less recent historical problems. He spent much time on his memoirs—too much time from a biographer's prejudiced viewpoint, for *Old Diplomacy* and *My Indian Years* as published represent at least a third draft. Unpublished sections of the second draft have been used in this work, but Hardinge destroyed his first draft along with a certain amount of personal correspondence. He was as circumspect about his private life as he expected others to be. For this reason, for example, he refused to allow Sir Sidney Lee to consult his papers for Lee's biography of King Edward VII. But Hardinge obviously enjoyed reconstructing the past, particularly in *On Hill and Plain*, a sportsman's account of hunting in India published in 1933.[62]

He did not enter into contemporary issues with any great heat, speaking no more than half a dozen times in the House of Lords. His only notable foray into public life was in connection with the general strike of 1926. Hardinge blamed both miners and mine-owners for causing the strike, but he was all for a strong line towards the strikers and what at least in its inception "was an attempt at revolution and nothing else." He acted as president of the Organization for the Maintenance of Supplies (O.M.S.), the object of which was to keep supplies and vital services going in the event of a strike by enrolling drivers and other technicians (a hundred thousand were on the final list). Although outwardly independent and voluntary, it had strong government support and contacts with the British fascist movement, possibly through cousin Arthur Hardinge, who sat on that party's executive. Hardinge thoroughly enjoyed himself during the actual strike, for he became a special constable and joined a flying squad of motor cars "in which I drove my own car through all the worst districts of South London." He and other retired figures of prominence such as Earl Jellicoe lent prestige to the organization; his activity in this matter was an exception to his general disengagement from home politics in other than a symbolic and decorative way—but then many took sides in 1926.[63]

Far more fixed in Hardinge's attention was India. His first postretirement appointment in 1923 was to serve as chairman of the Delhi Advisory Committee; his last remarks in the House of Lords in 1942 were to argue against India's claim for independence. Generally, Hardinge tried not to interfere in a direct way on the various committees on which he served, realizing how much had altered in the many years since he left India. He did represent India directly as Indian chief delegate to the League of Nations at Geneva in 1923 and again in 1924, but the assignment entailed little real work aside from keeping his fellow delegates in line. Hardinge spoke occasionally, principally on the opium traffic, but he was more interested in escaping from the sessions for long drives through France.[64]

In 1931–32, he was able to fulfil his pledge to return to India. It was a trying but memorable trip, from the first sight of his own statue on the Apollo Bundar to Bombay. Visits by a special two-car rail caravan followed to Hyderabad and Bangalore, Ajanta and Ellora, and a week in Mysore (which honored him with Hardinge Circle). Hardinge bagged his last seven tigers and thoroughly enjoyed himself, although such exertions tired him greatly. The viceregal honors he was accorded in Calcutta by the viceroy, Lord Irwin, demonstrated why the tradition against visits by ex-viceroys was a good one. But Hardinge's greatest enthusiasm was reserved for New Delhi, where he was met by Lutyens. He drove down Hardinge Avenue, and his first view of the new government buildings left him breathless: "when I came close to them I was thrilled and came to the conclusion that they had worked out even finer than I had ever expected. They are simply glorious. . . . I am more satisfied than words can express. The results are well worth all the worry and trouble I had when Viceroy and it is beautiful." Lady Hardinge Hospital, with which he had kept up closely in the intervening years (and to which he had made several donations), pleased him also—it was now greatly expanded, with 250 beds. In February he opened a long-delayed Lady Hardinge Serai at Phangarj for poor travelers, pleased again that two such memorials honored Winifred.[65]

On his return, however, he proved to have the same conservative views of change in India that he had before his visit. In 1928 he had already made a rare public intervention in the House of Lords against placing the loyal Indian princes under the authority of the Legislative Assembly. But large-scale concessions in the further Indianization were a "leap in the dark" in his view—and he had been, in his own eyes, a progressive, even radical viceroy in this sense. Participation in provincial affairs was a reality, but in this and subsequent remarks, Hardinge pleaded that self-government should be proven at this level before it was extended to the central government.[66]

Hardinge's liberalism, like that of most of his generation, had been outpaced in India by events. In European affairs, similarly, caution was his watchword. He spoke against unilateral sanctions against Mussolini in 1935, both to avoid "the slippery slope leading to war" with an old friend and ally in Italy, and because the sooner Abyssinia came under a civilizing power the better, although Italy's aggression was of course misguided. He criticized the British delegation (meaning Robert Cecil, now Viscount Cecil of Chelwood) for a provocative attitude. To Cecil, this was "outrageous"—if anything, the delegaton had been far too patient.[67]

Hardinge's view went further than Abyssinia. As he put in to

The Times in 1937, "the task to which we have set ourselves is no longer to make the world safe for democracy, but to make the coexistence of democracies and dictatorships safe for the world." He congratulated the government for the Anglo-German Naval agreement of 1935; he signed the "Declaration of Peace" of the "Friends of the League" in 1937; in 1939 he advocated broad propaganda efforts to let Germany know there was no need to fear encirclement, no need for war.[68] But war did come, as Hardinge, in his eighties was well aware, with Oakfields on the direct plane and V-bomb route to London. He died in 1944, and was buried in wartime austerity in Fordcombe churchyard, a few miles from South Park, the second successful governor-general of India named Hardinge to be sheltered in this family ground.

Charles Hardinge was a diplomatist first and foremost. He was a competent professional, the product of his era. No deep speculative thinker, he was not the man to challenge the givens of his Edwardian generation—the rightness of the monarchy, the empire, the raj in India—but he regarded them without the elaborate speculative framework provided by men such as the *Round Table* group on the nature of the commonwealth. As an ordinary man, he had ordinary faults: a tendency to hasty conclusions on individuals; a certain coldness in personal relations; intolerance of human foibles, particularly incompetence. Despite party labels, he was a conservative, above all in his last years, whether the context was labor at home, progress in India, or fascism in Europe.

His attributes were several. He had the necessary intelligence, tact, flexibility, and patience to exercise his craft well. He had energy and he had ambition, but never too much of the latter quality which, too artlessly disguised, has ruined many a man. He had extraordinary luck, aided by his own abilities, in his marriage to Winifred, the patronage of Dufferin, and above all the unflagging support of King Edward VII. He had courage, physically to face bombs in India, morally to take a stance which won enemies, such as on South Africa, or in the defense of his convictions in that difficult hour before the House of Lords in 1917. He had empathy, the ability to grasp something of the meaning of prewar India and to win the admiration of many Indians. Above all, however, he had a sense of justice which covered lesser faults and which explained much of his success as a diplomat turned administrator in India.

Hardinge had his critics, officially in the Mesopotamian commission, in remote subordinates on occasion, in historians sometimes for his role in bringing about the war.[69] But he was a success, certainly in the visible trappings which marked achievement in his age (aside from riches): his appointment as viceroy, his collection of honors (surely something of a record for nonmilitary and nonroyal personages in British history). His career had both triumph and disaster: triumph as a rising star during the Russo-Japanese War, as a builder of the Entente, as a defender of his office and his profession, as his Foreign Office reforms bear witness. India too was a success, until the last arguable advances on Baghdad. But the war years were disappointing, and he found no answer then or later to the continued deterioration of his profession and his employer. The nadir was the Paris Conference where Hardinge, ignored and humiliated, could only administer the staff and watch developments with cynicism and despair.

But as ambassador to Paris, despite the new diplomacy in general or Lloyd George's method in particular, he proved once again the utility of the trained ambassador, or the art of gentle diplomatic persuasion, of realistic analysis and prediction. Hardinge was at his very best not as under secretary or viceroy, but as ambassador: it is the irony of his career that despite forty-three successful years in the Diplomatic Service, he was ambassador in the traditional sense for less than five. His epitaph, however, is not to be found in the brief eulogy pronounced in the House of Lords, although Viscount Cranborne's tribute was warm enough: "Everybody respected him and everybody trusted him."[70]—but in the words of Dryden with which Hardinge closed *Old Diplomacy:*

Happy the man, and happy he alone,
He, who can call to-day his own;
He, who secure within, can say,
To-morrow do thy worst for I have lived today.
Be fair, or foul, or rain, or shine,
The joys I have possessed, in spite of fate, are mine,
Not heaven itself upon the past has power,
But what has been, has been, and I have had my hour.

Abbreviations Used in Notes

Add.Ms.	British Library, Additional Manuscripts.
BD	*British Documents on the Origins of the War, 1898–1914.*
DBFP	*Documents on British Foreign Policy, 1919–1939.*
FO	Foreign Office Records, Public Record Office.
H	Lord Hardinge of Penshurst.
HP(C)	Hardinge Papers, Cambridge University.
HP(M)	Hardinge Papers, Kent County Archives, Maidstone.
HP(SP)	Hardinge Papers, South Park.
Lib. Corresp.	Librarian's Department Correspondence, Foreign Office Library.
OD	Lord Hardinge, *Old Diplomacy* (London, 1947).
OD Ms.	An earlier draft of *Old Diplomacy* located at South Park.
Parl. Deb.	Hansard's *Parliamentary Debates.*
priv.	Private.
RA	Royal Archives, Windsor Castle.
RIBA	Royal Institute of British Architects.

Notes

Notes to Chapter I

1. *OD*, 1. All subsequent unidentified quotations in this chapter and chapters 2–5 are from this work.

2. Charles Stewart Hardinge in his biography of his father, *Viscount Hardinge by his Son and Private Secretary in India*, (Oxford, 1891), 142, says that Lord Hardinge declined the East India Company annuity; George Bruce, *Six Battles for India: the Anglo-Sikh Wars, 1845-6, 1848-9* (London, 1969), 101, 122, 126–27.

3. Hardinge to Lady Hardinge, 1 March 1846, in J. T. Bikrama Hasrat, ed., *The Punjab Papers* (Hoshiapur, Punjab, 1970), 104.

4. Charles Stewart Hardinge, *Recollections of India, Drawn on Stone by J.D. Harding, from the original drawings by. . .* (London, 1847); J. D. Harding was no relation. A few letters from Charles Stewart are to be found in his father's papers, McGill University Library, Montreal, and they show clearly his desire to record his experiences in India through his art.

5. OD Ms., 8.

6. Zara S. Steiner, *The Foreign Office and Foreign Policy, 1898-1914* (Cambridge, 1969), 175.

7. Dufferin to Viscount Hardinge, 3 May 1881, HP(C) 1.

8. Dufferin to Viscount Hardinge, 1 June 1882, Sanderson to Dufferin, 9 June 1882, Dufferin to H, 30 September 1884. HP(C) 1.

9. H to Dufferin, 12 October and Granville to Dufferin, 9 November 1881, HP(C) 1.

10. OD Ms., 48.

11. *Ibid.*

12. H to Salisbury, 1 December 1887, FO 78/4033, and to Salisbury, 3 January

1889 (quoted), FO 78/4229. H was chargé 25 November–17 December 1887, 7 May–1 June 1888, 6 August 1888–22 January 1889, and 21 November 1890–11 April 1891.

13. O'Conor to Salisbury, 6 March, enclosing H to O'Conor, 3 March 1888, FO 78/4136, and O'Conor to Salisbury, 23 December 1887, FO 78/4033.

14. H to Sir E. Barrington, 27 September, 8 October, and 4 December, and Barrington to H, 3 October and 30 November 1888, HP(C) 1.

15. Letters from Winifred of 1889–90 are in memorial album, HP(SP); Philip Magnus, *King Edward the Seventh* (Harmondsworth, Middlesex, 1967), 279–80. A jaundiced view of the Alingtons is given in Sonia Keppel, *Edwardian Daughter* (London, 1958), 19–24, 33–36.

16. H to Salisbury, 12 January, 29 March, and 2 April, and O'Conor to Salisbury, 11 April 1891, FO 78/4377.

17. Great Britain, *Parliamentary Papers*, Treaty Series No. 1, 1893.

18. Queen to Rosebery, 19 January, and Rosebery to queen, 20 January 1893, RA O 28/12 and 16.

19. H to Rosebery, 22 and 28 December 1892, FO 104/96.

20. H, Paris diary, 11 April 1896, HP(SP).

21. OD Ms., 98.

22. H, Paris diary, 1 July 1896, HP(SP).

23. OD Ms., 111–12; H, *On Hill and Plain* (London, 1933), 101–10.

24. H telegram to Durand, 29 March, Durand to H, 11 July 1897, HP(C) 1.

25. H to Salisbury, 7 April 1897, FO 60/584, and to Sanderson, 28 February 1897, HP(C) 1.

26. H priv. to Sanderson, 6 January, 1 February (quoted), and 2 March 1898, and to Salisbury, 7 May 1897, and Lynch Co. to H, 21 April 1898, HP(C) 2.

27. H. priv. to Sanderson, 2 March 1898, HP(C) 2.

28. See Briton Cooper Busch, *Britain and the Persian Gulf, 1894–1914* (Berkeley, 1967).

29. H to Sanderson, 28 August 1897, HP(C) 2. See Firuz Kazemzadeh, *Russia and Britain in Persia, 1864–1914* (New Haven, 1968).

30. See FO 60/584, particularly H to Salisbury, 13 March 1897; Kazemzadeh, 410.

31. Durand to Salisbury, 31 March 1898, FO 60/595.

Notes to Chapter II

1. H priv. to Sanderson, 1 November 1900, HP(C) 3.

2. H priv. to Bertie, 14 November 1901, FO 800/176.

3. H to Salisbury, 10 October 1900, FO 65/1601. Hardinge was chargé 3 June–3 July and 27 September–10 December 1899; 13 September–26 November 1900; 28 September–2 December 1901; 15 June–12 August and 8 October–12 December 1902.

4. H to Lansdowne, 23 November 1900 (quoted), FO 65/1602; H priv. to Bertie, 20 October, and Bertie priv. to H, 6 November 1901, HP(C) 3.

5. Ian H. Nish, *The Anglo-Japanese Alliance* . . . (London, 1966), 189–90.

6. H quoted in Peter Fleming, *Bayonets to Lhasa*. . . (London, 1961), 39.

7. Scott to Salisbury, 3 May 1899, FO 65/1578; H to Lansdowne, 9 October 1901, FO 65/1623; and 4 November 1902, FO 65/1643.

8. H to Salisbury, 18 October 1899, FO 65/1580.

9. H priv. to Sanderson, 2 November 1899, HP(C) 3.

10. H priv. to Sanderson, 2 November and 9 December HP(C) 3; and H to Salisbury, 30 October 1899, FO 65/1580.

11. Scott to Lansdowne, 6 March, H priv. to Sanderson, 7 March, and Lansdowne to Scott, 21 March 1901, HP(C) 3.

12. H priv. to Sanderson, 27 November 1902, HP(C) 3.

13. Spring Rice priv. to H, 25 July 1900, HP(C) 3.

14. Bertie, reporting his own words to Barrington, priv. to Knollys, 8 February 1902, RA W42/72.

15. H priv. to Bertie, 30 July 1902; Lascelles private to Hardinge, 16 January 1903, HP(C) 3.

16. Knollys priv. to H, 15 January 1903, HP(C) 3; George Monger, *The End of Isolation* (London, 1963), 89–90; Philip Magnus, *King Edward the Seventh* (Harmondsworth, Middlesex, 1967), 373–78.

17. Sanderson's arrangement in note circulated in F.O., 6 February 1903, FO 366/386.

    Villiers kept the Americas and Campbell the Far East. Zara S. Steiner, *The Foreign Office and Foreign Policy, 1898–1914* (Cambridge, 1969), 13, is in error giving Villiers continued control of Consular and Treaty Departments in 1903, proving that even a leading expert can become mired in these constant changes of staff and assignments.

18. H priv. to Lascelles, 25 March 1903, FO 800/14.

19. Sir Frederick Ponsonby (first Lord Sysonby), *Recollections of Three Reigns* (New York, 1952), 224–31; H, *A Short Record of the King's Journey. . .* (London, 1903).

20. H priv. to Winifred Hardinge, 5 April 1903, HP(SP).

21. Gordon Brook-Shepherd, *Uncle of Europe. . .*(London, 1975), 172–73; *OD*, 87.

22. H priv. to Winifred, 11 April 1903, HP(SP); Ponsonby, 230–31.

23. H priv. to Bertie, 4 April 1903, FO 800/183.

24. H priv. to Winifred, 22, 24, and 28 April 1903, HP(SP); *OD*, 93–94.

25. *OD*, 94; Ponsonby, 244.

26. H priv. to Winifred, 3 May 1903, HP(SP).

27. Bertie priv. to H, 14 January, HP(C) 3; H priv. to Lascelles, 10 March 1903, FO 800/14.

28. H priv. to Bertie, 25 May 1903, FO 800/163, quoted in Steiner, 72; Cranborne was parliamentary under secretary, 1900–1903.

29. H priv. to Bertie, 25 May, FO 800/163; Steiner, 72, and appendices on proposed reforms; Villiers to Sanderson, 27 April 1903, FO Lib. Corresp. 3A.

30. Sanderson note, 13 May 1903, FO Lib. Corresp. 3A.

31. Ray Jones, *The Nineteenth-Century Foreign Office. . .*(London, 1971), 114–18; Lansdowne minutes, 15 and 22 May, and 20 June, Sanderson minutes, 25 and 27 May 1903, FO Lib. Corresp. 3A.

32. H priv. to Bertie, 2 January 1904, FO 800/183; Jones, 121.

33. Steiner, 79.

34. Monger, chapter 6.

35. H priv. to Lascelles, 10 and 25 March 1903, FO 800/14.

36. Lansdowne memo, 10 September 1903, quoted in Monger, 133.

37. H priv. to Curzon, 26 October, and Curzon priv. to H, 21 November 1903, HP(C) 3.

38. H to Lansdowne, 22 November, *BD* IV; H priv. to Spring Rice, 29 November, Spring Rice File, HP(SP); and priv. to Knollys, 29 November 1903, RA W44/10; Monger, 143.

39. H priv. to Bertie, 15 June, and Knollys priv. to Bertie, 28 November 1903,

FO 800/173.

40. H priv. to Bertie, 4 December 1903, FO 800/163.

41. Knollys priv. to H, 17 December, HP(C) 7; and priv. to Bertie, 23 December, and H priv. to Bertie, 24 December 1903, FO 800/163; and 8 February 1904, FO 800/176.

42. King Edward to H, and H to king, both 15 February, HP(C) 7; H priv. to Bertie, undated (but at least 18 February), 26 February, and 3 March 1904, FO 800/183.

43. H priv. to Bertie, 20 March 1904, FO 800/183, and undated letter (quoted) referred to in note 42 above.

44. H priv. to Bertie, 11 and 14 March 1904, FO 800/183.

45. H priv. to Bertie, 20 March 1904, FO 800/183.

46. Ponsonby, 267–71; Magnus, 413–14; H priv. to Lansdowne, 6 December 1904, FO 800/141; Brook-Shepherd, 128; Sir Sidney Lee, *King Edward VII . . .* (London, 1927), II, 184–85; Rogers Platt Churchill, *The Anglo-Russian Convention of 1907* (Cedar Rapids, Iowa, 1939), 64–65. Quoted remark from H priv. to Spring Rice, 22 April 1904 (Spring Rice file), HP (SP).

Notes to Chapter III

1. H diary, 16–17 May 1904, HP(C) 5.

2. H priv. to Knollys, 23 April and 25 May 1904, RA W44/90, 103; Lord Newton, *Lord Lansdowne: A Biography* (London, 1929), 310–11.

3. H to Lansdowne, 28 May, *BD* IV; and priv. to Lansdowne, 25 May 1904, FO 800/140.

4. H priv. to Lansdowne, 25 May, FO 800/140; on Plehve, H diary, 3 June 1904, HP(C) 5.

5. H to Lansdowne, 5 June, and no. 282, 8 June (quoted), FO 65/1680; and 30 June, *BD* IV; and priv. to Sanderson, 9 June 1904, HP(C) 6.

6. H diary, 29 May, HP(C) 5; H to Lansdowne, 20 June 1904, *BD* IV; H priv. to Sanderson, 3 June; and to Valentine Chirol (quoted), 20 June, HP(C) 6; Chirol priv. to H, 14 June, HP(C) 7; and H priv. to Chirol, copy, 3 June 1904, FO 800/2.

7. H priv. to Knollys, 6 July 1904, HP(C) 6.

8. Findlay telegram to Lansdowne, 9 July; H telegram to Lansdowne no. 31, 21 July, and no. 35, 23 July, and to Lansdowne (quoted), 19 July, and priv. to

Lansdowne, 6 December 1904, FO 418/19.

9. Lansdowne priv. to H (quoted), 27 July, FO 800/140; H to Lansdowne, 28 July, and telegram no. 99, 24 August 1904, FO 418/19.

10. H diary, 28 July 1904, HP(C) 5.

11. H priv. to Lansdowne, 18 August and 1 and 15 September, FO 800/141; H priv. to king, 18 and 25 August, RA W44/104, 196; H diary, 13 August 1904, HP(C) 5.

12. H priv. to Sanderson, 3 June, HP(C) 6; H diary, 21 October 1904, HP(C) 6.

13. H to Lansdowne, 28 October 1904, *BD* IV; Bertie priv. to H, 21 September, HP(C) 7; H telegram to Lansdowne, 10 September, and telegram no. 127, 21 September, FO 418/19; priv. to Bertie, 29 September, HP(C) 6, and 29 September 1904, FO 65/1681.

14. H diary, 14 October, HP(C) 5; H to Lansdowne, 10 October, FO 418/27; and priv. to Lansdowne, 13 October 1904, FO 800/141.

15. H to Bertie (quoted), 28 September, FO 800/176; Lansdowne telegram no. 174 to H and H telegram no. 146 to Lansdowne, 24 October 1904, *BD* IV.

16. H to Winifred, 15 October 1904, HP(SP).

17. Lansdowne to H, 25 and 26 October 1904, *BD* IV.

18. H priv. to Lansdowne, 27 October 1904, FO 800/141.

19. H telegram no. 160 to Lansdowne and Lansdowne to H, 27 October, *BD* IV; account in *OD* is based on diary, 12 November 1904, HP(C) 5.

20. H telegram no. 164 to Lansdowne, 28 October, Lansdowne to H. 29 October, *BD* IV, and priv. to H, 29 October, FO 800/141; *OD*, 108, is taken from priv. to Lansdowne, 5 November 1904, FO 800/141. See George Monger, *The End of Isolation* (London, 1963), 170–75; David Walder, *The Short Victorious War. . .* (New York, 1973), chapters 13–14.

21. H priv. telegram to Lansdowne, 29 October, FO 800/141; H to Lansdowne, 31 October 1904, *BD* IV.

22. H. priv. to Lansdowne, 4 November 1904, FO 800/141.

23. H to Lansdowne, 7 November 1904, *BD* IV.

24. Knollys priv. to H, 15 November, H priv. to Prince Louis of Battenburg, 17 December 1904, HP(C) 6.

25. H to Lansdowne, 2 December, *BD* IV; Knollys priv. to H, 15 November, HP(C) 7; H priv. to Knollys, 24 November 1904, RA W45/76; Monger, 235.

26. *OD*, 111–12, based on H priv. to Lansdowne, 14 December 1904, FO 800/141.

27. H to Lansdowne, 7 and 23 November 1904, FO 65/1682.

28. H to Lansdowne, 21 and 28 December 1904, FO 65/1682; H priv. to Knollys, 18 January, RA W45/101; Knollys priv. to H, 11 January, HP(C) 7; H priv. to Barrington, 31 January 1905, FO 800/141.

29. H to Lansdowne, 23 January 1905, FO 418/21.

30. H to Lansdowne, 27 January 1905, FO 418/21.

31. H to Lansdowne, 26 and 30 January, and 6 February, FO 65/1698; *The Times*, 31 January on Hardinge's vigorous protest; H priv. to Sanderson and Knollys, both 1 February, HP(C) 6; to Lansdowne, 2, 14, and 18 February, FO 418/21; priv. to Knollys, 8 February 1905 (quoted), RA W45/109.

32. H priv. to Lansdowne, 4 January 1905, FO 800/141.

33. H to Lansdowne, 15 and 25 March (quoted), FO 65/1699; priv. to Knollys, 29 March, RA W45/150; priv. to Lansdowne, 29 March, and priv. telegram no. 52, 29 March 1905, FO 800/141.

34. Lansdowne priv. to H, 3 April, FO 800/141; H priv. to Lansdowne, 4 (quoted) and 11 April 1905, *BD* IV.

35. H to king, 31 May, and to Knollys, 6 June 1905 (quoted), RA W46/33,36.

36. H to Lansdowne, 6 June, FO 418/23; and 5 June, *BD* IV; and priv. to Lansdowne, 7 June 1905, FO 800/141.

37. H priv. to Lansdowne, 18 July, FO 800/141; priv. to Knollys, 21 June and 5 and 19 July, RA W46/48, 64, 70; priv. to Sanderson, 21 June, FO 65/1701; and to Lansdowne, 20 June 1905, *BD* IV.

38. H to Lansdowne, 4 July 1905, FO 418/24.

39. H priv. to Sanderson, 5 July 1905, HP(C) 6.

40. H to Lansdowne, 18 July 1905, FO 418/25.

41. H to Lansdowne, 18 July and 1 and 20 August, FO 418/24; and 28 August 1905 (quoted), FO 418/25.

42. H priv. to Bertie, 14 August, FO 800/184; priv. to Lansdowne, 16 August 1905, FO 800/141; Monger, 174 (quoted) and 201; Rogers Platt Churchill, *The Anglo-Russian convention of 1907* (Cedar Rapids, Iowa, 1939), 68–69.

43. H to Lansdowne, 1 and 15 August, *BD* IV: priv. to Lansdowne, 1 August, FO 800/141; and to Knollys, 2 August 1905, RA W46/144; Monger, 206.

44. H priv. to Lansdowne, 30 August, FO 800/141; telegrams no. 161 and no.

168 to Lansdowne, 2 and 8 September, Lansdowne telegram no. 224 to H, 4 September; H to Lansdowne, 6 and 9 September 1905, *BD* IV.

45. H to Lansdowne, 6 September, *BD* IV; priv. to Knollys, 13 (quoted) and 27 September 1905, HP(C) 6.

46. H to Lansdowne, 26 September 1905, *BD* IV.

47. Lansdowne to H, 3 October 1905, *BD* IV.

48. H priv. to Lansdowne, 5 October, FO 800/141; to Lansdowne, 4 October 1905, *BD* IV.

49. H to Lansdowne, 8, 14, and 21 October *BD* IV; priv. to Knollys, 10 October 1905, HP(C) 6.

50. H to Grey, 6 and 10 January, *BD* IV, appendix 3; 7 January 1906, FO 371/122.

51. H priv. to king, 11 January, RA W48/6; and priv. to Grey, 11 January 1906, FO 800/72.

52. H priv. to Bertie, 9 June, and Bertie priv. to Mallet, 29 June 1904, FO 800/ 176.

53. H priv. to Bertie, 9 August 1904, FO 800/176.

54. Bertie priv. to H, 28 November 1904; Knollys priv. to H 11 January 1905, HP(C) 7; H priv. to Bertie, 17 January 1905, FO 800/176.

55. H priv. to Bertie, 16 July (quoted), FO 800/163; Bertie priv. to H, 5 and 25 July 1904, HP(C); Lansdowne priv. to Bertie, 1 January 1905, FO 800/183.

56. H priv. to Bertie, 14 August 1905, FO 800/184.

57. Mallet priv. to Bertie, undated (October 1905), FO 800/184; Bertie priv. to H, 27 August 1905, HP(C) 7; H priv. to Bertie, 11 (quoted) and 25 September 1905, FO 800/163.

58. Lister priv. to Bertie, 12 December 1905, FO 800/163; quoted in Zara S. Steiner, *The Foreign Office and Foreign Policy, 1898–1914* (Cambridge, 1969), 75.

59. H priv. to Spring Rice, 26 November 1905, HP(SP); and priv. to Nicolson, 15 February 1906, FO 800/338.

Notes to Chapter IV

1. Peter Rowland, *The Last Liberal Governments: Unfinished Business, 1911–*

1914 (New York, 1971), 170–71; Zara S. Steiner, *The Foreign Office and Foreign Policy, 1898–1914* (Cambridge, 1969), 83–87, 92–95, 100–12.

2. Keith Robbins, *Sir Edward Grey* (London, 1971), 133.

3. *OD*, 122, and OD Ms., HP(SP), II, 213.

4. H to Spring Rice, 6 February 1906, HP(SP); priv. to Knollys, 6 and 14 April, and to king, 24 April 1907, RA W51/71, 72A, and 73; Lord Vansittart, *The Mist Procession* (London, 1958), 85–86; Steiner, 104–6.

5. See particularly Grey's tribute, Viscount Grey of Fallodon, *Twenty-five Years, 1892–1916* (New York, 1925), I, xviii.

6. On Crowe, see Richard Alfred Cosgrove, "Sir Eyre Crowe and the English Foreign Office, 1905–1914," Ph.D. dissertation, University of California, Riverside, 1967.

7. For example, C. J. Lowe and M. L. Dockrill, *The Mirage of Power: British Foreign Policy 1902–1922* (London, 1972), I, 19.

8. See G. R. Searle, *The Quest for National Efficiency: A Study in British Politics and Political Thought, 1899–1914* (Berkeley, 1971).

9. H notes for under secretaries, 3 (quoted) and 9 February, FO 366/1136; H priv. to Nicolson, 8 February 1906, FO 900/338.

10. H minutes, 21 and 28 February 1906, 29 July, and 3 August 1907, and 20 January 1908, FO 366/116.

11. Press: Steiner, 189 and 191, for example. Diplomatic service: Sir John Tilley and Stephen Gaselee, *The Foreign Office* (London, 1933), 166; H priv. to Nicolson, 6 December 1908, FO 800/341, and 27 October 1909, FO 800/343; and priv. to Villiers, 20 March 1908, FO 800/24; and Steiner, 18. King's Messengers: H priv. to King Edward, 7 April 1909, HP(C) 18. Foreign Office and court: H priv. to Townley, 28 May 1908, HP(C) 13; and priv. to Knollys, 25 May 1907 (quoted), FO 366/1136.

12. H priv. to Holderness, 22 October 1915, HP(C) 121.

13. Bertie to Grey, 16 January 1906, *BD* III.

14. Nicolson priv. to Grey, 21 January FO 371/171; H priv. to Spring Rice, 23 January 1906 (quoted, "unconditional" crossed out in the original), HP(SP); Grey, I, 71, 77–78; Harold Nicolson, *Sir Arthur Nicolson* (London, 1930), chapter 7; Eugene N. Anderson, *The First Moroccan Crisis, 1904–1906* (Hamden, Conn., 1966), and S. L. Mayer, "Anglo-German Rivalry at the Algeciras Conference," in Prosser Clifford and William Roger Louis, eds., *Britain and Germany in Africa: Imperial Rivalry and Colonial Rule* (New Haven, 1967), 215–44.

15. H priv. to Spring Rice, 6 February (1906), HP(SP).

16. Nicolson to Grey, 4 February, FO 371/172; Grey toyed with the idea of resignation; Grey priv. to Campbell-Bannerman, 4 February 1906, Add.Ms. 41207.

17. H priv. to Nicolson, 8 February, FO 800/338; but see Grey priv. to Campbell-Bannerman, 9 January 1906, Add.Ms. 41218, noting that Germany *was* making warlike preparations.

18. H priv. to Nicolson, 15 and 22 February 1906, FO 800/338.

19. Grey memo, 20 February *BD* III. On Sinai, FO 371/60–63, particularly skeptical minute, 3 February 1906, 4195/1880, FO 371/60.

20. H note, 23 February, 1906, *BD* III; George Monger, *The End of Isolation* (London, 1963), 275–76.

21. Spring Rice telegram to Grey and Grey telegram to Spring Rice, 22 February, FO 371/172; Spring Rice telegram no. 42 to Grey, 24 February 1906, with minutes by Crowe, H, and Grey, FO 371/173 and *BD* III.

22. H priv. to Lascelles, 26 February and 6 March (quoted) 1906, FO 800/13.

23. H minutes, ca. 9 and 10 March, on Nicolson telegrams, 8 and 9 March, FO 371/173; H priv. to Nicolson, 15 March 1906, FO 800/338; Monger, 277–79.

24. H priv. to Spring Rice, 5 and 21 (quoted) March 1906, HP(SP).

25. Knollys priv. to H, 4 March, HP(C) 9; H priv. to Spring Rice, 21 March, HP(SP); Grey to Campbell-Bannerman, 31 March 1906, Add.Ms. 52514; Philip Magnus, *King Edward the Seventh*, (Harmondsworth, Middlesex, 1967) 442–47; Sir Sidney Lee, *King Edward VII* (London, 1927), II, 515–21.

26. H Priv. to Grey, 20 and 26 April FO 800/92, and Grey memo for Benckendorff, 10 May 1906, FO 371/50.

27. H priv. to Knollys, 16 and 28 July, and Knollys priv. to H, 30 July 1906, RA W49/75, 82–3; Hardinge's report on the trip, dated 16 August 1906, is in FO 800/92 (*BD* III); Gordon Brook-Shepherd, *Uncle of Europe* (London, 1975), 259–61.

28. H priv. to Knollys, 19 August, RA W49/93; Grey priv. to Campbell-Bannerman, 20 August 1906, Add.Ms. 41218; Magnus, 467; Monger, 303.

29. H priv. to king, 26 August 1906, RA W49/97; on the Hague Conference, E. L. Woodward, *Great Britain and the German Navy* (Oxford, 1935), chapter 6; for an example of view of Hardinge, Monger, 317.

30. Grey to Campbell-Bannerman, 13 September, Add.Ms. 41218; Nicolson telegram no. 225 to Grey, 17 September, with H minute, and other documents in FO 371/169; H minute (quoted) on Nicolson to Grey, 4

November 1906, *BD* IV. It helped that King Edward invited Isvolski for a brief trip from Paris to London; Magnus, 475.

31. H memo, 16 November 1906, *BD* IV.

32. H priv. to Grey, 3 October and 25 December, FO 800/92; H priv. to Knollys, 23, 30, and 31 October 1906, and 6 January 1908, RA W50/28, 33–4, and 52/88; Steiner, 98–99; Lee, II, 327–28; Richard Hough, *Admiral of the Fleet: The Life of John Fisher* (New York, 1970), 202–6.

33. H to king, 9 October, and to Knollys, 17 October 1906, RA W50/18, 23.

34. H priv. to Bertie, 6 and 12 October, and Bertie priv. to H, 9 October 1906, FO 800/184.

35. H priv. to king, 14 September HP(C) 9, and to Knollys, 11 November 1906, RA W50/44.

36. King to Campbell-Bannerman, 20 November 1906, RA R27/100 and Add. Ms 52513.

37. Knollys priv. to H, 24 November 1906, HP(C) 9.

38. Grey to Campbell-Bannerman, 21 November, Add.Ms. 41207; king priv. to Campbell-Bannerman, 23 November, Add.Ms.52513; H priv. to Knollys, 30 November 1906, RA W50/86.

39. Crowe memo, 1 January, Sanderson memo, 21 February 1907, FO 371/257; Steiner, 112; Cosgrove, 105ff. Sir Frederick Ponsonby (first Lord Sysonby), *Recollections of Three Reigns* (New York, 1952), 292–93 discusses Christmas at Crichel.

40. H to Knollys, 1 January, RA W50/146: note for Grey, 14 January 1907, FO 371/334.

41. Grey priv. to Campbell-Bannerman, 11 January 1907, Add.Ms. 52514; Monger,. 318–22.

42. H priv. to Knollys, 17 and 18 February 1907, RA W51/22–3.

43. H to king 23 March, RA W51/51; H memo, 25 March, with minutes, and Crowe minute on Bertie to Grey, 31 March 1907, *BD* VII, no. 19–22.

44. H telegram to Grey, 9 April, and Grey memo for Cabinet, 26 April 1907, *BD* VII; *OD*, 135–37; Brook-Shepherd, 279–83.

45. H minute, ca. 14 January 1907, 1507/9, FO 371/295.

46. H minute, 20 January, enclosing King Haakon to King Edward, 9 January, FO 371/295; H minute, 18 February, *BD* VIII, no. 91; Nicolson to Grey, 19 June, H minute 24 June, and note for Grey, 29 June, and Dr. Fridhöf Nansen to King Edward, 3 July, with H minute, 10 July, FO 371/295; Bertie to Grey, 9 July, *BD* VIII; Sir A. Herbert (Christiana) to Grey, 25 July

1907, FO 371/338.

47. H priv. to Nicolson, 12 November 1907, *BD* VIII.

48. H priv. to Nicolson, 27 January, FO 800/339; Spring Rice to Grey, 6 February 1907, FO 371/369.

49. Nicolson to Grey, 17 and 23 February, and Spring Rice telegram to Grey, 4 March, FO 371/369: H priv. to Nicolson, 22 February 1907 (quoted), FO 800/339.

50. Grey priv. to Spring Rice, 15 April, FO 800/241; Nicolson to Grey, 22 April 1907, *BD* IV.

51. H priv. to Nicolson, 19 March and 15 May (quoted), FO 800/339; Nicolson to Grey, 22 April 1907, with H minute, *BD* IV; the Gulf issue is discussed in Briton Cooper Busch, *Britain and the Persian Gulf, 1894–1914* (Berkeley, 1967), chapter 11.

52. Grey to Spring Rice, 21 June, *BD* IV; Nicolson telegram to Grey, 16 June, with H minute (quoted), FO 371/324; Nicolson telegram to Grey, 24 June, with H minute, 25 June, FO 371/370; H priv. to Nicolson, 26 June 1907, FO 800/339.

53. Grey priv. to Campbell-Bannerman, 31 August, Add.Ms. 52514; Grey and other letters quoted in *OD*, 146–47; H priv. to Nicolson, 4 September, *BD* IV (and for text of agreement, 618–20); H to king, 26 August and 1 and 4 September 1907, RA W52/15, 18, 20.

54. Monger, 301–2.

Notes to Chapter V

1. Lascelles to Grey, 6 February, with H minute, 11 February 1907, FO 371/258; Zara S. Steiner, *The Foreign Office and Foreign Policy, 1898–1914* (Cambridge, 1969), 98–99.

2. H priv. to Knollys, 19 July, RA W59/9; H memo, 19 August, *BD* VI no. 25; H priv. to Grey, 21 August 1907, FO 800/92.

3. H priv. telegram to Lascelles, 11 September, and letters of 2 and 8 October, Grey priv. to Lascelles, 18 September, FO 800/24; H priv. to Grey, 2 October, *BD* VI; H minute, 7 October 1907, RA W52/38.

4. H priv. to Nicolson, 7 and 21 January, FO 800/341; Nicolson to Grey, 30 January, with H minute, ca. 3 February, and Nicolson to Grey, 4 February, with H minute, 8 February 1908, FO 371/581.

5. H priv. to Nicolson, 12 November 1907, *BD* VIII; to Knollys, 16 February

1908, RA W52/118; *The Times*, 26 February; Bertie to Grey, 9 March, with H minute, 10 March 1908, FO 371/582.

6. Crowe and H minutes, 19 February and undated March 1908, FO 800/92.

7. H priv. to Lascelles, 19 May 1908, HP(C) 13.

8. H priv. to Nicolson, 13 April 1908, *BD* V.

9. H priv. to king, 7 May, HP(C) 14 (quoted in Philip Magnus, *King Edward the Seventh* [Harmondsworth, Middlesex, 1967], 495); to Villiers, 20 March and 14 May, FO 800/24; and to Knollys, 30 May 1908, RA W53/95.

10. H memo, 12 June, *BD* V; Sir Sidney Lee, *King Edward VII* (London, 1927), II, 590–94; Viscount Grey of Fallodon, *Twenty-five Years, 1892–1916* (New York, 1925), II, 202–9; H priv. to Adam Block (Constantinople), 2 June, HP(C) 3; and to Grey, 12 June 1908, enclosing his report, FO 800/92.

11. H priv. to O'Bierne, 24 June, and to Barclay, 30 June 1908, HP(C) 3, 13; Magnus, 498–500; Keith Robbins, *Sir Edward Grey* (London, 1971), 186–87; an example of criticism of the absence of a minister: Reginald, Viscount Esher, *Journals and Letters*, II, (London, 1934), 322.

12. Grey priv. to Marling, 2 July (drafted by H), FO 371/576; and H priv. to Marling, 8 July 1908, HP(C) 13.

13. H priv. to Barclay, 28 July 1908, HP(C) 13.

14. Grey memo 31 July, *BD* VI, appendix 3, and 6 August, *BD* VI; Lee, 614–20 (wrongly dates 31 July memo); Gordon Brook-Shepherd, *Uncle of Europe* (London, 1975), 300–312 (repeating Lee's error); Magnus, 502–5.

15. H memo, 16 August, Lascelles to Grey, 14 August, *BD* VI; H priv. to Knollys, 17 August 1908, RA W54/7.

16. Brook-Shepherd, p. 302.

17. F. R. Bridge, *Great Britain and Austria-Hungary, 1906–1914* (London, 1972), 93, 102–5, 126, 145.

18. H memo, 16 August 1908, Austrian portion in *BD* V, appendix 4.

19. Grey priv. to H, 23 August, and H priv. to Grey, 25 August, HP(C) 14 and *BD* VI (former quoted in *OD*, 164); Grey note, 22 August 1908, FO 800/92; and see *The Times*, 24 October 1924.

20. Russian embassy to Grey, 30 September, with H minute, and H notes for Grey, 25 and 28 September, FO 371/550; H priv. to Grey, 27 September, FO 800/92; and to Nicolson, 30 September 1908, *BD* V; Bridge, 108–9; Harold Nicolson, *Sir Arthur Nicolson* (London, 1930), chapter 10.

21. Buchanan telegram to Grey, 1 October, with H minute, Bertie to Grey, 4

October, with H minute, FO 371/550; H priv. to Grey, 3 October, FO 800/92; H memo, 3 October, *BD* V; H priv. to Knollys, 5 October 1908, RA W54/95.

22. H priv. to Knollys, 4 October RA W54/93a; Nicolson telegram to Grey, 5 October, with H minute, *BD* V; Lowther to Grey, 5 October, with H minute, and Grey to Bertie, 6 October, FO 371/550; and H minute, 8 October 1908, 34802/31738, FO 371/551.

23. H priv. to Bertie, 5 October FO 800/161; and to Buchanan, 6 October 1908, HP(C) 12.

24. Grey to Goschen, 7 October, *BD* V; Lowther telegram to Grey, 8 October 1908, with H and Grey minutes, FO 371/551.

25. Grey to Nicolson, 12 October, FO 371/552; H priv. to Bertie, 12 October 1908, HP(C) 13.

26. H priv. to Nicolson, 13 October, and Grey memo for Cabinet, 14 October 1908, *BD* V; Robbins, 189.

27. H priv. to Goschen, 20 October, HP(C) 13; Grey priv. to Nicolson, 26 October, H priv. to Nicolson, 28 October, Nicolson to Grey, 3 November 1908, *BD* V; Magnus, 510–11; for Turkish conference, see FO 371/553–5.

28. H to king, 24 October, and Knollys, 3 November, RA W54/119, 129; OD Ms., II, 290. Cassel had not intended that his request for a G.C.B., made to Knollys, should ever go to Asquith and Grey; H priv. to Grey, 27 December 1908, FO 800/92; and to Knollys, 12 January 1909, RA W54/149.

29. H priv. to Bertie, 29 October, de Salis, 3 November and 29 December (quoted), and Bryce, 4 December, HP(C) 13; Bertie to Grey, 5 December, with H minute, 6 December 1908, *BD* V.

30. H priv. to Villiers, 19 November 1908, FO 800/24.

31. H priv. to Nicolson, 4 January 1909, *BD* V (no. 500, ed. note).

32. H priv. to Grey, 9 January, FO 800/93; and to Goschen, 12 January 1909, HP(C) 17. H (*OD*, 174) claimed to have opened the king's collar; Magnus, 512, says the queen did: the fallability of recollection at work. See on the trip, Brook-Shepherd, chapter 15.

33. H memo, 11 February 1909, *BD* VI; Grey, II, 185–86.

34. Grey telegrams to Nicolson, 15 February (two of date), FO 371/750; Grey priv. to Nicolson, 16 February; Nicolson, 297; H priv. to Cartwright, 23 February 1909, HP(C) 17.

35. Goschen telegram to Grey, 23 February, with minutes, *BD* V; H priv. to Spring Rice (quoted), 26 February 1909, HP(C) 17.

36. H priv. to Nicolson, 15 March, FO 800/343; to Knollys, 26 February (quoted) and 7 March, RA W55/8, 11; priv. to Goschen, 23 March 1909, HP(C) 17; Robbins, 197–204, makes too much of this remark. Winston Churchill, it should be added, was not "Sir" Winston in 1909.

37. H priv. to Cartwright (quoted), 6 April, HP(C) 17; and to king, 31 March and 7 April 1909, Magnus, 514.

38. H priv. to Nicolson, 30 March 1909, *BD* V.

39. H memo, undated (April 1909), FO 800/93 and *BD* V, appendix 3; Grey priv. to Nicolson, 2 April, and H priv. to Nicolson, 12 and 30 April, and 12 May 1909, FO 800/342.

40. H priv. to Goschen, 30 March 1909, HP(C) 17.

41. H priv. to Spring Rice (quoted), 4 June, and to Goschen, 3 May 1909, HP (C) 17.

42. Secret service expenditure: OD Ms., II, 320. H priv. to Goschen, 27 July, HP(C) 17; priv. to Grey, 25 August, enclosing memo, Mallet to Grey, 26 August, and Tyrrel to Grey, 27 August, FO 800/93, and *BD* VI for 25 August letter; Grey notes of 31 August, *BD* VI; H priv. to O'Beirne (quoted), 14 September 1909, HP(C) 17.

43. Goschen to Grey, 15 October and 4 November (latter with H minute), *BD* VI; H priv. to Goschen, 18 and 27 October 1909, HP(C) 17.

44. H priv. to Lowther, 28 May, 29 June, 9 August, 21 September, and 5 October 1909, HP(C) 17; and to Goschen, 4 April 1910, HP(C) 21.

45. H priv. to Nicolson, 24 November and 8 December 1909, *BD* VI; Stuart A. Cohen, *British Policy in Mesopotamia, 1903–1914* (London, 1976), 154, 180.

46. H priv. to Nicolson, 9 June (quoted), FO 800/342; to Barclay, 27 October, 1909 HP(C) 17; Goschen telegram to Grey, 10 April and 11 April 1910 letter with grey, H minutes, *BD* VI.

47. H priv. to Goschen (quoted), 11 January, and to Lowther, 24 January, HP (C) 21; H priv. to Knollys, 27 January (quoted) and 12 February 1910, RA W55/90, 103.

48. H priv. to Knollys, 2 March, RA GV K2552/17; and to Goschen (quoted), 2 March 1910, HP(C) 21.

49. Margot Asquith, *Autobiography* (Boston, 1963), 166–67.

50. H priv. to Knollys, 3 May (2 of date), RA W55/109–10; OD Ms., II, 329 (quoted); H priv. to R. Graham (quoted), 19 May 1910, HP(C) 21.

51. Knollys to H, 1 February 1909, HP(C) 18 (quoted in *OD*, 173; see also *My Indian Years*, chapter 1).

52. Probyn to Birdwood, 24 February (quoted) and 4 March, *Birdwood Papers* (India Office Library); Minto to Bigge, 7 March, RA GV N51/20; and to Clarke, 20 June 1910, Add.Ms. 50837.

53. Magnus, 230, 297, and 528; Lee, II, 710–14; Martin Gilbert, ed., *Servant of India. . . Correspondence and Diaries of Sir James Dunlop Smith* (London, 1966), 228 (Morley asked Dunlop Smith about expenses); Stephen Koss, *John Morley at the India Office, 1905–1910* (New Haven, 1969), 117–22, and *Lord Haldane* (New York, 1969), 119; Stanley Wolpert, *Morley and India, 1906–1910* (Berkeley, 1967), 5, 61–62; Sir Almeric Fitzroy, *Memoirs*, II (London, n.d.), 415. Others mentioned were Churchill and the Master of Elibank.

54. Esher to H, 24 May 1910, HP(M) VP1/1; Esher, II, 361–65, 442, 446–47, and III, 3, 5, 8; Gilbert, 241.

55. Congratulatory letters: HP(M) VP1/1; Philip Magnus, *Kitchner: Portrait of an Imperialist* (New York, 1959), 252.

56. HP(M) VP1/1 correspondence.

57. H to Grey, 11 June, FO 800/93; Grey to Nicolson, 12 June 1910, FO 800/343.

Notes to Chapter VI

1. H, *My Indian Years* (London, 1948), 1. Uncited quotations in chapters 6–8 are from this work.

2. H, *Speeches by Lord Hardinge of Penshurst, Viceroy and Governor-General of India*, vol. 1 (Calcutta, 1913–16), 20 October 1910.

3. H priv. to Gorst, 23 April, HP(C) 21; and to Crewe, 3 June 1910, Crewe Ms., C/18.

4. H priv. to Lady Minto, 7 July 1910, HP(M) VP1/1.

5. H priv. to Morley, 6 July 1910, HP(M) VP1/1; to Crewe, 14 March 1911, HP(C) 118; and to Cromer, 10 August 1910, FO 633/19. David Dilks, *Curzon in India*, (London, 1969), I, 83; Nigel Nicolson, *Mary Curzon* (London, 1977), 106.

6. Correspondence on appointments in HP(M) VP1/1.

7. H priv. to Bigge, 29 July, and to Knollys, 5 September 1910, RA GV P522/1 and N473/6; John W. Wheeler-Bennett, *King George VI* (London, 1958), 165–68.

8. H diary, 2–4 November 1910, HP(M) VP2.

9. Clarke to Chirol, 5 and 14 June, 7, 13, and 15 July, 21 November, and 5 December 1910, Add.Ms. 50833; Lord Sydenham of Combe, *My Working Life* (London, 1927), 245–46.

10. H, *My Indian Years*, draft Ms., HP(SP), 1.

11. H priv. to Sanderson, 1 December 1910, HP(SP).

12. H priv. to Bertie, 25 January 1911, FO 800/174.

13. Minto priv. to H, 28 July, and Hirtzel priv. to Morley, 24 August, HP(M) VP1/1; and H priv. to Crewe, 22 December 1910, HP(C) 117; H, *My Indian Years,* draft Ms., HP(SP), 24.

14. H priv. to Ritchie, 7 December 1910, HP(C) 117.

15. H diary, 25 and 28 November, and 9 December, HP(M) VP2; H priv. to Morley, 30 November 1910, HP(M) VC5; H, *My Indian Years*, draft Ms., 14.

16. H priv. to Crewe, 1 December 1910 and 11 January 1911, and Crewe priv. telegram to H, 30 December 1910, HP(C) 117, 95; James Pope-Hennessy, *Lord Crewe, 1858-1945* (London, 1955), 83–86.

17. Baker priv. to H, 28 and 31 January, and H priv. to Baker, 30 January 1911, HP(C) 81.

18. H priv. to Crewe, 2 February, and telegram (no. 43, Home Department) to secretary of state, 10 February 1911, HP(C), 117, 95; H speech to Imperial Legislative Council, 20 March 1911, H, *Speeches*, I.

19. Hardinge chose Hewett because he was impressed with an exhibition at Allahabad which Hewett had overseen; H priv. to Curzon, 19 January 1911, HP(M) VC5.

20. Chirol priv. to H, 9 November, H to Chirol, 8 December, Crewe priv. to H, 18 November, and H priv. to Crewe, 8 December 1910, HP(M) VC5 and VA16.

21. Crewe priv. to H, 30 December 1910, HP(C) 117; Gen. Sir O'Moore Creagh, *Autobiography* (London, n.d.), 375–76.

22. H priv. to Crewe, 1, 4, and 25 (quoted) January 1911, HP(C) 117; Curzon priv. to H, 28 December 1910, HP(M) VC5; H priv. to king (quoted), 5 January 1911, RA GV P522/5.

23. Crewe priv. to H, 27 January 1911, HP(C) 117.

24. H priv. to Crewe, 16 February, HP(C) 117; priv. to Baker, 13 February, Jenkins and Baker priv. letters to H, both 14 February 1911, HP(M) VA23; H diary, 26 November 1910, HP(M) VP2.

25. Hare to Du Boulay, 20 February, HP(M) VA23; H priv. to Crewe, 22 February 1911, HP(C) 117.

26. H to Crewe, 1 December 1910 and 17 January 1911, HP(C) 117; H priv. to Chirol, 16 February, HP(M) VC5.; viceroy telegram no. 55 to secretary of state, 17 February 1911, HP(C) 95.

27. H to king, 2 March, RA GV P522/8; Crewe priv. telegram to H, 28 February, HP(C) 95; H priv. to Crewe (quoted), 2 March 1911, HP(C) 117.

28. H priv. to Sanderson, 12 January (quoted) and 2 March, HP(SP); priv. to Wilson, 14 May, and to Curzon, 18 May 1911, HP(M) VA17.

29. Crewe priv. to H, 2 February, HP(C) 117; H priv. to Chirol, 16 February 1911, HP(M) VC5.

30. H to Curzon, 8 May, Curzon to H, 24 July, HP(M) VA17, 18; Crewe priv. to H, 20 June 1911, HP(C) 117.

31. Curzon priv. to H, 8 January, HP(M) VC5; H priv. to Sanderson, 16 March 1911, HP(SP).

32. H. priv. to Ritchie, 29 March, and to Morley, 5 and 11 April, HP(C) 117; H, *Speeches,* I; H diary, 29 March–13 April 1911, HP(M) VP2.

33. H priv. to Sanderson, 15 May 1911, HP(SP).

34. H diary, 5 and 23 May, HP(M) VP2; Jenkins priv. to H, and H priv. to Morley (quoted), 25 May 1911, HP(C) 81, 117 (latter quoted in Stephen Koss, *John Morley at the India Office, 1905–1910* (New Haven, 1969), 108).

35. H priv. to Chirol, 28 May, and to Hare, 9 June, and Hare priv. to H, 7 July 1911, HP(C) 81, 82.

36. H priv. to Crewe, 8 June, and Jenkins priv. to H, 14 June 1911, HP(C) 117, 82.

37. H priv. to Crewe, 1 and 29 June, and 3 and 10 August, and to Morley, 9 March, HP(C) 117; H priv. to Butler, 27 May, Eur.Ms. F.116/39 (India Office Library); viceroy telegram no. 153 Education Department to secretary of state, 10 June HP(C) 95; Clarke to Chirol, 31 July 1911, Add.Ms. 50834.

38. H priv. to Jenkins, 18 June, HP(M) VA23. "My scheme": H diary, 11 August, HP(M) VP2; priv. to king, 23 August 1910, RA GV P522/11; and priv. to Sanderson, 17 January 1911, HP(SP). On the question of the wording and authorship of the proposal, see S. Z. H. Zaidi, "The Partition of Bengal and Its Annulment: A Survey of the Schemes of Territorial Redistribution of Bengal (1902–1911)" (Ph.D. diss., University of London, 1964), and Matiur Rahman, *From Consultation to Confrontation: A Study of the Muslim League in British Indian Politics, 1906–1912* (London,

1970), 232–36. A small file of Jerkins's papers in the India Office Library (Eur.Ms. C. 255) adds little.

39. Carlyle memorandum, 16 August 1911, computes the legislative figures to be, in the west, ten Bengalis, two Muslim Bengalis, versus ten Biharis; and, in the east, ten Muslims versus nine Hindu Bengalis and two officially appointed Bengalis; HP(M) VC23.

40. H note, 20 June, with minutes of various council members, and Wilson priv. to H, 22 June 1911, HP(M) VA23.

41. H priv. to Butler, 29 June, Eur.Ms. F116/39 (Butler Ms.); priv. to Crewe 6 (quoted) and 13 July 1911, HP(C) 117.

42. Crewe priv. to H, 28 July, and 11 and 15 August, and priv. telegram, 7 August 1911, VA23.

43. H, *My Indian Years*, draft Ms., 53 HP(SP); Cd. 5979 (1911) "East India Coronation Durbar"; H priv. to Crewe, 16 May, and Crewe priv. to H, 28 June, HP(C) 118; and memo, 1 July, RA GV P522/21; H priv. to Clarke (quoted), 2 July 1912, HP(C) 84.

44. H priv. to Sanderson, 1 January 1912, HP(SP).

45. Cmd. 5979 (especially Crewe to H in council, 1 November); H priv. to Crewe, 17 August 1911, HP(C) 117.

46. Crewe priv. to H, 14 September, HP(C) 117; viceroy priv. telegram to secretary of state, 21 September and telegram 82–C, 30 October 1911, HP(C) 95.

47. H, *My Indian Years,* draft Ms., 60, HP(SP).

48. B. J. Gould, *The Jewel in the Lotus: Recollections of an Indian Political* (London, 1957), 12.

49. H, *My Indian Years,* draft Ms., 75, HP(SP); His Highness Maharaja Sir Sayaji Rao Gaekwar Bahadur of Baroda to H, 14 December 1911, HP(C) 82.

50. John Fortescue, *Narrative of the Visit to India of their Majesties . . .* (London, 1912), 179–80; see also Aga Khan, *Memoirs* (London, 1954), 120.

51. H diary, 7 January 1912, HP(M) VP3; H undated note, Crewe Ms. (Cambridge University Library), I/2.

Notes to Chapter VII

1. *Parl. Deb.*, Commons, 5th vol. 28, 26 July 1911, col. 1664–1783; H priv. to

Guy Fleetwood Wilson, 5 June 1911, Eur.Ms. E.224/4A (G.F. Wilson Ms., India Office Library).

2. H priv. to Crewe, 11 January and 2 February, HP(C) 117; priv. to Wilson, 2 February, Eur.Ms. E.224/4A (Wilson Ms.); H memo, with council minutes, 2 February 1911, CAB 19/8.

3. H diary, 4 and 8 August, HP(M) VP2; H priv. to Crewe, 10 August 1911, HP(C) 117.

4. Wilson priv. to H, 19 August, HP(C) 82; H priv. to Crewe, 24 August 1911, 27 March and 26 September 1912, HP(C), 117, 118; Creagh priv. to H, 9 September 1912, HP(C) 84, and Gen. Sir O'Moore Creagh, *Autobiography* (London, n.d.), H diary, 1 September, HP(M) VP2; Wilson priv. to H, 16 August 1911, Eur.Ms. E.224/4B (Wilson Ms.).

5. H priv. to Morley, 23 March, Eur.Ms. D.573/26 (Morley Ms., India Office Library); and to Nicolson, 29 March 1911, HP(C) 92; see Briton Cooper Busch, *Britain and the Persian Gulf, 1894–1914* (Berkeley, 1967).

6. H priv. to Crewe, 21 September, enclosing note of 30 August (quoted), HP(C) 117; to Chirol, 8 July, and to A. Hardinge, 25 July, HP(C) 92; and to Sanderson, 15 October 1911, HP(SP).

7. Crewe priv. to H, 9 November 1911, HP(C), 117; Reginald, Viscount Esher, *Journals and Letters* (London, 1934), III, 58 (6 September 1911).

8. Samuel R. Williamson, Jr., *The Politics of Grand Strategy* (Cambridge, Mass., 1969), 171–72; Sir Austen Chamberlain, *Politics from Inside* (New Haven, 1937), 484; General Sir James Marshall-Cornwall, *Haig as Military Commander* (New York, 1973), 76–79.

9. H priv. to Jenkins, 20 December, HP(C), 82; H note, 23 December, with council minutes, and telegram to Ritchie, 30 December 1911, and 6 January 1912, HP(M) VA24.

10. Wilson priv. to H, 26 December, and to Hailey, 27 December 1911, 7 and 25 January, and 18 September, Eur.Ms. 200/1 (Hailey Ms., India Office Library); H priv. to Chirol, 28 February and 7 March 1912, and telegrams to secretary of state, 3, 18, and 19 March, secretary of state telegram to viceroy, 28 February 1913, and priv. letter, 16 May 1912, HP(M) VA24.

11. Chirol priv. to H, 21 December; H priv. to Morley, 27 December, 1911, and to Chirol, 1 January 1912, HP(M) VC5.

12. *Parl. Deb.*, Lords, fifth series vol. 11, col. 137–87, 21 February, and 189–243, 22 February 1912.

13. H priv. to Chirol, 12 February and 12 and 27 March HP(M)VC5; Wilson priv. to H, 10 February 1912, Eur.Ms. E.224/5 (Wilson Ms.).

14. H priv. to Sanderson, 12 February, HP(SP) Sanderson Corresp.; priv. to

Butler, 3 February, Eur.Ms. F.116/39 (Butler Ms., India Office Library); and priv. to Crewe, 25 January, and 15 and 26 February 1912, HP(C) 118; Sir Malcolm C. C. Sutton, *The India Office* (London, 1926), 39–40.

15. H priv. to Crewe, 10 April, HP(C) 118; and to Wilson, 12 April 1912, Eur.Ms. E.244/5 (Wilson Ms.).

16. H priv. to Crewe, 3 April, HP(C) 118; and to Chirol, 10 April 1912, HP(M) VC5.

17. Lutyens to Lady Lutyens, 14, 20 (both quoted), and 29 April 1912, Lutyens Ms., RIBA (collection arranged in boxes by year); Christopher Hussey, *The Life of Sir Edwin Lutyens* (London, 1950), 250–66.

18. Lutyens to Baker, 8 May, Baker Ms., RIBA; H priv. to king, 8 May 1912, RA GV P522/17. Lutyens to Lady Lutyens, 21 and 24 May, Lutyens MS.; H priv. to Crewe, 2 and 30 May, HP(C), 118; first site report, 13 June 1912, Cmd. 6885 (East India, Delhi).

19. H priv. to Chirol, 27 June, HP(M) VC5; *Parl. Deb.*, Lords, fifth series, vol. 12, col. 75–160; H priv. to R. W. Gillan, 28 June 1912, HP(C) 83.

20. H priv. to Crewe, 30 July, HP(C) 118; H notes, 31 July (quoted) and 14 August, to Capt. G. S. C. Swinton, 1 August, and telegram to governor-general of Australia, 3 August 1912, HP(M) VA25; H priv. to Lutyens, 19 August 1912, HP(M) VA25; Hardinge confused a visit of July, when he objected to the site picked, and another of November, where he and Hailey picked Raisana; Hussey, 265–73.

21. H telegram to Swinton, 25 November, HP(M) VA25; Chirol to Geoffrey Robinson, 13 November and 10 December (quoted), Chirol Ms., New Printing House Square Archives of *The Times*; Lutyens to Lady Lutyens, 13, 16, and 19 December 1912, Lutyens Ms.

22. H priv. to Crewe, 11 July, and to Clarke (quoted), 25 July 1912, HP(C) 118, 84.

23. H priv. to Wilson, 18 July, Eur.Ms. E.224/5 (Wilson Ms.); to Crewe, 4 November, HP(C) 118; and to Carmichael, 2 August, HP(C) 84; *Parl. Deb.*, Commons, fifth series, vol. 41, col. 1901–2, 30 July 1912. A popular misconception is that Hardinge secured Gokhale's appointment: Percival Spear, *A History of India* (Baltimore, 1956) II, 179.

24. H priv. to Montagu, 22 April, and to Chirol, 29 May 1913, HP(M) VC6.

25 H priv. to Chirol, 19 June, to Islington, 1 September, HP(M) VC6; and to Holderness, 26 June 1913, HP(C) 119.

26. Crewe priv. to H, 18 June, and H priv. to Crewe, 18 June and 16 October 1914, HP(C) 120; Cmd. 8382 (Royal Commission on Public Services in India).

27. H priv. to Clarke, 1 February 1912, HP(C) 83; H, *On Hill and Plain* (London, 1933), ii–iii; see Hardinge's introduction to K. M. Panikkar, *Maharaja of Bikaner* (Oxford, 1937).

28. H, *On Hill and Plain*, 21; H priv. to Crewe, 13 October, and to E. S. Montagu, 29 October, HP(C) 118; and to Sanderson, 29 October 1912, HP(SP) Sanderson Corresp.

29. H diary, 21 November 1912, HP(M) VP3.

30. Chirol to Robinson, 10 December, Chirol Ms.; viceroy telegram (Finance Department) to secretary of state, 21 September 1912, HP(C) 96; H, *My Indian Years*, chapter 5, gives full details of the tour.

31. Except as noted, the account of the bomb episode is based upon Crewe Ms. I/11, files and diagrams; National Archives of India, Home Dept., Political Files, March 1913, 96–116, and December 1914, 11; accounts written to King George by Lady Hardinge (26 December), McMahon (25 December), Creagh and Wilson (both 26 December), RA GV R522/16 and N431/1–3; H letters of January-February, HP(C) 119; Creagh, 288–91; Cmd. 6642 (Attempt upon the Life of the Viceroy) and enclosures. No corner of India escaped the effect; for a small sample, see E. M. Forster, *The Hill of Devi* (New York, 1953), 27–28.

32. Manhar Kooverba, Maharani of Panna, *Lady Hardinge of Penshurst* (Richmond [1916]), 23–25.

33. Chirol to Gertrude Bell, 27 December 1912, copy in FO 633/21 (Cromer Ms.).

34. H, *Speeches by Lord Hardinge of Penshurst, Viceroy and Governor-General of India,* vol. 1 (Calcutta, 1913), 23 December 1912.

35. Arun Chandra Guha, *First Spark of Revolution: The Early Phase of India's Struggle for Independence, 1900–1920* (Bombay, 1971), 190–91, 309–10; Arun Coomer Bose, *Indian Revolutionaries Abroad, 1905–1922* (Patna, 1971), 146–51.

36. Wilson priv. to Crewe, 26 December, Eur.Ms. E.224/8–9 (Wilson Ms.); Wilson note and council minutes, 27–29 December, 1912; National Archives of India, Home Dept., Political "A" proceedings, March 1913, 96–116, and other documents in this file, especially reports of Hailey and Cleveland and others on investigations.

37. Du Boulay to Hailey, 19 February, and H priv. to Wilson, 30 March, HP(C) 84–5; Wilson priv. to Hirtzel, 10 February, and priv. telegrams to private secretary to secretary of state, 28 January and 26 February 1913, Eur.Ms. E.224/3, 8–9 (Wilson Ms.).

38. Lutyens to Lady Lutyens, 1 January 1913, Lutyens Ms.; India album, 1913, HP(SP); H to king, 5 November 1912 discusses hospital efforts, RA GV

P522/24; Phyllis Clarke to Chirol, 31 December 1912, Add.Ms. 50834 (Sydenham Ms.).

39. H, *Speeches*, I, 27 January 1913; Lady Hardinge to king, 4 February 1913, RA GV P522/31.

40. *Parl. Deb.*, Commons, fifth series, vol. 50, col. 10, 10 March; H priv. to Crewe, 23 and 30 January 1913, HP(C) 119. Security: R. H. Craddock to Sir James Meston, 19 July 1913, Eur.Ms. F.136/3 (Meston Ms.).

41. Lutyens to Lady Lutyens, 2 and 7 January, 13, 16 (Taj), 21, and 22 February, and 1 March 1913, Lutyens Ms.; Lutyens to Baker, 29 December 1912, Baker Ms.; H in council to Crewe, 27 February, HP(M) VA25; H priv. to Crewe, 12 February, HP(C) 119; Lutyens and Baker to H, 8 March, Baker Ms.; H priv. to king, 13 March 1913, RA GV P522/34; Hussey, 283–6.

42. Baker to H, 21 March, H to Lutyens, 28 March (quoted) and 30 April, and Lutyens to H, 1 May 1913, HP(M) VA25.

43. Lutyens and Baker letters to H, 11 July, HP(M) VA26; H priv. to Hailey, 13 and 18 August, Eur.Ms. E.220/1 (Hailey Ms., India Office Library); Crewe priv. to H, 14 November, HP(C) 119; Lutyens to Lady Lutyens, 23 November, and 5, 9 (quoted), and 18 December 1913, Lutyens Ms.; Hussey, 311–20.

44. Lutyens to Lady Lutyens, 2, 15, and 21 January, 1, 4, 18, and 25 February, and 2 and 28 March, Lutyens Ms.; H priv. to Crewe, 12 February, HP(C) 120; H notes, 16 February and 30 June, priv. telegram to private secretary to secretary of state, 23 March, and priv. to Holderness, 16 June, HP(M) VA26.

45. H priv. to Crewe, 2 April 1914, HP(C) 120.

46. H priv. to Syndenham, 14 March, to Carmichael, 18 March, and to Crewe, 3 April 1913, HP(C) 85, 119; see Lady Carmichael of Skirling, *Lord Carmichael of Skirling* (London, n.d.).

47. H priv. to Craddock, 27 March, HP(C) 85; and to Wilson, 15 April, Eur.Ms. F.224/6–7 (Wilson Ms.); to Crewe, 1 May 1913, HP(C) 119.

48. H priv. to Carmichael, 10 and 21 May, and 7 June, HP(C) 85; and priv. to king, 11 June 1913, RA GV P522/39.

49. H priv. to Butler, 9 April, Eur.Ms. F. 116/4 (Butler Ms.); to Chirol, 8 May, HP(M) VC6; to Crewe, 31 July, HP(C) 119, and *Legislative Council Proc.*, 1913–14, 17 September 1913.

50. Meston priv. to H, 12 and 24 July, and H priv. to Meston, 13 September; viceroy telegram to secretary of state, Home Dept., 5 August; and H priv. to Crewe, 27 August 1913, HP(C) 86, 85, 97, 119.

51. Craddock priv. to H, 11 September, Meston priv. to H, 16 September, HP(C) 86; H priv. to king, 9 October, RA GV P522/47; to Crewe, 9 and 15 October, and to Butler, 1 October, HP(C) 119, 85; speech, 14 October 1913 (quoted), H, *Speeches*, II. Craddock to H, 19 October, H priv. to Chirol, 7 November, HP(C) 86; and 15 April, HP(M) VC6; Montagu priv. to Crewe, 20 October 1913, Crewe Ms. C/34.

52. H priv. to Crewe, 22 October, to Willingdon, 24 October (quoted), HP(C) 119, 86; and to Sanderson, 9 November 1913, HP(SP).

53. H priv. to Syndenham (Clarke), 27 March 1913, HP(C) 85.

54. *Visit of His Excellency the Viceroy to Mysore State, November 1913* (privately printed, n.d.), HP(SP); *Autumn Tour of His Excellency the Viceroy and Governor General, 1913* (Simla, 1913), HP(SP).

55. Crewe priv. telegram to H, 3 December, H telegrams to Crewe, 19 December 1910, no. 2, 2 January, and no. 90, 14 March 1911, HP(C) 95; Crewe priv. to H, 8 December 1910, HP(C) 117.

56. H priv. to Crewe, 31 July and 31 August, and Crewe priv. to H, 31 October, H priv. telegram to Crewe, 3 November, and Gokhale telegram to Du Boulay, 19 November 1913, HP(C) 119, 97, 86; Stanley A. Wolpert, *Tilak and Gokhale* (Berkeley, 1962), 251–56.

57. H priv. to Clarke, 26 November, HP(C) 86; priv. to king, 20 November, RA GV P552/49; and to Crewe, 20 November 1913, HP(C) 119.

58. Viceroy telegram to secretary of state (Commerce Dept.), 22 November, HP(C) 97; H, *Speeches*, II, 24 November 1913.

59. H priv. to Crewe and Crewe priv. to H, 27 November, and telegrams (2), 25 November, H priv. telegram to Crewe, 29 November 1913, HP(C) 119, 97. Robert A. Huttenback, *Gandhi in South Africa* (Ithaca, 1971), 320 (quoted).

60. Crewe priv. to H, 11 December, and H priv. to Crewe, 4 December, HP(C) 119; Asquith priv. to Crewe, 4 December, Crewe Ms. C/40; H priv. to Sanderson, 11 December 1913, HP(CP) Sanderson Corresp.

61. H to king, 1 January, RA GV P522/51; Robertson, Pretoria, telegrams to viceroy, 22 January and 4 February, and priv. letter (Capetown) to H, 2 March 1914, HP(M) VC6.

62. *Legislative Council Proc.*, 1913–14, 17 March 1914 (and H, *Speeches*, II).

Notes to Chapter VIII

1. H priv. to Crewe, 7 January and 20 March, HP(C) 120; H priv. to Sander-

son, 25 February, 13 May, and 24 June, HP(SP); Lutyens to Lady Lutyens, 28 March, Lutyens Ms.; H priv. to Chirol, 24 June 1914, HP(M) VC6.

2. Clippings and letters in Hardinge's memorial album to Winifred, HP(SP); Winifred to king, 3 and 4 July 1914, RA GV AA48/17–18.

3. Chirol to Robinson, 19 July 1914, quoting from Hardinge's undated letter, *The Times* archives; information on Robinson's leader from G. Phillips, archivist of *The Times*, is gratefully acknowledged.

4. Du Boulay to Wigram, 22 July; H priv. to king, 6 August 1914, RA GV N527/16 and P522/57.

5. Correspondence to, from, and regarding Edd, memorial album, HP(SP); Crewe priv. to Willingdon, 2 October, Crewe Ms. C/61; H to king, 24 September and 13 October 1914, RA GV P522/61, 63.

6. H priv. to Chirol, 12 November; Chirol priv. to H, 23 December, HP(M) VC6.

7. Crewe priv. to H, 24 December 1914, HP(C) 120; H priv. to king, 23 January 1915, RA GV P522/67.

8. H priv. to king, 9 October 1914, RA GV P522/47.

9. H to king, 24 August, RA GV P522/58, and to Butler (also quoted), 12 September 1914, Eur.Ms. F.116/41 (Butler Ms.).

10. H priv. to Crewe (quoted), 20 August, minute, 11 August, and priv. letter to Willingdon, 24 August 1914, HP(C) 120, 88.

11. H priv. to Crewe, 27 August 1914, HP(C) 120.

12. H priv. to Carmichael, 2 September, and to Crewe, 9 September, HP(C) 88, 120; Home Department Poli. Proc. November 1914, 1–27 Part A.

13. L. F. Rushbrook Williams, "India and the War," in Henry H. Dodwell, ed., *The Cambridge History of the British Empire*, V (Cambridge, 1932), 478–79.

14. H priv. to Crewe, 9, 17, and 23 (quoted) September, HP(C) 120; priv. to Duff, 20 September, HP(C) 88; and to Stamfordham, 30 September 1914, RA GV P522/62.

15. H priv. to Nicolson, 8 October HP(M) VC6; and to Crewe, 6 August 1914, HP(C) 120.

16. On the war in Mesopotamia, see Briton Cooper Busch, *Britain, India, and the Arabs, 1914–1921* (Berkeley, 1971), chapter 1, and sources cited there. Hardinge's role is given particular attention in Douglas Goold, "Lord Hardinge and the Mesopotamia Expedition and Inquiry, 1914–1917," *Historical Journal* 19 (1976): 919–45.

17. H priv. to king, 29 October 1914, RA GV P522/64.

18. Duff priv. to H, 27 November, and H priv. to Crewe, 2 December, HP(C), 88, 120; Home Political Proc., December 1914, no. 27.

19. McMahon to H, 4 December 1914, HP(M) VC6; H, *My Indian Years*, draft Ms., HP(SP), 171–72; Busch, 20–22, and references there cited.

20. H note, 26 December 1914, Foreign Department, Secret War Files (National Archives of India), February 1915, 101–19; H priv. telegrams to Crewe, 30 December 1914, Crewe Ms. I/20, and 20 January 1915, HP(C) 99.

21. Crewe priv. to Stamfordham, 11 January 1915, RA GV N730/1.

22. H priv. to Nicolson, 4 February 1915, FO 800/377; Secret War Files, September 1915, 217–29; Gulf trip photograph album, HP(M); Lt. Col. Sir Arnold T. Wilson, *Loyalties, Mesopotamia, 1914–1917* (Oxford, 1930), 32–33; Marian Kent, *Oil and Empire: British Policy and Mesopotamian Oil, 1900–1920* (New York, 1976), 119.

23. H priv. to Crewe, 17 February 1915, HP(C)121.

24. H to Crewe, 17 February, HP(C) 121; and to Curzon (quoted), 18 February, Eur.Ms. F. 112/163; and note on Basra, 24 February, copies in priv. letter to Nicolson, 1 March 1915, FO 800/377 and HP(M) UR5.

25. Viceroy telegrams to secretary of state, 16 and 24 February (2 of date), and priv. letter to Crewe, 25 February 1915, HP(C) 99, 121.

26. Crewe priv. to H, 5, 12, and 19 March, and 2 April, H priv. to Crewe, 24 March, viceroy telegram (Foreign Dept.) to secretary of state, 23 March 1915, HP(C)121, 99.

27. H to king, 4 June, RA GV P522/56; and priv. telegram to Crewe, 12 June 1914, HP(C) 98; Home Dept. Poli. Proc. November 1914, 97–177; Arun Coomer Bose, *Indian Revolutionaries Abroad, 1905–1922* (Patna, 1971), chapter 2; Arun Chandra Guha, *First Spark of Revolution: The Early Phase of India's Struggle for Independence, 1900–1920* (Bombay, 1971), chapter 35; H priv. to Crewe, 8 October, HP(C) 88.

28. H priv. to king, 17 March, RA GV P522/69; and to Crewe, 22 January 1915, HP(C) 121.

29. H, *Speeches by Lord Hardinge of Penshurst, Viceroy and Governor-General of India,* vol. 3 (Calcutta, 1913–16), 18 March; H priv. to Crewe, 24 March 1915, HP(C) 121.

30. H. priv. to Crewe, 1 and 29 April, to Chamberlain, 27 May, to Holderness, 23 June, HP(C) 121; and to king, 12 April 1915, RA GV P522/70.

31. Crewe memo for king, 15 April, and Stamfordham to Crewe (quoted, 26

April, RA GV N812/1-2; Crewe priv. to H, 15 April, HP(C) 121; Chirol priv. to H, 7 May 1915, HP(M) VC7.

32. H priv. to Crewe, 13 May, HP(C) 99; Nicolson priv. to H, 22 April, Chirol priv. to H, 24 May, H priv. to Chirol 2 June, and to Nicolson, 17 May, and 21 June 1915, HP(M) VC7.

33. H priv. to Graham (Cairo), 30 May, HP(M) VC7; to Chamberlain, 27 May, HP(C) 121; and to Sanderson, 1 June 1915, HP(SP).

34. Chirol to H, 1 June, and H priv. to Chirol, 9 June, HP(M) VC7; Chamberlain priv. telegram to H, 7 June, and H priv. letter to Chamberlain, 17 June 1915, HP(C) 99, 121.

35. H priv. to Chamberlain, 27 May, and 10 June 1915, HP(C) 121; Sir Charles Petrie, *Life and Letters of Rt. Hon. Sir Austen Chamberlain* (London, 1940), II, 33–43.

36. H priv. to McMahon, 16 July, and to Chamberlain (quoted), 30 July, and Chamberlain priv. to H, 30 July, and 26 August 1915, HP(C) 94, 121.

37. H priv. to Chamberlain (quoted), 17 April, to Chirol, 23 September, HP(C)121; and to earl of Onslow (quoted), 23 September 1915, HP(M) VC7.

38. Chamberlain priv. to H, 7, 8, 13, 22, and 29 October 1915, HP(C) 121; Busch, 31; Petrie, 36–39.

39. H priv. to Nicolson, 14 October, FO 800/380; to Stamfordham (quoted), 14 October, RA GV P522/79; and to Lt. Col. Sir George Roos-Keppel, 20 October 1915, HP(C) 89.

40. H priv. to Chamberlain, 22 October, and telegram, 23 October 1915, HP(C) 121, 99.

41. Viceroy telegram (Foreign Dept.) to secretary of state, 4 November 1915, HP(C) 99.

42. H priv. telegrams to Chamberlain, 8 and 10 November 1915, HP(C) 99.

43. H priv. to Chamberlain, 12 and 26 November, and 17 (quoted), 24 (enclosing Duff to H, 15 December) and 31 December, and to Holderness, 29 December, Chamberlain priv. to H, 3 and 9 December, HP(C) 121; H priv. to Nixon, 17 December 1915, HP(C) 90; Petrie, 39–40.

44. H priv. to Chamberlain, 7 January (2 of date), HP(C) 122; H priv. to Nicolson, 11 January 1916, FO 800/381; Petrie, 42–43; Field Marshal Lord Birdwood, *Khaki and Gown* (London, 1941), 216, notes Lake was in poor health at the time in any case.

45. H priv. to Chamberlain, 11 and 25 February, Chamberlain priv. to H, 24

February, HP(C) 122; and priv. to Willingdon, Chamberlain Ms. (Birmingham Univ. Library) AC 12/33; H priv. telegram to Chamberlain, 25 February, HP(C) 100; and priv. to Nicolson, 18 February 1916, FO 800/381.

46. H priv. to Crewe, 23 December 1914, and 20 August 1915, HP(C) 120, 121; Craddock to Du Boulay, 25 March, and H priv. to Butler (quoted), Good Friday, 1915, HP(C) 89.

47. H priv. to Crewe, 24 March, and 29 July, HP(C) 121; to Sanderson, 24 May, HP(SP), Sanderson corresp., encloses speech; H priv. to king, 6 May 1915, RA GV P522/71.

48. H priv. to Willingdon, 18 June 1915, HP(C) 89.

49. H's memo of October 1915, with all earlier notes and correspondence, HP(C) 116; H priv. to Birdwood (quoted), 6 August 1915, HP(M) VC7.

50. H priv. to Chamberlain, 10 and 17 September, and 16 November; Chamberlain priv. to H, 23 and 30 September 1915 and 6 January 1916, HP(C) 121, 122; Hardinge was able to initiate a new commission to study ways to give more attention to industry—and, as a natural result of the war, India emerged with far more government interest and participation in the industrial side of the economy than before the war.

51. C. A. Andrews to H, 2 November 1915, HP(M) VC7; H priv. to Chamberlain, 3 March, HP(C) 122; H, *Speeches*, III, 20 March 1916.

52. H priv. telegram to Crewe, 17 May, HP(C) 99; H to G. B. Allen, 1 July, and Allen to H, 27 October, HP(M) VC7; Chamberlain priv. to H, 2 September, HP(C) 121; and to Asquith, 21 September 1916, Chamberlain Ms., AC15/1/5; H priv. to Chamberlain, 24 September 1915, HP(C) 121.

53. H priv. to Chirol, 30 September, HP(M) VC7; to Butler (quoted), 28 December 1915, Eur.Ms. F.116/42; to Chamberlain, 6 January, HP(C) 122; and to Sanderson, 26 January, HP(SP), Sanderson corresp.; Chirol to Robinson, 15 February 1916, Chirol Ms.

54. H priv. to Birdwood, 16 March, HP(M) VC7; and to Chamberlain, 10 and 30 March 1916, HP(C) 122.

55. H priv. to Butler, 10 February 1916, HP(C) 91; R. P. Masani, *Britain in India* (Bombay, 1960), 106–8.

56. H priv. to Chirol, 17 June, and 17 December 1914, and 25 January 1916, HP(M) VC6, 7; Chirol to Robinson, 15 February 1916 (''land of regrets''), Chirol Ms.

57. H, *Speeches*, III, (25 March 1916); Simla speech quoted in Prithwis Chandra Ray, *Life and Times of C. R. Das* (London, 1927), 134–35.

58. Legis. Council, *Proc.* 1915–16 (24 March 1916); S. R. Mehrotra, ''The

Politics behind the Montagu Declaration of 1917," in C. H. Philips, ed., *Politics and Society in India* (New York, 1962), 83; "guarded liberalism"; Max Beloff, *Imperial Sunset* (New York, 1970), I, 162.

59. Masani, 84. Similar appreciative Indian comments: K. M. Panikkar, *Maharaja of Bikaner* (Oxford, 1937), 169–70; S. R. Mehrotra, *India and the Commonwealth, 1885–1929* (New York, 1965), 83; from an Anglo-Indian in Sir Stanley Reed, *The India I Knew 1897–1947* (London, 1952), 155–87; and from a well-known British historian in Pereival Spear, *A History of India* (Baltimore, 1956), II, 179: "Beneath a formal and rather frigid exterior he concealed a talent for handling people and an unusual understanding of the Indian mind."

60. Martin Gilbert, ed., *Servant of India. . .Correspondence and Diaries of Sir James Dunlop Smith* (London, 1966), 4.

61. H priv. to Gertrude Bell, 29 March, HP(M) VC7; and to king, 17 March 1916, RA GV P522/87.

Notes to Chapter IX

1. Nicolson priv. to Grey, 22 April, Crewe priv. to Grey, 24 April, FO 800/96; H to Foreign Office, 3 May, F.O. memorandum (unsigned), 8 May, F.O. to Treasury, 12 May, FO 366/786; Nicolson priv. to H, 1 June 1916, HP(C) 22; Keith Robbins, *Sir Edward Grey* (London, 1971), 324.

2. Asquith to H, 3 May, Grey to H, 4 May, H to Asquith, 5 May, HP(C) 22; H priv. to Butler, 15 May 1916, Eur.Ms. F116/43 (Butler Ms.).

3. Asquith to H, 6 and 9 May, HP(C) 22; H priv. to Butler (quoted), 15 May, Eur.Ms. F.116/43 (Butler Ms.); H priv. to Hamilton Grant, 4 June 1916, Eur.Ms. D660 (Hamilton Grant Ms., India Office Library); Viscount Sandhurst, *From Day to Day, 1916–1921* (London, 1929), 53.

4. Cmd. 8279 (Royal Commission on the Rebellion in Ireland), quoted, and Cmd. 8311 (minutes of evidence and appendix of documents); H priv. to Hamilton Grant (misgovernment), 14 June, Eur.Ms. D.660 (Grant Ms.); and to Birdwood (wretched commission), 1 July 1916, HP(C) 23.

5. H priv. to Errington, 27 June, HP(C) 22; and to Bertie, 27 June 1916, FO 800/176; OD Ms., II, 347.

6. H priv. to Errington, 12 July, HP(C) 23; and to Bertie, 21 December 1916, FO 800/163.

7. Bertie note, London, 19 December 1914, FO 800/163.

8. Graham priv. to H, 20 and 25 July, and 22 August, H undated (1916) priv.

to Graham, Sybil Graham to H, 27 July, HP(C) 22 and 23; H priv. to Bertie, 21 September, and Bertie note, 16 August 1916, FO 800/163, 175.

9. Bertie priv. to H, 25 June 1916, HP(C) 22. On the Foreign Office in the war, see Roberta M. Warman, "The Erosion of Foreign Office Influence in the Making of Foreign Policy, 1916–1918," *Historical Journal* 15 (1972); 133–159.

10. H priv. to Buchanan (quoted), undated (1916), and to Chirol (quoted), 4 January 1917, HP(C) 27 and 29; Sydney H. Zebel, *Balfour: A Political Biography* (Cambridge, 1973), 66.

11. H priv. to Butler, 28 December 1916, Eur.Ms. F.116/43 (Butler Ms.).

12. H priv. to Bertie, 12 December and Bertie priv. to H, 16 December 1916, FO 800/163.

13. OD Ms., II, 354; Bertie priv. to H, 6 and 24 August 1916, HP(C) 24 give examples of complaints.

14. H priv. to Bertie, 19 September 1906, FO 800/172, is an early example of the "dog at the fair"; H priv. to Rodd, 18 May 1917, HP(C) 32.

15. H priv. to A. Hardinge, 7 November 1916, to Gertrude Bell, 27 March 1917, to Chirol, 31 January 1917, HP(C) 27, 30, 29; to Butler, 28 March 1917, Eur.Ms. F.116/43 (Butler Ms.); and to Chamberlain, 18 August, and Chamberlain priv. to H, 21 August 1916, Chamberlain Ms., AC12/100–1.

16. Curzon memo to Cabinet, 13 June 1916, copy in HP(C) 23; Curzon to Chamberlain, 2 July, Chamberlain Ms., AC14/1/7c; H priv. to Chirol, 5 July (quoted), and 9 August, to Chamberlain, 12 July, to Chelmsford, 14 September 1916, and to Chamberlain, 27 February 1917, HP(C) 23 and 29; H to Hailey, 28 March 1916, and 20 March, 7 May, and 31 October 1917, Eur.Ms. D. 200/1 (Hailey Ms.), show his continuing interest in Delhi and pledge to return.

17. H priv. to Nicolson, 25 May, and to Graham, 30 May 1915, HP(M) VC7.

18. H (acting for Grey) to Crewe, 11 September with F.O. minutes, and H minute on Italian communication, 1 November, 188501, 220218/173725, FO 371/2780; H priv. to Rodd, 13 September (quoted), 15 November 1916, and 14 February 1917, and priv. to Bertie, 27 April 1917 (Imperiali), HP(C) 27, 29, and 30.

19. OD Ms., III, 12 (quoted); H priv. to Bertie (quoted), 24 April 1917, HP(C) 30.

20. *Parl. Deb.,* Commons, fifth series, vol. 91, col. 110 (5 March); H priv. to McKenna, 6 March 1917, HP(C) 30.

21. H priv. to Chirol, 4 January 1917, HP(C) 29.

22. H priv. to Grey and to Bertie, 2 September 1916, FO 800/96 and 172; see for details FO 371/2620–1.

23. H priv. to Grey (quoted), 3 September, and to Bertie, 5 (quoted), 15, 19, and 26 September 1916, FO 800/96 and 172. Compton Mackenzie, *Greek Memories* (London, 1939), 217–18, explains why Hardinge was so convinced of Constantine's position: the source was letters intercepted in the German diplomatic bag. Sir Basil Thompson, *The Allied Secret Service in Greece* (London, 1941), 138, not only unjustly blamed Hardinge for Greek policy, but also prematurely recorded his death.

24. Grey memorandum for War Committee, 20 September, FO 371/2621; H priv. to Bertie, 10 October, FO 800/172; to Rodd, 14 December, and to Elliott, 21 December 1916, HP(C) 28.

25. H priv. to Grant, 4 October, Eur.Ms. D.660/11 (Hamilton Grant Ms.); and minute, 13 December 1916, 251807/63430 FO 371/2796.

26. H priv. to Chirol, 9 August, to Buchanan, 26 August, HP(C) 24; and to Bertie, 15 September 1916, FO 800/178.

27. H priv. to Spring Rice, 21 December 1916, and to Sir Esme Howard, 28 April 1917, HP(C) 28 and 31.

28. H priv. to Spring Rice (quoted), 21 December 1916, to A. Hardinge, 12 February, to Chirol, 8 March 1917, HP(C) 28 and 30; and to Butler, 28 December 1916, Eur.Ms. F.116/43 (Butler Ms.).

29. H priv. to Buchanan, 1 February 1917, HP(C) 20; and to Bertie, 6 and 19 March, FO 800/179; Buchanan telegrams to Balfour, both with H minutes, no. 313, 14 March, and no. 473, 6 April 1917, FO 371/2995–96.

30. H priv. to Chirol (quoted), 18 April, and to Rodd, 26 May 1917, HP(C) 31 and 32.

31. H priv. to Chamberlain, 1 May and 26 July (quoted), Chamberlain priv. to H, 21 July, and Mallet priv. to H, 6 May, HP(C) 22; H priv. to Birdwood, 1 July 1916, HP(C) 23.

32. Mesopotamian Commission, printed evidence, CAB 19/8 (Public Record Office), especially appendix 13, Crewe note of 11 September 1916.

33. H statement, undated, CAB 19/8, 754–773; oral evidence thirty-first day, 19 December 1916; H priv. to Grant, 28 August 1917, HP(C) 33.

34. Final report is Cmd. 8610, 1917.

35. H priv. to Chirol ("narrow-minded"), 21 June, HP(C) 33; Curzon memo for Cabinet, 16 June 1917, Eur.Ms. F.112/164 (Curzon Ms.).

36. H priv. to Chirol ("drastic and cruel"), 21 June, Crewe to H, 21 and 27

June, and Curzon to H, 27 June, HP(C) 33; H priv. to Chamberlain, 30 June 1917, Chamberlain Ms., AC48/26.

37. *Parl. Deb.*, fifth series, Lords, vol. 25, col. 725–45 (3 July 1917); the *Times,* 4 July 1917; Stamfordham to king, 3 July 1917, RA GV K1135/1; letters of sympathy in HP(C) 33.

38. Balfour priv. to Lloyd George, 9 July 1917, Lloyd George Papers, F3/2/23 (Beaverbrook Library); Harold Nicolson, *King George the Fifth* (London, 1952), 319; Stephen Roskill, *Hankey, Man of Secrets* (London, 1970–71) I, 407.

39. Stamfordham priv. to king, 9 July 1917, RA GV K1135/4.

40. Stamfordham priv. to king, 11 July, RA GV K1135/6; H priv. to Balfour, 10 July 1917 (two of date), Add.Ms. 49748 (Balfour Ms.). Nicolson, 319–20, notes that the king told Stamfordham to advise Hardinge to resign; although correct, this instruction was given on the eleventh, and Stamfordham had already spoken to Hardinge in this sense the day before; see king's telegram to Stamfordham, 11 July 1917, RA GV K1135/7.

41. *Parl. Deb.*, Lords, fifth series, vol. 25, col. 919–1039, 12 July 1917. On Chamberlain's resignation, file in Chamberlain Ms., AC15/4; Sir Charles Petrie, *Life and Letters of Rt. Hon. Sir Austen Chamberlain* (London, 1940), 83–88.

42. *Parl. Deb.*, Commons, fifth series, vol. 753, col. 2153–2268.

43. H priv. to Balfour, 13 July 1917, Add.Ms. 49748 (Balfour Ms.).

44. *Parl. Deb.*, Commons, fifth series, vol. 96, col. 468–511, 18 July 1917; see also Curzon announcement, Lords, fifth series, vol. 25, col. 1066–67.

45. H priv. to Grant, 28 August 1917, Eur.Ms. E.660/15 (Grant Ms.).

46. H priv. to Buchanan, 25 June and 25 July 1917, HP(C) 33.

47. H priv. to Bertie, 11 September 1917, FO 800/175. Warman discusses these intrigues, correctly noting that Hardinge was unaware of Henderson's real mission (to evaluate Buchanan); she has overlooked the campaign against Arthur Hardinge.

48. H priv. to Bertie (quoted), 21 February FO 800/191; Derby priv. to Bertie, 17 April, Curzon to Bertie, 23 April 1917, FO 800/175; and H priv. to Granville, 10 May 1918, HP(C) 37; OD Ms. III, 34; Randolph S. Churchill, *Lord Derby* (New York, 1960), 349–62.

49. H memo for Balfour, 16 March 1917, HP(C) 30.

50. H priv. to Wingate, 7 May 1917, HP(C) 32.

51. H priv. to Bertie, 9 January 1918, FO 800/175; and to Butler, 15 January 1920, HP(C) 42.

52. Cecil priv. to Balfour, 8 January 1918, Add.Ms. 49738 (Balfour Ms.); Treasury to F.O., 24 January 1917, and other documents in FO 366/787; Warman, 141.

53. F.O. memorandum, 14 March, and circular, 25 May 1918, FO 366/787.

54. F.O. report on staff, 11 July, FO 366/787; H priv. to Rodd, 26 October 1916, on commercial responsibilities, HP(C) 26; Z. A. B. Zeman, *A Diplomatic History of the First World War* (London, 1971), 179–80.

55. H priv. to Wingate (quoted) 25 July, HP(C) 38; Balfour to H, 28 August, H to Balfour, 29 August and 10 October, and H to Cecil, 20 August 1918, Add.Ms. 49748 (Balfour Ms.); HP(C) 39; Cecil to Sykes, 7 September, and to Montagu, 18 September, Sykes to Cecil, 9 September, Add.Ms. 51094 (Cecil Ms.).

56. H priv. to Buchanan, 25 June 1917, HP(C) 33.

57. H priv. telegram to Buchanan, 23 October, Buchanan priv. telegram to H, 25 November, 201697A/3743; H minute, 19 November 218943/7684; H minute on Buchanan no. 1867, 25 November, 1918, 226633/3743, FO 371/2999.

58. H priv. to Wingate, 28 August 1918, HP(C) 38; Arno J. Mayer, *Politics and Diplomacy of Peacemaking* (New York, 1967), 312–15; Richard H. Ullman, *Anglo-Soviet Relations, 1917–1921* (Princeton, 1961–72) II, 13–18.

59. Ovey to F.O., 12 November FO 371/344; H minute, 6 December 1918, quoted in Ullman, II, 89.

60. Arthur Willert, *The Road to Safety* (London, 1952), 46, 110–11, 115–16; Reginald Pound and Goeffrey Harmsworth, *Northcliffe* (London, 1959), 550, 590–91; Michael G. Fry, *Illusions of Security: North Atlantic Diplomacy, 1918–22* (Toronto, 1972), 33–34, 83–85.

61. C. J. Lowe and M. L. Dockrill, *The Mirage of Power: British Foreign Policy 1902–1922* (London, 1972), II, 290–93; William Roger Louis, *Great Britain and Germany's Lost Colonies, 1914–1919* (Oxford, 1967), 48–49; Ian H. Nish, *Alliance in Decline: A Study in Anglo-Japanese Relations, 1908–1923* (London, 1922), 186–87; V. H. Rothwell, "The British Government and Japanese Military Assistance, 1914–1918," *History* 56 (1971): 35–45.

62. OD Ms., III, 214 (democracy); Isiah Friedman, *The Question of Palestine, 1914–1918* (New York, 1973) 62, 135, 143, 149 (quoted); Doreen Ingrams, ed., *Palestine Papers, 1917–1922* (New York, 1973), 8.

63. OD Ms., III, p. 23a. Warman, 159, concludes that "undoubtedly, Hardinge could have helped the Foreign Office" by taking a firm stand against the process of erosion of influence, but this vision of hindsight is not sup-

ported by any specific suggestions.

Notes to Chapter X

1. H priv. to Balfour, 10 October, and to Wingate (quoted), 28 November 1918, HP(C) 39.

2. H minutes on P.I.D. file, PC 54, FO 371/4352; and PC 56 and 65, FO 371/4354.

3. H priv. to Gertrude Bell (quoted), 6 December, HP(C) 39; and to Butler, 8 December 1918, Eur.Ms. F.116/43 (Butler Ms.).

4. Stephen Roskill, *Hankey, Man of Secrets* (London, 1970–71), I, 395, and II, 22, quoted (22 November 1918).

5. Foreign office delegates lists and other documents on preparations, FO 608/162; United States, Department of State, *Papers Relating to the Foreign Relations of United States: The Paris Peace Conference, 1919* (Washington, 1947) XI, 537–47, 557–67, 601; Sir James Headlam-Morley, *A Memoir of the Paris Peace Conference, 1919* (London, 1972), xli–xliii; H to Drummond, 27 January 1919 (Sykes), FO 800/329.

6. Hankey memo, 22 January, FO 608/162; Hankey to Jones, 18 January, Ray Jones, *The Nineteenth-Century Foreign Office* (London, 1971), 73; Lord Hankey, *The Supreme Control at the Paris Peace Conference, 1919: A Commentary* (London, 1963), 27–29.

7. Roskill, II, 48–49, 99; Headlam-Morley, 90; Harold Nicolson, *Peacemaking 1919* (New York, 1965), 108–9, 311; F. S. Marston, *The Peace Conference of 1919: Organization and Procedure* (London, 1944), 98; Lord Riddell, *Intimate Diary of the Peace Conference and After, 1918–1923* (London, 1933), 14 (23 January 1919); David Lloyd George, *Memoirs of the Peace Conference* (New Haven, 1939) I, 132; H priv. to Graham, 24 January 1919 (quoted), HP(C) 40.

8. Lord Vansittart, *The Mist Procession* (London, 1958), 210, 218; Randolph S. Churchill, *Lord Derby* (New York, 1960), 376–77 (Malcolm's poem); Nicolson to Vita Sackville-West, 16 February 1919, Nicolson Papers, Sissinghurst Castle, Kent (my thanks to Nigel Nicolson for this reference).

9. H priv. to Granville, 13 January, HP(C) 40; Balfour priv. telegram to Curzon, 21 January 1919, Add.Ms. 49734 (Balfour Ms.); H priv. to Butler, 15 January 1920, HP(C) 42.

10. H priv. to Graham and to Elliot, both 24 January 1919, HP(C)40; Richard H. Ullman, *Anglo-Soviet Relations, 1917–1921* (Princeton, 1961–72), II,

110–11; Arno J. Mayer, *Politics and Diplomacy of Peacemaking* (New York, 1967), 428–32.

11. Minutes of Astoria conferences, 30–31 January, 33951–3/4156, FO 371/4156; H priv. to Chirol, 21 February 1919, HP(C) 40; Nicolson, 252–53.

12. H priv. to Chirol, 8 February, HP(C)40; and to Curzon (quoted), 11 February 1919, Eur.Ms. F. 111/212 (Curzon Ms.).

13. H priv. to Butler, 25 February, to Wingate, 19 March, HP(C) 40; and priv. to Curzon (quoted), 28 February, Eur.Ms. F.111/212 (Curzon Ms.); Parker priv. to H, 4 April, and H to Parker, 5 April 1919, HP(C) 41.

14. H priv. to Drummond, 29 March, and to Chirol (quoted), 13 May 1919, HP(C) 40.

15. H priv. to Butler, 5 July, HP(C) 41; Campbell to Crowe, 26 September, and Derby to Crowe, 1 October 1919, FO 800/243 (Crowe Ms.); Crowe's reports are in *DBFP*, first series, volumes 3 and 4.

16. Arnold Wilson priv. to Cox, 9 May 1919, Add.Ms. 52455 (A. Wilson Ms.).

17. H priv. to Butler, 23 April 1919, HP(C) 40.

18. H priv. to Butler, 15 January (quoted), and 22 June 1920, HP(C) 42.

19. H priv. to Butler, 11 October 1920, HP(C) 43.

20. Doreen Ingrams, ed., *Palestine Papers 1917–1922* (New York, 1973), 89.

21. Vansittart, 233.

22. C. J. Lowe and M. L. Dockrill, *The Mirage of Power: British Foreign Policy 1902–1922* (London, 1972), II, 335, quoting H to Graham, 10 April 1920.

23. H priv. to Hohler, 15 December 1919, and to Chirol, 12 January 1920, HP(C) 41 and 42.

24. H priv. telegram to Curzon (Paris), 13 January, file 6, FO 608/271; telegram to Wardrop (Tiflis), 15 January, and Curzon telegram to H, 20 January 1920, *DBFP* III, 645, 652.

25. H to Goode, 13 February, minute 1 and 21 March, *DBFP* XIII, 500, and XII, 510, 522; H priv. to Curzon (quoted), 22 March 1920, Eur.Ms. F. 112/199 (Curzon Ms.).

26. Lowe and Dockrill, II, 329; Ullman, III, 14–19 and 130, n. 69.

27. H note for Curzon, 22 January, enclosing Graham to H, 20 January, HP(C) 42; *DBFP* IX, 569, 572 discuss kaiser; Jones, 121; OD Ms., III, 64, 67 (quoted).

28. OD Ms., III, 64, 67 (quoted).

29. H priv. to Butler, 9 April, and to Rumbold, 13 July 1920, HP(C) 42, 43; OD Ms., III, 76.

30. H priv. to Rumbold, 13 July, to Graham (quoted), 18 August, HP(C) 43; to Crewe, 4 October, Crewe Ms. C/18; and to Curzon, 15 October 1920, Eur.Ms. F. 112/199 (Curzon Ms.).

31. H priv. to Curzon, 24 and 30 August, Eur.Ms. F. 112/199; F.O. to H, 27 November 1920, HP(M) O29; H priv. to Curzon, 16 October 1922, HP(C) 45.

32. H priv. to Curzon, 23 September, Eur.Ms. F. 112/119 (Curzon Ms.); and to F.O., 16 October 1920, F.O. Librarians Memoranda, vol. 6.

33. H priv. to Curzon, 30 November 1920 and 13 June 1921, HP(C) 44; James Pope-Hennessy, *Lord Crewe, 1858–1945* (London, 1955), 162; Kenneth Rose, *Superior Person: A Portrait of Curzon and His Circle in Late Victorian England* (London, 1969), 6–7, quoted.

34. H diary, Paris, I, 8, 23 December 1920, HP(SP).

35. H to Curzon, 2 December 1920, *DBFP* X, 409. Hardinge's views on various aspects of Anglo-French relations are examined in detail by J. Douglas Goold, "Lord Hardinge as Ambassador to France, and the Anglo-French Dilemma over Germany and the Near East, 1920–1922," *Historical Journal* 21 (1978): 913–37.

36. OD Ms., III, 81, quoted; H priv. to Curzon, 3 December, and Curzon to H, 5 December 1920, HP(C) 44; H diary, Paris, I, 7 January 1921 (quoted), HP(SP).

37. H to Curzon, 12 December, *DBFP* XIII, 194, 348; Curzon priv. to H, 19 December 1920, Eur.Ms. F. 112/199 (Curzon Ms.).

38. H telegrams to Curzon, 27 December 1920 and 3 January 1921, *DBFP* X, 27 and XVI, 560; H diary, Paris, II, 7 April 1921, HP(SP).

39. H priv. to Curzon, 13 January, Eur.Ms. F. 112/199 (Curzon Ms.); H diary, Paris, I, 19 January (quoted), HP(SP); H to Curzon, 17 January 1921, FO 425/387.

40. H priv. to Curzon, 23 January, HP(C) 44; H diary, Paris, I, 24–31 Jan. (29 January quoted) 1921, HP(SP).

41. H diary, Paris, III, 8 and 15 February and 24 November 1921; IV, 3 September and 27 November 1922, HP(SP). OD Ms., III, 90; HP(SP).

42. H diary, Paris, I, 25 February, HP(SP): H priv. to Curzon, 22 February, 11 March, and 24 April 1921, HP(C) 44.

43. H priv. to Curzon, 20 April 1921, HP(C) 44; Ruhr, reparation, and Silesian matters are followed in *DBFP* XVI.

44. H to Curzon, 3 June 1921, *DBFP* XVI 636; also 172–84.

45. H priv. to Curzon, 13 June, HP(C) 1921; H diary, Paris, II, 20 and 21 June 1921, HP(SP); *DBFP* XVII, 229–34, XVI, 186–93.

46. H diary, Paris, II, 8 August 1921, HP(SP).

47. H diary, Paris, II, 12 August 1921, HP(SP).

48. H priv. to Curzon, 23 August 1921, HP(C) 44.

49. H priv. to Curzon, 30 September and 6, 9, and 30 November 1921, Eur.Ms. F. 111/200 (Curzon Ms.); *DBFP* XVII, 70, 76, 84, 113.

50. H priv. to Curzon, 12 November 1921, HP(C), 44.

51. H to Curzon, 13 January 1922, FO 425/389.

52. H diary, Paris, IV, 21 May, 17 June, 16 July, HP(SP); H priv. to Curzon, 19 March, FO 425/389; and 1 September 1922, Eur.Ms. F.112/200 (Curzon Ms.).

53. H diary, Paris, IV, 6 September 1922, HP(SP).

54. Ibid., 24 September 1922, HP(SP).

55. Ibid., 24 (quoted) and 25 September 1922, HP(SP); OD Ms., III, 122–23.

56. H priv. to Curzon, 11 and 20 October 1922 (both quoted), HP(C) 45.

57. Curzon priv. to H, 13 and 20 June, HP(C) 45; H priv. to Curzon (quoted), 18 June 1922, Eur.Ms. F.112/200 (Curzon Ms.); OD Ms., III, 117.

58. H priv. to Curzon, 2 and 12 September, HP(C) 45; Curzon to Lloyd George, 13 September 1922, Lloyd George Papers F.13/3/31.

59. H priv. to Crewe, 23 November, Crewe Ms. C/18; H diary, Paris, IV, 13 and 15 (quoted) December, HP(SP); and H priv. to Curzon (quoted), 20 December 1922, Eur.Ms. F.112/200 (Curzon Ms.).

60. Correspondence in HP(M) O28/1.

61. H priv. to Butler, 25 May 1923, 29 October 1924, 23 July 1926, 11 February 1927, Eur.Ms. F.116/43 (Butler Ms.); John W. Wheeler-Bennett, *King George VI* (London, 1958), 580; the abdication crisis and Alec are discussed at length in Helen Hardinge, *Loyal to Three Kings* (London, 1967), in addition to the standard sources.

62. Correspondence in HP(M) O29; and Ponsonby to H, 20 May 1927, RA GV BB2/1135.

63. *Parl. Deb.*, Lords, fifth series vol. 54, col. 1436–37, 26 June 1923; H to Butler, 23 July and 2 October 1926 (both quoted), Eur.Ms. F.116/43 (Butler Ms.); Christopher Farman, *The General Strike: May 1926* (London,

1974), 60–64.

64. H diary, League of Nations representation, HP(SP).

65. H to Butler, 1 June 1923, Eur.Ms. F.116/43 (Butler Ms.); H to Baker, 4 January 1923, Baker Ms.; *Parl. Deb.,* Lords, fifth series, vol. 124, col. 136; H diary, Indian trip, HP(SP); H to Peel, 28 August and 8 September 1923, HP(M) O30.

66. *Parl. Deb.,* Lords, fifth series, vol. 72, col. 403–4, 5 December 1928, and fifth series, vol. 87, col. 355–58, 5 April 1933 (also see HP(M) ZP4 and ZI13).

67. *The Times,* 27 August 1935; *Parl. Deb.,* Lords, fifth series, vol. 98, col. 111–18, 22 October, and 1197, 24 October 1935 (Cecil response).

68. *The Times,* 24 May 1937, and 12 June 1939 (and file of clippings of local Kent papers, HP(M) ZP1); Brig. Gen. Sir George Cockerill, *What Fools We Were* (London [1944]), 125.

69. Perhaps the most bitter personal criticism is from Sir Francis Oppenheimer, *Stranger Within: Autobiographical Pages* (London, 1960), who railed against what he conceived to be Hardinge's bias against commercial representatives which blocked his own promotion; for criticisms of Hardinge's policies, Wilhelm Gall, *Sir Charles Hardinge und die englische Vorkriegspolitik 1903–1910* (Berlin, 1939).

70. *Parl. Deb.,* Lords, fifth series, vol. 133, col. 115–17, 26 September 1944.

Select Bibliography

MANUSCRIPT COLLECTIONS

Official Correspondence

Commonwealth Relations Office, India Office Records, London.
Home Department Political Confidential Proceedings, 1910–16.
Legislative Council Proceedings, 1910–16.
Political and Judicial Department Files (L/P&J/6), 1911–16.
Political Department, Political and Secret Subject Files (L/P&S/7), 1911–16.

Foreign Office Library, London
Foreign Office Librarian's Memoranda.

National Archives of India, New Delhi.
Home Department Proceedings. Political Files, 1911–20.
Foreign Department Proceedings. Secret External and War Files, 1910–16.

Public Record Office, London.
Cabinet Files, 23–24 (Cabinet minutes and memoranda), 27 (Cabinet Committees), 29 (Preparations for Peace).
Foreign Office Files, series 27 (France, 1893–96), 60 (Persia, 1897–98), 65 (Russia, 1899–1905), 78 (Turkey: Bulgaria, 1887–1901), 104 (Rumania, 1892–93), 366 (Chief Clerk's Department), 371 (post-1905), 608 (Peace Conference).

Private Correspondence

Baker, Sir Herbert. Royal Institute of British Architects.

Balfour, Arthur James, First Earl of. FO 800; British Museum Add.Mss. 49683–49962.

Bertie, Francis, First Viscount. FO 800.

Birdwood, Sir William R., First Baron Birdwood of Anzac and Totnes. India Office Library, uncatalogued.

Butler, Sir Spencer Harcourt. I.O.L. Eur.Ms. F.116.

Campbell-Bannerman, Sir Henry. British Museum Add.Mss. 52512–52521.

Cecil, Robert, Viscount Cecil of Chelwood. FO 800; British Museum Add.Mss. 51071–51204.

Chamberlain, Sir Austen. University of Birmingham Library.

Chelmsford, First Viscount (Frederic J. N. Thesiger). I.O.L. Eur.Ms. E. 264.

Chirol, Sir Valentine. New Printing House Archives of *The Times*.

Crewe, First Marquess of (Robert O. A. Crewe-Milnes). Cambridge University Library.

Crowe, Sir Eyre. FO 800.

Curzon, George Nathaniel, First Marquis Curzon of Kedleston. I.O.L. Eur.Ms. F.112.

Dunlop Smith, Sir James. I.O.L. Eur.Ms. F.166.

Edward VII. Royal Archives, Windsor.

George V. Royal Archives, Windsor.

Grant, Sir Hamilton. I.O.L. Eur.Ms. D 660.

Grey, Sir Edward, First Viscount Grey of Fallodon. FO 800.

Hailey, William Malcolm, First Baron Hailey of Shapur, Punjab, and Newport Pagnall. I.O.L. Eur.Ms. E.220.

Hardinge, Sir Charles, First Baron Hardinge of Penshurst. Cambridge University Library; Kent County Record Office, Maidstone; Hardinge Family Papers, South Park, Penshurst, Kent; FO 800.

Hardinge, Sir Henry, First Viscount Hardinge of Lahore. McGill University Library, Montreal.

Jenkins, Sir John Lewis. I.O.L. Eur.Ms. C.255.
Lansdowne, Fifth Marquess of. FO 800.
Lascelles, Sir Frank C. FO 800.
Lloyd George, David, Earl Lloyd George of Dwyfor. Beaverbrook Library.
Lutyens, Sir Edwin Landseer. Royal Institute of British Architects.
Meston, Sir James S., First Baron Meston of Agra and Dunottar. I.O.L. Eur.Ms. F. 136.
Morley of Blackburn, John, First Viscount. I.O.L. Eur.Ms. D.573.
Nicolson, Sir Arthur. FO 800; Sissinghurst Castle, Kent.
Roos-Keppel, Sir George. I.O.L. Eur.Ms. D.613.
Sanderson, Sir Thomas H. FO 800.
Spring Rice, Sir Cecil A. FO 800.
Syndenham of Combe, Baron (Sir George Syndenham Clarke), British Museum Add.Mss. 50831–50841.
Villiers, Sir Francis Hyde. FO 800.
Wilson, Sir Guy Fleetwood. I.O.L. Eur.Ms. C.255.

PUBLISHED WORKS CITED IN THE TEXT

Aga Khan. *The Memoirs of Aga Khan: World Enough and Time*. London: Cassell, 1954.
Anderson, Eugene N. *The First Moroccan Crisis, 1904–1906*. 1930. Reprint. Hamden, Conn.: Archon Books, 1966.
Asquith, Margot. *Autobiography*. Edited by Mark Bonham Carter. Boston: Houghton Mifflin, 1963.
Beloff, Max. *Imperial Sunset*. Vol. 1. New York: Knopf, 1970.
Birdwood, Field Marshal Lord, of Anzac and Totnes. *Khaki and Gown: An Autobiography*. London: War, Lock, 1941.
Bose, Arun Coomer. *Indian Revolutionaries Abroad, 1905–1922*. Patna: Bharati Bhawan, 1971.

Bridge, F. R. *Great Britain and Austria-Hungary, 1906–1914: A Diplomatic History.* London: Weidenfeld & Nicolson, 1972.

Brook-Shepherd, Gordon. *Uncle of Europe: the Social and Diplomatic Life of Edward VII.* London: Collins, 1975.

Bruce, George. *Six Battles for India: the Anglo-Sikh Wars, 1845–6, 1848–9.* London: Arthur Barker, 1969.

Busch, Briton Cooper. *Britain and the Persian Gulf, 1894–1914.* Berkeley: University of California Press, 1967.

———. *Britain, India, and the Arabs, 1914–1921.* Berkeley: University of California Press, 1971.

———. *Mudros to Lausanne: Britain's Frontier in West Asia, 1918–1923.* Albany, N.Y.: State University of New York Press, 1976.

Carmichael of Skirling, Lady. *Lord Carmichael of Skirling: A Memoir Prepared by his Wife.* London: Hodder & Stoughton, n.d.

Chamberlain, Sir Austen. *Politics from Inside: An Epistolary Chronicle, 1906–1914.* New Haven: Yale University Press, 1937.

Churchill, Rogers Platt. *The Anglo-Russian Convention of 1907.* Cedar Rapids, Iowa: Torch Press, 1939.

Cockerill, Brig. Gen. Sir George. *What Fools We Were.* London: Hutchinson, 1944.

Cohen, Stuart A. *British Policy in Mesopotamia, 1903–1914.* London: Ithaca Press, 1976.

Cosgrove, Richard Alfred. "Sir Eyre Crowe and the English Foreign Office, 1905–1914." Ph.D. dissertation, University of California at Riverside, 1967.

Creagh, Gen. Sir O'Moore. *Autobiography.* London: Hutchinson, n.d.

Das, M. N. *India Under Morley and Minto.* London: Allen & Unwin, 1964.

Dilks, David. *Curzon in India.* 2 vols. New York: Taplinger, 1969.

Esher, Reginald, Viscount. *Journals and Letters.* Vols. 2 and 3.

London: Ivor Nicholson and Watson, 1934–39.

Farman, Christopher. *The General Strike: May 1926.* London: Panther, 1974.

Fitzroy, Sir Almeric. *Memoirs.* Vol. 2. London: Hutchinson, n.d.

Fleming, Peter. *Bayonets to Lhasa: The First Full Account of the British Invasion of Tibet in 1904.* London: Hart-Davis, 1961.

Forster, E. M. *The Hill of Devi.* New York: Harcourt, Brace, 1953.

Fortescue, John. *Narrative of the Visit to India of their Majesties King George V and Queen Mary and of the Coronation Durbar Held at Delhi, 12th December 1912.* London: Macmillan, 1912.

Friedman, Isaiah. *The Question of Palestine, 1914–1918: British-Jewish-Arab Relations.* New York: Schocken, 1973.

Fry, Michael G. *Illusions of Security: North Atlantic Diplomacy 1918–22.* Toronto: University of Toronto Press, 1972.

Gall, Wilhelm. *Sir Charles Hardinge und die englische Vorkriegspolitik 1903–1910.* Berlin: Verlag Dr. Emil Ebering, 1939.

Gilbert, Martin. *Servant of India: A Study of Imperial Rule from 1905–1910 as Told through the Correspondence and Diaries of Sir James Dunlop Smith.* London: Longmans, 1966.

Goold, J. Douglas. "Lord Hardinge and the Mesopotamia Expedition and Inquiry, 1914–1917." *Historical Journal* 19 (1976): 919–45.

———. "Lord Hardinge as Ambassador to France, and the Anglo-French Dilemma over Germany and the Near East, 1920–1922." *Historical Journal* 21 (1978): 913–37.

Gould, B. J. *The Jewel in the Lotus: Recollections of an Indian Political.* London: Chatto and Windus, 1957.

Great Britain. Foreign Office. *British Documents on the Origins of the War, 1898–1914.* Edited by G. P. Gooch and Harold Temperley. 11 vols. in 13. London: H.M.S.O., 1926–38.

———. *Documents on British Foreign Policy, 1919–1939.*

Edited by Rohan Butler, J. P. T. Bury, and E. L. Woodward. First series, vols. 1–18. London: H.M.S.O., 1947–72.

———. Parliament. *Parliamentary Debates* and *British and Foreign State Papers*. London: H.M.S.O., 1892–1922.

Grey of Fallodon, Viscount. *Twenty-Five Years, 1892–1916*. 2 vols. New York: Frederick A. Stokes, 1925.

Guha, Arun Chandra. *First Spark of Revolution: the Early Phase of India's Struggle for Independence, 1900–1920*. Bombay: Orient Longman, 1971.

Hankey, Lord. *The Supreme Control at the Paris Peace Conference, 1919: A Commentary*. London: Allen & Unwin, 1963.

Hardinge, Charles, first baron Hardinge of Penshurst. *My Indian Years, 1910–1916*. London: John Murray, 1948.

———. *Old Diplomacy*. London: John Murray, 1947.

———. *On Hill and Plain*. London: John Murray, 1933.

———. *A Short Record of the King's Journey, March 30–May 5, 1903*. London: John and Edward Bumpus, 1903.

———. *Speeches by Lord Hardinge of Penshurst, Viceroy and Governor-General of India*. 3 vols. Calcutta: Government Printing Office, 1913–16.

Hardinge, Charles Stewart. *Recollections of India, Drawn on Stone by J. D. Harding, from the Original Drawings by . . . .* London: Thomas M'Lean, 1847.

———. *Viscount Hardinge (by His Son and Private Secretary in India)*. Oxford: Clarendon Press, 1891.

Hardinge, Helen. *Loyal to Three Kings*. London: William Kimber, 1967.

Hasrat, Bikrama J. T., ed. *The Punjab Papers: Selections from the Private Papers of Viscount Hardinge . . . 1836–1849 on the Sikhs*. Hoshiarpur, Punjab: V. V. Research Institute Press, 1970.

Headlam-Morley, Sir James. *A Memoir of the Paris Peace Conference, 1919*. London: Methuen, 1972.

Hough, Richard. *Admiral of the Fleet: the Life of John Fisher*. New York: Macmillan, 1970.

Hussey, Christopher. *The Life of Sir Edwin Lutyens.* London: Country Life, 1950.

Huttenback, Robert A. *Gandhi in South Africa: British Imperialism and the Indian Question, 1860–1914.* Ithaca: Cornell University Press, 1971.

Ingrams, Doreen, ed. *Palestine Papers 1917–1922: Seeds of Conflict.* New York: Braziller, 1973.

Jones, Ray. *The Nineteenth-Century Foreign Office: An Administrative History.* London: Weidenfeld & Nicolson, 1971.

Kazemzadeh, Firuz. *Russia and Britain in Persia 1868–1914: A Study in Imperialism.* New Haven: Yale University Press, 1968.

Kent, Marian. *Oil and Empire: British Policy and Mesopotamian Oil, 1900–1920.* New York: Barnes & Noble, 1976.

Keppel, Sonia. *Edwardian Daughter.* London: Hamish Hamilton, 1958.

Koss, Stephen. *John Morley at the India Office, 1905–1910.* New Haven: Yale University Press, 1969.

———. *Lord Haldane: Scapegoat for Liberalism.* New York: Columbia University Press, 1969.

Lee, Sir Sidney. *King Edward VII: A Biography.* Vol. 2. London: Macmillan, 1927.

Lloyd George, David. *Memoirs of the Peace Conference.* 2 vols. New Haven: Yale University Press, 1939.

Louis, William Roger. "Great Britain and German Expansion in Africa, 1884–1919." In *Britain and Germany in Africa: Imperial Rivalry and Colonial Rule,* edited by Prosser Gifford and William Roger Louis. pp. 3–46. New Haven: Yale University Press, 1967.

Lowe, C. J., and M. L. Dockrill. *The Mirage of Power: British Foreign Policy, 1902–1922.* 3 vols. London: Routledge & Kegan Paul, 1972.

Mackenzie, Compton. *Greek Memories.* London: Chatto & Windus, 1939.

Magnus, Philip. *King Edward the Seventh.* New York: Dutton,

1964.

———. *Kitchener: Portrait of an Imperialist.* New York: Dutton, 1964.

Majumdar, R. C. "Lord Hardinge." In *History and Culture of the Indian People,* vol. II ("Struggle for Freedom"), edited by R. C. Majumdar. pp. 161–97. Bombay: Bharatiya Vidya Bhavan, 1969.

Manhar Kooverba, maharani of Panna. *Lady Hardinge of Penshurst, C.I., Vice-Reine of India. A Tribute to Her Memory.* Richmond, England: R. W. Simpson, 1916.

Marshall-Cornwall, Gen. Sir James. *Haig as Military Commander.* New York: Crane, Russak, 1973.

Marston, F. S. *The Peace Conference of 1919: Organization and Procedure.* London: Oxford University Press, 1944.

Masani, R. P. *Britain in India: An Account of British Rule in the Indian Subcontinent.* Bombay: John Brown, Oxford University Press, 1960.

Mayer, Arno J. *Politics and Diplomacy of Peacemaking: Containment and Counterrevolution at Versailles, 1918–1919.* New York: Knopf, 1967.

Mehrotra, S. R. *India and the Commonwealth, 1885–1929.* New York: Praeger, 1965.

———. "The Politics behind the Montagu Declaration of 1917." In *Politics and Society in India,* edited by C. H. Philips, pp. 71–96. New York: Praeger, 1962.

Monger, George *The End of Isolation: British Foreign Policy 1900–1907.* London: Thomas Nelson, 1963.

Newton, Lord. *Lord Lansdowne: A Biography.* London: Macmillan, 1929.

Nicolson, Harold. *King George the Fifth: His Life and Reign.* London: Constable, 1952.

———. *Peacemaking 1919.* New York: Grosset & Dunlap, 1965.

———. *Sir Arthur Nicolson, Bart., First Lord Carnock: A Study in the Old Diplomacy.* London: Constable, 1930.

Nicolson, Nigel. *Mary Curzon.* London: Weidenfeld & Nicolson, 1977.

Nish, Ian H. *Alliance in Decline: A Study in Anglo—Japanese Relations, 1908-1923.* London: University of London, Athlone Press, 1972.

———. *The Anglo-Japanese Alliance: The Diplomacy of Two Island Empires, 1894-1907.* London: University of London, Athlone Press, 1966.

Openheimer, Sir Francis. *Stranger Within: Autobiographical Pages.* London: Faber & Faber, 1960.

Panikkar, K. M. *His Highness the Maharaja of Bikaner: A Biography.* Oxford: Oxford University Press, 1937.

Petrie, Sir Charles. *The Life and Letters of the Right Hon. Sir Austen Chamberlain.* 2 vols. London: Cassell, 1940.

Ponsonby, Sir Frederick, first Lord Sysonby. *Recollections of Three Reigns.* New York: E. P. Dutton, 1952.

Pope-Hennessy, James. *Lord Crewe, 1858-1945: The Likeness of a Liberal.* London: Constable, 1955.

Pound, Reginald, and Geoffrey Harmsworth. *Northcliffe.* London: Cassell, 1959.

Rahman, Matiur. *From Consultation to Confrontation: A Study of the Muslim League in British Indian Politics 1906-1912.* London: Luzac, 1970.

Ray, Prithwis Chandra. *Life and Times of C. R. Das.* London: Oxford University Press, 1927.

Reed, Sir Stanley, *The India I Knew 1897-1947.* London: Odhams Press, 1952.

Riddell, Lord, *Intimate Diary of the Peace Conference and After, 1918-1923.* London: Gollancz, 1933.

Robbins, Keith. *Sir Edward Grey: A Biography of Lord Grey of Fallodon.* London: Cassell, 1971.

Rose, Kenneth. *Superior Person: A Portrait of Curzon and his Circle in Late Victorian England.* London: Weidenfeld & Nicolson, 1969.

Roskill, Stephen. *Hankey, Man of Secrets.* 2 vols. London: Collins, 1970–71.

Rothwell, V. H. *British War Aims and Peace Diplomacy, 1914-1918.* Oxford: Clarendon Press, 1971.

Rowland, Peter. *The Last Liberal Governments: Unfinished Business, 1911–1914.* New York: St. Martin's, 1971.

Sandhurst, Viscount. *From Day to Day, 1916–1921.* London: Edward Arnold, 1929.

Seton, Sir Malcolm C. C. *The India Office.* London: Putnam's, 1926.

Spear, Percival. *A History of India.* Vol. 2. Baltimore: Penguin Books, 1956.

Steiner, Zara S. *The Foreign Office and Foreign Policy, 1898–1914.* Cambridge: Cambridge University Press, 1969.

Sydenham of Combe, Col. Lord. *My Working Life.* London: John Murray, 1927.

Sykes, Brig. Gen. Sir Percy. *The Right Honourable Sir Mortimer Durand.* London: Cassell, 1926.

Thomson, Sir Basil. *The Allied Secret Service in Greece.* London: Hutchinson, 1931.

Tilley, Sir John, and Stephen Gaselee. *The Foreign Office.* London: Putnam, 1933.

Ullman, Richard H. *Anglo-Soviet Relations, 1917–1921.* 3 vols. Princeton: Princeton University Press, 1961–72.

United States. Department of State. *Papers Relating to the Foreign Relations of the United States: The Paris Peace Conference, 1919.* Vols. 3–12. Washington, D.C.: U.S.G.P.O., 1943–47.

Vansittart, Lord. *The Mist Procession: The Autobiography of . . . .* London: Hutchinson, 1958.

Walder, David. *The Short Victorious War: The Russo-Japanese Conflict, 1904–5.* New York: Harper & Row, 1973.

Warman, Roberta M. "The Erosion of Foreign Office Influence in the Making of Foreign Policy, 1916–1918." *Historical Journal* 15 (1972): 133–59.

Wheeler-Bennett, John W. *King George VI.* London: Macmillan, 1958.

Willert, Arthur. *The Road to Safety: A Study in Anglo-American Relations.* London: Derek Verschoyle, 1952.

Williams, L. F. Rushbrook. "India and the War." In *The Cam-*

bridge History of the British Empire, vol. 5, pp. 476–88, edited by Henry H. Dodwell, Cambridge: Cambridge University Press, 1932.

Williamson, Samuel R., Jr. *The Politics of Grand Strategy: Britain and France Prepare for War, 1904–1914*. Cambridge, Mass.: Harvard University Press, 1969.

Wilson, Lt. Col. Arnold T. *Loyalties, Mesopotamia, 1914–1917*. Oxford: Oxford University Press, 1930.

Wolpert, Stanley A. *Morley and India, 1906–1910*. Berkeley: University of California Press, 1967.

———. *Tilak and Gokhale*. Berkeley: University of California Press, 1962.

Woodward, E. L. *Great Britain and the German Navy*. Oxford: Clarendon Press, 1935.

Zebel, Sydney H. *Balfour: A Political Biography*. Cambridge: Cambridge University Press, 1973.

Zeman, Z. A. B. *A Diplomatic History of the First World War*. London: Weidenfeld & Nicolson, 1971.

Index

Index

Index

Index

Index

Index

Index